D1103850

Learning by Playing

Learning by Playing

VIDEO GAMING IN EDUCATION

EDITED BY FRAN C. BLUMBERG

OXFORD
UNIVERSITY PRESS

OXFORD
UNIVERSITY PRESS

Oxford University Press is a department of the University of Oxford.
It furthers the University's objective of excellence in research, scholarship,
and education by publishing worldwide.

Oxford   New York
Auckland   Cape Town   Dar es Salaam   Hong Kong   Karachi
Kuala Lumpur   Madrid   Melbourne   Mexico City   Nairobi
New Delhi   Shanghai   Taipei   Toronto

With offices in
Argentina   Austria   Brazil   Chile   Czech Republic   France   Greece
Guatemala   Hungary   Italy   Japan   Poland   Portugal   Singapore
South Korea   Switzerland   Thailand   Turkey   Ukraine   Vietnam

Oxford is a registered trademark of Oxford University Press
in the UK and certain other countries.

Published in the United States of America by
Oxford University Press
198 Madison Avenue, New York, NY 10016

© Oxford University Press 2014

Library of Congress Cataloging-in-Publication Data
Learning by playing : frontiers of video gaming in education / edited by Fran C. Blumberg.
   pages cm
Includes bibliographical references and index.
ISBN 978-0-19-989664-6
1. Educational technology.   2. Education—Effect of technological innovations on.
3. Video games and children.   I. Blumberg, Fran C.
LB1028.3.L3775 2014
371.33—dc23
2013034455

9 8 7 6 5 4 3 2 1
Printed in the United States of America
on acid-free paper

Contents

Part Three   GAME DESIGN PERSPECTIVES: HOW SHOULD WE DESIGN EDUCATIONAL VIDEO GAMES?

Part Four   LEARNING IN PRACTICE: HOW SHOULD WE STUDY LEARNING IN VIDEO GAMES FOR TRANSFER TO ACADEMIC TASKS?

Part Five   CONCLUSION

Contributors

Ugochi Acholonu, Graduate School of Education, Stanford University, Stanford, California

Debby E. Almonte, National Assessment of Educational Progress, Princeton, New Jersey

Jared S. Anthony, Division of Psychological and Educational Services, Fordham University, New York, New York

Dylan Arena, Kidaptive, Inc., Palo Alto

Jodi Asbell-Clarke, EdGE at TERC, Cambridge, Massachusetts

James Bachhuber, Education Development Center, Center for Children and Technology, New York, New York

Yishai Barkhardori, Division of Psychological and Educational Services, Fordham University, New York, New York

Susan M. Barnett, Department of Policy Analysis and Management, Cornell University, Ithaca, New York

John R. Best, Djavad Mowafaghian Centre for Brain Health, University of British Columbia, Vancouver, British Columbia

Jennifer Biedler, Blacksburg High School, Blacksburg, Virginia

Erica Biely, Center for Digital Games Research, University of California, Santa Barbara, Santa Barbara, California

John B. Black, Teachers College, Columbia University, New York, New York

Fran C. Blumberg, Division of Psychological and Educational Services, Fordham University, New York, New York

Bradley J. Bond, Department of Communication Studies, University of San Diego, San Diego, California

Walter R. Boot, Department of Psychology, Florida State University, Tallahassee, Florida

Patricia J. Brooks, Department of Psychology, College of Staten Island and the Graduate Center of City University of New York, New York, New York

Sandra L. Calvert, Children's Digital Media Center, Georgetown University, Washington, DC

Sandra Crespo, College of Education, Michigan State University, East Lansing, Michigan

Anne Dickmeis, Leuven School for Mass Communication Research, University of Leuven, Leuven, Belgium

K. Anders Ericsson, Department of Psychology, Florida State University, Tallahassee, Florida

Michael A. Evans, School of Education, Virginia Tech, Blacksburg, Virginia

Shalom M. Fisch, MediaKidz Research & Consulting, Teaneck, New Jersey

Matthew Gaydos, Department of Educational Psychology, University of Wisconsin-Madison, Madison, Wisconsin

Douglas A. Gentile, Department of Psychology, Iowa State University, Ames, Iowa

J. Ronald Gentile, Department of Educational Psychology, State University of New York at Buffalo, Buffalo, New York

C. Shawn Green, McPherson Eye Research Institute, University of Wisconsin-Madison, Madison, Wisconsin

Christopher L. Groves, Department of Psychology, Iowa State University, Ames, Iowa

Naoko Hashimoto, Counseling Center, Syracuse University, Syracuse, New York

Célia Hodent, Epic Games, Cary, North Carolina

Shih-Chieh Doug Huang, Teachers College, Columbia University, New York, New York

Osvaldo Jiménez, Department of Computer Science, University of the Pacific, Stockton, California

Brett D. Jones, Department of Educational Psychology, Virginia Tech, Blacksburg, Virginia

Saadia A. Khan, Teachers College, Columbia University, New York, New York

Andrew Leno, Division of Psychological and Educational Services, New York, New York

Richard Lesh, School of Education, Indiana University, Bloomington, Indiana

Michael H. Levine, Joan Ganz Cooney Center, Sesame Workshop, New York, New York

Debra A. Lieberman, Center for Digital Games Research, University of California, Santa Barbara, Santa Barbara, California

Vincent Melfi, Department of Statistics and Probability, Michigan State University, East Lansing, Michigan

Elizabeth Motoki, School of Education, Indiana University, Bloomington, Indiana

Susana Peinado, Department of Communication, University of California, Santa Barbara, Santa Barbara, California

Kasey L. Powers, Department of Psychology, College of Staten Island and the Graduate Center of City University of New York, New York, New York

Gerard Robertson, Division of Psychological and Educational Services, Fordham University, New York, New York

Keith Roe, Leuven School for Mass Communication Research, University of Leuven, Leuven, Belgium

Elizabeth Rowe, EdGE at TERC, Cambridge, Massachusetts

John L. Sherry, Department of Communication, Michigan State University, East Lansing, Michigan

Amanda E. Staiano, Pennington Biomedical Research Center, Louisiana State University, Baton Rouge, Louisiana

Lori Takeuchi, Joan Ganz Cooney Center, Sesame Workshop, New York, New York

Chan L. Thai, Department of Communication, University of California, Santa Barbara, Santa Barbara, California

Sarah E. Vaala, Annenberg Public Policy Center, University of Pennsylvania, Philadelphia, Pennsylvania

Jong Sung Yoon, Department of Psychology, Florida State University, Tallahassee, Florida

Corinne Zimmerman, Department of Psychology, Illinois State University Normal, Illinois

Akane Zusho, Division of Psychological and Educational Services, Fordham University, New York, New York

Part One

INTRODUCTION AND OVERVIEW

1

Academic Lessons from Video Game Learning

FRAN C. BLUMBERG, DEBBY E. ALMONTE,
YISHAI BARKHARDORI, AND ANDREW LENO

The chapters presented in this volume are largely based on presentations and ideas exchanged during a National Science Foundation–sponsored conference (awarded to the first author), Academic Lessons from Video Game Learning: Screen2Screen, convened in October 2010 at the Lincoln Center–New York City campus of Fordham University. During this three-and-a-half day meeting, twenty researchers and practitioners in developmental and cognitive psychology, cognitive science, communications, media, educational technology, and game design (see appendix to this chapter for a list) came together to share their work and to discuss whether and how the learning experienced via video game play transferred to or positively affected the knowledge and skills obtained within formal educational settings (see chapter 9 for a general model of learning in the context of video games). In its most general sense, transfer of learning (as discussed in greater detail in chapters 2 and 13) occurs when learning in one context affects one's learning or ability to carry out a task in another context. As noted in our conference discussions, evidence supporting transfer of learning in formal and informal learning contexts remain mixed (see chapters 3, 14, and 21 for some of the different perspectives). For example, Masson, Bub, and Lalonde (2011) found that middle school students' playing of a game emphasizing the trajectories of objects in motion improved their understanding of the shape of the trajectories but not their conceptual understanding of object motion. Similarly, Sims and Mayer (2002) had earlier demonstrated that college students' experience playing *Tetris* improved their performance on later tests of mental rotation ability but only when *Tetris*-like shapes were used.

Despite mixed evidence of transfer, interest in the promise of recreational video game play for reinvigorating classroom learning continues. For example, science, technology, engineering and math (STEM) education initiatives, based in the Oval Office, federal agencies such as the National Science Foundation, and private foundations such as the MacArthur Foundation have fueled an expanding library of educational games (see White House, 2010; MacArthur Foundation, 2012). These games have not been uniformly well-received by the child and adolescent populations that they are designed to serve (Kato, 2012; Papastergiou, 2009; Van Eck, 2006). Reasons for this less than enthusiastic reception (as considered in chapters 10 and 11) may reflect the vastly differing budgets allotted to educational versus recreational games, which have ramifications for the look and feel of the games (although the success of *Angry Birds* despite its relatively low development budget of $140,000 presents a counterexample; see Crossley, 2011). Users of these games also may perceive the presentation of content or skills to be learned as disconnected from or not well integrated into the goals of the games (Sherry, 2013a). Further, players may perceive educational games as too cognitively demanding or as insufficiently challenging (see Blumberg & Ismailer, 2009). These circumstances clearly affect conclusions about the efficacy of educational games for promoting content learning and skill acquisition in the classroom setting.

Why Develop Educational Video Games?

OVERALL APPEAL

Regardless of students' tempered interest in playing educational games, the proliferation of these games continues. One clear reason is the appeal of video game play. This appeal, which is found among a diverse age range and among both females and males, has been attributed to the curiosity, fantasy, and challenge inherent in game play, as noted by Malone (1981) in his seminal article on motivation for playing digital games. Notably, the games available at the time in which Malone's article appeared were two-dimensional and fairly primitive in their graphics by today's standards (e.g., *Donkey Kong*). However, factors cited by Malone remain relevant today when considering motivation for playing video games (see chapters 6 and 19 for greater consideration of motivation in the context of video game play).

More recently, other features have been cited as contributing to the appeal of video game play. These features include *interactivity*, whereby players initiate and receive feedback about their actions, which affects their game play experience (Renkl & Atkinson, 2007; Ritterfeld et al., 2009); *agency* or *control*, which refers to players' ability to manage aspects of their game play, such as the use of the control mechanisms or the unfolding of the story line (Skalski, Lange, Tamborini, Helton, Buncher, & Lindmark, 2011; Qin, Rau, & Salvendy, 2009; Wood, Griffiths, Chappell, & Davies, 2004); *identity*, which refers to players' opportunity to form relationships and linkages with game characters or to become game characters via avatar construction (see Blascovich & Bailenson, 2011; Lane et al., 2013; Trepte, Reinecke, & Behr, 2010); *feedback*, which refers to the information players receive about the efficacy of their game actions, which in turn scaffolds the course of their game play (Lane et al., 2013; Lieberman, 2006); and *immersion*, which refers to players' sense of presence or integration within the game (see Tamborini & Skalski, 2006). Immersion has been linked to the attainment of the highly plea-surable state of flow (Csikszentmihalyi, 1988; Sherry, 2004; Weber, Tamborini, Westcott-Baker, & Kantor, 2009), whereby game play is perceived as all-absorbing and seemingly automatic despite the cognitive resources needed to master the game (see Csikszentmihalyi, 1990). Collectively, these features and others high-lighted in this volume are expected to promote sustained and enjoyable game play. In the context of educational game play in particular, one presumed corol-lary is that more game play provides more opportunity for learning.

Regardless of the truth of this corollary, which the conference members con-sidered in some detail and demonstrated in their work (see chapter 20), it is also true that many individuals play video games. For example, the most recent find-ings reported by the Entertainment Software Association (ESA, 2013) indicate that recreational games are played by 58% of the U.S. population and that 45% of players are female. Of those who play video games, 32% are younger than age 18. In fact, 8–18 year olds have been found to spend as much as 90 minutes per day involved in video game play (Rideout, Foehr, & Roberts, 2010). The ESA also reports that game players access games via their smartphones (36%). As the num-ber of game apps available for smartphones increases, one might expect increases in the amount of time individuals engage in game play, particularly among adoles-cents, who are leading users of smartphones (see Nielsenwire, 2012).

ENHANCED COGNITIVE SKILLS

Educational game development also may continue to expand, given the type of learning that occurs within game play in general. For example, as noted by Gee (2003; 2008) and Squire (2006), video game play serves to captivate and challenge its players as they use the type of reasoning skills that they may be expected to show in more formal learning settings (see chapters 5 and 17). The most compel-ling reason pertains to the accumulating evidence, among primarily adult par-ticipants, that links frequent video game play to enhanced problem-solving and inductive reasoning (Blumberg, Rosenthal, & Randall, 2008; Fisch, Lesh, Motoki, Crespo, & Melfi, 2011; Greenfield et al., 1994; Pillay, 2002), mental rotation and spatial visualization (Okagaki & Frensch, 1994), spatial distribution of attention and visual selective attention (Boot, Kramer, Simmons, Fabiani, & Gratton, 2008; Green & Bavelier, 2003, 2006, 2007; Karle, Watter, & Shedden, 2010), metacog-nition (VanDeventer & White, 2002), and memory (Boot et al., 2008). Recent findings also show that executive functioning (Best, 2013; Staiano, Abraham, & Calvert, 2012) may be enhanced through the playing of exergames (e.g., *WiiFit*). (See chapters 4 and 15 for greater consideration of cognitive skills enhanced via exergame play.) Recent findings also indicate that frequent action game play may

facilitate neural plasticity and the enhancement of cognitive skills that help prepare us for "learning to learn" (see Bavelier, Green, Pouget, & Schrater, 2012; see
also chapter 3).

What Do We Need to Know About Game Play?

While researchers have examined the nexus of video game play, learning, and
acquisition of cognitive skills among college age participants (Boot et al., 2008;
Green & Bavelier, 2007; Green, Li, & Bavelier, 2009; Greenfield, Camaioni, et al.,
1994; Greenfield, DeWinstanley, Kilpatrick, & Kaye, 1994; Spence & Feng, 2010),
very little is known about the ramifications of video game play for the child and
adolescent participants for whom many educational games are designed (see
Blumberg & Altschuler, 2011; Blumberg, Altschuler, Almonte, & Mileaf, 2013;
DeLisi & Wolford, 2002; Salonius-Pasternak & Gelfond, 2005).

   What we do know is that the extent to which cognitive skills are enhanced
via video games is largely dependent on the frequency of play. We also know
that the types of strategies that children and adolescents use may be influenced by age and frequency of play. Surprisingly, the developmental appropriateness of a given educational game is seldom considered as a critical aspect
of the game development process or assessment of game efficacy. This situation, in fact, was addressed by conference members, given the importance of
the developmental appropriateness of a game for learning (see Blumberg &
Ismailer, 2009; Sherry, 2013b; and chapter 12 for game design strategies
that could be used to rectify this situation). For example, frequent players
show greater proficiency in spatial skills (DeLisi & Wolford, 2002; Okagaki &
Frensch, 1994; Subrahmanyam & Greenfield, 1994), planning and metacognition (VanDeventer & White, 2002), and visual attention skills (Dye &
Bavelier, 2010) than infrequent players. Child and adolescent players who play
frequently also show different strategies for game play from those who play
infrequently. For example, Blumberg and Sokol (2004) found that second-
and fifth-grade frequent players reported greater use of self-reliant strategies
such as trial and error than infrequent players, who reported greater use of
other-dependent strategies, such as watching others play or asking others for
help. Hamlen (2011) found that fourth- and fifth-grade frequent players were
more likely than infrequent players to cite repetition and cheat codes as ways
to master a game (see chapter 16 for further consideration of strategies used
to master games). Very recently, Blumberg and Randall (2013) found that in
the think-aloud protocols of fifth- through seventh-graders who were learning to play a novel video game, fifth- and sixth-graders made greater reference
to short-term goals and mastery of specific actions within the game than the
seventh-graders.

Overall, the lack of research concerning what children and adolescents learn in the context of video game play, and what skills might be facilitated by that play, compromises what we can say about the type of learning or skill acquisition that occurs during game play (see Sherry & Dibble, 2009), much less what transfers from game play to classroom settings. Exploration of this issue was one of the motivations for the conference.

Another motivation was how best to enrich the study of children and adolescents' learning in the context of video game play by drawing on relevant perspectives from other disciplines, such as media and communications (see chapters 8 and 18) and other areas of study, such as expert performance (see chapter 7).

The chapters that follow reflect the fruits of our discussions and presentations as supplemented by contributions from other scholars and practitioners whose work concerns effective game design and the study of factors contributing to children and adolescents' learning in the context of video games and digital media in general. The hope is that readers of this volume will see themselves, as we did during the conference, as being one step closer to bridging a significant gap as noted by Levine, Takeuchi, and Vaala (chapter 22, p. 333), "...between the promise of game-based learning and the current reality. This gap is especially evident in transforming games from effective research trials into financially sustainable products that can reach and affect students through either formal or informal channels."

Structure of the Book

This volume includes four sections in addition to this first chapter, which comprises Part One. In Part Two, "Theoretical and Cognitive Perspectives: How Should We Think about Learning in Video Games?," diverse theoretical perspectives are presented that have ramifications for understanding how children and adolescents acquire content knowledge and cognitive skills.

Part Three, "Game Design Perspectives: How Should We Design Educational Video Games?" shares different views from practitioners and researchers about the game design process and the specific features that comprise an effective educational game.

Part Four, "Learning in Practice: How Should We Study Learning in Video Games for Transfer to Academic Tasks?" reviews findings from research programs examining the impact of recreational and educational games on children and adolescents' skills and content knowledge. Also included within this section are chapters examining the relationship between media use in general and school learning and a meta-analysis examining the extent to which cognitive skills obtained through video game play transfer beyond the game setting.

Part Five, the conclusion, includes a single chapter intended as a closing statement on the text and as a challenge for readers to consider best ways to use educational games and educational technology to improve learning among all students.

Authors' Note

We extend our thanks to John Randall for his support and insight throughout the Academic Lessons from Video Game Learning: Screen2Screen conference and the preparation of this chapter. The conference was supported by a grant from the National Science Foundation to the first author (DRL, #0921710).

References

Bavelier, D., Green, C. S., Pouget, A., & Schrater, P. (2012). Brain plasticity through the lifespan: Learning to learn and action video games. *Annual Review of Neuroscience, 35*, 391–416.

Best, J. R. (2013). Exergaming in youth. Effects on physical and cognitive health. *Zeitschrift für Psychologie, 221*(2), 72–78.

Blascovich, J., & Bailenson, J. (2011). *Infinite Reality: Avatars, Eternal Life, New Worlds, and the Dawn of the Virtual Revolution.* New York: HarperCollins.

Blumberg, F. C. & Altschuler, E. (2011). From the playroom to the classroom: Children's views of video game play and academic learning. *Child Development Perspectives, 2*, 99–103.

Blumberg, F. C., Altschuler, E. A., Almonte, D. E., & Mileaf, M. M. (2013). The impact of recreational video game play on children and adolescents' cognition. In F. C. Blumberg & S. M. Fisch (Eds.), *New Directions for Child and Adolescent Development, 139*, 41–50.

Blumberg, F. C. & Fisch, S. M. (2013). Introduction: Digital games as a context for cognitive development, learning, and developmental research. In F. C. Blumberg & S. M. Fisch (Eds.), *New Directions for Child and Adolescent Development, 139*, 1–9.

Blumberg, F. C. & Ismailer, S. S. (2009). What do children learn from playing video games? In U. Ritterfeld, M. Cody & P. Vorderer (Eds.). *Serious Games: Mechanisms and Effects.* New York, NY: Routledge, Taylor, and Francis.

Blumberg, F. C. & Randall, J. D. (2013). What do children and adolescents say they do during video game play? *Journal of Applied Developmental Psychology, 34*, 82–88.

Blumberg, F. C., Rosenthal, S. F., & Randall, J. D. (2008). Impasse-driven learning in the context of video games. *Computers in Human Behavior, 24*, 1530–1541.

Blumberg, F. C., & Sokol, L. M. (2004). Boys' and girls' use of cognitive strategy when learning to play video games. *Journal of General Psychology, 131*(2), 151–158.

Boot, W. R., Kramer, A. F., Simmons, D. J., Fabiani, M., & Gratton, G. (2008). The effects of video game playing on attention, memory, and executive control. *Acta Psychologica, 129*, 387–398.

Crossley, R. (2011). Angry Birds cost Rovio $140K, has made $70M. Retrieved from http://www.develop-online.net/news/37242/Angry-Birds-cost-Rovio-100k-has-made-50m

Csikszentmihalyi, M. (1988). The flow experience and its significance for human psychology. In M. Csikszentmihalyi & I. S. Csikszentmihalyi, (Eds.), *Optimal experience: Psychological studies of flow in consciousness* (pp. 15–35). Cambridge, UK: Cambridge University Press.

Csikszentmihalyi, M. (1990). *Flow. The psychology of optimal experience.* New York, NY: Harper Perennial.

De Lisi, R., & Wolford, J. L. (2002). Improving children's mental rotation accuracy with computer game playing. *The Journal of Genetic Psychology, 163*, 272–282.

Dye, M. W. G. & Bavelier, D. (2010). Differential development of visual attention skills in school-age children. *Vision Research, 50*, 452–459.

Entertainment Software Association (2013). 2013: Essential facts about the computer and video game industry. Retrieved June 16, 2013 from http://www.theesa.com/facts/pdfs/ESA_EF_2013.pdf

Fisch, S. M., Lesh, R., Motoki, E., Crespo, S., & Melfi, V. (2011). Children's mathematical reasoning in online games: Can data mining reveal strategic thinking? *Child Development Perspectives*, 5, 88–92.

Gee, J. P. (2003). *What video games have to teach us about learning and literacy.* New York, NY: Palgrave/MacMillan.

Gee, J. P. (2008). Learning and games. In K. Salen (Ed) *The ecology of games: Connecting youth, games, and learning* (pp. 21–40). Cambridge, MA: The MIT Press.

Green, C. S. & Bavelier, D. (2003). Action video game modifies visual selective attention. *Nature*, 423(6939), 534–538.

Green, C. S. & Bavelier, D. (2006). Effect of action video games on spatial distribution of visuospatial attention. *Journal of Experimental Psychology: Human Perception and Performance*, 32, 1465–1478.

Green, C. S. & Bavelier, D. (2007). Action video game experience alters the spatial resolution of attention. *Psychological Science*, 18, 88–94.

Green, C. S., Li, R., & Bavelier, D. (2009). Perceptual learning during action video game playing. *Topics in Cognitive Science*, 2, 1–15.

Greenfield, P. M., Camaioni, L., Ercolani, P., Weiss, L., Lauber, B. A., & Perucchini, P. (1994). Cognitive socialization by computer games in two cultures: Inductive discovery or mastery of an iconic code? *Journal of Applied Developmental Psychology*, 15, 59–85.

Greenfield, P. M., DeWinstanley, P., Kilpatrick, H., & Kaye, D. (1994). Action video games and informal education: Effects on strategies for dividing visual attention. *Journal of Applied Developmental Psychology*, 15, 105–123.

Hamlen, K. R. (2011). Children's choices and strategies in video games. *Computers in Human Behavior*, 27(1), 532–539.

Karle, J. W., Watter, S., & Shedden, J. M. (2010). Task switching in video game players: Benefits of selective attention but not resistance to proactive interference. *Acta Psychologica*, 134, 70–78.

Kato, P. M. (2012). Evaluating efficacy and validating games for health. *Games for Health Journal: Research, Development, and Clinical Applications*, 1(1), 74–76

Lane, H. C., Cahill, C., Foutz, S., Auerbach, D., Noren, D., Lussenhop, C., & Swartout, W. (2013). The effects of a pedagogical agent for informal science education on learner behaviors and self-efficacy. *Proceedings of 16th International Conference on Artificial Intelligence in Education*, LNAI 7926 (pp. 309–319). Berlin/Heidelberg, Germany: Springer.

Lieberman, D. A. (2006). What can we learn from playing interactive games? In P. Vorderer & J. Bryant (Eds.), *Playing Video Games. Motives, Responses, and Consequences* (pp. 379–397). Hillsdale, NJ: Lawrence Erlbaum Associates.

MacArthur Foundation Digital Media Digital Learning Initiative (2012, September). Digital Media and Learning. Retrieved from http://www.macfound.org/media/article _pdfs/ Digital_Media_Learning_Info_Sheet.pdf

Malone, T. W. (1981). Toward a theory of intrinsically motivating instruction. *Cognitive Science*, 4, 333–369.

Masson, M. E. J., Bub, D. N., & Lalonde, C. E. (2011). Video-game training and naïve reasoning about object motion. *Applied Cognitive Psychology*, 25, 166–173.

Nielsenwire (2012). Young adults and teens lead growth among smartphone owners. Nielsenwire. Retrieved from http://blog.nielsen.com/nielsenwire/online_mobile/young-adults-and-te ens-lead-growth-among-smartphone-owners/

Okagaki, L. & Frensch, P. (1994). Effects of video game playing on measures of spatial performance: Gender effects in late adolescence. *Journal of Applied Developmental Psychology*, 15, 33–58.

Papastergiou, M. (2009). Digital game-based learning in high school computer science education: Impact on educational effectiveness and student motivation. *Computers & Education*, 52, 1–12.

Pillay, H. (2002). An investigation of the cognitive processes engaged in by recreational computer game players: Implications for skills of the future. *Journal of Research on Technology in Education*, 34, 336–350.

Qin, H., Rau, P. L., & Salvendy, G. (2009). Measuring player immersion in the computer game narrative. *International Journal of Human-Computer Interaction, 25*, 107–133.

Renkl, A., & Atkinson, R. K. (2007). Interactive learning environments: Contemporary issues and trends. An Introduction to the special issue. *Educational Psychology Review, 19*, 235–238.

Rideout, V., Foehr, U. G., & Roberts, D. F. (2010). *Generation M2: Media in the Lives of 8–18 Year-Olds*. Menlo Park, CA: Henry J. Kaiser Family Foundation.

Ritterfeld, U., Shen, C., Wang, H., Nocera, L., & Wong, W. L. (2009). Multimodality and interactivity: Connecting properties of serious games with educational outcomes. *Cyberpsychology & Behavior, 12*, 691–697.

Salonius-Pasternak, D. E. & Gelfond, H. S. (2005). The next level of research on electronic play: Potential benefits and contextual influences for children and adolescents. *Human Technology: An Interdisciplinary Journal on Humans in ICT Environments, 1*, 5–22.

Satwicz, T., & Stevens, R. (2008). Playing with representations: How do kids make use of quantitative representations in video games? *International Journal of Computers for Mathematical Learning, 13*, 179–206.

Sherry, J. L. (2004). Flow and media enjoyment. *Communication Theory, 14*, 328–347.

Sherry, J. L. (2013a). The challenge of audience reception: A developmental model for educational game engagement. In F. C. Blumberg & S. M. Fisch (Eds.), *New Directions for Child and Adolescent Development, 139*, 11–20.

Sherry, J. L. (2013b). Formative research for STEM educational games: Lessons from the Children's Television Workshop. *Zeitschrift für Psychologie, 221*(2), 90–97.

Sherry, J. L., & Dibble, J. (2009). The impact of serious games on childhood development. In U. Ritterfeld, M. Cody, & P. Vorderer (Eds.), *Serious games: Mechanisms and effects* (pp. 145–166). New York, NY: Routledge.

Sims, V. K. & Mayer, R. E. (2002). Domain specificity of spatial expertise: The case of video game players. *Applied Cognitive Psychology, 16*, 97–115.

Skalski, P., Lange, R., Tamborini, R., & Shelton, A. (2007). Mapping the road to fun: Natural video game controllers, presence, and game enjoyment. Conference Papers—International Communication Association, 1.

Skalski, P., Tamborini, R., Shelton, A., Buncher, M., & Lindmark, P. (2011). Mapping the road to fun: Natural video game controllers, presence, and game enjoyment. *New Media & Society, 13*(2), 224–242.

Spence, I. & Feng, J. (2010). Video games and spatial cognition. *Review of General Psychology, 14*, 92–104.

Squire, K. (2006). From content to context: Videogames as designed experience. *Educational Researcher, 35*, 19–29.

Staiano, A. E., Abraham, A. A., & Calvert, S. L. (2012). Competitive versus cooperative exergame play for African American adolescents' executive function skills: Short-term effects in a long-term training intervention. *Developmental Psychology, 48*, 337–342.

Subrahmanyam, K. & Greenfield, P. M. (1994). Effect of video game practice on spatial skills in girls and boys. *Journal of Applied Developmental Psychology, 15*, 13–32.

Tamborini, R., & Skalski, P. (2006). The role of presence in the experience of electronic games. In P. Vorderer & J. Bryant (Eds.), *Playing Video Games. Motives, Responses, and Consequences* (pp. 225–240). Hillsdale, NJ: Lawrence Erlbaum Associates.

Trepte, S., Reinecke, L., & Behr, K. (2010). Avatar creation and video game enjoyment: Effects of life-satisfaction, game competitiveness, and identification with the avatar. Paper presented at the annual meeting of the International Communication Association, Suntec Singapore International Convention & Exhibition Centre, Suntec City, Singapore.

The White House, Office of the Press Secretary (2010). President Obama to announce major expansion of "Educate to Innovate" campaign to improve science, technology, engineering and math (STEM) education [Press release]. Retrieved from http://www.whitehouse.gov/the-press-office/2010/09/16/president-obama-announce-major-expansion-educate-innovate-campaign-impro

Van Eck, R. V. (2006). Digital game–based learning. *Educause Review*, (March/April), 17–30.

VanDeventer, S. S., & White, J. A. (2002). Expert behavior in children's video game play. *Simulation & Gaming, 33*, 28–48.

Wood, R., Griffiths, M. D., Chappell, D., & Davies, M. (2004). The structural characteristics of video games: A psycho-structural analysis. *CyberPsychology & Behavior, 7*, 1–10.

Weber, R., Tamborini, R., Westcott-Baker, A., & Kantor, B. (2009). Theorizing flow and media enjoyment as cognitive synchronization of attentional and reward networks. *Communication Theory, 19*, 397–422.

Appendix

Conference Members, October 9–11, 2010, Academic Lessons from Video Game Learning: Screen2Screen

Jay Bachhuber EDC/Center for Children and Technology	Shalom M. Fisch MediaKidz Research & Consulting	Michael Levine Joan Ganz Cooney Center
Susan Barnett Cornell University	Nick Fortugno Playmatics	Alex Quinn EDC/Center for Children and Technology
John R. Best* University of Georgia	Matt Gaydos* University of Wisconsin-Madison	Katie Salen Parsons, The New School/ Institute of Play
John Black Teachers College, Columbia University	Douglas A. Gentile Iowa State University	John Sherry Michigan State University
Mark Blades University of Sheffield	C. Shawn Green University of Minnesota	Corinne Zimmerman llinois State University
Fran Blumberg Fordham University	Osvaldo Jiménez* Stanford University	
Sandra L. Calvert Georgetown University	David Klahr Carnegie Mellon University	
Mike Edwards Parsons, The New School	Kathleen Kremer Fisher-Price	
K. Anders Ericsson Florida State University	H. Chad Lane ICT, University of Southern California	

Notes: All affiliations are those that were current at the time of the conference. Participants whose names are followed by an * were postdoctoral fellows or graduate students at the time of the conference, who won scholarships to attend.

Part Two

THEORETICAL AND COGNITIVE PERSPECTIVES: HOW SHOULD WE THINK ABOUT LEARNING IN VIDEO GAMES?

2

Virtual to Real Life—Assessing Transfer of Learning from Video Games

SUSAN M. BARNETT

In many ways, it seems as if video games should be treated differently from other potential learning experiences that might bring about transfer. They are new and unfamiliar to many, especially older adults; the games rely on technologies that weren't around a generation ago. Some games have the added cachet of being branded a bad influence on modern youth, and some are said to be so exciting to play that people become addicted to them. All these qualities give video games a mysterious distinction that could tempt an uninformed commentator to jump to the conclusion that our existing understanding of the attributes of and constraints on transfer of learning do not apply here. One might hope that all that has to be done is to dress up some academic content as a game, place it in front of some children, and voila! If video games are so captivating that users can get addicted to them, surely games can be used to teach anything. However, learning is still learning, even if it is wrapped up in electronically assisted and captivating packaging. As has been amply demonstrated elsewhere (see Barnett & Ceci, 2002), the history of research on learning and transfer also suggests that it cannot be taken for granted that learning will transfer, or indeed that any learning will necessarily occur from a given set of experiences. In fact, quite the opposite is often claimed (see, e.g., Detterman, 1993).

Transferability of Learning

Famous psychologists have been debating the transferability of learning for more than 100 years. At the beginning of the twentieth century, Judd (1908) stated, "Every experience has in it the possibilities of generalization" (p. 38), while Thorndike and Woodworth (1901) claimed the contrary, stating, "There is no inner necessity for improvement of one function to improve others closely similar to it, due to a subtle transfer of practice effect" (p. 386). More recently, Halpern (1998) claimed, "Numerous studies have shown that critical thinking...can be learned in ways that promote transfer to novel contexts" (p. 449), but Detterman (1993) argued, "Reviewers are in almost total agreement that little transfer occurs" (p. 8).

In his classic educational psychology text, Klausmeier (1961) asserted, "A main reason for formal education is to facilitate learning in situations outside school" (p. 352). Thus, if critics are correct in asserting that transfer very rarely happens, the justification for educational and training expenditures may need to be reevaluated: as Detterman suggests, "Cognitive psychologists, and other people who should know better, continue to advocate a philosophy of education that is totally lacking in empirical support" (p. 16). This debate is as important for video game learning as it is for traditional, nondigital, educational endeavors. If Detterman is right, the whole enterprise may be doomed to failure.

Barnett and Ceci (2002) reviewed evidence of transfer of learning from hundreds of studies across several decades in search of conclusive proof of transferable learning. They sought to get definitive answers as to whether transfer really happened. They also sought to determine why what seems like such a simple question has led eminent researchers to form such divergent opinions for so long. The answer was twofold. First, the question is not a simple one, because it is not well-defined and, second, because the answer depends on the circumstances, the answer may differ depending on the situation to which one hopes to generalize findings.

Defining the question requires defining successful transfer. One possible definition is "the carrying over of an act or way of acting from one performance to another" (Woodworth & Schlosberg, 1954, p. 734). But there are no clear, agreed-upon criteria for what constitutes "carrying over." For example, does it count as true transfer if the experimenter has to drop loud hints to the participants to let them know that they should be able to carry over what they have just learned to a new set of apparently unrelated problems? One researcher may count the resulting behavior from this situation as successful transfer while another might not. Much disagreement comes from situations that essentially compare apples and oranges. For some purposes, aspects such as spontaneity may be crucial, whereas for others they may be unnecessary. For example, if the hope is that learners will apply acquired mathematical and statistical literacy to critical evaluation of issues and policies they read about in the news, spontaneity is required: there will be no omnipresent experimenter to remind them of the applicability of that knowledge. On the other hand, if the goal is to use the same mathematical and statistical literacy to analyze the results of a quantitative academic study, the analyst can look up the applicability of particular procedures in a textbook or ask a friend for advice, and depending on these prompts or hints is less of a problem.

Another proposed definition of successful transfer is "the ability to extend what has been learned in one context to new contexts" (Bransford, Brown, & Cocking, 1999, p. 39). Again, however, there is no clear, agreed-upon definition of a "new context." If a study participant learns a mathematics algorithm and applies it successfully to a novel problem on the next page of the math textbook five minutes later, is "page 29 at 2:33 p.m." a new context from "page 28 at 1:58 p.m."? Or does the participant need to apply the learned algorithm to, for example, calculating required quantities of flour and other ingredients while baking a cake at home that weekend? How different does a context have to be to be truly "new" and therefore count as transfer? Again, resolution to this question may come from agreement as to the goal of the education or training effort. If the goal is transfer to a later work or home context, researching immediate transfer in the laboratory doesn't answer all these relevant questions. Generalizing from lab research to home and work can only be justified if elsewhere it has been shown that these contextual differences are irrelevant.

Thus, before judgment can be rendered regarding the value of video games as a tool to teach transferable learning, evidence must be assessed regarding the success of transfer from video games to academic subjects and other desired aspects of daily life. Further, before conclusions can be reached regarding the generalizability of specific findings, it is important to clearly define what is meant by successful transfer for that purpose. For example, in a given case, does transfer count if it only occurs when the circumstances of application make it obvious to the transferee that transfer is required, either by overt prompting or by more subtle hints, or should spontaneity be a requirement? Similarly, should transfer be considered successful if the learning experience changes one performance attribute, for example speed of response, but not others, such as accuracy or response quality? Further, if the success of transfer is assessed only in contexts that are very similar to the context of learning, it is unknown whether transfer would be successful in more remote contexts. Research elsewhere has shown that many dimensions of the learning and transfer context may affect transfer success (for examples, see Barnett & Ceci, 2002). Thus, generalizability of findings may be limited unless these dimensions are taken into account.

Effects of Learning Content on Transfer

Many characteristics of learning and transfer tasks may affect transfer success. Three attributes that have received some attention from transfer researchers are (1) the possible effects of the type of skill that is being learned; (2) the aspect of performance being changed; and (3) the memory demands of the improvement being assessed (see Table 2.1 as drawn from Barnett & Ceci, 2002).

The type of learned skill can vary from a very specific, routinized procedure to a broader, more general principle or heuristic as in the use of hierarchical classification to organize understanding. This specificity-generality continuum has been a topic of investigation in transfer and learning research for some time. For

Table 2.1 **Characteristics of the Learning and Transfer Tasks**

	A. Content: What transferred		
Learned skill	Procedure	Representation	Principle or heuristic
Performance change	Speed	Accuracy	Approach
Memory demands	Execute only	Recognize and execute	Recall, recognize and execute

From: Barnett, S. M., & Ceci, S. J. (2002). When and where do we apply what we learn?: A taxonomy for far transfer. *Psychological Bulletin, 128*, 4, 612–637, APA, reprinted with permission.

example, Brown (1989) and Brown and Kane (1988) found that preschool-aged children studying mimicry in the animal kingdom could transfer principles such as "hide using mimicry as a defense mechanism" from one creature to another. Some learned only one particular aspect of this defense, such as looking like a dangerous creature (e.g., a beetle might look like a wasp, a caterpillar might look like a poisonous snake), while others learned a more general approach from a variety of methods (e.g., a fly might sound like a bee, a marsupial might freeze and play dead, an insect might looks like a twig). Those who learned the more general approach transferred more successfully than those who learned the specific mechanism.

Similarly, the nature of the performance change being measured can affect the success of transfer. For example, Vasta, Knott, and Gaze (1996) found that training on a water jug level task eradicated a previously found sex difference in performance when the outcome measure being assessed was answering the problem correctly, but not when success was defined as articulation of the correct principle. Classic work by Reed, Ernst, and Banerji (1974) on analogical transfer also found that transfer success differed depending on whether the measure of transfer was solution speed or the number of errors made.

One of Detterman's (1993) most powerful criticisms of studies purporting to demonstrate successful transfer of learning concerns the third content dimension—the memory demands of the transfer task. He notes that many studies only find successful transfer if the participants are told, either directly or by indirect hints, that they are supposed to be transferring their learning to a particular new task. However, as Detterman points out, a major component of the challenge of transferring learning is often determining when and where information that has been learned is relevant. In the real world outside academic settings, one is rarely told which specific learned skills or information to apply. Thus, for many purposes, spontaneity may be considered a requirement for proof of true, generalizable transfer success.

Effects of Context on Learning and Transfer

Another challenging aspect of transfer research is ensuring that learning has been transferred to truly new contexts, often referred to as "far contexts" in the learning and transfer literature. At first blush, it is not obvious that context matters for learning and transfer. Surely, one might think, a learning experience should be the same, and the resulting learning the same, no matter where, when, or why it occurs, if the task and procedures are the same—end of story. It shouldn't matter whether that learning is occurring at school, at home, or on the sports field. However, evidence suggests otherwise.

In a classic study of children's learning, at home and in the laboratory, Ceci and Bronfenbrenner (1985) investigated the effect of varying the physical context of learning. Groups of children were asked to bake cupcakes. While the cupcakes were in the oven for 30 minutes, the children were allowed to play an appealing game (*Pac-Man*). The learning aspect of the task was the implicit requirement to keep track of time, without wasting too much effort staring continuously at the clock. At the beginning of the baking time, the children glanced at the clock frequently to check how fast time was passing. Once they learned how fast time was passing and their internal clock was calibrated, they should have needed to check the clock less frequently, allowing them to concentrate on the more enjoyable experience of playing the game, until the time was almost up. At this point, they might have been expected to check more frequently to ensure that they didn't burn the cupcakes. This pattern was indeed shown by one group of children—those who participated in the experiment at home. However, children who participated in the same experiment in the laboratory behaved differently (except for a group of older boys). Those in the lab kept looking at the clock more and more frequently as time passed, throughout the entire 30 minutes, without taking a break. They never learned to calibrate their internal clock (or at least did not demonstrate any improved ability to do so). Thus, the simple fact of being in a laboratory rather than a home setting changed how they approached the task and the learning they demonstrated. Thus, the physical context affected learning.

Physical context also affects the transferability of learning. A well-known example of this type of contextual effect is Godden and Baddeley's classic study (1975) showing that word lists learned underwater were more easily retrieved when the learner was again underwater than when memory was attempted on dry land. Thus, if an experimenter seeks to show that learning can be transferred to a new context, and if the purpose of the educational effort being evaluated requires transfer to a different physical context, the training and testing must occur in different physical contexts. Otherwise, generalization of study results will be limited.

What other aspects of context might also affect learning and transfer? Barnett and Ceci (2002) specified six dimensions (see Table 2.2). For each of these

Table 2.2 **Characteristics of the Learning and Transfer tasks: Context**

		B. Context: where transferred from/to			
	Near ←--→ Far				
Knowledge domain	Mouse vs. rat	Biology vs. botany	Biology vs. economics	Science vs. English	Science vs. cooking
Physical context	Same room at school	Different room at school	School vs. research lab	School vs. home	School vs. at the beach
Temporal context	Same session	Next day	2 weeks later	Months later	Years later
Functional context	Both clearly academic	Both academic but one non-evaluative	Academic vs. filling in tax forms	Academic vs. informal questionnaire	Academic vs. at play
Social context	Both individual	Individual vs. pair	Individual vs. small group	Individual vs. large group	Individual vs. nation?
Modality	Both written, same format	Both written, multiple choice vs. essay	Book learning vs. oral exam	Lecture vs. wine tasting	Lecture vs. wood carving

From: Barnett, S. M., & Ceci, S. J. (2002). When and where do we apply what we learn?: A taxonomy for far transfer. *Psychological Bulletin, 128*, 4, 612–637, APA, reprinted with permission.

dimensions, they described evidence from the learning and transfer literature suggesting that the success of transfer might be affected. Some dimensions—knowledge domain and temporal context—make intuitive sense. For example, applying an understanding of population growth learned in the context of wheat farming to barley farming might be expected to be easier than applying the same understanding to the context of human colonization, a much more distant knowledge domain.

Similarly, aspects of temporal context, such as elapsed time between training and transfer, might be expected to affect transfer success. For most purposes, to be useful, learning must be enduring, but some learning may be fleeting, so transfer tests should evaluate the longevity of learning and transfer, if results are to be generalizable to different contexts. Although applying learning right away might be expected to be easier than applying that same learning months or even years later, this is not always the case: time can have more puzzling effects. For example, in a physics learning study, Craig, Chi, and VanLehn (2009) found no difference between three groups of learners on a short-term transfer task but did find a difference on longer-term retention and transfer measures. Thus, temporal context must be considered when generalizing from transfer studies.

The relevance of some of the other context dimensions is more questionable and begs further exploration. For example, the literature on the phenomenon of functional fixedness suggests that functional context might affect transfer. The functional context is the purpose of the task, or the mindset it invokes—whether the purpose is to play, to learn, or to earn money, for example. We do not know whether functional context affects transfer. Functional fixedness (see Duncker, 1945) refers to the fact that the use of objects is often so tied to their original purpose that it's hard for people to think of using them in other ways. For example, you may look for a screwdriver, not realizing that a dime in your pocket could get the job done. Similarly, academic learning may be tied in our mind to academic situations and not readily transfer to work or play, or video gaming skills may be tied to play (even if conducted at school) and not transferred readily to work. Unfortunately, much transfer research is conducted within a single functional context, so transfer across contexts is rarely tested.

Social context is another dimension that might affect transfer success, but for which evidence is currently scarce. Although schools may be increasingly using collaborative approaches, little is known about their effect on transfer (Druckman & Bjork, 1994). Some learning studies do exist. For example, Chi, Roy, and Hausmann (2008) compared learning from textbooks and watching tutoring videos collaboratively and individually, and found a benefit of collaboration. They attribute the benefit of collaboration to interaction resulting in deep learning, which has been associated with far transfer (see Barnett & Ceci, 2002).

The modality dimension is also not well understood. In one interesting example, Herrnstein, Nickerson, de Sanchez, and Swets (1986) compared transfer measures in various modalities, including written questions and questions read aloud by the teacher, and a practical design task and an oral argumentation task. Although transfer was found on most of the measures, transfer success varied between test modalities, with the largest benefits generally found on tests closest to the modality of original training.

Thus, there is some evidence to suggest that these dimensions of transfer context might affect transfer success. If these dimensions indeed do matter, it is possible that a particular learning experience might transfer successfully to a context that is near to the context of learning on some or all of these dimensions, but not to a far context. For example, an academic lesson about photosynthesis learned in the classroom from a textbook might successfully transfer to a paper-and-pencil test in the same classroom the next day, but the learner might not be able to show evidence of that learning while doing yard work that weekend. Similarly, knowledge acquired during video game play might not be accessible outside of that context. We do not know whether this is the case, but we do know enough about transfer to know that it cannot be taken for granted that learning that has been demonstrated in one near context will necessarily transfer to another far context. Barnett and Ceci's (2002) taxonomy of transfer content and context provides a framework to guide design of future transfer tests to ensure that aspects relevant to generalizability are investigated.

Evidence for Far Transfer

Even outside the world of video games, there are few documented examples of successful transfer to a far context. It is so much easier to study learning and transfer in the context of a single session, in the same location, and in the same domain. Two notable exceptions are a study of elementary school children by Chen and Klahr (1999) and a study of university students by Fong, Krantz, and Nisbett (1986). Chen and Klahr's study involved training and transfer of the "control of variables" strategy for scientific reasoning. In addition to more immediate tests in a near context, Chen and Klahr tested what they termed "remote" transfer. Specifically, they evaluated transfer of learning several months later (a far temporal context), in different domains and using a different testing format (different modality). Testing was also conducted by different experimenters, providing a different physical context. Despite the successful near transfer found among both third- and fourth-grade children, only the fourth-grade group showed evidence of successful far transfer. Thus, evidence of successful near transfer cannot be assumed to mean that far transfer will also occur.

Fong et al.'s (1986) creative study of far transfer used a transfer test disguised as a household survey, and was conducted at home over the phone. Their training phase was a university statistics course, and the transfer test involved questions about sports, for which statistical principles were relevant. For example, one question posed was "In general, the major league baseball player who wins Rookie of the Year does not perform as well in his second year. This is clear in major league baseball in the past 10 years. In the American League, eight Rookies of the Year have done worse in their second year; only two have done better. In the National League, the Rookie of the Year has done worse the second year 9 times out of 10. Why do you suppose the Rookie of the Year tends not to do as well his second year?" Answers were coded for evidence of good statistical reasoning. A typical response that does not show evidence of good statistical reasoning would be, "The Rookie of the Year doesn't do as well because he's resting on his laurels; he's not trying as hard in his second year." A response that does show evidence of good statistical reasoning would be, "A player's performance varies from year to year. Sometimes you have good years and sometimes you have bad years. The player who won the Rookie of the Year award had an exceptional year. He'll probably do better than average in his second year, but not as well as he did when he was a rookie." Students tested at the end of the semester, after taking the statistics course, showed more evidence of good statistical reasoning on the survey questions than those tested at the beginning, before taking the course, though only for some of the questions. Transfer was shown to a far context along many dimensions, including physical context (lecture hall versus home), functional context (academic class versus a household survey), and modality (lectures and written work versus a phone conversation).

These two studies show that far transfer of learning is possible. However, their partial success also cautions that it cannot be assumed that far transfer will always occur, just because evidence for near transfer has been shown. Regardless, these studies set the standard against which future tests of far transfer, whether from video game learning or other, more conventional educational formats, can be assessed.

Evaluating Evidence for Video Game Transfer

Digital games have been hypothesized to offer a number of potential instructional benefits as a learning medium (O'Neil, Wainess, & Baker, 2005), including inter-activity, which outside the world of video games has been associated with deeper understanding and more successful far transfer (Barnett & Ceci, 2002; Bransford, Brown, & Cocking, 1999; Reed & Saavedra, 1986; Halpern, 1998). However, "while effectiveness of game environments can be documented in terms of intensity and longevity of engagement (participants voting with their money or time), as well as the commercial success of the games, there is much less solid information about what outcomes are systematically achieved by the use of individual and multi-player games to train participants in acquiring knowledge and skills.... What is missing is how games should be evaluated for education and training purposes" (O'Neil et al., 2005, p. 456). To attain this goal, it's been suggested that assessment be built into the learning games themselves: "Games that teach also need to be games that test," (Michael & Chen, 2005). However, such near transfer tests may not necessarily translate to successful far transfer to contexts outside video games, depending on the particular goal of the training program.

Even when the transfer goal is clear, that is, when the purpose is to train employees for particular work-related tasks, transfer testing cannot simply focus on that set of tasks in the work environment, without bearing in mind that a demonstration of successful transfer cannot necessarily be generalized to different training and transfer situations. That is, if a pilot test of a particular training program, which shows successful transfer, is conducted in an unrealistic environment where the transfer required is only to near contexts (testing soon after training in the same location by the same individuals), the findings may not generalize to real world applications of the same training program when scaled up. For example, Rosser, Lynch, Cuddihy, Gentile, Klonsky, and Merrell (2007) studied the relationship between surgeons' video gaming experience and performance on a laparoscopic surgery skills game. They found a significant relationship. However, as pointed out by Curet (2007), scores on the laparoscopic surgery skills game did not necessarily relate to skill at actual surgery. Perhaps, for example, surgeons performing under the stress of a real life on the line might behave differently from when they are merely playing (that is, in a different functional context).

The problem of how to assess transfer is even more complex when assessing the benefits of games for other educational purposes, because the desired outcomes may be less clear. In both cases, research on transfer of learning from video games can be evaluated by situating findings in the taxonomy of transfer content and context described above. One area in which video game play has been found to improve performance in transfer tasks for a potentially important skill is in three-dimensional (3-D) mental rotation: the visualization and imaginary rotation of an object that is presented as a two-dimensional drawing. This concept was introduced to the field by Shepard and Metzler in 1971 and further explored by Vandenberg and Kuse (1978), who popularized the classic mental rotation test. Each stimulus in this test is a two-dimensional image of a 3-D object. Each object is shown at different orientations and participants are required to recognize, as quickly as possible, which images represent rotated versions of the same object. Reliable gender differences are found on this measure, in favor of males.

The male superiority on tests of 3-D mental rotation has been the subject of a great deal of discussion in the debate surrounding the disproportionate number of men at the top of science, technology, engineering, and mathematics (STEM) fields (see Ceci, Williams, & Barnett, 2009). The overrepresentation of men in these fields has been attributed by some (see Summers, 2005) to innately superior mathematical skills. Although males were once thought to do better, on average, than females on all aspects of mathematics, in the face of more recent evidence, the supposed area of superiority has been narrowed to spatial skills only, and even more recently narrowed again to the particular skill of 3-D mental rotation, a skill for which there is reasonably robust evidence of superior average male performance. Whether this skill is linked to the overrepresentation of men in STEM jobs is currently unknown, but the finding has led to increased interest in understanding causes of differences in 3-D mental rotation skills. The argument for an innate difference in ability between males and females has been bolstered by findings of gender differences among kindergartners (Casey, Andrews, Schindler, Kersh, Samper, & Copley, 2008). However, evidence from innovative video game training studies (Terlecki & Newcombe, 2005; Feng, Spence, & Pratt, 2007) argues in favor of an experience-based explanation. If 3-D mental rotation may be a factor limiting the advancement of women in STEM fields, it is important to understand whether video game play can improve 3-D mental rotation skills in a durable way that transfers.

Feng, Spence, and Pratt (2007) trained participants by having them play a 3-D first-person shooter game (*Medal of Honor*) for several sessions in their laboratory. Such games require intense visual monitoring and attention. The hypothesis explored was whether spatial attention distribution, a "basic capacity that supports higher-level spatial cognition" (p. 850), could be modified by playing a video game and whether improving individuals' spatial attention distribution would also lead to improved higher level mental rotation ability (3-D mental rotation). The control group played a different 3-D computer game (a maze puzzle game) that did not involve focused attention on a target and was therefore not expected to improve distribution of spatial attention. Spatial attention was assessed using the Uniform Field of View task, in which participants are required to indicate the direction in which a target has very briefly appeared, after a visual mask. Mental rotation ability was assessed using Vanderberg and Kuse's (1978) test, described above, in which different 2-D representations of a 3-D object must be recognized as representing the same object. Results confirmed the hypothesis and showed a reduction in the preexisting gender difference on both measures.

So does this mean that video game play can solve the problem of the dearth of women at the top of STEM fields? Clearly, the answer partly depends on the relevance of these skills to the success of women—compared to the relevance of other possible skill differences and societal and discriminatory factors—which learning studies such as that by Feng et al. (2007) do not address. It also depends on whether improvements shown in these kinds of studies robustly transfer. In general, the further the contexts to which transfer is demonstrated in the experimental situation (testing in a physical context remote from the context of learning; learning and transfer tasks differing in purpose and in contrasting modalities; testing after a substantial time has passed since learning occurred; etc.), the further we can be confident the skills will transfer outside of the experimental situation.

As can be seen in Table 2.3, apart from the knowledge domain, all aspects of context for the Feng, Spence, and Pratt (2007) posttest were near to the context of training. Assessments were conducted soon after training, in the same lab, and both training and transfer tests were overtly research-oriented, involved working individually, and were computer-based. However, the knowledge domain, involving transfer from shooting virtual soldiers to locating the direction of dots on a screen and mentally rotating abstract shapes, can be considered somewhat far transfer. Also, the follow-up test assessed durability of the enhancement an impressive five months later.

Presumably, transfer of these skills would be desirable in many contexts: in book and lab work; at school, in research institutions or in the workplace; in test performance; and at a later time, months or even years later. Thus, for example, it is important to know whether similar improvements would have been found if the training and transfer tasks had not both been computer-based. Would a team of engineers designing a bridge be better at visualizing their plans and detecting design issues from various perspectives if they were trained on *Medal of Honor*? Would a study group have enhanced success on their trigonometry exam? What is the likelihood that improving these skills will have an effect on women's success in STEM fields? Greene, Li, and Bavelier (2009) have suggested that action video game experience teaches individuals to "form templates for, or extract the relevant statistics of, the task at hand" (p. 1). What we lack is an understanding of how and when aspects of STEM jobs might tap into such skills.

Table 2.3 **Transfer Context of Feng, Spence, and Pratt (2007) Experiment 2**

	Context: where transferred from/to	
	Near ←--→ Far	
Knowledge domain		Shooting virtual soldiers vs. locating dots and rotating abstract shapes
Physical context	Same lab	
Temporal context	Soon after training (posttest)	About 5 months later (follow-up)
Functional context	Both clearly research	
Social context	Both individual	
Modality	Both computer-based	

Based on: Feng, J., Spence, I., & Pratt, J. (2007). Playing an action video game reduces gender differences in spatial cognition. *Psychological Science, 18,* 850–855.

Similarly, transfer success for these skills may be sensitive to the content of the tasks. For example, would the video game training enhance mental rotation performance measures that are not time-pressured tests? This issue is important, because many aspects of STEM professionals' work do not require quick responses, but rather deliberate and prolonged thought. Studies such as these represent only the beginning of investigation into these exciting possibilities. Future research might fruitfully investigate transfer situations that involve other aspects of task content and that require far transfer on more of the dimensions highlighted by the simple framework detailed above. Further, many very different sorts of experience fall under the broad label of "video game" (Klopfer, Osterweil, & Salen, 2009) and a wide variety of people play these games, from stereotypical gamers, who dedicate countless hours deeply immersed in their games, to more casual players who play when they happen to be bored, and others who use games as a way to interact with friends. Although the dedicated gamers often come to mind when video games are mentioned, they only represent 11% of players, according to the researchers. Further, multilevel first-person shooter games with lengthy plots and complex graphics, played on a dedicated gaming platform such as an Xbox, offer a very different learning experience from simple driving games, dance-step copying and music-playing games, basic sports simulations (such as *Wii* tennis), slower moving computer-based simulations (such as managing a family of Sims or building an ancient civiliza-tion), socially interactive Internet games played within non-game-specific com-munities such as Facebook, and cell-phone-based digital versions of board and card games. Intentionally educational variants of these formats would likely offer very diverse learning experiences. These diverse learning experiences also would translate to very different transfer challenges. What all these games have in common is that they have a digital component. As a transfer challenge, some video games might have more in common with chess than with a first-person shooter game, while others might share skills in common with deer hunting. Transfer from different kinds of games needs to be assessed on a case-by-case basis. For all these various forms of learning games, understanding how these learning experiences transfer across the dimensions of content and context detailed earlier should allow us to better evaluate the utility of educational investment in video game learning.

References

Barnett, S. M., & Ceci, S. J. (2002). When and where do we apply what we learn?: A taxonomy for far transfer. *Psychological Bulletin, 128*, 612–637.

Bransford, J. D., Brown, A. L., & Cocking, R. R. (1999). *How people learn: Brain, mind, experience, and school*. Washington, DC: National Academy Press.

Brown, A. L. (1989). Analogical learning and transfer: What develops? In S. Vosniadou & A. Ortony (Eds.), *Similarity and analogical reasoning* (pp. 369–412). Cambridge, UK: Cambridge University Press.

Brown, A. L., & Kane, M. J. (1988). Preschool children can learn to transfer: Learning to learn and learning from example. *Cognitive Psychology, 20*, 493–523.

Casey, B. M., Andrews, N., Schindler, H., Kersh, J. E., Samper, A., & Copley, J. (2008). The development of spatial skills through interventions involving block building. *Cognition & Instruction, 26*, 269–309.

Ceci, S. J., & Bronfenbrenner, U. (1985). "Don't forget to take the cupcakes out of the oven": Prospective memory, strategic time-monitoring, and context. *Child Development, 56*, 152–164.

Ceci, S. J., Williams, W. M., & Barnett, S. M. (2009). Sex differences in mathematical and spatial ability. In B. A. Kerr (Ed.), *Encyclopedia of giftedness, creativity, and talent*. Thousand Oaks, CA: Sage.

Chen, Z., & Klahr, D. (1999). All other things being equal: Acquisition and transfer of the Control of Variables Strategy. *Child Development, 70*, 1098–1120.

Chi, M. T. H., Roy, M., & Hausmann, R. G. M. (2008). Observing tutorial dialogues collabora-tively: Insights about human tutoring effectiveness from vicarious learning. *Cognitive Science, 32*, 301–341.

Craig, S. D., Chi, M. T. H., & VanLehn, K. (2009). Improving classroom learning by collaboratively observing human tutoring videos while problem solving. *Journal of Educational Psychology. 101*, 779–789.

Curet, M. J. (2007). The impact of video games on training surgeons in the 21st century—Invited critique. *Archives of Surgery, 142*, 186.

Detterman, D. K. (1993). The case for the prosecution: Transfer as an epiphenomenon. In D. K. Detterman & R. J. Sternberg (Eds.), *Transfer on trial: Intelligence, cognition, and instruction.* (pp. 1–24). Norwood, NJ: Ablex Publishing Corp.

Druckman, D., & Bjork, R. A. (1994). *Learning, remembering, believing: Enhancing human performance.* Washington, D. C.: National Academy Press.

Duncker, K. (1945). On problem-solving. *Psychological Monographs, 58,* 113.

Feng, J., Spence, I., & Pratt, J. (2007). Playing an action video game reduces gender differences in spatial cognition. *Psychological Science, 18,* 850–855.

Fong, G. T., Krantz, D. H., & Nisbett, R. E. (1986). The effects of statistical training on thinking about everyday problems. *Cognitive Psychology, 18,* 253–292.

Godden, D. R., & Baddeley, A. D. (1975). Context dependency in two natural environments on land and underwater. *British Journal of Psychology, 66,* 325–331.

Green, C. S., Li, R., & Bavelier, D. (2009). Perceptual learning during action video game playing. *Topics in Cognitive Science, 2,* 202–216.

Halpern, D. F. (1998). Teaching critical thinking for transfer across domains. *American Psychologist, 53,* 449–455.

Herrnstein, R. J., Nickerson, R. S., de Sanchez, M., & Swets, J. A. (1986). Teaching thinking skills. *American Psychologist, 41,* 1279–1289.

Judd, C. H. (1908). The relation of special training to general intelligence. *Educational Review, 36,* 28–42.

Klausmeier, H. J. (1961). *Educational psychology. Learning and human abilities.* NY: Harper.

Klopfer, E., Osterweil, S., & Salen, K. (2009) Moving learning games forward: Obstacles, opportunities & openness. The Education Arcade, MIT. Retrieved from http://education.mit.edu/papers/MovingLearningGamesForward_EdArcade.pdf.

Michael, D., & Chen, S. (2005). Proof of learning: Assessment in serious games. Retrieved from http://www.gamasutra.com/view/feature/2433/proof_of_learning_assessment_in_.php.

O'Neil, H. F., Jr., Wainess, R., & Baker, E. L. (2005). Classification of learning outcomes: Evidence from computer games literature. *Curriculum Journal, 16,* 455–474.

Reed, S. K., Ernst, G. W., & Banerji, R. (1974). The role of analogy in transfer between similar problem states. *Cognitive Psychology, 6,* 436–450.

Reed, S. K., & Saavedra, N. A. (1986). A comparison of computation, discovery, and graph methods for improving students' conception of average speed. *Cognition and Instruction, 3,* 31–62.

Rosser, J. C., Lynch, P. J., Cuddihy, L., Gentile, D. A., Klonsky, J., & Merrell, R. (2007). The impact of video games on training of surgeons in the 21st century. *Archives of Surgery, 142,* 181–186.

Shepard, R., & Metzler. J. (1971). Mental rotation of three dimensional objects. *Science, 171,* 972, 701–703.

Summers, L. H. (2005). Remarks at NBER on diversifying the science and engineering workforce. Cambridge, MA: National Bureau of Economic Research. Retrieved from http://www.president.harvard.edu/speeches/2005/nber.html.

Terlecki, M. S., & Newcombe, N. S. (2005). How important is the digital divide? The relation of computer and videogame usage to gender differences in mental rotation ability. *Sex Roles, 53,* 433–441.

Thorndike, E. L., & Woodworth, R. S. (1901). The influence of improvement in one mental function upon the efficiency of other functions. II. The estimation of magnitudes. *Psychological Review, 8,* 384–395.

Vandenberg, S. G., & Kuse, A. R. (1978). Mental rotations, a group test of three-dimensional spatial visualization, *Perceptual and Motor Skills, 47,* 599–604.

Vasta, R., Knott, J., & Gaze, C. (1996). Can spatial training erase the gender differences on the water-level task? *Psychology of Women Quarterly, 20,* 549–567.

Woodworth R. S., & Schlossberg, H. (1954). *Experimental Psychology.* New York: Holt, Rinehart & Winston.

3

The Perceptual and Cognitive Effects of Action Video Game Experience

C. SHAWN GREEN

Introduction

For decades, the prevailing view in the field of cognitive neuroscience was that, upon reaching maturity, the adult brain settles into a relatively fixed, unchanging state. Consistent with such an interpretation, for instance, significant effort was put into delineating more or less plastic stages of development (e.g., critical periods; Wiesel & Hubel, 1963). More recently, however, this view has shifted substantially, with current research establishing that the brain possesses an enormous capacity for reorganization throughout the lifespan (Bavelier, Levi, Li, Dan, & Hensch, 2010). Even some critical periods that were previously believed to be quite rigid have since been shown to be flexible and in fact can often be reopened via behavioral means (e.g., through dark exposure; He, Ray, Dennis, & Quinlan, 2007). Such research on neural plasticity has spurred tremendous interest in the development of training regimens to improve brain function in domains ranging from motor skill, to vision and hearing, to broader classes of high-level cognition.

However, while we now know that the human brain retains some level of plasticity even into old age (obviously not at equivalent levels in each age range), a major obstacle remains. This obstacle has been dubbed the "curse of specificity" (Bavelier, Green, Pouget, & Schrater, 2012), and it refers to the fact that although humans show increases in performance on virtually any task given appropriate practice, the enhancements are typically limited to the exact characteristics of the trained task; little or no transfer of learning is observed to even seemingly highly similar untrained tasks (Fahle, 2005). For instance, in seminal work by Fiorentini and Berardi (1980) in the domain of perceptual learning, participants were trained to discriminate between two complex gratings. Over the course of three sessions of training, performance improved from chance levels all the way to ceiling levels. Yet, when the gratings were altered in seemingly minor ways (e.g., in orientation or spatial frequency), subject performance

29

returned to chance levels. Similar specificity has been seen for low-level features such as retinal location, motion direction, motion speed, or even the trained eye. Furthermore, although such specificity has been perhaps most thoroughly described in the field of perceptual learning, it has been documented in essentially all fields that focus on learning, including motor learning, training of high-level cognitive skills such as working memory, and even in education (Barnett & Ceci, 2002; Redick et al., 2013; Tremblay, Houle, & Ostry, 2008). It should be intuitively obvious how significant an impediment such specificity can be for those whose goal is to construct learning paradigms for practical purposes such as rehabilitation (where success necessarily requires benefits that extend beyond the exact laboratory setup).

Interestingly, there are a variety of types of experience, which often correspond to real-world activities that have been shown to produce learning that extends beyond the specifics of the trained contexts. Music training is one such domain. In one study, for example, children who received musical training (vocal or keyboard), showed significantly larger improvements on the Wechsler Intelligence Scale for Children (which clearly bears little resemblance to vocal or keyboard training) than did children who received drama training (Schellenberg, 2004). Similarly, in the athletics domain there are myriad examples wherein individuals with extensive experience playing a given sport demonstrate enhanced abilities at basic laboratory tests (Kida, Oda, & Matsumura, 2005; Lum, Enns, & Pratt, 2002). There is the further focus of this review—playing action video games (Green & Bavelier, 2012).

Before examining these effects, we briefly discuss what makes a game an "action" video game. While there are no quantitative rules that can be applied to perfectly separate the various video game genres, there is a set of qualitative features that all action games share. In particular, action video games are those that involve exceptional speeds (both in terms of the velocity of moving items and the brevity of transient events). These games also involve extraordinary perceptual load (whereby the individual must track many objects), cognitive load (which entails considering many possible outcomes), and/or motor load (which involves engaging in multiple action plans). The games also involve temporal and spatial unpredictability and require a high degree of peripheral processing. Games that fit these criteria include so-called first-person shooter games like the *Call of Duty* series, third-person shooter games like the *Gears of War* series, and some car driving games. To one not familiar with the various video game genres, these may seem like unimportant points, but we have seen that the effects of playing various video games depends highly on the games' content and structure (Cohen, Green, & Bavelier, 2007). Simply put, not all games produce the same types of benefits, if they provide benefits at all.

Here we review the ever-growing literature on the effects of video game experience on vision, attention, and cognitive skills. Although the paradigms that will be reviewed were designed to test processes that are thought to be relatively independent, at the conclusion we will suggest that the results of each can potentially be accounted for by a single common underlying mechanism. As the majority of the literature has compared the performance of expert action video game players (VGPs: usually defined as individuals who play more than five hours a week of action video games) against non-action video game players (NVGPs: who play no action games, though they may play other game genres), we will adopt this focus for our review. However, as simple population differences do not themselves prove a causal link, we will specifically highlight studies that have demonstrated such a link through well-controlled training paradigms.

Spatial Characteristics/Resolution of Vision and Attention

Results from several different paradigms have established an enhanced ability to process spatial information across the visual field in VGPs. For instance, a number of labs have now compared VGP and NVGP performance on the Useful Field of View (UFOV) task, a modified visual search task initially developed by Ball, Beard, Roenker, Miller, & Griggs (1988). Briefly, this task requires participants to localize a very quickly flashed target shape from among a field of distractor shapes. VGPs have demonstrated far superior localization performance on this task as compared to NVGPs in both college-aged adults (Feng, Spence, & Pratt, 2007; Green & Bavelier, 2003, 2006a) and school-aged children (Dye & Bavelier, 2010). Furthermore, the same result has been repeatedly observed in NVGPs specifically brought to the lab and trained on action video games, thus establishing a causal link between video game playing and enhanced performance (Feng et al., 2007; Green & Bavelier, 2003, 2006a; Spence, Yu, Feng, & Marshman, 2009). Similar results have been also seen in the "swimmer task" developed by West and colleagues (West, Stevens, Pun, & Pratt, 2008), and the crowding paradigm (Green & Bavelier, 2007), which both require participants to localize targets from within a field of distracting objects. It is worth noting that in each of these cases, the stimuli did not in any way resemble the rich and complex environments of action video games (they instead used incredibly simple sets of lines and basic shapes). Performance was also tested well into the periphery of the field of vision (e.g., as far as 25° to 30°), which is beyond the typical field of view used while playing (Green & Bavelier, 2007). This type of transfer across both stimulus type and retinal location stands in stark contrast with the perceptual learning literature reviewed previously. Finally, the VGP advantage in spatial abilities is not limited to tasks that have employed displays with extremely limited presentation times. A clear VGP advantage has also been shown in visual search tasks that use reaction time as the primary dependent measure (i.e., the search display is present until the subject finds the target and presses the relevant key). More specifically, these studies have shown that VGPs require less time to process each item across the display (Castel, Pratt, & Drummond, 2005; Hubert-Wallander, Green, Sugarman, & Bavelier, 2011).

Differences in low-level spatial resolution in tasks that are not commonly thought to be limited by visual attention have also been considered (i.e., tasks in which targets appear at a known time and place in the absence of distractors and thus "attention" as it is typically conceived of would not be called upon). For instance, acuity was measured by assessing the smallest T that could be correctly identified as right side up or upside-down (Green & Bavelier, 2007). Similarly, contrast sensitivity was measured via a 2-interval forced choice (2IFC) task in which one interval contained a low-contrast Gabor patch—that is, a sinusoidal grating vignetted by a Gaussian envelope (Li, Polat, Makous, & Bavelier, 2009). In both cases VGPs demonstrated enhanced performance compared to NVGPs (although only in the latter case was there a significant effect of action video game training). Together this overall body of results demonstrates an enhancement in the spatial characteristics and resolution of visual and attentional processing that is due to playing action video games.

Temporal Characteristics/Resolution of Vision and Attention

Differences in the temporal characteristics of vision in VGPs have been measured using a variety of paradigms. For instance, in the standard attentional blink paradigm (Shapiro, Arnell, & Raymond, 1997), participants view a stream of visually presented letters, all of which are black except one target letter, which is white. Although participants can typically successfully identify the white letter, its presence creates a momentary "blink" of attention and thus they often fail to detect a second target that is presented shortly after. The magnitude of this blink is significantly reduced in both adult and child VGPs (Dye & Bavelier, 2010; Green & Bavelier, 2003) and in adults after action video game training (Green & Bavelier, 2003). Similarly, VGPs are capable of performing orientation discrimination tasks at a significantly shorter presentation time than NVGPs (Li et al., 2009) and have significant reductions in the negative effects of backward masking (Li, Polat, Scalzo, & Bavelier, 2010). Again, as was true of the spatial tasks, these temporal processing measures were sterile laboratory tasks completely unlike action video game environments. Thus, these findings suggest that a more general enhancement occurs in the temporal characteristics of visual processing after action video game training.

Capacity/Flexible Allocation of Attentional Resources

In addition to the spatial and temporal aspects of attention, one's attentional capacity and how these attentional resources are distributed are also modified via action video game training. For instance, the multiple object-tracking task measures the number of moving target items that can be successfully tracked within a field of moving items, which act as distractors and are visually identical to the target items. In one version of the task, VGPs were able to track approximately two more items than NVGPs at a criterion level of performance (Green & Bavelier, 2006b) with similar effects being reported in child action gamers (Dye & Bavelier, 2010; Trick, Jaspers-Fayer, & Sethi, 2005). A training study showed the same results, demonstrating a causative link (Green & Bavelier, 2006b). The same basic enhancement in capacity has also been observed in an enumeration paradigm. In this task, white squares were briefly flashed on a black background followed by a mask. Participants were asked to determine the number of squares that were presented. VGPs were able to accurately count a greater number of quickly flashed items than NVGPs given the same display duration (Green & Bavelier, 2006b).

Executive Functions

Several authors have noted performance increases in action video game players on tasks that are commonly thought to tap executive functions. For instance, one common measure of executive function and attentional control is the time it takes to switch between competing tasks. Many different labs have noted a reduction in the size of this "switch cost" in VGPs and in action game trainees (Colzato, van Leeuwen, van den Wildenberg, & Hommel, 2010; Karle, Watter, & Shedden, 2010; Strobach, Frensch, & Schubert, 2012). Furthermore, in our own work we have shown that this effect is not due to a simple increase in the ability of VGPs to map decisions onto button presses (Green, Sugarman, Medford, Klobusicky, & Bavelier, 2012). Indeed, the overall size of the VGP advantage held even when all participants were allowed to give a vocal response rather than to execute a button press response (the assumption being that VGP participants should not be disproportionately practiced at speaking). A second executive-type skill on which VGPs show an advantage is multitasking. For instance, the UFOV task discussed earlier can be performed with or without a concurrent central identification task. While the presence of this additional task greatly interferes with the ability of NVGPs to search, VGPs are able to perform both tasks with little performance decrement (Green & Bavelier, 2006a).

Work from our lab has also addressed the common belief that the RT differences can be explained by video game players potentially showing more impulsivity than NVGPs (Dye, Green, & Bavelier, 2009b). To assess this issue, the Test of Variables of Attention (TOVA) was administered to VGPs and NVGPs. This test requires participants to monitor a display and make a timed response to a stimulus if it appears at one location, while withholding a response to the same stimulus if it appears at another location (i.e., the test is a go/no-go task). In different blocks of trials, the target (go) can appear either frequently or infrequently. The TOVA therefore offers a measure of both impulsivity (i.e., whether the subject is able to withhold a response to a nontarget when most of the stimuli are targets) and a measure of sustained attention (i.e., whether the subject is able to stay on task and respond quickly to a target when most of the stimuli are nontargets). VGPs responded more quickly than did NVGPs on both task components, with equivalent accuracy. The fact that the advantage was equivalent regardless of block (mostly go trials or mostly no-go trials) suggests that VGPs are faster but not more impulsive than NVGPs and equally capable of sustaining their attention.

Possible Neural Changes Underlying These Effects

There are several underlying neural mechanisms that may support the enhanced attentional skills noted in VGPs. One that has been recently tested is the ability of VGPs to filter or suppress task irrelevant items. Mishra, Zinni, Bavelier, and Hillyard (2011) measured EEG signals while VGPs and NVGPs performed a selective attention task. Multiple streams of letters flashed to the left, right, and above fixation, but on any given trial the participants were instructed to attend to only one stream (looking for the occasional digit to appear in the stream) and ignore the other streams. To quantify neural processing, the authors made use of the Steady State Visually Evoked Potential (SSVEP) technique, wherein the various streams are presented at different temporal frequencies (i.e., one stream might be presented at a rate of one item every 83 ms or 12 Hz; another stream might be presented at a rate of one item every 67 ms or 15 Hz, etc). Because neural populations tend to phase lock, the amount of power at these frequencies can then be extracted from the EEG signal and used as a measure of the amount of processing devoted to the stimuli flashing at each frequency. The authors were thus able to assess the neural processing devoted to both the attended and unattended streams. While the two groups showed an equivalent increase in processing devoted to the attended stream, the VGPs showed far greater suppression of processing resources devoted to the unattended stream. Other recent work also indicates major changes in the brain systems that mediate top-down attention in VGPs. For example, a recent fMRI study indicates that recruitment of the fronto-parietal network thought to underlie attention is weaker as attentional demands increase in VGPs, which is consistent with the proposal of increased efficiency in top-down attention in VGPs (Bavelier, Achtman, Mani, & Focker, 2011). Indeed, a decrease in blood-oxygen-level-dependent (BOLD) signal along with enhanced behavioral performance (e.g., faster reaction times or higher d') appears to be a signature of skills that become less effortful and more automatized (Raichle et al., 1994).

Exogenous Attention Does Not Appear to Be Strongly Affected by Action Game Experience

Not all aspects of visual processing appear to be altered via experience with action video games. Interestingly, an aspect that one may have predicted a priori to be significantly taxed by action video games—namely the ability to orient attention toward exogenous cues—does not appear to be altered via action video game experience. Several studies, using both the classic Posner cueing paradigm and the Attentional Network Test, have now examined the time course with which attention is automatically pulled by exogenous cues (Castel et al., 2005; Dye, Green, & Bavelier, 2009a; Hubert-Wallander et al., 2011). Although, as has been seen throughout the literature, VGPs responded faster to targets independent of cueing condition, there was no systematic change indicative of an enhancement of exogenous attention (although see West et al., 2008, for a positive result).

A Common Mechanism—Faster Integration

Based on the results reviewed thus far, any possible single mechanistic explanation must be able to predict (1) increases in VGP accuracy in tasks where participants are asked to make unspeeded perceptual judgments about quickly flashed displays; and (2) decreased RTs in tasks where participants are asked to respond to perceptual stimuli as quickly as possible, noting that previous work has eliminated explanations that refer to additive components of a task, such as simple speeding up of motor execution once response selection has occurred (Dye et al., 2009b). Perhaps the simplest single mechanism that could potentially explain these results is an increase in the rate at which perceptual information is integrated. According to this view, VGPs should be more accurate than NVGPs in accuracy-based tasks because they are able to extract more information from the flashed displays, whereas in speeded tasks this faster integration would be manifested as quicker RTs.

However, while certainly suggestive, none of the previous tasks previously reviewed were ideal to examine this hypothesis. Therefore, as a more specific test

of the hypothesis that VGP experience results in faster integration of information, we made use of a perceptual decision-making task that requires the integration of information over time (Green, Pouget, & Bavelier, 2010).

The coherent dot motion direction discrimination task has been used extensively both in the human literature (Palmer, Huk, & Shadlen, 2005) and animal
literature (Roitman & Shadlen, 2002) to assess the rate at which information
is accumulated over time. In this task participants are asked to determine the
motion direction of many simultaneously moving dots. RT and accuracy in this
task are known to reflect the information that is accumulated until the subject makes a decision and executes a motor response. When many of the dots
move in a consistent direction (high coherence), RTs are generally very fast
and accuracy is high. Conversely, as the percentage of consistently moving dots
approaches zero, RTs become slow and accuracy approaches chance-level.

The motion direction discrimination task is of particular interest because
psychometric models of this decision task indicate that performance (both
accuracy and RT) on the task can be captured by three main variables: (1) the
rate at which information is accumulated over time, which is a function of both
the quality of the stimulus itself as well as the sensitivity of the system to the
stimulus (how well the system is able to detect the given stimulus); (2) the
stopping rule, or the threshold at which the system stops accumulating evidence and the motor decision is made; and (3) a residual amount of time that
is common to all tasks and reflects motor planning and execution (independent of the stopping rule and accumulation rate). This formalism allows us to
examine the qualitative pattern of results, and to ask in a quantitative fashion
which component of the decision making process is modified by action video
game experience.

As predicted based on the wealth of previous experimental data reviewed
above, VGPs were found to be significantly faster than NVGPs across all levels of coherence. A significant interaction between coherence and group indicated once again that an additive component could not explain the results.
Interestingly however, accuracy was perfectly equivalent between groups.
While fitting this particular pattern of results (nonadditive reduction in reaction time and equivalent accuracy) using standard quantitative models (Palmer
et al., 2005) requires a perfect trade-off between an increase in sensitivity and a
decrease in decision threshold, we found—using a newly proposed neural model
of the task (Beck et al., 2008)—that the difference between VGPs and NVGPs
could be captured via a change in a single parameter, namely, the conductance of
the connections between the input and integration layers. Consistent with our
hypothesis above, this parameter does indeed control the amount of information that is processed per unit time.

Furthermore, because the prediction of an increase in the rate at which
information is processed need not include only *visual* information, an auditory
analog of the motion direction task was also developed. In this experiment,

a pure tone embedded in a white noise mask was presented in one ear, while white noise alone was presented in the other (both were normalized to the same mean amplitude). The participants' task was to indicate the ear in which the tone was presented as quickly and accurately as possible. In a manner consistent with adjusting the coherence level of the motion stimulus, the ratio of the amplitude of the target tone to the white noise mask was manipulated in order to test performance across the range of possible accuracy levels and reaction times. As was the case in the motion discrimination task, VGPs were found to be significantly faster than NVGPs, but with equivalent accuracy. Again, this pattern was well-captured by a single change in the conductance parameter of the neural model.

Although a thorough discussion is beyond the scope of this review, it is interesting to examine these results through the theory of Bayesian decision-making. From this perspective, the best a subject can do is to calculate the probability that the various possible options are correct given the current evidence, a probability distribution known as the posterior distribution over choices (denoted $p(c \mid e)$ where c are the choices and e is the evidence). According to Bayes's rule, calculation of the posterior depends on knowledge of the likelihood, or the statistics of the evidence (denoted $p(e \mid c)$)—or in other words, given that the correct option is choice n, what is the probability of receiving the current evidence? Initially, there is no way for participants to know this (i.e., because they have never before seen choice n, there is no way to know the probability of receiving various types of evidence given n) and thus the posterior over choices that they compute will be suboptimal. Over time, the statistics of the evidence can be learned, which in turn will lead to a more accurate posterior being calculated. All of the tasks that have been reviewed in this paper can be formalized in this manner with one slight addition: the insertion of time into the equation. Although it may be initially unintuitive for those tasks employing briefly flashed displays, each of the tasks is an integration task at its root; information is presented over time that must be accumulated. The quantity of interest is therefore the probability of the choice given the evidence that has accrued from the beginning of the trial until the current time. Assuming independence across time, this quantity is simply the product of the posterior at each time step. Failing to perform this multiplication step accurately at each time step will also result in the computation of a suboptimal posterior. The reason this situation is of particular interest to us is that the neural model used to fit the data above has a clear probabilistic interpretation. Increasing the conductance parameter is the same as having better knowledge of the statistics of the evidence or more accurately performing the above multiplication step. Because, as mentioned above, there is no a priori way for participants to know the statistics of the evidence, this suggests that the VGP advantage may be explained in terms of the ability to very rapidly and accurately learn these statistics—in essence the VGPs have "learned to learn."

Summary of the Effects of Action Video Games

Over the past decade, a growing body of literature has indicated that action video game experience has the potential to enhance basic perceptual, motor, or cognitive processes. While each report in the literature has posited a different independent enhancement—whether in the capacity of visual attention; the spatial resolution or temporal resolution of visual attention; the ability to divide attention; the efficiency of visual search; the susceptibility to distractors; or the formation of stimulus-response mappings—we have put forth the hypothesis that a single mechanistic change, an increase in the rate at which sensory information accrues, can account for the majority of the findings in the literature. Such a mechanism would indeed predict the major patterns of results that have been seen. Tasks with accuracy as the primary dependent measure largely consist of quickly flashed displays. An increase in the efficiency with which sensory information is accumulated from the display would result in greater accuracy, which is what is observed in VGPs. In tasks with RT as the primary dependent measure, accuracy is typically near ceiling, making these tasks essentially a "race" toward the correct answer. An increase in the rate at which information is accumulated would result in faster RTs, which again is what is observed in VGPs. From a Bayesian perspective, the ability to accumulate sensory evidence depends highly on knowledge of sensory statistics, which must be learned through experience with a task. Viewed through this framework, what action video game experience teaches individuals is to quickly and accurately learn these statistics—essentially to "learn to learn." This type of learning would explain why the effects of video game experience transfer so widely beyond the game environment and may serve as a hallmark for training regimes that will lead to highly general learning.

Lessons for Educational Games

Although researchers and entrepreneurs alike have recognized the potential of video games to make real-world impact in classroom settings, thus far the successes have been somewhat limited, particularly in contrast to the widespread benefits to general perceptual and cognitive abilities conveyed by action video games. A number of key differences between commercial action video games and typical educational games may explain this disparity in outcome. First, action video games, as part of the very nature of the experience, place players in biophysiological states known to promote learning and plasticity. For instance, for more than one hundred years psychologists have argued that some level of physiological arousal, such as that engendered by action video games (Barlett, Branch, Rodeheffer, & Harris, 2009), more strongly promotes learning than very low arousal states (Yerkes & Dodson, 1908). Furthermore, the emotional content and richly structured storylines and scenarios result in strong activation of the dopaminergic system (Koepp et al., 1998), which in addition to being implicated in the processing of reward (Dayan & Daw, 2008), also appears to play a role in permitting plasticity (Bao, Chan, & Merzenich, 2001). Educational games in contrast have often eschewed these factors in favor of utilizing the highly repetitive "practice-makes-perfect" structure that is easily afforded by computerized paradigms. Unfortunately, doing so strips games of any potential power, instead creating what amounts to little more than flashcards. Among those that create and study video games, these types of games have earned the pejorative nickname "chocolate covered broccoli" in that they are little more than basic and boring drills dressed up in a thin video game shell. Furthermore, in addition to arousal and reward, there are a number of other factors present in action video games (and indeed, in most successful commercial games in general), which theoretical work suggests should strongly promote transfer (Bavelier et al., 2012; Schmidt & Bjork, 1992). Perhaps most important is that in most commercial games, the information to be learned is used in many contexts and domains. Such variety has often been lacking in educational games, which may further explain their relative lack of efficacy. Finally, the idea of "learning to learn" is not a new one in psychology (Binet, 1909; Harlow, 1949; Thorndike & Woodworth, 1901). It may be worth considering how to structure an educational video game such that it not only promotes the learning of the specific material at hand but also enhances the ability of users to acquire content in new situations (Bavelier et al., 2012).

References

Ball, K. K., Beard, B. L., Roenker, D. L., Miller, R. L., & Griggs, D. S. (1988). Age and visual search: expanding the useful field of view. *Journal of the Optical Society of America A, 5,* 2210–2219.

Bao, S., Chan, V., & Merzenich, M. (2001). Cortical remodelling induced by activity of ventral tegmental dopamine neurons. *Nature, 412,* 79–83.

Barlett, C., Branch, O., Rodeheffer, C., & Harris, R. (2009). How long do the short-term violent video game effects last? *Aggressive Behavior, 35,* 225–236. doi: 10.1002/ab.20301

Barnett, S. M., & Ceci, S. J. (2002). When and where do we apply what we learn?: A taxonomy for far transfer. *Psychological Bulletin, 128,* 612–637.

Bavelier, D., Achtman, R. L., Mani, M., & Focker, J. (2011). Neural bases of selective attention in action video game players. *Vision Research.* doi: 10.1016/j.visres.2011.08.007

Bavelier, D., Green, C. S., Pouget, A., & Schrater, P. (2012). Brain plasticity through the life span: Learning to learn and action video games. *Annual Review of Neuroscience, 35,* 391–416.

Bavelier, D., Levi, D. M., Li, R. W., Dan, Y., & Hensch, T. K. (2010). Removing brakes on adult brain plasticity: From molecular to behavioral interventions. *Journal of Neuroscience, 30,* 14964–14971.

Beck, J. M., Ma, W. J., Kiani, R., Hanks, T., Churchland, A. K., Roitman, J., Shadlen, M. N., Latham, P. E., & Pouget, A. (2008). Probabilistic population codes for Bayesian decision making. *Neuron, 60,* 1142–1152.

Binet, A. (1909). *Les idées modernes sur les enfants.* Paris, France: E. Flammarion.

Castel, A. D., Pratt, J., & Drummond, E. (2005). The effects of action video game experience on the time course of inhibition of return and the efficiency of visual search. *Acta Psychologica (Amst), 119*, 217–230.

Cohen, J. E., Green, C. S., & Bavelier, D. (2007). Training visual attention with video games: not all games are created equal. In H. O'Neil & R. Perez (Eds.), *Computer games and adult learning*. Amsterdam, The Netherlands: Elsevier.

Colzato, L. S., van Leeuwen, P. J., van den Wildenberg, W. P., & Hommel, B. (2010). DOOM'd to switch: Superior cognitive flexibility in players of first person shooter games. *Frontiers in Psychology, 1*, 8.

Dayan, P., & Daw, N. D. (2008). Decision theory, reinforcement learning, and the brain. *Cognitive, Affective, and Behavioral Neuroscience, 8*, 429–453.

Dye, M. W. G., & Bavelier, D. (2010). Differential development of visual attention skills in school-age children. *Vision Research, 50*, 452–459.

Dye, M. W. G., Green, C. S., & Bavelier, D. (2009a). The development of attention skills in action video game players. *Neuropsychologia, 47*, 1780–1789.

Dye, M. W. G., Green, C. S., & Bavelier, D. (2009b). Increasing speed of processing with action video games. *Current Directions in Psychological Science, 18*, 321–326.

Fahle, M. (2005). Perceptual learning: specificity versus generalization. *Current Opinion in Neurobiology, 15*, 154–160.

Feng, J., Spence, I., & Pratt, J. (2007). Playing an action video game reduces gender differences in spatial cognition. *Psychological Science, 18*, 850–855.

Fiorentini, A., & Berardi, N. (1980). Perceptual learning specific for orientation and spatial frequency. *Nature, 287*, 43–44.

Green, C. S., & Bavelier, D. (2003). Action video game modifies visual selective attention. *Nature, 423*, 534–537.

Green, C. S., & Bavelier, D. (2006a). Effect of action video games on the spatial distribution of visuospatial attention. *Journal of Experimental Psychology: Human Perception and Performance, 32*, 1465–1478.

Green, C. S., & Bavelier, D. (2006b). Enumeration versus multiple object tracking: The case of action video game players. *Cognition, 101*(1), 217–245.

Green, C. S., & Bavelier, D. (2007). Action-video-game experience alters the spatial resolution of vision. *Psychological Science, 18*, 88–94.

Green, C. S., & Bavelier, D. (2012). Learning, attentional control and action video games. *Current Biology, 22*, R197–R206.

Green, C. S., Pouget, A., & Bavelier, D. (2010). Improved probabilistic inference as a general mechanism for learning with action video games. *Current Biology, 23*, 1573–1579.

Green, C. S., Sugarman, M. A., Medford, K., Klobusicky, E., & Bavelier, D. (2012). The effect of action video games on task switching. *Computers in Human Behavior, 12*, 984–994.

Harlow, H. F. (1949). The formation of learning sets. *Psychological Review, 56*, 51–65.

He, H.-Y., Ray, B., Dennis, K., & Quinlan, E. M. (2007). Experience-dependent recovery of vision following chronic deprivation amblyopia. *Nature Neuroscience, 10*, 1134–1136.

Hubert-Wallander, B., Green, C. S., Sugarman, M., & Bavelier, D. (2011). Changes in search rate but not in the dynamics of exogenous attention in action videogame players. *Attention Perception and Psychophysics, 73*, 2399–2412.

Karle, J. W., Watter, S., & Shedden, J. M. (2010). Task switching in video game players: Benefits of selective attention but not resistance to proactive interference. *Acta Psychologica (Amst), 134*(1), 70–78.

Kida, N., Oda, S., & Matsumura, M. (2005). Intensive baseball practice improves the Go/Nogo reaction time, but not the simple reaction time. *Cognitive Brain Research, 22*, 257–264.

Koepp, M., Gunn, R., Lawrence, A., Cunningham, V., Dagher, A., Jones, T., Brooks, D. J., Bench, C. J., & Grasby, P. (1998). Evidence for striatal dopamine release during a video game. *Nature, 393*, 266–268.

Li, R., Polat, U., Makous, W., & Bavelier, D. (2009). Enhancing the contrast sensitivity function through action video game training. *Nature Neuroscience, 12*, 549–551.

Li, R., Polat, U., Scalzo, F., & Bavelier, D. (2010). Reducing backward masking through action game training. *Journal of Vision, 10*(14), 1–33.

Lum, J., Enns, J., & Pratt, J. (2002). Visual orienting in college athletes: Explorations of athlete type and gender. *Research Quarterly for Exercise and Sport, 73*, 156–167.

Mishra, J., Zinni, M., Bavelier, D., & Hillyard, S. A. (2011). Neural basis of superior performance of action videogame players in an attention-demanding task. *Journal of Neuroscience, 31*, 992–998.

Palmer, J., Huk, A. C., & Shadlen, M. N. (2005). The effect of stimulus strength on the speed and accuracy of a perceptual decision. *Journal of Vision, 5*, 376–404.

Raichle, M. E., Fiez, J. A., Videen, T. O., MacLeod, A.-M. K., Pardo, J. V., Fox, P. T., & Petersen, S. E. (1994). Practice-related changes in human brain functional anatomy during nonmotor learning. *Cerebral Cortex, 4*(Jan/Feb), 8–26.

Redick, T. S., Shipstead, Z., Harrison, T. L., Hicks, K. L., Fried, D. E., Hambrick, D. Z., Kane, M., & Engle, R. W. (2013). No evidence of intelligence improvement after working memory training: A randomized, placebo-controlled study. *Journal of Experimental Psychology: General, 142*, 359–379.

Roitman, J., & Shadlen, M. (2002). Response of neurons in the lateral intraparietal area during a combined visual discrimination reaction time task. *Journal of Neuroscience, 22*, 9475–9489.

Schellenberg, E. G. (2004). Music lessons enhance IQ. *Psychological Science, 15*, 511–514.

Schmidt, R. A., & Bjork, R. A. (1992). New conceptualizations of practice: Common principles in three paradigms suggest new concepts for training. *Psychological Science, 3*, 207–217.

Shapiro, K. L., Arnell, K. M., & Raymond, J. E. (1997). The attentional blink. *Trends in Cognitive Sciences, 1*, 291–296.

Spence, I., Yu, J. J., Feng, J., & Marshman, J. (2009). Women match men when learning a spatial skill. *Journal of Experimental Psychology: Learning, Memory, and Cognition, 35*, 1097–1103.

Strobach, T., Frensch, P. A., & Schubert, T. (2012). Video game practice optimizes executive control skills in dual-task and task switching situations. *Acta Psychologica, 140*(1), 13–24.

Thorndike, E. L., & Woodworth, R. S. (1901). The influence of improvement in one mental function upon the efficiency of other functions. *Psychological Review, 8*, 247–261.

Tremblay, S., Houle, G., & Ostry, D. J. (2008). Specificity of speech motor learning. *Journal of Neuroscience, 28*, 2426–2434.

Trick, L. M., Jaspers-Fayer, F., & Sethi, N. (2005). Multiple-object tracking in children: The "Catch the Spies" task. *Cognitive Development, 20*, 373–387.

West, G. L., Stevens, S. S., Pun, C., & Pratt, J. (2008). Visuospatial experience modulates attentional capture: Evidence from action video game players. *Journal of Vision, 8*(16), 1–9.

Wiesel, T., & Hubel, D. (1963). Effects of visual deprivation on morphology and physiology of cells in the cat's lateral geniculate body. *Journal of Neurophysiology, 26*, 978–993.

Yerkes, R. M., & Dodson, J. D. (1908). The relation of strength of stimulus to rapidity of habit-formation. *Journal of Comparative Neurology and Psychology, 18*, 459–482.

4

Relations between Video Gaming and Children's Executive Functions

JOHN R. BEST

Among other abilities, successful classroom learning requires ignoring distractions in the environment, overriding automatic impulses and emotional reactions, and directing cognition and behavior toward goal achievement. At the center of these abilities are executive functions (EFs), which refer to those cognitive processes that underlie controlled, goal-directed cognition and behavior. EFs are a collection of interrelated yet distinguishable components, which include the updating of working memory (monitoring and adding/deleting items from working memory), inhibitory control (overriding automatic responses), and shifting (switching between different mental tasks) (Miyake, Friedman, Emerson, Witzki, Howerter, & Wager, 2000).

Studies show that individual differences in EFs in early childhood uniquely contribute to future academic achievement (e.g., Cameron et al., 2012) and to classroom behavior (e.g., Riggs, Blair, & Greenberg, 2003). In light of its important role in school functioning, researchers have investigated various strategies to boost children's EFs with the hope that this will transfer to improvements in learning and academic achievement (Diamond & Lee, 2011). This chapter focuses on one nascent area of research that investigates the utility of interactive video games in improving EFs. This brief review differs from previous ones on the effects of video games on cognitive and brain function (e.g., Bavelier, Green, Pouget, & Schrater, 2012). First, the focus of this review is specifically on the effects of video gaming on EFs, rather than on multiple aspects of cognition. Second, traditional sedentary games (i.e., games played via button presses on a handheld controller or keyboard) and exergames (i.e., games played via gross motor movements of the upper and lower body) will be considered. Third, the focus will be on children and adolescents (though research on younger and older adults will be included where applicable).

Sedentary Video Gaming

Examination of the positive effects of interactive video gaming on cognition dates back several decades. Greenfield (1984) argued that video games (at that time, they were largely confined to public arcade games such as *Pac-Man*) engage the player in cognitively and visually complex experiences that require substantial visuospatial processing, cognitive flexibility, and an ability to deduce rule structures. As these demands increase with progression through the game levels, interactive video games could have been training certain visualspatial and cognitive skills; however, Greenfield cautioned that while it is possible that these skills may transfer to other domains outside of video gaming expertise, this proposition was far from a foregone conclusion.

Researchers continue to explore these issues brought up by Greenfield nearly three decades ago, and in recent years, researchers have begun to address the specific question of whether video game playing enhances EFs. Much of this research has focused on action video games, which contain high perceptual, cognitive, and motor loads and include fast-paced first-person shooter games such as *Halo* and *Call of Duty*. The high cognitive loads of these games likely place demands on EFs, such as maintaining and rapidly manipulating information in working memory (e.g., "What is my current task in the game and how does my task change once I achieve X?") and shifting between different task sets (e.g., "When confronted with enemy X, I should do Y, and when confronted by enemy W, I should do Z").

The EF most frequently studied in video game studies is shifting, which is assessed by having participants respond repeatedly to one dimension of an object when one cue is present (e.g., when the background is blue, they must respond to the color of the object); later they respond to an alternative dimension when a different cue is present (e.g., when the background is yellow, they must respond to the shape of the object). Participants typically experience a switch cost when the mental set changes; for example, they respond more slowly and less accurately when they transition from responding to an object's color to responding to its shape. Cross-sectional research indicates that self-reported action video game players (AVGPs; those who report ≥ 5 hours per week of action game play) have superior shifting ability, as indicated by smaller switch costs, compared to non-action game players (nAVGPs; those who report little or no action game play) (Andrews & Murphy, 2006; Boot, Kramer, Simons, Fabiani, & Gratton, 2008; Cain, Landau, & Shimamura, 2012; Colzato, van Leeuwen, van den Wildenberg, & Hommel, 2010; Green, Sugarman, Medford, Klobusicky, & Daphne, 2012; Karle, Watter, & Shedden, 2010). Importantly, improved shifting appears not to be confined to manual responses (which may result from more efficient mapping of a stimulus to a manual response that would occur from heavy use of a handheld controller) but generalizes to the vocal modality (Green et al., 2012, Experiment 1).

Given the correlational nature of the above results, it could be that individuals with better shifting are more likely to be successful at active video games and therefore more likely to become regular players, or it may be that AVGPs differ from nAVGPs on some other, unaccounted for, dimension. Thus, training studies that randomly assign nAVGPs to either training on action video games or to an active control condition in which slower-paced games are used (e.g., puzzle or simulation games) are needed to establish a causal link between action gaming and improved shifting ability. One study has shown that 50 hours of training on active video games marginally improves shifting in comparison to an equivalent amount of time training on slower-paced games (Green et al., 2012, Experiment 4). A second study found no effect of 20 hours of active game training on shifting (Boot et al., 2008), perhaps suggesting that 20 hours of active video game play is insufficient for enhancing the shifting component of EF.

Other EFs have been studied less frequently. In one correlational study, AVGPs outperformed nAVGPs in updating of working memory but not in inhibitory control (Colzato, van den Wildenberg, Zmigrod, & Hommel, 2012), whereas in a second study, AVGPs did not show improved updating of working memory (Boot et al., 2008). A third study showed that AVGPs have an advantage at controlling visual attention and inhibiting eye movements to interfering stimuli (Chisholm & Kingstone, 2011). While it is difficult to draw firm conclusions from these limited studies, it is important to note that some of the inconsistencies in results may arise from differences in EF tasks used. For example, both Colzato and colleagues (2012) and Chisholm and Kingstone (2011) assessed inhibitory control generally speaking, but it can be argued that the ability to override a previously activated motor response (assessed in the Colzato study) is quite different from selectively attending to target stimuli while inhibiting visual attention to irrelevant stimuli (assessed in the Chisholm study). Whereas the former ability likely relies more on reactive control (i.e., implementing inhibitory control processes after stimulus presentation), the latter would require proactive control (i.e., the ability to maintain top-down control throughout the task), and as argued by Chisholm and Kingstone, AVGPs appear to show superiority in top-down proactive control, but not in reactive control.

In addition to considering the methodological issues that may give rise to inconsistent results, researchers should attempt to formulate unifying theories that account for what effects video gaming may have on EFs. One noteworthy example is recent work by Green, Bavelier, and colleagues (Bavelier et al., 2012; Green & Bavelier, 2012), in which the authors posit that playing high-paced action video games improves the player's ability to use task-relevant information and ignore irrelevant information, which in turn permits the player to learn more quickly and efficiently from the environment. This improved ability to "learn to learn" would likely benefit multiple aspects of cognition, including EFs, such as the ability to shift between mental sets and to quickly learn new rule structures (as needed in shifting tasks). Whether improved "learning to learn" accounts for differential effects on EFs (e.g., between proactive and reactive inhibitory control) should be considered in future research.

All of the aforementioned research was conducted with young adults, typically university students. Given the importance of EFs both in childhood development and in the aging process (Best, Miller, & Jones, 2009), determining whether video games can positively affect EFs at both ends of the lifespan will be valuable. To date, few studies have been conducted in these populations. One study with older adults examined the effects of training on a real-time strategy game (*Rise of Nations*) on EFs (Basak, Boot, Voss, & Kramer, 2008). Real-time strategy games are not quite as fast-paced or as violent as action video games (and therefore may be more positively received by older adults), but they do require constant engagement through maintaining and manipulating game priorities in working memory and shifting between these priorities. For example, in *Rise of Nations* players must balance between engaging in activities that bolster their offense, defense, and their economy. Older adults who trained on this game for 23.5 hours over 4–5 weeks demonstrated improved shifting and updating of working memory compared to a no-treatment control group. The results may suggest that training on real-time strategies games can help prevent or slow down cognitive aging by preserving EFs; however, given the lack of an active control group, it is difficult to conclude that the positive effects were due specifically to video game playing and not to some other factors (e.g., the social interaction inherent in completing a laboratory study—that is, the Hawthorne effect).

Studies with children and adolescents are also limited. Two correlational studies reported that youth with significant video game experience show improved multiple-object tracking (Trick, Jaspers-Fayer, & Sethi, 2005), which relies in part on the updating of working memory, but greater interference from incongruent visuospatial stimuli (Dye, Green, & Bavelier, 2009), which relies in part on inhibitory control. In this latter study, the authors argue that the increased interference effect in AVGPs may not necessarily reflect a decrement in inhibitory control but instead may reflect a greater spread of attention, that is, enhanced processing of peripheral stimuli by AVGPs. This argument is based on the fact that AVGPs were not slower than nAVGPs at processing interfering stimuli; instead, AVGPs responded more slowly than would be expected based on their overall faster visual processing compared to nAVGPs.

To my knowledge, no training studies have been conducted with children using entertainment video games like action video games or real-time strategy games. However, several training studies have tested the effects of playing computerized cognitive training games on children's EFs. Cognitive training games are interactive games designed to target specific cognitive processes and improve those processes via repeated and progressively more challenging tasks. The most common cognitive training games target working memory by having children attempt to maintain and manipulate more and more information in working memory over successive game levels. These games are similar to traditional video games in that they are interactive and played with a keyboard or remote, but differ in that their primary focus is not entertainment, and therefore, they often have limited game elements (e.g., narrative, variety of game content). Recent meta-analyses of computerized cognitive training studies (Melby-Lervag & Hulme, 2012; Wass, Scerif, & Johnson, 2012) suggest that while these games often yield short-term improvements to the targeted EFs (suggesting near transfer), there is inconsistent evidence that these improvements result in far transfer to more generalized abilities (e.g., verbal ability) or academic achievement (e.g., arithmetic skills).

Although it is far from clear that cognitive training games have a robust effect across the developmental spectrum, these meta-analyses provide some evidence that younger children benefit from this type of training more so than older children or adults, perhaps indicating sensitive periods in earlier development during which training may have a more robust effect—both in terms of far transfer and of long-term maintenance of the effect. There is also some tentative evidence that cognitive training that incorporates more game elements (i.e., training that appears more like a entertainment video game) improves children's motivation to complete the training and induces greater transfer than cognitive training without these elements (Prins, Dovis, Ponsioen, ten Brink, & van der Oord, 2011). Thus, future research should examine whether games that incorporate the elements of entertainment games (narrative, rapid visual and cognitive processing, variety of content) and of cognitive training games (adaptive training of specific EFs such as working memory) have stronger effects on EFs than games that do not have this combination of elements. Moreover, studies using large age ranges are needed to determine whether sensitive periods of robust training effects truly exist.

It should be noted that sedentary video games are not without their potential negative effects. Some correlational research suggests that video game experience may be associated with poorer inhibitory control in young adults (e.g., Bailey, West, & Anderson, 2010) and with greater impulsiveness and attention problems in children and adolescents (e.g., Gentile, Swing, Lim, & Khoo, 2012). Furthermore, youth may be more prone to overeat while playing sedentary video games compared to doing other activities (Lyons, Tate, Ward, & Wang, 2012), which may contribute to the increases in childhood obesity over recent decades. As Gentile (2011) recently argued, video games are neither all good nor all bad; rather, some elements of video games may contribute to positive outcomes, whereas others may contribute to negative outcomes. Rigorous study of these elements is needed to better understand what types of games will have positive or negative effects, for what populations of players, in what amounts, and in what contexts. Overall, interventions aimed to improve children's EFs should likely use a diversity of strategies, perhaps including certain types of sedentary video games.

Exergaming

Exergames are a relatively new genre of video games that require gross motor movements (e.g., swinging the arms; running in place) instead of or in addition to the traditional button presses of sedentary video games. One of the most iconic exergames, *Dance Dance Revolution (DDR)*, was introduced in the late 1990s and requires the player to mimic dance steps presented on the video screen in rhythm with various musical selections (Behrenshausen, 2007). In its original form, *DDR* was a stand-alone arcade game that used pressure-sensitive footpads to sense the player's movement. In recent years, *DDR* and other exergames have become available for home use as a result of advances in sensor technologies. In 2006 Nintendo introduced the Wii, which uses a wireless remote embedded with accelerometers and optical sensors to measure arm motion and rotation. Along with additional peripherals (e.g., a pressure-sensitive response pad), the Wii remote allows players to engage in whole-body movement to execute moves for their virtual characters. More recently, Microsoft introduced the Kinect as an add-on peripheral for the Xbox 360 console, which uses optical sensing to track the movement of players in three dimensions and translates whole-body movement into virtual activity. This obviates an external controller altogether. The prevalence of exergaming in youth has increased concurrently with increasing sophistication and diminishing costs of exergame consoles. Indeed, recent representative surveys indicate that between 25% and 40% of adolescents in the U.S. and Canada play exergames on a regular basis (Fulton, Song, Carroll, & Lee, 2012; O'Loughlin, Dugas, Sabiston, & O'Loughlin, 2012).

Exergames have many of the perceptual and cognitive demands of action video games but also have significant physical demands through their requirement of gross motor movement. These physical demands could also contribute to the player's EFs in light of the following. First, experimental research indicates that physical activity (PA), both in acute and chronic forms, improves children's cognitive function, especially their EFs (for a review, see Best, 2010). Second, children with greater physical fitness show better EFs than children with poor physical fitness (Hillman, Buck, Themanson, Pontifex, & Castelli, 2009). Third, there are close interrelations among the biological pathways underlying energy metabolism, motor control, and cognition, which suggests that an individual's brain functions optimally when that individual maintains a certain level of PA (Vaynman & Gomez-Pinilla, 2006).

To date, only three studies have examined the effects of exergames on children's EFs. Two of these studies tested normally developing children (Best, 2012; Staiano, Abraham, & Calvert, 2012), and one tested children diagnosed with autism spectrum disorder (ASD) (Anderson-Hanley, Tureck, & Schneiderman, 2011). All three studies tested the acute effects of active video gaming on EFs, that is, the effects immediately following a bout of gaming. In the first study, Best

(2012) determined whether an exergame that contained significant cognitive engagement (i.e., a Wii game that became progressively more difficult as the child mastered easier elements) has a stronger impact on children's inhibitory control than an exergame without significant cognitive engagement (i.e., a Wii game that required only repetitive running in place). The results demonstrated that playing either exergame for approximately 25 minutes enhanced children's inhibitory control compared to watching a video or playing a sedentary video game for an equivalent period of time, suggesting that the increases in arousal induced by the physical demands of exergaming may contribute more to the immediate improvement to this EF than do the priming effects caused by the cognitive demands. Staiano and colleagues (2012) examined whether playing competitive versus cooperative exergames have different effects of adolescents' EFs. After completing 10 weeks of training on Wii EA Sports in either a cooperative or competitive fashion, the participants played the game one last time for 15 minutes and then completed EF assessments that primarily assessed shifting. Participants in a control condition received no training during the 10-week period and completed the EF assessment following a 5-minute period of sitting. In support of the primary hypothesis, adolescents who played the exergame in a competitive fashion showed improvements in EF compared to adolescents in either the cooperative exergame or control conditions. However, counter to the researchers' predictions, adolescents who played the cooperative exergame did not demonstrate improved EF in comparison to adolescents who were in the control condition. The authors argue that playing the exergame in a competitive fashion may place stronger demands on EF than would playing in a cooperative fashion (see Decety, Jackson, Sommerville, Chaminade, & Meltzoff, 2004), leading to a significant improvement to EF performance following competitive exergaming only. As both these studies show, exergames can serve as a useful experimental tool to test the effects on children's EFs of different types of gaming experiences (e.g., playing games with significant cognitive engagement versus limited cognitive engagement; playing games in a competitive versus cooperative fashion).

In the third study, Anderson-Hanley and colleagues (2011) examined the effects of exergaming on the EFs and repetitive behaviors of children and adolescents diagnosed with ASD. Along with significant difficulties in social interaction and verbal and nonverbal communication, children with ASD often show repetitive behavior, such as repeating the same phrase over and over or obsessively lining up toys. In two separate pilot studies, the researchers found that playing DDR or playing a cybercycle game (a stationary bike connected to an interactive video game) for 20 minutes reduced repetitive behavior and improved the updating of working memory relative to watching a 20-minute video. The researchers suggest that the reductions in repetitive behavior may be mediated in part by improvements to EFs caused by exergaming.

To date, the limited experimental research with children and adolescents has examined the immediate effects of exergaming on EFs. (See also Gao & Mandryk,

2012, and O'Leary, Pontifex, Scudder, Brown, & Hillman, 2011, for acute exer-gaming studies with young adults). While more research is needed in this realm, future research should also examine the chronic effects of exergaming that occur after a period of training. Chronic exergaming may lead to long-term changes to brain structure and neurophysiology, leading to enduring effects on players' EFs. For example, Staiano and colleagues had adolescents train on an exergame for 10 weeks; however, the researchers examined shifting performance immediately after playing the exergame, which disallows teasing apart the chronic from the acute effects.

Two studies with older adults have tested the effects of chronic exergaming (i.e., exergame training) and are germane to the current discussion. In one study, Maillot, Perrot, and Hartley (2012) tested whether exergame training improves physical and cognitive functioning in sedentary older adults. Participants in the treatment group played a variety of exergames on the Nintendo Wii in pairs and individually during two 1-hour sessions per week for 12 weeks. Participants in the control condition were asked to maintain their sedentary lifestyles for the duration of the study. Not only did participants in the training group improve on several measures of physical fitness and functioning (e.g., number of arm curls, distance covered during a 6-minute walk), they also showed gains in multiple EFs as well as in processing speed in comparison to the no-treatment control. In a second study, Anderson-Hanley and her colleagues (2012) examined whether exergame training for three months has a stronger impact on older adults' EFs compared to traditional PA training of an equal period of time. The researchers found that participants in the treatment group (playing a cybercycle game on average three sessions per week) demonstrated greater benefits to the three primary EFs (i.e., inhibitory control, updating of working memory, and shifting) compared to older adults who participated in training on a traditional stationary bike. Participants in the treatment group also showed greater concentrations of brain-derived neu-rotropic factor in the blood, which is a protein that promotes neuroplasticity in the brain. Importantly, both groups showed similar fitness gains as a result of PA training, which suggests that the cognitive demands and the interactive nature of cybercycling may have contributed to the improvements in EFs and brain health beyond the benefits provided by enhanced physical fitness. An important next step will be to conduct similar training studies in children to determine whether the interactive and cognitively demanding nature of exergaming can provide addi-tional benefits to EFs over noninteractive forms of PA.

Concluding Thoughts: Transfer to Academics?

As highlighted at the start of this chapter, EFs are important to academic achieve-ment and uniquely predict children's future academic success. This chapter has presented tentative evidence from nascent areas of research that both traditional sedentary video games and exergames may bolster EFs at various times in the lifespan. An important next step—applicable to all age groups but especially to children—is to determine whether video games could improve academic outcomes via improved EFs. This research differs from other lines of research that look at whether video games can teach certain educational content important to academic outcomes; instead, this research would examine whether playing certain video games (not necessarily games with explicit educational content) has an effect on academic outcomes mediated by changes in EFs.

To my knowledge, only training studies using cognitive training games have begun to test this possibility. Loosli, Buschkuehl, Perrig, and Jaeggi (2012) found that two weeks of training on an interactive computer game that emphasized working memory improved reading ability in typically developing 9- to 11-year-olds. Similarly, Chein and Morrison (2010) found that four weeks of working memory training improved reading comprehension in young adults, which appeared to be mediated by improvements in working memory from pre- to posttest. However, a limitation of both studies is that the control group received no sort of intervention, and therefore, the improvements in the training groups may be due to some factors unrelated to the training per se (e.g., a Hawthorne effect). Video game training may be most beneficial for those individuals who present with poor EFs. For example, one study (Holmes, Gathercole, & Dunning, 2009) demonstrated that six weeks of computerized working memory training improved mathematics performance in children with poor working memory. Importantly, this effect was found in comparison to a nonadaptive version of the training program (i.e., the difficulty remained low throughout the 6-week training period), suggesting that the adaptive, interactive nature of the game caused the positive effect on academic achievement. An interesting aspect of this study was that the effect on mathematics was not evident immediately following training, but instead six months afterwards. The authors argue that there may be a time lag during which the improvement in EFs translates into improvement in academic achievement.

Exergaming may also have an effect on academic outcomes mediated by improved EFs. In part, this could occur via mechanisms described above; that is, similar to sedentary games, certain cognitive demands may boost EFs, and in turn, academic achievement. Additionally, the physical demands of exergaming may influence academic outcomes. This possibility arises from experimental evidence that both acute physical activity (Hillman, Pontifex, Raine, Castelli, Hall, and Kramer, 2009; Pontifex, Saliba, Raine, Picchietti, & Hillman, 2012) and chronic physical activity (Davis et al., 2011) improve children's academic achievement, in addition to improving their EFs. Another possibility is to combine educational games with exergames to teach specific academic content in a physically active fashion. Previous research has shown that implementing a physically active curriculum in the classroom improves academic achievement beyond a traditional, sedentary curriculum (Donnelly & Lambourne, 2011).

In general, much more research is needed to examine the effects of sedentary and active video games on EFs, and in turn, on academic outcomes. This research is especially lacking in children and adolescents. When feasible, future research should use randomized, controlled designs that engage children in specific types of interactive gaming experiences to address questions with important theoretical and practical implications. Some questions relate specifically to the type of video game experience: Do fast-paced, action video games have the strongest effects on EFs or do games that train children to maintain more and more information in working memory work better? Should games combine elements from multiple genres? Would games that require physical exercise be best? Other questions relate to developmental and individual differences: Do younger children gain more benefits than older children? Do children with EF deficits benefit more than children without such deficits? Still others involve the causal relations between EFs and academic achievement: If certain video game experiences improve EFs, do these improvements translate into improved academic achievement generally or to improvements in specific aspects of academic achievement? Are these effects evident immediately or only after a delay? Overall, addressing these sorts of questions will help us better understand what types of video game experiences contribute to EF performance and its development and how these may be used to improve academic outcomes.

References

Anderson-Hanley, C., Arciero, P. J., Brickman, A. M., Nimon, J. P., Okuma, N., Westen, S. C.,...Zimmerman, E. A. (2012). Exergaming and older adult cognition: a cluster randomized clinical trial. *American Journal of Preventive Medicine, 42*, 109–119.

Anderson-Hanley, C., Tureck, K. & Schneiderman, R. L. (2011). Autism and exergaming: effects on repetitive behaviors and cognition. *Psychology Research and Behavior Management, 4*, 129–137.

Andrews, G., & Murphy, K. (2006). Does video game playing improve executive function? In M. A. Vanchevsky (Ed.), *Frontiers in cognitive psychology* (pp. 145–161). Hauppauge, NY: Nova Science Publishers.

Bailey, K., West, R., & Anderson, C. A. (2010). A negative association between video game experience and proactive cognitive control. *Psychophysiology, 47*, 34–42.

Basak, C., Boot, W. R., Voss, M. W., & Kramer, A. F. (2008). Can training in a real-time strategy video game attenuate cognitive decline in older adults? *Psychology and Aging, 23*, 765–777.

Bavelier, D., Green, C. S., Pouget, A., & Schrater, P. (2012). Brain plasticity through the life span: learning to learn and action video games. *Annual Review of Neuroscience, 35*, 391–416.

Behrenshausen, B. G. (2007). Toward a (kin)aesthetic of video gaming: The case of Dance Dance Revolution. *Games and Culture, 2*, 335–354.

Best, J. R. (2010). Effects of physical activity on children's executive function: Contributions of experimental research on aerobic exercise. *Developmental Review, 31*, 331–351.

Best, J. R. (2012). Exergaming immediately enhances children's executive function. *Developmental Psychology, 48*, 1501–1510.

Best, J. R., Miller, P. H., & Jones, L. L. (2009). Executive functions after age 5: Changes and correlates. *Developmental Review, 29*, 180–200.

Boot, W., Kramer, A., Simons, D., Fabiani, M., & Gratton, G. (2008). The effects of video game playing on attention, memory, and executive control. *Acta Psychologica, 129*, 387–398.

Cain, M. S., Landau, A. N., & Shimamura, A. P. (2012). Action video game experience reduces the cost of switching tasks. *Attention, Perception & Psychophysics, 74*, 641–647.

Cameron, C. E., Brock, L. L., Murrah, W. M., Bell, L. H., Worzalla, S. L., Grissmer, D., & Morrison, F. J. (2012). Fine motor skills and executive function both contribute to kindergarten achievement. *Child Development, 83*, 1229–1244.

Chein, J. M., & Morrison, A. B. (2010). Expanding the mind's workspace: Training and transfer effects with a complex working memory span task. *Psychonomic Bulletin & Review, 17*, 193–199.

Chisholm, J. D., & Kingstone, A. (2011). Improved top-down control reduces oculomotor capture: The case of action video game players. *Attention, Perception, & Psychophysics, 74*, 257–262.

Colzato, L. S., van den Wildenberg, W. P., Zmigrod, S., & Hommel, B. (2013). Action video gaming and cognitive control: playing first person shooter games is associated with improvement in working memory but not action inhibition. *Psychological Research, 77*, 234–239.

Colzato, L. S., van Leeuwen, P. J. A., van den Wildenberg, W. P., & Hommel, B. (2010). DOOM'd to switch: superior cognitive flexibility in players of first person shooter games. *Frontiers in Psychology, 1*, 8.

Davis, C. L., Tomporowski, P. D., McDowell, J. E., Austin, B. P., Miller, P. H., Yanasak, N. E.,...Naglieri, J. A. (2011). Exercise improves executive function and achievement and alters brain activation in overweight children: A randomized, controlled trial. *Health Psychology, 30*, 91–98.

Decety, J., Jackson, P. L., Sommerville, J. A., Chaminade, T., & Meltzoff, A. N. (2004). The neural bases of cooperation and competition: an fMRI investigation. *NeuroImage, 23*, 744–751.

Diamond, A., & Lee, K. (2011). Interventions shown to aid executive function development in children 4 to 12 years old. *Science, 333*, 959–964.

Donnelly, J. E., & Lambourne, K. (2011). Classroom-based physical activity, cognition, and academic achievement. *Preventive Medicine, 52*, S36–S42.

Dye, M. W. G., Green, C. S., & Bavelier, D. (2009). The development of attention skills in action video game players. *Neuropsychologia, 47*, 1780–1789.

Fulton, J. E., Song, M., Carroll, D. D., & Lee, S. M. (2012). Active video game participation in U.S. youth: Findings from the National Youth Physical Activity and Nutrition Survey, 2010. *Circulation, 125*, AP260.

Gao, Y., & Mandryk, R. L. (2012). The acute cognitive benefits of casual exergame play. Paper presented at the Proceedings of the 2012 ACM annual conference on Human Factors in Computing Systems.

Gentile, D. A. (2011). The multiple dimensions of video game effects. *Child Development Perspectives, 5*, 75–81.

Gentile, D. A., Swing, E. L., Lim, C. G., & Khoo, A. (2012). Video game playing, attention problems, and impulsiveness: Evidence of bidirectional causality. *Psychology of Popular Media Culture, 1*, 62–70.

Green, C. S., & Bavelier, D. (2012). Learning, attentional control, and action video games. *Current Biology, 22*, R197–R206.

Green, C. S., Sugarman, M. A., Medford, K., Klobusicky, E., & Daphne, B. (2012). The effect of action video game experience on task-switching. *Computers in Human Behavior, 28*, 984–994.

Greenfield, P. M. (1984). *Mind and media: The effects of television, video games, and computers.* Cambridge, MA: Harvard University Press.

Hillman, C. H., Buck, S. M., Themanson, J. R., Pontifex, M. B., & Castelli, D. M. (2009). Aerobic fitness and cognitive development: Event-related brain potential and task performance indices of executive control in preadolescent children. *Developmental Psychology, 45*, 114–129.

Hillman, C. H., Pontifex, M. B., Raine, L. B., Castelli, D. M., Hall, E. E., & Kramer, A. F. (2009). The effect of acute treadmill walking on cognitive control and academic achievement in preadolescent children. *Neuroscience, 159*, 1044–1054.

Holmes, J., Gathercole, S. E., & Dunning, D. L. (2009). Adaptive training leads to sustained enhancement of poor working memory in children. *Developmental Science, 12,* F9–F15.

Karle, J. W., Watter, S., & Shedden, J. M. (2010). Task switching in video game players: Benefits of selective attention but not resistance to proactive interference. *Acta Psychologica, 134,* 70–78.

Loosli, S. V., Buschkuehl, M., Perrig, W. J., & Jaeggi, S. M. (2012). Working memory training improves reading processes in typically developing children. *Child Neuropsychology, 18,* 62–78.

Lyons, E. J., Tate, D. F., Ward, D. S., & Wang, X. (2012). Energy intake and expenditure during sedentary screen time and motion-controlled video gaming. *The American Journal of Clinical Nutrition, 96,* 234–239.

Maillot, P., Perrot, A., & Hartley, A. (2012). Effects of interactive physical-activity video-game training on physical and cognitive function in older adults. *Psychology and Aging, 27,* 589–600.

Melby-Lervåg, M., & Hulme, C. (2013). Is working memory training effective? A meta-analytic review. *Developmental Psychology, 49,* 270–291.

Miyake, A., Friedman, N. P., Emerson, M. J., Witzki, A. H., Howerter, A., & Wager, T. D. (2000). The unity and diversity of executive functions and their contributions to complex "frontal lobe" tasks: A latent variable analysis. *Cognitive Psychology, 41,* 49–100.

O'Loughlin, E. K., Dugas, E. N., Sabiston, C. M., & O'Loughlin, J. L. (2012). Prevalence and correlates of exergaming in youth. *Pediatrics, 130,* 806–814.

O'Leary, K. C., Pontifex, M. B., Scudder, M. R., Brown, M. L., & Hillman, C. H. (2011). The effects of single bouts of aerobic exercise, exergaming, and videogame play on cognitive control. *Clinical Neurophysiology, 122,* 1518–1525.

Pontifex, M. B., Saliba, B. J., Raine, L. B., Picchietti, D. L., & Hillman, C. H. (2013). Exercise improves behavioral, neurocognitive, and scholastic performance in children with attention-deficit/hyperactivity disorder. *The Journal of Pediatrics, 162,* 543–551.

Prins, P. J. M., Dovis, S., Ponsioen, A., ten Brink, E., & van der Oord, S. (2011). Does computerized working memory training with game elements enhance motivation and training efficacy in children with ADHD? *Cyberpsychology, Behavior, and Social Networking, 14,* 115–122.

Riggs, N. R., Blair, C. B., & Greenberg, M. T. (2003). Concurrent and 2-year longitudinal relations between executive function and the behavior of 1st and 2nd grade children. *Child Neuropsychology, 9,* 267–276.

Staiano, A. E., Abraham, A. A., & Calvert, S. L. (2012). Competitive versus cooperative exergame play for African American adolescents' executive function skills: Short-term effects in a long-term training intervention. *Developmental Psychology, 48,* 337–342.

Trick, L. M., Jaspers-Fayer, F., & Sethi, N. (2005). Multiple-object tracking in children: The "Catch the Spies" task. *Cognitive Development, 20,* 373–387.

Vaynman, S., & Gomez-Pinilla, F. (2006). Revenge of the "sit": How lifestyle impacts neuronal and cognitive health through molecular systems that interface energy metabolism with neuronal plasticity. *Journal of Neuroscience Research, 84,* 699–715.

Wass, S. V., Scerif, G., & Johnson, M. H. (2012). Training attentional control and working memory—Is younger, better? *Developmental Review, 32,* 360–387.

5

Developing Scientific Thinking in the Context of Video Games: Where to Next?

CORINNE ZIMMERMAN

In October 2010, a group of experts gathered at Fordham University in New York City for two days to discuss the academic potential of video games. There were game designers, researchers, and educators. I was invited to participate in the conversations as someone with expertise on the development of scientific thinking skills (Zimmerman, 2000, 2007). Claims have been made that video games may facilitate scientific thinking (e.g., Barab & Dede, 2007; Steinkuehler & Duncan, 2008). As someone with only cursory knowledge of current gaming (but an early adopter of the home version of Atari Pong and an avid player of the VIC-20 versions of *Frogger* and *Asteroids*), I was curious to explore this issue more. As a novice of the *new* gaming technologies, I conducted an informal analysis of the content and structure of a number of educationally relevant video games (e.g., *River City, WolfQuest, Quest Atlantis, ThinkerTools, WhyVille*), which led me to believe that this new generation of games does include elements that are relevant to scientific thinking—such as problem-solving, self-directed experimentation, hypothesis testing, and causal reasoning.

Much has been written on the rationale for including video games in educational contexts in general, and in science education in particular (e.g., Annetta, 2008; Barab et al., 2009; Mayo, 2009; NRC, 2011). Arguments for the educational use of games include their potential for "complex forms of learning and participation... discursive richness, depth of collaborative inquiry, opportunities for consequentiality, rich perception-action cycles, and exploration of situated identities" (Barab, Gresalfi, & Ingram-Goble, 2010, p. 525). A particularly compelling argument relates to issues of motivation: video games are known for (and designed for) keeping players engaged. The behavioral persistence, extended time-on-task, lack of fear of failure, leveling up, and mastery approaches are all characteristics of games that educators would love to exploit. Moreover, the engagement seen in game play is consistent with various theories of motivation (Deci & Ryan, 2000), the concept of psychological flow

(Csíkszentmihályi, 1975, 1990), and with educational research and theory, such as the benefits of self-directed, collaborative, and participatory learning (e.g., Gauvain, 2001; O'Loughlin, 1992).

My intention, developed after the conversations at the Academic Lessons from Video Game Learning conference, was to write about the research that is relevant for those working at the intersection of game development and academic skill development, with a specific focus on scientific thinking skills. My goal was to create a document that would provide a common knowledge base for game designers working at this intersection: if game designers knew more about the development of scientific thinking skills, they could be more informed engineers of the potential learning environments within the video game context. Similarly, knowing how scientific thinking is assessed and measured is important if we are to examine claims about the effectiveness of particular video games with respect to the transfer of relevant skills and knowledge to academic settings.

I begin with a brief review of the research on video games and science, showing that there is still much work to be done. My main goal for this chapter is to provide a focused review of the research on scientific thinking that is relevant for game developers interested in creating or modifying video games to promote these thinking skills. This review is embedded within a set of suggestions for the next phase of the research agenda on the academic potential of video games. My second goal is to outline the next steps, in a somewhat sensible but arbitrary order, that could be considered by educators and researchers interested in using video games to scaffold and develop scientific thinking skills.

Past Research on Video Games and Learning in Science

In the time between outlining the goals for my chapter and writing it, several relevant books and papers have been published. With respect to reviewing the research literature at the intersection of video game play and scientific thinking, I will briefly focus on three recent sources that have already synthesized much of the literature.

The National Research Council recently published a book-length report titled *Learning Science through Computer Games and Simulations* (NRC, 2011). The committee responsible for the report was charged with investigating whether computer games and simulations have the potential to address the various challenges faced by science educators. Computer simulations include dynamic visualizations of phenomena and processes that are not typically observable because of complexity (e.g., ecological systems), because of size (e.g., subatomic structure, planetary motion), because they occur over a long timescale (e.g., population growth, seafloor spreading), or because they occur very quickly (e.g., synaptic transmission).

Their analysis of video games focused on "serious games" – those that support inquiry approaches to science education. Games were defined as including elements of fun and enjoyment, but also feedback to measure progress toward a player's goals, and use of strategies and rules for controlling the game environment (NRC, 2011; see also McGonigal, 2011). Generally, compared to games, simulations were found to have a greater influence on science learning. The overall conclusion of the 2011 NRC report was that the current state of research on the use of video games to support learning in science is "inconclusive." However, an entire chapter is devoted to the future research agenda to continue to explore the "great potential" that games and simulations have for science learning.

Another relevant publication is the volume edited by Tobias and Fletcher (2011): *Computer Games and Instruction* provides a synthesis of research on serious games. The growing body of research on games designed for learning contexts is summarized, followed by commentary from various experts in the field of video game research. Although not specific to science, the overall conclusion of this volume echoes that of the NRC (2011) report, with the suggestion that additional research is necessary to demonstrate the effectiveness of games in educational contexts. Young et al. (2012) also reviewed research on video games and academic achievement in math, science, language learning, history, and physical education. Their overall conclusion was that "many educationally interesting games exist, yet evidence for their impact on student achievement is slim" (p. 61). Despite delivering bad news, the authors also provide recommendations for future research.

Outlining a New Agenda

This sample of recent reviews supports the conclusion that there is insufficient and inconclusive evidence that video games have any causal status with respect to academic achievement. However, there are compelling reasons why we should continue to do research to explore whether elements of game play can be exploited for educational gain. In Figure 5.1, I outline several steps for the next phases of such a research agenda. I independently generated many of these critiques and suggestions, but I note when they are consistent with views expressed by others interested in the academic potential of games. Note that the order of steps in Figure 5.1 is somewhat arbitrary. For example, steps 3 through 5 could go in any order. Similarly, the information in steps 2 through 6 *should* inform the development of high-quality learning games (step 1). However, I will agree with Prensky (2011) that research on the educational effectiveness of a game should come only after the initial research and development steps toward game design have been completed. I will focus on steps 1 through 6 in this chapter. Step 7 is beyond the scope of this chapter and includes many domain-general guidelines for good research, regardless of content area. Specific suggestions with respect to video

Step 1: Develop High-Quality Learning Games

Step 2: Specify More Precise Research Questions

Step 3: Identify the Science Education Problems That Need Solutions

Step 4: Specify the Big Picture Learning Goals (e.g., NRC, 2010, 2011, 2012)

Step 5: Consult the Basic Research on Scientific Thinking

Step 6: Specify Learning Goals, Learning Activities, Games, and Learning Outcomes

Step 7: Improve the Quality of Research (e.g., adequate intervention time, adequate statistical power, industry-education partnerships, longitudinal research)

Step 8: Iterate

Figure 5.1 An outline of the possible next steps for research on video games in science education.

games can be found in Dede (2011), Gee (2011), NRC (2011), Prensky (2011), and Young et al. (2012).

STEP 1: DEVELOP HIGH-QUALITY LEARNING GAMES

Prensky (2011) outlines a compelling argument that research on the academic potential of video games is not worth doing if time and effort has not been spent on the development of high-quality instructional video games. Prensky suggests 10 criteria for assessing whether a game is "high quality." A sample of characteristics includes (1) a balance between content to be learned and elements that engage learners to voluntarily participate in game play; (2) a correspondence between the teaching goal, the game's goal, and the learner's goal; (3) a high level of complexity (e.g., multiple goals, levels, and skills); (4) a built-in leveling-up process that requires the evaluation of learning or skills; (5) the ability to adapt to the learner's successes and failures and make adjustments. Adaptivity is a particularly important feature of commercial entertainment games, and Prensky (2011) argues that it should be a critical component of instructional games. Many commercial games implement artificial intelligence programming to determine in real time whether a player's performance indicates the need for scaffolding or additional challenges, and the game automatically changes in response to learner performance, much the way intelligent tutoring systems do (Anderson, Corbett, Koedinger, & Pelletier, 1995; VanLehn et al., 2005)

Prensky (2011) also describes 10 design principles that commercial games incorporate to create engaging game play. Many are relevant to learning scientific inquiry skills via game play. For example, making players heroes may not sound educationally relevant. However, players of *River City* take on the role of a researcher who must determine the cause of an outbreak of illness. Giving students goals in the context of role-playing as scientists or engineers may then contribute to identification with science and science learning. Similarly, the design principle to "make players decide and see the results" (p. 272) is a critical component of engagement in game play. Making decisions and receiving feedback are prototypically important parts of engaging in scientific inquiry activities (described in more detail, below). I direct the reader interested in further exploring this topic to Prensky (2001, 2011) and McGonigal (2011).

The take-away message is that any research program or individual study focused on using video games to scaffold academic skills in science must ensure that those games are of high quality and are engaging. None of the following steps of a research agenda is relevant if an inadequate instructional game is incorporated into a science curriculum.

STEP 2: SPECIFY MORE PRECISE RESEARCH QUESTIONS

As a research question, "Are video games good for science learning?" is vague and underspecified. Several authors have also noted this flaw in the existing research: such a broad research question is unanswerable (Gee, 2011). To illustrate a more nuanced version of a research question, consider the following:

Under what conditions, and for whom, can video games facilitate or improve science achievement relative to achievement attained in a comparison group or groups?

Now we can unpack the constituent elements of this question.

Under what conditions: A variety of educationally relevant conditions could be enumerated including, for example, whether games are used for instruction or assessment, or whether the goal is to teach science concepts or science process skills. It may be that some games are better suited for content within particular science domains, or for individual or collaborative learning. We need to determine which types of conditions afford learning via a gaming context.

For whom: Participant groups must be specified to avoid making assumptions about "one size fits all." Is an intervention effective for at-risk students, advanced placement students, or for particular age groups (i.e., preschool, elementary, middle, or high school)? It is also important to specify participant characteristics to answer questions about aptitude-treatment interactions.

Video games: "Video games" (and simulations) are very broad categories (Tobias & Fletcher, 2011). Games can and should be defined along dimensions of quality, complexity, genre, time scales, extent of collaboration, competitiveness, and so on. It is important to note whether a game was designed for entertainment but has instructional potential or whether it was designed as an instructional game.

Science achievement: As will be discussed in more detail below, K–12 science education is quite broad, and includes concepts, processes, and crosscutting ideas, all
of which need to be taught and assessed in developmentally appropriate ways.
Comparison group(s): Prensky (2011), for example, has noted that it is time to go
beyond research implementing the prototypical "treatment vs. standard practice" research design.

Previous reviews that support the common conclusion that research to date
is "inconclusive" may, in part, be due to overly broad research questions. Dede
(2011) discusses the need for more precision in research questions, and provides
samples for research on educational games in general. For the sake of illustration,
a sample of his questions (p. 240) adapted for science content might include:

- To what extent can educational games replicate authentic science inquiry
  activities that learners can master?
- Are there particular individual difference characteristics of learners (e.g., the
  tendency to approach inquiry with either an "experimenter" or a "theorist"
  mindset/strategy; Dunbar & Klahr, 1989; Zimmerman, Raghavan, & Sartoris,
  2003) that predict which students will (or will not) find educational games and
  simulations motivating and effective?
- In hands-on inquiry tasks, students show a different pattern of performance
  when they are given the goals of a "scientist" or "engineer" (Schauble, Klopfer,
  & Raghavan, 1991). Does this same pattern generalize to role-playing in
  video games?

STEP 3: IDENTIFY THE SCIENCE EDUCATION PROBLEMS
THAT NEED SOLUTIONS

The NRC (2011) identified several problems in science education that may potentially be addressed by inclusion of games in science curricula. The first problem is
attracting and retaining individuals into science careers. The workforce requires
professionals trained in science, technology, engineering, and mathematics
(STEM). For decades there has been a declining interest in STEM careers, a high
dropout rate from STEM majors, and a lack of diversity among STEM professionals (e.g., NRC, 2012). The second problem concerns the scientific literacy of *every-
body else*. We live in a scientifically and technologically advanced culture, so many
personal, professional, and public policy decisions require an understanding of
the concepts, processes, and nature of science. We witness the consequences of
scientific illiteracy when we consider, for example, climate change denial, anti-
vaccination lobbying, end-of-world prophesies, and school boards voting to
include creationism in the science curriculum (to name only a few). The apparent
"antiscience" sentiments of citizens and misinformed politicians are alarming to

scientists and educators. Therefore, changes are needed in how science is taught to make it clear that science is relevant for all.

If we buy the argument that science is a necessary component of modern education for all citizens, the next problem involves how best to teach it across the curriculum. The natural, social, and physical sciences all include abstract phenomena that may be difficult to visualize and represent because of magnitude, time scales, or complexity. Video games and computer simulations have enormous potential to help address the problem of communicating abstract concepts. Science educators are also faced with the problem of teaching students a number of challenging cognitive and metacognitive thinking skills that are required for conducting research. Although claims about "scientists in the crib" have been made, decades of research on the development of scientific thinking show a long slow trajectory that requires educational scaffolding (Zimmerman, 2000, 2007; Klahr, Zimmerman, & Jirout, 2011). Professionals in STEM careers are immersed in disciplinary training for years to overcome the cognitive heuristics and biases that may work well enough for everyday problem solving. Finally, science educators recognize that students should be exposed to learning experiences that reflect how authentic science is conducted and communicated. The problem is how best to engage students in authentic inquiry and argumentation that is developmentally appropriate (NRC, 2011).

STEP 4: SPECIFY THE BIG PICTURE LEARNING GOALS

Once again, we can rely on the National Research Council to do the heavy lifting for us. The newly published science education standards (NRC, 2012) focus on elements within three dimensions. The first dimension, *Scientific and Engineering Practices*, includes authentic science process skills, with additional specification for science versus engineering contexts. For example, "asking questions" (in science) and "defining problems" (in engineering) are the first skills listed. The other domain-general skills are used across disciplines (e.g., conducting investigations, interpreting data, using evidence, constructing explanations (science), or designing solutions (engineering). Many of the practices listed here overlap with the specific set of cognitive and metacognitive skills studied by developmental psychologists of science, and thus, we already know a great deal about them (see step 5).

The second dimension includes *Crosscutting Concepts*, such as cause and effect, systems and system models, patterns, and stability and change (NRC, 2012). The third dimension, *Disciplinary Core Ideas*, specifies core ideas in four disciplinary areas (i.e., physical sciences, life sciences, Earth and space science, and engineering, technology, and the applications of science). For example, molecules, organisms, ecosystems, heredity, and evolution are some of the core ideas included within life sciences. Learning the wide range of discipline-specific content may be difficult to adapt to game play: Roth (2008) points out that there are thousands of possible science concepts that can be taught. Prensky (2011) notes that "building a game for every topic is probably not necessary" (p. 268). However, big-picture crosscutting concepts, such as systems, patterns, and causality, are perfect for simulation and games.

STEP 5: CONSULT THE BASIC RESEARCH ON SCIENTIFIC THINKING

In previous writings, I have maintained that science education can and should be informed by basic psychological research on how people think and reason about science. More specifically, educational interventions should be developed and tested in the context of what we know about scientific thinking skills and how they develop across the school years. The types of science activities that children are capable of during the preschool and elementary years (e.g., Klahr et al., 2011) are different from the inquiry activities that children are capable of later (Zimmerman & Croker, 2013).

Scientific thinking includes the set of reasoning and problem-solving skills involved in generating, testing, and revising hypotheses or theories. In the case of fully developed skills, one can also reflect metacognitively on the processes of knowledge acquisition and knowledge change that result from inquiry activities. Scientific thinking involves intentional information seeking (Kuhn, 2011), and is the product of individual reasoning and collaborative cognition that is supported by the social and physical environment (Morris, Croker, Masnick, & Zimmerman, 2012). Given this broad definition of scientific thinking, we can study anyone engaged in the process, from young children making observations in a school classroom (e.g., Chinn & Malhotra, 2002) to a research team in a laboratory discussing the results of a set of experiments (e.g., Dunbar, 1995).

In typical studies of scientific thinking, participants are presented with a multivariable causal system (e.g., a computer simulation or physical apparatus). The participant's goal is to investigate the system: propose hypotheses, make predictions, conduct experiments, collect and evaluate evidence, make inferences, and draw conclusions in the form of either new or updated knowledge. As an exemplar, Schauble (1996) had students conduct experiments in hydrodynamics, where the goal was to determine which variables have an effect on boat speed. Participants could vary the depth of the canal, and the size, shape, and weight of the boat. Such studies may take place over the course of a brief one-hour session, or researchers may collect data from participants as they negotiate multiple cycles of inquiry over the course of weeks.

I have previously reviewed and synthesized this body of work (Zimmerman, 2000, 2007; Zimmerman & Croker, 2013) and will focus on trends that are evident across a variety of studies on the development of scientific thinking. First, prior knowledge matters; how much prior knowledge, the domain of knowledge (e.g., social vs. physical science), and the strength of prior knowledge all influence inquiry and inference skills on scientific reasoning tasks. Second, scientific reasoning is guided by our assessment of the plausibility of a hypothetical cause. That is, we make judgments about the world in ways that "make sense" or are consistent with what we already know about how things work. In general, plausibility is a known constraint with respect to belief formation and revision (Holland, Holyoak, Nisbett, & Thagard, 1986) and is a domain-general heuristic that is used to guide the choice of which hypotheses to test and which experiments to run (Klahr, Fay, & Dunbar, 1993). Because we use the strength of our existing beliefs and assessments of plausibility when engaged in scientific reasoning, children and adults often choose to maintain their prior beliefs rather than changing them to be in line with newly acquired evidence (e.g., Chinn & Brewer, 1993; Chinn & Malhotra, 2002).

Third, across numerous studies, children and adults have a difficult time disconfirming a causal belief, compared to disconfirming a noncausal belief or confirming an existing belief. In exploring multivariable systems, there are both causal and noncausal variables. The causal status of some variables will be inconsistent with prior belief, and some researchers incorporate known robust misconceptions into the system (e.g., many children and adults believe that heavier objects fall and sink faster than lighter objects). During inquiry, people may generate evidence inconsistent with a *causal* belief. In other cases, a variable initially believed to be *noncausal* will be found to have an effect. A common finding is that it is generally more difficult to integrate evidence that disconfirms a prior causal belief (which involves restructuring one's belief system) than it is to integrate evidence that disconfirms a prior noncausal belief (which involves incorporating a newly discovered causal relation). In the example of sinking objects, it is difficult to give up the belief that weight matters, but it is easy to add the belief that shape (sphere vs. cube) speeds up or slows down an object (see Penner & Klahr, 1996).

Finally, much has been written in the scientific reasoning literature about the importance of causal mechanisms. In particular, a useful heuristic in scientific reasoning tasks is the need for a plausible causal mechanism to explain the relationship between potential causes and their effects (Koslowski, 1996). Although we are good at noticing the many examples of covariation between events in the world, we tend to make a causal inference only when it can be supported by a mechanism or explanation. Similarly, when a plausible causal mechanism exists to explain why a putative cause and effect should be linked, it is difficult to let go of a belief when there is mismatch between prior belief and new evidence suggesting no causal effect. A consideration of a causal mechanism is also important because for many scientific phenomena, mechanisms are either unobservable (e.g., force, radiation, natural selection) or are unobservable to the naked eye (e.g., genes, neurotransmitters), a limitation that could be overcome with games and simulations.

I have described four generalized findings from the basic psychological literature on scientific thinking to illustrate a sample of what we know about how people learn via inquiry. Findings related to prior knowledge, plausibility, belief change, and causal mechanisms are examples of moderating factors that should be considered when using or designing educational video games with scientific inquiry activities. The first take-away message is that belief change is not always straightforward and linear, which needs to be taken into account when using instructional games that include experimentation and other science process skills. As we negotiate cycles of inquiry, generate and evaluate evidence, assess the plausibility of correlations, and consider putative causal mechanisms, the prior knowledge we bring to the task can either facilitate or hinder progress toward learning goals. That is, existing knowledge can have either a positive or a negative impact, and in teaching and learning situations involving science, it is necessary to analyze the content and structure of games for expectations about the nature and extent of necessary prior knowledge. If an instructional game deals with an area of science for which there are robust misconceptions, the process of belief change or belief replacement (i.e., replacing naïve impetus theory with Newtonian mechanics) may be less than straightforward.

The second take-away message is that games can be analyzed or designed with respect to known psychological findings. Adaptive games can, for example, assess a learner's errors and then supply missing relevant knowledge. In particular, when we are aware of robust science misconceptions, if cycles of inquiry and evidence-generating activities do not result in belief change consistent with scientific consensus, games can provide remedial instruction via adaptive programming. For example, a simple simulation that animates the difference between Copernican and Tychonian planetary motion[1] could be used to demonstrate counterfactual behaviors of such systems. These are but two illustrations of why basic research is relevant in the creation and adaptation of instructional interventions.

STEP 6: SPECIFY LEARNING GOALS, LEARNING ACTIVITIES, GAMES, AND LEARNING OUTCOMES

The next step involves reducing the grain size from big picture outcomes to specific learning goals, learning activities, and measurable outcomes. If we imagine a world in which high-quality instructional games provide the motivation to engage in and practice various scientific inquiry skills, and to learn science content (e.g., concepts and theories), what types of learning outcomes should we be measuring?

One suggestion for improving educational research is to ensure that learning goals are specified for any intervention (whether traditional or game-based). For example, the learning goals specified by the NRC (2011) report on video games and simulations include (1) motivation to learn science; (2) conceptual understanding of facts, theories, arguments, and models in the various domains of science; (3) science process skills such as asking questions, observing, generating hypotheses, and conducting experiments; (4) understanding the nature of science as an individual, social, and cultural endeavor; (5) participation in science discourse, including use of scientific language in communication and argumentation; and (6) developing an identity as a science learner who uses and generates scientific knowledge.

In Table 5.1 I have attempted to illustrate a mapping between some of these learning goals (2, 3, and 5, above) and the types of activities that would need to be incorporated into a classroom, game, or simulation activity, along with some suggestions of the style of game that could be used or developed. Where possible, I have included a concrete suggestion of an already available game that encompasses some of the necessary features. Many of these fit across several of the game style categories. For example, *Kibble Space Program* is a game that encompasses invention and experimentation, in which the goal is to design and test rockets. *Spore* is a strategy game in which one starts as a single-cell organism, and throughout the game evolves into a more complex life form, thus illustrating concepts relevant to cell division, heredity, and evolutionary theory. Games specifically designed for science education purposes (e.g., *River City, Quest Atlantis*) cross a number of game styles. Note also that additional work is needed to further classify games by appropriate age range. Ideally, the next step would be to determine specific game features that provide the learning opportunities for each goal, rather than just general styles or genres.

A final step is to consider the types of assessments that have been used to assess scientific process skills. In microgenetic studies of self-directed experimentation, a variety of measures are employed to assess progress over time. In Table 5.2 I have included a sample of these measures (adapted from Zimmerman, 2007, p. 194).

Summary and Conclusions

The ultimate goal of this volume is to focus on how skills and knowledge acquired during video game play might transfer to academic settings. In particular, as educators, we are interested in finding out how we can take advantage of the features of video games that players find so motivating and engaging, and apply them to formal learning settings. I am particularly interested in the development and transfer of scientific thinking skills. The conceptualization and measurement of transfer has been a contentious issue in psychology and education for decades. One reason that transfer is so tricky is summed up nicely in a quote from Steve Jobs's 2005 Stanford commencement speech: "You can't connect the dots looking forward; you can only connect them looking backwards." Transfer, from the educator's perspective, is a prospective concept: we hope that skills and knowledge will be applicable to some future time or situation. As students, however, transfer

Table 5.1 **Mapping Learning Goals to Learning Activities and Possible Game Styles**

Sample Learning Goals[1]	Sample Learning Activities	Possible Game/Simulation Styles
Conceptual Understanding[2]		
Facts	Reading	Game show (e.g., *Jeopardy*)
Theories	Questions	Flashcard games
Systems and system models	Associations	Strategy (e.g., *Spore*)
	Memorization	Simulations of phenomena, systems, theory in action (e.g., *WolfQuest, Whyville'sWhyReef*)
Science/Engineering Process Skills		
Asking questions/defining problems	Asking questions	Role Play (e.g., *Whyville*)
Developing and using models	Proposing hypotheses	Adventure (e.g., *Whyville's Hot Air Balloon Race*)
Planning and carrying out investigations	Decision-making	"Detective" (e.g., *River City, WhyFlu*)
Using mathematics and computation	Experimentation	Puzzle games
Constructing explanations	Inquiry	Construction games
Designing solutions	Observing	Simulation games
	Measuring	Invention games (e.g., *Kibble Space Program*)
	Evaluating evidence	
	Building models	
	Explaining	
	Inference	
Science Discourse		
Communication	Group discussions	Role playing
Engaging in argument from evidence	Group decision-making	Multiplayer (e.g., *Quest Atlantis, Moonbase Alpha*)
Obtaining, evaluating, and communicating information	Imitation/coaching	Built-in tutors
	Argumentation	Online game forums

Note: Adapted from Prensky (2011, p. 269). [1] The three sample learning goals are from the NRC (2011) report. Three additional learning goals are outlined, including motivation; understanding the nature of science; and identification as a science learner. Specific examples under each learning goal are sampled from two dimensions (Dimension 1: Scientific and Engineering Practice, and Dimension 2: Crosscutting Concepts) of the new science standards (NRC, 2012). [2] Under conceptual understanding, it would make sense to include specific facts and theories listed under Dimension 3: Core Ideas in Four Disciplinary Areas (e.g., under life sciences, examples could include facts about the structure and function of molecules, organisms, and theories such as biological evolution, and system models could include the interaction and dynamics of ecosystems). However, including all of the concepts from the core scientific disciplines would make the table unwieldy.

Table 5.2 **A Sample of Measurable Learning Outcomes**

Element of Scientific Thinking	*Learning Outcomes That Can Be Assessed*
Conceptual understanding	Assessment of initial/final beliefs (i.e., belief change)
	Types of hypotheses selected (e.g., causal, single/multiple, plausible)
	Theory-based predictions
	Retention and use of concepts
Science process skill: Planning and carrying out an experimental investigation	Selection of variables and variable levels
	Use of hypothesis-testing strategies (i.e., change one variable at a time; hold one variable at a time; change all variables)
	Record keeping, record consultation
Science process skill: Evidence evaluation	Type of inferences (i.e., causal/inclusion, noncausal, indeterminate, false inclusion)
	Justification for inferences (i.e., theory-based vs. evidence-based)

is often a retrospective concept. As Prensky (2011) points out, transfer is not a property of a game or educational intervention; rather, "the ability to transfer knowledge or skills to another domain is a property, or a skill, of people" (p. 266). If we are aware that the educational goal is to transfer learning from one situation to another, we must teach for transfer.

Two of the skills identified as important for a 21st century STEM workforce are nonroutine problem-solving and adaptability (NRC, 2010).[2] To engage in nonroutine problem-solving, one must experience routine problem-solving. To manage uncertainty, change, and novelty, one needs experience in adapting to rapidly changing conditions. "When we build transfer training into the gameplay, the answer to 'does this game transfer?' will almost certainly be 'yes,' because the players have been taught to do it through playing" (Prensky, 2011, p. 267). To promote skills and knowledge transfer in our students, these must be built into the design of educational interventions, whether through traditional or innovative game play, so that they can be made explicit and practiced. A hallmark of sophisticated scientific thinking is metacognitive reflection on knowledge change (Kuhn, 2011). I see no difference in promoting explicit metacognitive training as is done for STEM apprentices. We need to have students practice building bridges between knowledge domains and skill sets so that they can one day build their own bridges when the need arises.

Author Notes

The author thanks Trinity Aodh, Fran Blumberg, Steve Croker, Devin Gill, Robert Hausmann, Carrie Lavis, and Brad Morris for helpful comments and suggestions.

Notes

1. http://dd.dynamicdiagrams.com/wp-content/uploads/2011/01/orrery_2006.swf
2. The others are complex communication/social skills, self-management, and systems thinking.

References

Anderson, J. R., Corbett, A. T., Koedinger, K. R., & Pelletier, R. (1995). Cognitive tutors: Lessons learned. *Journal of the Learning Sciences, 4*, 167–207.

Annetta, L. A. (2008). Video games in education: Why they should be used and how they are being used. *Theory Into Practice, 47*, 229–239.

Barab, S. A., & Dede, C. (2007). Games and immersive participatory simulations for science education: An emerging type of curricula. *Journal of Science Education and Technology, 16*, 1–3.

Barab, S. A., Gresalfi, M., Ingram-Goble, A. (2010). Transformational play: Using games to position person, content, and context. *Educational Researcher, 39*, 525–536.

Barab, S. A., Scott, B., Siyahhan, S., Goldstone, R., Ingram-Goble, A., Zuiker, S. J., & Warren, S. (2009). Transformational play as a curricular scaffold: Using videogames to support science education. *Journal of Science Education and Technology, 18*, 305–320.

Chinn, C. A., & Brewer, W. F. (1993). The role of anomalous data in knowledge acquisition: A theoretical framework and implications for science instruction. *Review of Educational Research, 63*, 1–49.

Chinn, C. A., & Malhotra, B. A. (2002). Children's responses to anomalous scientific data: How is conceptual change impeded? *Journal of Educational Psychology, 94*, 327–343.

Csíkszentmihályi, M. (1975). *Beyond boredom and anxiety: The experience of play in work and games.* San Francisco, CA: Jossey-Bass.

Csíkszentmihályi, M. (1990). *Flow: The psychology of optimal experience.* New York, NY: Harper & Row.

Deci, E. L., & Ryan, R. M. (2000). The "what" and "why" of goal pursuits: Human needs and the self-determination of behavior. *Psychological Inquiry, 11*, 227–268.

Dede, C. (2011). Developing a research agenda for educational games and simulations. In S. Tobias and J. D. Fletcher (Eds.), *Computer games and instruction* (pp. 233–250). Charlotte, NC: Information Age Publishing.

Dunbar, K. (1995). How scientists really reason: Scientific reasoning in real-world laboratories. In R. J. Sternberg & J. E. Davidson (Eds.), *The nature of insight* (pp. 365–395). Cambridge, MA: MIT Press.

Dunbar, K., & Klahr, D. (1989). Developmental differences in scientific discovery processes. In D. Klahr & K. Kotovsky (Eds.), *Complex information processing: The impact of Herbert A. Simon* (pp. 109–143). Hillsdale, NJ: Lawrence Erlbaum Associates.

Gauvain, M. (2001). *The social context of cognitive development.* New York, NY: Guilford.

Gee, J. P. (2011). Reflections on empirical evidence on games and learning. In S. Tobias and J. D. Fletcher (Eds.), *Computer games and instruction* (pp. 223–232). Charlotte, NC: Information Age Publishing.

Holland, J. H., Holyoak, K. J., Nisbett, R. E., & Thagard, P. R. (1986). *Induction.* Cambridge, MA: The MIT Press.

Klahr, D., Fay, A., & Dunbar, K. (1993). Heuristics for scientific experimentation: A developmental study. *Cognitive Psychology, 25,* 111–146.

Klahr, D., Zimmerman, C., & Jirout, J. (2011). Educational interventions to advance children's scientific thinking. *Science, 333,* 971–975.

Koslowski, B. (1996). *Theory and evidence: The development of scientific reasoning.* Cambridge: MA: MIT Press.

Kuhn, D. (2011). What is scientific thinking and how does it develop? In U. Goswami (Ed.), *Handbook of childhood cognitive development.* (2nd ed., pp. 497–523) Oxford, UK: Wiley-Blackwell.

Mayo, M. J. (2009). Video games: A route to large-scale STEM education? *Science, 323,* 79–82.

McGonigal, J. (2011). *Reality is broken: Why games make us better and how they can change the world.* New York: Penguin.

Morris, B. J., Croker, S., Masnick, A. M., & Zimmerman, C. (2012). The emergence of scientific reasoning. In H. Kloos, B. J. Morris, & J. L. Amaral (Eds.), *Current topics in children's learning and cognition* (pp. 61–82). Rijeka, Croatia: InTech. http://dx.doi.org/10.5772/53885

National Research Council. (2010). *Exploring the intersection of science education and 21st century skills: A workshop summary.* Washington, DC: National Academies Press.

National Research Council. (2011). *Learning science through computer games and simulations.* Washington, DC: National Academies Press.

National Research Council. (2012). *A Framework for K–12 Science Education: Practices, Crosscutting Concepts, and Core Ideas.* Washington, DC: National Academies Press.

O'Loughlin, M. (1992). Rethinking science education: Beyond Piagetian constructivism toward a sociocultural model of teaching and learning. *Journal of Research in Science Teaching, 29,* 791–820.

Penner, D. E., & Klahr, D. (1996). The interaction of domain-specific knowledge and domain-general discovery strategies: A study with sinking objects. *Child Development, 67,* 2709–2727.

Prensky, M. (2001). *Digital game-based learning.* New York, NY: McGraw Hill.

Prensky, M. (2011). Comments on research comparing games to other instructional methods. In S. Tobias and J. D. Fletcher (Eds.), *Computer games and instruction* (pp. 251–278). Charlotte, NC: Information Age Publishing.

Roth, W. M. (2008). The nature of scientific conceptions: A discursive psychological perspective. *Educational Research Review, 3,* 30–50.

Schauble, L. (1996). The development of scientific reasoning in knowledge-rich contexts. *Developmental Psychology, 32,* 102–119.

Schauble, L., Klopfer, L. E., & Raghavan, K. (1991). Students' transition from an engineering model to a science model of experimentation. *Journal of Research in Science Teaching, 28,* 859–882.

Steinkuehler, C., & Duncan, S. (2008). Scientific habits of mind in virtual worlds. *Journal of Science Education and Technology, 17,* 530–543.

Tobias, S., & Fletcher, J. D. (Eds.) (2011). *Computer games and instruction.* Charlotte, NC: Information Age Publishing.

VanLehn, K., Lynch, C., Schulze, K., Shapiro, J. A., Shelby, R., Taylor, L., Treacy, D., Weinstein, A., & Wintersgill, M. (2005). The Andes physics tutoring system: Lessons learned. *International Journal of Artificial Intelligence in Education, 15,* 147–204.

Young, M. F., Slota, S., Cutter, A. B., Jalette, G., Mullin, G., Lai, B., Simeoni, Z.... Yukhymenko, M. (2012). Our princess is in another castle: A review of trends in serious gaming for education. *Review of Educational Research, 82,* 61–89.

Zimmerman, C. (2000). The development of scientific reasoning skills. *Developmental Review, 20,* 99–149.

Zimmerman, C. (2007). The development of scientific thinking skills in elementary and middle school. *Developmental Review, 27,* 172–223.

Zimmerman, C., & Croker, S. (2013). Learning science through inquiry. In G. Feist & M. Gorman (Eds.), *Handbook of the psychology of science* (pp. 49–70). New York, NY: Springer Publishing.

Zimmerman, C., Raghavan, K., & Sartoris, M. L. (2003). The impact of the MARS curriculum on students' ability to coordinate theory and evidence. *International Journal of Science Education, 25,* 1247–1271.

6

Do Video Games Provide Motivation to Learn?

AKANE ZUSHO, JARED S. ANTHONY,
NAOKO HASHIMOTO, AND GERARD ROBERTSON

Much has been made of the "motivational pull" (Ryan, Rigby, & Przybylski, 2006) of video games. A common claim made about video games is that they are inherently engaging and therefore motivating (Prensky, 2006; Squire, 2011), and that researching video games can help us to better design educational environments (Gee, 2003; Squire, 2011). For example, Squire (2011) suggests that games can help individuals develop their academic interests and that incorporating game design principles can help to facilitate learning. Despite such theoretical musings about the potential motivational and academic benefits of video games, it is unclear whether or not the extant literature on video games is being framed explicitly in terms of current theories of achievement motivation. Thus, the overarching purpose of this chapter is to critically analyze the research on video games against the literature on achievement motivation. We therefore begin with a summary of the major theoretical frameworks of achievement motivation. From there, we turn to an analysis of the extant empirical research on video games and learning. We conclude with a brief discussion of future directions and research questions for ways that motivation, as an academic construct, can be used in the study of video games and learning in academic contexts.

WHAT IS MOTIVATION?

Motivation is typically defined as that which influences the initiation, direction, magnitude, perseverance, continuation, and quality of goal-directed behavior (Dweck & Elliott, 1983; Maehr & Meyer, 1997; Maehr & Zusho, 2009). In other words, it is a construct that helps to explain why individuals choose to approach or avoid a task; and once engaged, whether they put in effort and persist, or simply quit. It also encompasses thoughts and beliefs about a given task, including whether one finds a task to be interesting, enjoyable, challenging, important, or useful, and how one generally reacts to success or failure.

Considering that one of the primary claims about video games and motivation relates to engagement, it is important to note that motivation and engagement, albeit related constructs, are also distinguishable. Briefly, engagement is generally considered to be a broader construct than motivation to the extent that it encompasses cognitive, affective, and behavioral elements (Fredricks, Blumenfeld, & Paris, 2004). As Eccles and Wang (2012) point out, the conceptual overlap between motivation and engagement becomes blurriest when engagement is defined primarily in terms of affective engagement (e.g., liking or valuing of school). In an effort not to conflate motivation with engagement, we will focus our analysis on the literature on academic motivation rather than engagement.

History and General Theoretical Assumptions

Research on achievement motivation has a relatively brief history (Weiner, 1990). The roots of motivational psychology can be traced back to the era of behaviorism (1930s to 1950s) when primacy was placed on understanding what instigated an organism to move from a state of rest to a state of activity. Much of this research, then, operationalized motivation in terms of needs, drives, instincts, and energization (Weiner, 1990). Research by McClelland (1953) and Atkinson (1957) for example, popularized the motives to approach success and avoid failure.

With the cognitive revolution, there was a shift away from such mechanistic views to emphasize the role of individual perceptions. Researchers began to recognize that the effects of rewards were often contingent on how one perceived the reward; for example, rewards that were perceived as controlling were found to be less effective than rewards that were intended as positive feedback (Deci, 1975). Current theories of motivation can be considered to be largely social-cognitive in nature, given their focus on both individual perceptions of a specific learning situation and larger contextual influences, such as classroom environments and interactions with peers and teachers.

Contemporary theories of achievement motivation are guided by several assumptions (Maehr & Zusho, 2009). First, given its social-cognitive bases, they all typically assume that motivation is discernible through students' reports of their beliefs and perceptions, as well as through their behaviors, including choice of activities, level and quality of task engagement, persistence, and performance. Second, these theories assume that both personal (i.e., gender, ethnicity, age, personality) and contextual (e.g., classroom environment) factors influence how an individual approaches, engages in, and responds to achievement-related situations. Correspondingly, in contrast to earlier research (e.g., McClelland, 1953), which assumed motivation to be primarily a dispositional trait with some students being "more" or "less" motivated, motivation is increasingly recognized as situated and changeable across contexts, tasks, and instructional activities (Ames, 1992; Hickey & McCaslin, 2001; Maehr, 1974; Maehr & Nicholls, 1980). In short, a primary assumption of the research on motivation is that it is more a process than a product, and emphasis is accordingly placed more on exploring the conditions that aid in facilitating or undermining motivation.

Contemporary Theories of Motivation

A cursory review of the literature on achievement motivation will quickly reveal a number of theoretical frameworks of achievement motivation, including expectancy-value theory (Wigfield & Eccles, 2000), achievement goal theory (Maehr & Zusho, 2009), self-determination theory (Ryan & Deci, 2000), self-efficacy theory (Bandura, 1997), attribution theory (Weiner, 1985), and interest theory (Renninger & Hidi, 2002). Although there are theoretical nuances that distinguish these theories from each other, collectively they can be framed according to three primary questions (see also Eccles, Wigfield, & Schiefele, 1998):

- Can I do this task?
- Do I want to do this task and why?
- How do instructional or contextual factors shape motivation?

We direct the interested reader to more comprehensive reviews of these theories (Eccles, Wigfield, & Schiefele, 1998; Eccles & Wigfield, 2002).

CAN I DO THIS TASK?

Motivational constructs that relate to the question, "Can I do this task?" are considered to be types of *expectancies*, that is, constructs related to one's perceptions about future events. Schunk and Zimmerman (2006) classify expectancies into two categories. Specifically, they distinguish competence perceptions from control beliefs. The former relates to an individual's perceptions about the means, processes, and capabilities to successfully execute specific tasks, whereas the latter relates to the probability of accomplishing a desired outcome under certain conditions (Schunk & Zimmerman, 2006). Schunk and Zimmerman note that enhanced perceptions of one's competence and control are generally adaptive; however, simply feeling that one can accomplish a task does not necessarily indicate that an individual will feel that he or she is in control, particularly when the conditions of achieving success are challenging or uncertain.

A prime example of competence perceptions is that of self-efficacy beliefs, or beliefs related to one's capabilities to manage and deliver a specific course of action to accomplish a task (Bandura, 1997). Bandura describes self-efficacy as a multidimensional construct that varies across individuals. For example, some individuals may generally sense a strong feeling of efficacy, whereas others may not. Similarly, some individuals may perceive a strong sense of efficacy across a number of situations, whereas others may feel efficacious in certain contexts or domains. Bandura also suggests that efficacy levels may vary by challenge: some individuals may feel efficacious across both easy and difficult tasks, whereas others may feel efficacious only for easier tasks (Eccles & Wigfield, 2002). Apart from self-efficacy beliefs, agent-means beliefs, competence judgments, action-outcome expectancies, agency beliefs, and capacity/ability beliefs would also be considered examples of competence perceptions (Skinner, 1996).

Examples of control beliefs would include outcome expectations, as well as specific control beliefs such as mean-ends beliefs and causal attributions related to internal locus of control (e.g., one's belief in one's ability to write a quality paper) or external locus of control (e.g., one's belief that the professor will not reward a quality paper). Outcome expectations refer to beliefs that certain actions will result in certain outcomes, for example, the belief that studying will improve one's academic performance (Bandura, 1997). Means-end beliefs, like outcome expectations, refer to expectations that certain causes (e.g., effort, ability, luck, teachers, unknown causes) produce particular outcomes (Eccles & Wigfield, 2002). Attribution theory (Weiner, 1985) suggests that individuals' interpretation of their own success or failure rests on controllability, that is, whether or not the outcome was caused by things within their control (e.g., effort) or outside their control (e.g., aptitude, others' action, luck, mood).

DO I WANT TO DO THIS TASK AND WHY?

Just because individuals feels competent or in control does not necessarily mean that they will always be motivated to complete a task. Thus, certain motivational theories focus on the reasons for task engagement. These theoretical frameworks are focused on values and interest, intrinsic motivation, and achievement goal theory (see also Anderman & Wolters, 2006; Wigfield & Cambria, 2010).

Expectancy-value theory (Wigfield & Eccles, 2000) suggests that behavior is largely a function of the outcomes individuals expect and the value that they ascribe to those expected outcomes. In terms of values, modern expectancy-value theory submits that students are much more likely to choose a task when they feel that the task is important (attainment value), useful (utility value), and interesting/enjoyable (intrinsic interest value). Correspondingly, interest theory suggests that students are typically more engaged in tasks when they find them to be personally meaningful, relevant, and interesting (Hidi & Renninger, 2006). Interest theory further proposes that there are two kinds of interest: individual interest, which represents a more stable, long-term, predisposition to reengage in an activity; and situational interest, which represents a more temporary, in-the-moment form of enhanced attention and affect that results from environmental stimuli (e.g., use of computer games; Hidi & Renninger, 2006). Recent efforts in this area of inquiry have focused on the development of interest, specifically how situational interest can be leveraged to promote longer-term individual interest (Hidi & Renninger, 2006).

When students report high levels of interest and enjoyment, it is assumed that they are intrinsically motivated (Malone & Lepper, 1987). Two theories speak directly to intrinsic motivation: self-determination theory (SDT) and flow theory. Eccles and Wigfield (2002) suggest that these theories are complementary in that SDT outlines the longer-term conditions necessary for intrinsic motivation to flourish, whereas flow theory generally provides a more immediate account of what conditions need to be in place for an individual to achieve a state of flow.

More specifically, SDT suggests that all individuals, irrespective of their cultural backgrounds, have three innate psychological needs: needs for autonomy, competence, and relatedness. It further suggests that intrinsic motivation will flourish only under the "right" conditions, or when these three basic needs are met. SDT also assumes that the quality of motivation is enhanced when individuals are intrinsically motivated than extrinsically motivated, and that not all environments will facilitate intrinsic motivation (Deci & Ryan, 2000). Flow theory, in turn, proposes that enjoyment in an activity is realized in a flow state, which is generally characterized as a holistic sense of being fully immersed in an activity. This happens when challenges posed by a task align with individuals' ability: they merge action and awareness; are intensely focused on the task enough to lose a sense of self-awareness and time; and feel in total control of their actions and the environment (Csikszentmihalyi, 1996).

Finally, achievement goal theory stipulates that students' motivation and achievement-related behaviors can be understood by considering their goals for engaging in a task (Ames, 1992; Maehr & Zusho, 2009). Research framed within this tradition has focused on two primary achievement goals: goals focused on the development of competence (mastery) or on the demonstration of competence (performance). Researchers have since proposed a 2-by- 2 achievement goal framework that considers four main types of achievement goals: mastery-approach, mastery-avoidance, performance-approach, and performance-avoidance (Elliot & McGregor, 2001; Pintrich, 2000). Students who adopt mastery-approach goals focus on understanding course material, overcoming challenges, or increasing their level of competence, whereas mastery-avoidant students focus more on maintaining their skills and competence. Students who pursue performance-approach goals aim to demonstrate their ability relative to others or want to prove their self-worth publicly, whereas students who endorse performance-avoidance goals seek to avoid looking incompetent in relation to their others.

The focus of most of the research in this area has been on the causal relationship between individuals' goal endorsements and their academic-related behaviors and beliefs. Mastery goals, in particular mastery-approach goals, have been found to be related to adaptive cognitive, affective, and behavioral outcomes, such as the use of deep-level cognitive and metacognitive strategies. Research suggests that the endorsement of performance-approach goals may, at times, lead to higher levels of academic achievement (Maehr & Zusho, 2009). Notably, the effects of performance-avoidance goals have been found to be almost entirely negative (Maehr & Zusho, 2009). Research on mastery-avoidance goals is limited in comparison, and suggests these goals to be predictive of both positive and negative learning outcomes (Elliot & McGregor, 2001).

HOW DO INSTRUCTIONAL OR CONTEXTUAL FACTORS SHAPE MOTIVATION?

As mentioned earlier, one of the primary assumptions of contemporary theories of motivation is that motivation is not a fixed trait but is changeable depending on the situation or instructional context. Therefore, research on achievement motivation has increasingly centered on identifying the characteristics of environments that facilitate motivation (Perry, Turner, & Meyer, 2006). Much of this work has been framed according to a person-in-context approach that examines the relationship of the person and the impact of contextual factors and how they combine to shape motivation; as such, studies generally focus on the processes by which individuals—whether they are students or teachers—internalize social and contextual influences and how this process ultimately affects their motivation in that context (Nolen & Ward, 2008; Zusho & Clayton, 2011).

Perry and her colleagues (2006) suggest that individual motivation can be greatly affected by choice of task, instruction, and the social interactions that take place within a context. In terms of task, theory suggests that a task can trigger situational interest through variety and novelty, as well as through personal relevance (Hidi & Renninger, 2006; Perry et al., 2006). Both achievement goal and flow theory suggest that tasks that are moderately challenging can also promote deeper engagement in learning and a focus on understanding (Blumenfeld, 1992). Perry et al. (2006) note, however, that perceptions of what students consider being "meaningful," "challenging," and "interesting" will likely vary. Thus, tasks must be developed to account for differentiated engagement among learners and provide support where needed, to help students successfully struggle with challenging tasks.

In terms of instruction, research demonstrates that instructional practices that emphasize social comparison can promote a performance goal orientation, which may ultimately impede learning (Maehr & Zusho, 2009). In general, instructional practices, such as public and normative evaluation that emphasizes academic ability or course grades, are believed to promote social comparison. By contrast, students are more likely to adopt a mastery goal orientation when instructors value effort; do not penalize or embarrass students for making mistakes or taking longer to understand a concept; hold students accountable for their learning; support students when they encounter difficulties; relieve anxiety; and provide social support (Perry et al., 2006).

Finally, research demonstrates that when students feel like they belong to "caring communities," they are more likely to report heightened, adaptive motivational beliefs. This finding relates to SDT, which emphasizes that intrinsic motivation is most likely to flourish when the needs for relatedness, competence, and autonomy are met. For example, research by Wentzel (1997) suggests that when students are with "caring" teachers—that is to say, teachers who make class interesting, who talk and listen to students, who are fair and rely on democratic principles, and who consistently offer help—the students are more likely to put forth effort, and report greater internal control beliefs and prosocial goals. Research also finds that students consider teacher autonomy support as an indication of respect for students; not surprisingly, students generally do not like overly controlling policies or teachers who deliberately exert power over them (Perry et al., 2006). Taken together, the research on contextual influences on motivation suggests that environments that promote interest and competence, a sense of internal control, and belonging are most facilitative of motivation.

VIDEO GAMES AND MOTIVATION

Against this backdrop of the theoretical and empirical research on achievement motivation, we turn to the general research on video games. In reviewing this nascent body of work, we set several goals. First, we were interested in understanding what general theoretical claims were being made about the motivational benefits of video games, particularly in the context of academic learning. Second, we were interested in exploring what specific motivational frameworks, if any, guided the empirical research on motivation and video games. Third, we sought to investigate how these studies generally operationalized motivation. Finally, we explored whether there was any evidence to suggest that video gaming promoted motivation and learning.

Theoretical Claims about Video Games and Motivation

Theoretical claims about the potential instructional benefits of video games can be traced back to Malone (1981), who identified features of computer games that are believed to promote intrinsic motivation. Specifically, he argued that computer games are intrinsically motivating because they promote optimal challenge, fantasy, and curiosity. In terms of challenge, games provide specific, variable, personally meaningful goals whose attainment is made uncertain yet ultimately achievable by providing just-in-time, constructive performance feedback. Games also promote a sense of fantasy by allowing the user to interact with elements that are often not found in real life, which can make the task more interesting. This is especially true when the game promotes intrinsic fantasies, which occurs when the fantasy and the skills needed to progress are mutually dependent. That is, the fantasy feature of the game is dependent on the player's skill and the player's skill relies on constructive feedback provided by elements of the fantasy. Malone also argues that computer games arouse curiosity because the environment is often considered to be novel and surprising, but not completely unimaginable.

Building on this seminal work, Malone and Lepper (1987) proposed a more complete taxonomy of intrinsic motivations for learning, where they added "control" to the individual motivations of challenge, fantasy, and curiosity. Specifically, they argued that computer games are captivating because they give users a sense of control by showing them how their outcomes are dependent upon their actions (contingency) and by offering choice. In addition to these four individual motivations, Malone and Lepper also added an interpersonal dimension, arguing that certain forms of intrinsic motivation are dependent on others. For example, games can be designed to promote interpersonal competition, as well as to promote cooperation among team players. Games can also be motivating when they fulfill a need for approval by recognizing players' accomplishments by means of in-game performance feedback.

More recently, Gee (2003) and Squire (2011) have alluded to the motivational benefits of video games. Gee (2003) in particular outlines a number of design principles—36 in total—that can roughly be categorized according to Malone and Lepper's (1987) taxonomy. There are, for example, principles related to challenge (e.g., achievement, ongoing learning, regime of competence, incremental, explicit information on-demand, just-in-time principle), control (e.g., multiple routes), fantasy and curiosity (e.g., psychosocial moratorium, committed learning, identity and discovery), and cooperation (e.g., dispersed principle, affinity group principle).

Like Gee, Squire (2006, 2011), also offers his own design principle of video games. Squire (2011) suggests that "good educational games pique players' interests" (p. 36). In short, although he does not use this terminology, Squire sees effective game design as embedded in games that promote situational interest. This reasoning is in line with the work of Mitchell (1993), who argues that elements, such as computer games or puzzles, can "catch" or spark a player's interest.

Overall, many of the theoretical claims about the motivational benefits of video games are in line with the research discussed earlier on how instructional and contextual factors promote motivation to learn (Perry et al., 2006). Video games are engaging because they are designed to be interesting and challenging, but the skills necessary for mastery are ultimately attainable. Video games also promote a sense of control, as they allow users to make their own choices and enable them to realize a direct correlation between their actions and outcomes. Further, contemporary video games, such as massively multiplayer online role-playing games (MMORPG), are also inherently social and are designed to build community, thereby promoting a sense of belonging.

Theoretical Framing of Empirical Studies on Video Games

Considering the theoretical claims about the motivational benefits of video games together with the overarching literature on achievement motivation, it is reasonable to assume that video games could potentially promote both students' expectancies (i.e., sense of competence and control) and value for learning (i.e., interest, a focus on mastery, intrinsic motivation). In this section, we consider how current studies on video games and motivation have been framed and to what extent they coincide with the motivational theories reviewed earlier.

Across the studies reviewed, self-determination theory appears to be the most common motivational theory used to frame the research on video games and motivation (Chang & Zhang, 2008; Dickey, 2007; Przybylski, Ryan, & Rigby, 2009; Przybylski, Rigby, & Ryan, 2010; Ryan, Rigby, & Przybylski, 2006). Przbylski and his colleagues, for example, propose a motivational model of video game engagement that is based on cognitive evaluation theory, a subtheory of self-determination theory (Przybylski et al., 2010), which suggests that video games promote intrinsic motivation by satisfying the three psychological needs of competence, autonomy, and relatedness. They argue that the broad appeal of video games is directly related to need satisfaction, above and beyond differences in individual characteristics of players, and across game genres and content. For example, they propose that violence is not a primary motivator for game play; rather, satisfying the needs of competence, autonomy, and relatedness is a much more powerful reason for video game engagement. Their model of video game engagement also suggests that immersion in game play is based in large part on need satisfaction, and that it also might amplify the effect of video games on outcomes such as prosocial goals and decision making.

In line with self-determination theory, passion theory has been used to frame empirical studies on video games (Wang, Khoo, Liu, & Divaharan, 2008). Like Przybylski et al. (2010), we consider passion theory as a complement to self-determination theory, given its focus on autonomy and control; specifically, whether users engage in video game play because they *choose* to (harmonious passion), or because they feel *compelled* to (obsessive passion). To this end, passion theory is directly related to another subtheory of self-determination theory: organismic integration theory (OIT). OIT specifies that externally regulated behaviors, or behaviors that are controlled by rewards or other people, are more likely to lead to more maladaptive outcomes than internally regulated behaviors, or behaviors that are self-determined. Collectively, this line of research suggests that, in accordance with OIT, engagement in video games is enhanced when users are motivated by harmonious rather than obsessive passions.

Flow theory has also been used to frame research on video games (Hoffman & Nadelson, 2010; Sherry, 2004). Sherry (2004), in particular, argues that video games are designed to promote flow: they contain concrete and manageable goals and rules, variable levels of play that promote a sense of competence, clear feedback on game progress, and visually appealing graphics that help to focus attention and promote concentration. He further suggests that gender differences in video games could be explained, in part, by flow theory. For example, he suggests that structural features of video games, such as 3-D graphics that rely on spatial rotation ability for their interpretation, may favor boys over girls and may explain why certain video games are more engaging for boys.

Finally, reflecting back on the historical research on achievement motives (McClelland, 1953), some studies on video games focus on specific, dispositionally-based motives for game play. In general, this line of research assumes that video game play, in part, reflects individual differences, that contribute to distinct player "types" (Bartle, 1996). For example, Yee (2006) suggests that there are three primary factors that explain why individuals engage in video game play: achievement, social, and immersion. In terms of achievement, players are motivated to play because it fulfills their desire for (1) advancement, as indicated by a need for power, progress, accumulation and status; (2) mechanics, as represented by a general interest in analyzing and optimizing game rules and mechanics; and (3) competition, as indicated by a need for provoking, challenging, or dominating others. The social component, in turn, is represented by a desire to socialize, maintain, and develop long-term meaningful relationships with others, and to derive satisfaction from teamwork. Finally, the immersion component fulfills players' needs for discovery, role-playing, customization or personalization, and escapism.

Correspondingly, uses and gratification theory (Sherry & Lucas, 2003) suggests that individuals are motivated to play video games to access one (or more) of the following psychological states: (1) competition, (2) challenge, (3) diversion, (4) fantasy, (5) social interaction, and (6) arousal. Noting that many video games are embedded with cognitively demanding activities related to problem-solving or puzzles, Hoffman and Nadelson (2010) also suggest that video games may satisfy players' need for cognition, or preference to engage in effortful, thought-provoking activity (Cacioppo & Petty, 1982).

Despite claims about the role of games in promoting situational interest (Mitchell, 1993; Squire, 2011), we failed to find any studies on video games that were directly framed in terms of interest theory (Hidi & Renninger, 2006; Renninger & Hidi, 2002). Although empirical findings suggest that goal orientations may be linked with video game engagement (Hoffman & Nadelson, 2010), we were unable to locate any studies that were based mainly on achievement goal theory. Moreover, despite numerous claims about how video games promote competence through challenge, very few studies were framed entirely in terms of expectancies such as self-efficacy. Thus, more emphasis has been placed in the current literature on the value component of motivation (i.e., *why* individuals play video games), particularly as it relates to need s and motives and intrinsic motivation and less emphasis has been placed on the interest, expectancy, or goals components.

Measurement of Motivation in Video Games Studies

Although it appears that the empirical research on the role of motivation and video games is, largely, theoretically guided, this situation has not resulted in motivation being operationalized well or consistently across studies. Thus, in this section, we consider how "motivation" is being assessed across studies on video games. To facilitate that discussion we present a short commentary on how motivation is typically measured.

Historically, when motivation was conceptualized in terms of drives, instincts, needs and motives, it was common for researchers to rely on projective measures to assess motivation. For example, both the motive to approach success (i.e., need for achievement) and the motive to avoid failure were measured using the thematic apperception test (TAT). As social-cognitive views of motivation grew in popularity, the use of self-report survey measures became more common, reflecting the cognitive assumption that perceptions matter. For example, self-determination theory is typically assessed using survey instruments such as perceived competence scale, self-regulation questionnaires, and the intrinsic motivation inventory.

Recently, increasing attention has been placed on the problems endemic to self-reports. Urdan and Mestas (2006), for example, note that self-report measures typically define motivation for participants by providing specific statements designed by researchers that are purportedly related to the motivational construct of interest. This can be problematic if participants do not interpret the items in line with the researchers' intentions. Moreover, surveys preclude the researcher from following up on participant responses with specific questions, and may result in biased or inaccurate findings. Given these problems and others, calls for more qualitative investigations into motivational processes are becoming more frequent (Maehr & Zusho, 2009).

Turning back to the research on video games, consistent with the overall literature on achievement motivation in general and self-determination theory in particular, the majority of the studies we reviewed employed survey methodology. For example, Wang et al. (2008) used the Perceived Locus of Causality Scale to assess whether participants perceived their video game play to be regulated internally or externally; they also used the passion scale to assess harmonious and obsessive passion. Studies conducted by Przybylski and his colleagues generally used the need for satisfaction scale (Przybylski, Weinstein, Ryan, & Rigby, 2009; Ryan, Rigby, & Przybylski, 2006; Weinstein et al., 2009) and investigated how psychological needs predicted outcomes such as game enjoyment and intentions for future play (Ryan et al., 2006).

Notably, the quality of survey instruments used across studies was quite variable. For example, studies framed according to self-determination theory typically reported acceptable to good reliability statistics on scales (i.e., Cronbach alphas above. 7), and generally presented information on how the scales were adapted from previously validated measures (e.g., Przybylski, Weinstein, Murayama, Lynch, & Ryan, 2012). However, there were numerous studies in which the description of methods was limited, making it difficult to fully interpret results. For example, the study conducted by Eglesz, Fekete, Kiss, and Izso (2005) did not report how the survey instrument they used was developed and validated; nor did they report the psychometric statistics or what specific scales were included in their instrument. Consequently, although their results allude to differences in player motivations, it is not entirely clear how these motivations were operationalized. Similarly, Yee's (2006) study on types of motivations for play in online games did not provide any psychometric statistics on the 40 questions used to assess player motivations, although it was stated that these questions were generated based on Bartle's (1996) player types and previous qualitative information from earlier, unspecified surveys.

Thus, the vast majority of studies on video games use surveys of variable quality that rely mainly on quantitative statistics to investigate the relations between factors related to video games and motivation. We did, however, identify one study that also used qualitative methods. Specifically, Hoffman and Nadelson (2010) supplemented their surveys of video game players with more in-depth focused interviews of 25 undergraduate and graduate students who reported playing video games that involved problem solving or strategy for five or more hours per week. Specifically, the interviews focused on the reasons for engaging in video game play; the types of games participants preferred and the reasons for such preferences; their behaviors and perceptions related to tasks associated with video game play; and the nature of engagement and motivation for gaming.

Do Video Games Promote Motivation to Learn?

As mentioned earlier, one of the primary claims about video games is that they are, by design, engaging and therefore motivating, and that paying attention to their learning principles could potentially help educators to design better, more engaging learning environments (Gee, 2003; Squire, 2011). However, our review of the extant literature suggests that there is, at present, limited *empirical* evidence for this claim.

To be more specific, much of the current literature linking motivation to video game play does not take into consideration how these findings can be applied to educational settings (cf. Hoffman & Nadelson, 2010). Rather, most of these studies are ostensibly conducted by scholars who are more interested in: (1) observing how the satisfaction of certain needs and other psychological antecedents leads to enhanced enjoyment and engagement in the game (Przybylski et al., 2009a, b; Przybylski et al., 2012; Ryan, Rigby, & Przybylski, 2006); or (2) identifying different player "types" (Sherry & Lucas, 2003; Yee, 2006). Although this research generally suggests that gamers play video games for a number of cognitive, affective, and social reasons and that video games, by and large, satisfy the three basic psychological needs of competence, autonomy, and relatedness, the generalizabililty of these claims to K–12 populations is not known, considering that most studies focus on college students or adult populations.

There are, of course, a number of scholars who explicitly consider educational outcomes of video game play in their theory and research (e.g., Barab, Gresalfi, & Ingram-Goble, 2010; Gee, 2003; Shaffer, 2007; Squire, 2011). For example, Barab and colleagues (2010) state the importance of video games in helping to provide players with the opportunity to make meaningful decisions and foster skills for critical analysis and appraisal of consequences and risks. As we have demonstrated, such claims are generally supported by theories of achievement motivation and could therefore be considered to be theoretically sound. However, we could not identify any empirical studies conducted by these scholars that were framed explicitly in terms of specific theories of motivation and, moreover, considered how motivational factors such as expectancies and value were related to gains in academic achievement. By extension, then, there is very little evidence to support the claim that video games will lead to transfer of academic skills through motivation.

Conclusions and Future Directions

Based on the extant research on achievement motivation in general and video games in particular, several claims can be made about the role of video games in promoting motivation to learn. First, many of the design principles associated with video games (see Gee, 2003) allude to motivational elements, which are generally supported by the theory and research on achievement motivation, specifically the research linking certain instructional practices to enhanced perceptions of competence and value (Perry et al., 2006). Second, the majority of extant research on video games has been framed according to value-related theories of motivation, particularly those related to intrinsic motivation, such as self-determination theory or flow theory. Third, there is emerging evidence to suggest that video games satisfy basic psychological needs, and that satisfaction of these needs can help to explain why players find video games to be fun and engaging (Przybylski et al., 2010). Fourth, the quality of assessments used across studies examining the link between motivation and video games is variable. Finally, although empirical evidence suggests that video games are generally motivating, research demonstrating how video games can help to promote motivation (and transfer) in academic contexts is currently lacking.

Given the above, we suggest several directions for future research. From a practical standpoint, more targeted research linking video game play to academic contexts that is framed according to theories of achievement motivation is sorely needed. Specifically, we see potential for more qualitative, situated studies of motivation (e.g., Nolen & Ward, 2008) that employ within-subjects designs where researchers investigate, over extended periods of time, how students' nature of motivation and engagement varies when they participate in video game play (of their own choosing) versus when they engage in academics that does or does not incorporate educational games. We would also like to see quasi-experimental studies on video game play in schools (e.g., Barab et al., 2010) to also consider assessing students' expectancies and values related to both game play and academics. Additionally, there is a need to examine the claims put fourth by Barab and his colleagues (2010) that playing video games can promote transfer of academic skills. Specifically, studies are needed to assess whether the skills learned during game play transfer to similar or different tasks in the classroom, and the role motivational factors play in this process. Doing so would provide the much-needed link between video games, motivation, transfer, and achievement.

From a methodological standpoint, however, we also see that there is room for improvement in terms of how motivation is measured and operationalized across studies. Thus, before we can conduct more quantitative, experimental studies, there is an urgent need to improve and validate our current instruments for use with K–12 populations. We would also like to see expansion of methods to consider not only surveys but also more targeted, more in-the-moment investigations into video game play, such as those conducted by Blumberg and her colleagues (Blumberg, Rosenthal, & Randall, 2008).

Finally, theoretically, it appears that most of the current literature on motivation and video games has been framed according to self-determination theory. While we acknowledge that this is an important and comprehensive theory of motivation, we also see the need for more research to be framed according to interest theory, given its educational implications. In particular, this theoretical framework suggests that situational interest can ultimately develop into long-term personal interest. Considering that video games are a prime example of the catch component of situational interest, we see this particular motivational framework to be directly relevant to studies of video games. How exactly do video games promote situational interest, and for whom and under what conditions does this develop into individual interest? These are questions that still have to be addressed. Doing so could not only help to further the empirical research on video games but it could also help to substantiate the developmental model of interest (Renninger & Hidi, 2002).

We also see the potential for achievement goal theory to guide some of the research on video games, particularly as it relates to the social aspects of gaming. Achievement goal theory specifies that the quality of motivation may be compromised when students endorse goals that are primarily focused on the demonstration of competence (i.e., proving one's ability to others). It appears that much of the current research on video games assumes that the social aspect of gaming is almost entirely positive; however, we submit that this may not always be the case and that social comparison can sometimes have potentially detrimental effects (Maehr & Zusho, 2009).

In conclusion, like many others, we see the potential of video games to transform the educational landscape. However, we believe that much more work still needs to be done before we can fully realize the potential of video games to promote learning in academic contexts.

References

Ames, C. (1992). Classrooms: Goals, structures, and student motivation. *Journal of Educational Psychology, 84*, 261–271. doi: 10.1037//0022-0663.84.3.261

Anderman, E. M., & Wolters, C. (2006). Goals, values, and affect: Influences on student motivation. In P. A. Alexander & P. H. Winne (Eds.), *Handbook of educational psychology*. New York, NY: Simon & Schuster/Macmillan.

Atkinson, J. W. (1957). Motivational determinants of risk-taking behavior. *Psychological Review, 64*, 359–372. doi: 10.1037/h0043445

Bandura, A. (1997). *Self-efficacy: The exercise of self-control*. Gordonsville, VA: WH Freeman & Co.

Barab, S. A., Gresalfi, M., & Ingram-Goble, A. (2010). Transformational play using games to position person, content, and context. *Educational Researcher, 39*, 525–536. doi: 10.3102/0013189X10386593

Bartle, R. (1996). Hearts, clubs, diamonds, spades: Players who suit MUDs. *Journal of MUD Research, 1*(1), 19.

Blumberg, F. C., Rosenthal, S. F., & Randall, J. D. (2008). Impasse-driven learning in the context of video games. *Computers in Human Behavior, 24*, 1530–1541. doi: 10.1016/j.chb.2007.05.010

Blumenfeld, P. C. (1992). Classroom learning and motivation: Clarifying and expanding goal theory. *Journal of Educational Psychology, 84*, 272–281. doi: 10.1037//0022-0663.84.3.272

Cacioppo, J. T., & Petty, R. E. (1982). The need for cognition. *Journal of Personality and Social Psychology, 42*(1), 116–131. doi: 10.1037//0022-3514.42.1.116

Chang, J., & Zhang, H. (2008). Analyzing online game players: From materialism and motivation to attitude. *Cyberpsychology & Behavior, 11*, 711–714.

Csikszentmihalyi, M. (1996). *Creativity: Flow and the psychology of discovery and exploration*. New York, NY: HarperCollins.

Deci, E. L. (1975). *Intrinsic motivation: Theory and research*. New York: Plenum Press.

Deci, E. L., & Ryan, R. M. (2000). The "what" and "why" of goal pursuits: Human needs and the self-determination of behavior. *Psychological Inquiry, 11*, 227–268. doi: 10.1207/S15327965PLI1104_01

Dickey, M. D. (2007). Game design and learning: A conjectural analysis of how massively multiple online role-playing games (MMORPGs) foster intrinsic motivation. *Educational Technology Research and Development, 55*, 253–273. doi: 10.1007/s11423-006-9004-7

Dweck, C. S., & Elliott, E. S. (1983). Achievement motivation. In P. H. Mussen (Gen. Ed.) & E. M. Hetherington (Vol. Ed.), *Handbook of child psychology: Vol. IV. Social and personality development* (pp. 643–691). New York, NY: Wiley.

Eccles, J. S., & Wang, M. T. (2012). So what is student engagement anyway: Commentary on Section I. In S. Christenson, A. L. Reschy, & C. Wylie (Eds.), *Handbook of research on student engagement*. New York, NY: Springer.

Eccles, J. S., & Wigfield, A. (2002). Motivational beliefs, values, and goals. *Annual Review of Psychology, 53*(1), 109–132.

Eccles, J. S., Wigfield, A., & Schiefele, U. (1998). Motivation to succeed. In W. Damon (Series Ed.) & N. Eisenberg (Vol. Ed.), *Handbook of child psychology* (pp. 1017–1095). New York: Wiley.

Eglesz, D., Fekete, I., Kiss, O. E., & Izso, L. (2005). Computer games are fun? On professional games and players' motivations. *Educational Media International, 42*(2), 117–124. doi: 10.1080/09523980500060274

Elliot, A. J., & McGregor, H. A. (2001). A 2 x 2 achievement goal framework. *Journal of personality and social psychology, 80*, 501–519.

Fredricks, J. A., Blumenfeld, P. C., & Paris, A. H. (2004). School engagement: Potential of the concept, state of the evidence. *Review of Educational Research, 74*, 59–109.

Gee, J. P. (2003). What video games have to teach us about learning and literacy. New York, NY: Palgrave MacMillan

Hickey, D. T., & McCaslin, M. (2001). Comparative and sociocultural analyses of context and motivation. In S. S. Volet & S. Järvelä (Eds.), Motivation in learning contexts: Theoretical and methodological implications (pp. 33–56). Amsterdam: Pergamon/Elsevier.

Hidi, S., & Renninger, K. A. (2006). The four-phase model of interest development. *Educational Psychologist, 41*(2), 111–127. doi: 10.1207/s15326985ep4102_4

Hoffman, B., & Nadelson, L. (2010). Motivational engagement and video gaming: A mixed methods study. *Educational Technology Research and Development, 58*, 245–270. doi: 10.1007/s11423-009-9134-9

Maehr, M. L. (1974). Culture and achievement motivation. *American Psychologist, 29*, 887–896. doi: 10.1037/h0037521

Maehr, M. L., & Meyer, H. A. (1997). Understanding motivation and schooling: Where we've been, where we are, and where we need to go. *Educational Psychology Review, 9*, 371–409.

Maehr, M. L., & Nicholls, J. G. (1980). Culture and achievement motivation: A second look. In N. Warren (Ed.), *Studies in Cross-Cultural Psychology* (Vol. 3, pp. 221–267). New York, NY: Academic Press

Maehr, M. L., & Zusho, A. (2009). Achievement goal theory: The past, present, and future. In K. R. Wentzel & A. Wigfield (Eds.), *Handbook of motivation at school* (pp. 77–104). New York, NY: Routledge/Taylor & Francis Group.

Malone, T. W. (1981). What makes things fun to learn? A study of intrinsically motivating computer games. *Pipeline, 6*(2), 50–51.

Malone, T. W., & Lepper, M. R. (1987). Making learning fun: A taxonomy of intrinsic motivations for learning. *Aptitude, Learning, and Instruction, 3*, 223–253.

McClelland, D. C. (1953). *The achievement motive*. New York: Appleton-Century-Crofts.

Mitchell, M. (1993). Situational interest: Its multifaceted structure in the secondary school mathematics classroom. *Journal of Educational Psychology, 85*, 424. doi: 10.1037//0022-0663.85.3.424

Nolen, S. B., & Ward, C. J. (2008). Sociocultural and situative approaches to studying motivation. In M. Maehr, S. Karabenick, & T. Urdan (Eds.), *Advances in Motivation and Achievement* (Vol. 15, pp. 435–460). London: Emerald Group.

Perry, N. E., Turner, J. C., & Meyer, D. K. (2006). Classroom contexts for motivating learners. In P. Alexander & P. Winnie (Eds.), *Handbook of educational psychology: Second edition*, pp. 327–348. Mahwah, NJ: Lawrence Erlbaum Associates.

Pintrich, P. R. (2000). An achievement goal theory perspective on issues in motivation terminology, theory, and research. *Contemporary Educational Psychology, 25*(1), 92–104. doi: 10.1006/ceps.1999.1017

Prensky, M. (2006). Learning in the digital age. *Educational leadership*, 63(4), 8–13.

Przybylski, A. K., Rigby, C. S., & Ryan, R. M. (2010). A motivational model of video game engagement. *Review of General Psychology*, 14, 154–166. doi: 10.1037/a0019440

Przybylski, A. K., Ryan, R. M., & Rigby, C. S. (2009). The motivating role of violence in video games. *Personality and Social Psychology Bulletin*, 35, 243–259. doi:10.1177/0146167208327216

Przybylski, A. K., Weinstein, N., Murayama, K., Lynch, M. F., & Ryan, R. M. (2012). The ideal self at play: The appeal of video games that let you be all you can be. *Psychological Science*, 23(1), 69–76. doi: 10.1177/0956797611418676

Przybylski, A. K., Weinstein, N., Ryan, R. M., & Rigby, C. S. (2009). Having to versus wanting to play: Background and consequences of harmonious versus obsessive engagement in video games. *CyberPsychology & Behavior*, 12, 485–492. doi: 10.1089=cpb.2009.0083

Renninger, K., & Hidi, S. (2002). Student interest and achievement: Developmental issues raised by a case study. In A. Wigfield & J. S. Eccles (Eds.), *Development of achievement motivation* (pp. 173–195). San Diego, CA: Academic Press. doi: 10.1016/B978-012750053-9/50009-7

Ryan, R. M., & Deci, E. L. (2000). Self-determination theory and the facilitation of intrinsic motivation, social development, and well-being. *American Psychologist*, 55(1), 68–78. doi: 10.1037//0003-066X.55.1.68

Ryan, R. M., Rigby, C. S., & Przybylski, A. (2006). The motivational pull of video games: A self-determination theory approach. *Motivation and Emotion*, 30, 344–360. doi: 10.1007/s11031-006-9051-8

Schunk, D. H., & Zimmerman, B. J. (2006). Competence and control beliefs: Distinguishing the means and ends. *Handbook of Educational Psychology*, 2, 349–367.

Shaffer, D. W. (2007). Epistemic games as career preparatory experiences for students with disabilities. *Journal of Special Education Technology*, 22(3), 57–69.

Sherry, J. L. (2004). Flow and media enjoyment. *Communication Theory*, 14, 328–347. doi: 10.1093/ct/14.4.328

Sherry, J. and Lucas, K., (2003) Video Game Uses and Gratifications as Predictors of Use and Game Preference Paper presented at the annual meeting of the International Communication Association, Marriott Hotel, San Diego, CAOnline <.PDF>. 2009-05-26 from http://www.allacademic.com/meta/p111471_index.html

Skinner, E. A. (1996). A guide to constructs of control. *Journal of Personality and Social Psychology*, 71, 549–570. doi: 10.1037//0022-3514.71.3.549

Squire, K. (2006). From content to context: Videogames as designed experience. *Educational Researcher*, 35(8), 19–29. doi: 10.3102/0013189X035008019

Squire, K. (2011). *Video games and learning: Teaching and participatory culture in the digital age. Technology, education--connections (the TEC series).* New York, NY: Teachers College Press.

Urdan, T., & Mestas, M. (2006). The goals behind performance goals. *Journal of Educational Psychology*, 98, 354–365. doi: 10.1037/0022-0663.98.2.354

Wang, C. K., Khoo, A., Liu, W. C., & Divaharan, S. (2008). Passion and intrinsic motivation in digital gaming. *Cyberpsychology and Behavior*, 11, 39–45. doi: 10.1089/cpb.2007.000

Weiner, B. (1985). An attributional theory of achievement motivation and emotion. *Psychological Review*, 92, 548–573. doi: 10.1037//0033-295X.92.4.548

Weiner, B. (1990). History of motivational research in education. *Journal of Educational Psychology*, 82, 616–622. doi: 10.1037//0022-0663.82.4.616

Wentzel, K. R. (1997). Student motivation in middle school: The role of perceived pedagogical caring. *Journal of Educational Psychology*, 89, 411–419. doi: 10.1037//0022-0663.89.3.411

Wigfield, A., & Cambria, J. (2010). Students' achievement values, goal orientations, and interest: Definitions, development, and relations to achievement outcomes. *Developmental Review*, 30(1), 1–35. doi: 10.1016/j.dr.2009.12.001

Wigfield, A., & Eccles, J. S. (2000). Expectancy–value theory of achievement motivation. *Contemporary Educational Psychology*, 25(1), 68–81. doi: 10.1006/ceps.1999.1015

Yee, N. (2006). The labor of fun: How video games blur the boundaries of work and play. *Games and Culture, 1*(1), 68–71. doi: 10.1177/1555412005281819

Zusho, A., & Clayton, K. (2011). Culturalizing achievement goal theory and research. *Educational Psychologist, 46*, 239–260. doi: 10.1080/00461520.2011.614526

7

What We Know About How Experts Attain Their Superior Performance: Implications for the Use of Video Games and Game Training in Schools

K. ANDERS ERICSSON, JONG SUNG YOON, AND WALTER R. BOOT

The US school system aims to prepare students to achieve success in their professional careers and responsibilities as parents and adult citizens. It was long assumed that only a small group of individuals were born with the innate gifts (talents) necessary for superior achievement. However, recent evidence demonstrates that superior performance is primarily determined by acquired skills and other attributes that have been attained through extended periods of practice and training (Ericsson, 2006; Ericsson, Krampe, & Tesch-Römer, 1993). In this chapter, we briefly review evidence for the importance of skill acquisition and the development of complex skills and mechanisms that mediate superior adult performance. The emphasis on skill acquisition requires a new approach to the study of expertise that focuses on reproducing superior performance to study its mediating mechanisms in diverse domains of expertise, and determining whether and how these mechanisms are acquired through training. We describe the development of expert performance and comment on generalizable findings about the nature of effective training (deliberate practice). We conclude with commentary on general implications for training in schools with video games.

SCIENTIFIC ANALYSIS OF SUPERIOR AND EXPERT-LEVEL PERFORMANCE

An examination of the past few centuries reveals that, without exception, eminent individuals only reach the highest levels of performance within a single domain of expertise. Musicians achieve success only in music and not in sports, writing, or science. In fact, musicians do not reach the highest levels of performance on several different instruments, such as flute, violin, and piano, but typically specialize in a single instrument and often limit their solo performance to a specific type of music by a restricted set of composers. Similarly, athletes typically specialize in a single sport and often excel only in a single event, or sometimes very similar events, such as running both 5,000 meters and 10,000 meters. Scientists nearly always conduct award-winning research within a single academic discipline and frequently spend most of their research careers focused on a small number of scientific issues and questions. The classical Greek ideal of individuals mastering many arts, sports, sciences, and civic duties at a high level is simply not possible when individuals aspire to achieve at today's highest levels. From a review of the existence of polymaths—also sometimes referred to by the terms "Renaissance man" or "universal man"—(e.g., Leonardo da Vinci), ostensibly the vast majority of them lived many centuries or even millennia ago (Polymath, n.d.).

Research on the acquisition of very high levels of performance in science, arts, games, and sports has uncovered compelling explanations for the near complete lack of contemporary polymaths or individuals succeeding in several domains. Reviews (Ericsson, 2006; Ericsson & Lehmann, 1996) demonstrate that many years of intense engagement in activities in a particular domain is absolutely necessary to attain an elite level of performance in virtually all established domains with objective methods for measuring performance; time constraints do not allow for the acquisition of expert performance in multiple domains.

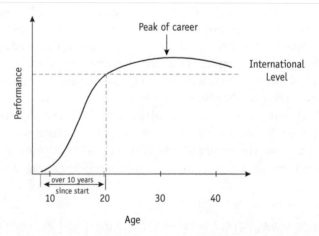

Figure 7.1 An illustration of the gradual increases in expert performance as a function of age in domains such as chess. The international level, which is attained after more than around 10 years of involvement in the domain, is indicated by the horizontal dashed line. (From "Expertise," by K. A. Ericsson and Andreas C. Lehmann, 1999, *Encyclopedia of Creativity.* Copyright by Academic Press.)

Furthermore, these reviews show that when performance is measured with the same objective adult standards in longitudinal studies, there is no evidence for sudden increases in performance during a short time interval (see Figure 7.1 for an illustration).

These findings are inconsistent with the traditional innate talent view based on the importance of inherited genetic factors (e.g., Lykken, 1998; Simonton, 1999), which emphasizes the natural maturation of high level performance without the need for relevant prior extended practice and experience. The effects of genetic factors on the development of individual differences in height and body size, which are beneficial for athletes, such as basketball players, are not influenced or dependent on particular types of practice and training (Ericsson, 1990). The reviews of empirical data (Ericsson, 2006; Ericsson & Lehmann, 1996) show in a wide range of domains that increasing levels of performance are reached only gradually with small increments, and that very high levels of performance are only attained after many years of engagement in domain-related practice activities. Even child prodigies in chess, whose performance is vastly superior to that of chess-playing children of the same age, demonstrate only gradual and steady increases in their chess-performance ratings over their development (Elo, 1978). These reviews also find that future expert performers improve their performance during childhood and adolescence while their bodies and brains are developing. More theoretically interesting is that their performance increases beyond the age of completed physical maturation (the late teens in industrialized countries) for many years and even decades. The age at which performers typically reach their highest level of performance of their career is in their mid- to late 20s for many vigorous sports; for those in the arts and sciences, the peak comes a decade later, in their 30s and 40s (Lehman, 1953; Schulz & Curnow, 1988). Evidence for continued development a full decade beyond physical maturity implies that engaging in activities in the domain is necessary for individuals to improve their performance. Finally, the most striking evidence for the necessity of vast experience in domain activities prior to attaining high levels of performance is that even the most "talented" need around ten years of intense involvement before they reach an international level. Bryan and Harter (1899) were the first psychologists to suggest that 10 years of professional experience was necessary to reach an expert level in telegraphy. With respect to world-class achievement, Simon and Chase (1973) were the first scientists to propose the 10-year rule for attaining elite achievement by showing that no modern chess master had reached the international level in less than around 10 years of chess playing. Subsequent reviews show that the 10-year rule extends to music composition (Hayes, 1981) along with a wide range of traditional sports, sciences, and arts (Ericsson, Krampe, & Tesch-Römer, 1993), and that exceptions to this rule are surprisingly rare. Overall, the necessity of consistent daily active engagement in domain-related activities to improve performance is well established.

Mere accumulation of experience in domain-related activities at any age, however, is not sufficient to reach an international level in established domains. The particular types of domain-related activities that one needs to engage in to increase one's performance to an expert level have special characteristics and require goal-directed training with feedback (we discuss deliberate practice later in the chapter). It is also important that the relevant training start early during development. Ericsson et al. (1993) reviewed many studies showing that the start of training and practice in the domain at very young ages is predictive of adult performance. For example, world class performers have systematically younger starting ages than less accomplished performers in domains such as swimming, tennis, chess, and music. An early start of training allows a child to gain an advantage over other same-aged children in performing in competitions. Moreover, recent research also shows that intense practice at very young ages may be effective during development windows when the body and nervous system are most malleable. More generally, recent reviews (Gaser & Schlaug, 2003; Hill & Schneider, 2006; Kolb & Whishaw, 1998) show that the function and structure of the brain is more markedly influenced by training and practice than previously thought possible. In particular, early and extended training has been shown to change the development of white matter in the brain (Bengtsson, Nagy, Skare, Forsman, Forsberg, & Ullén, 2005), the development of "turn-out" of ballet dancers (an essential ballet technique: a rotation of the leg causing the hip, knee and ankle joint to turn outward), the development of perfect pitch, and flexibility of fingers (Ericsson & Lehmann, 1996; Ericsson, Roring, & Nandagopal, 2007).

Research on general cognitive abilities among skilled performers is also consistent with the hypothesis that skilled performance is mediated by mechanisms that are constructed, acquired, and refined as the result of training and practice. This hypothesis can explain why it is so difficult to predict who will become expert performers based on tests of general ability during the first part of aspiring expert performers' careers (Ericsson & Lehmann, 1996). It can also account for the fact that individual differences in general mental ability, such as intelligence, have not been found to be significantly correlated among highly skilled performers with their attained level of performance in domains of expertise such as chess (Ericsson et al., 2007), Go (Masunaga & Horn, 2001), and music (Ruthsatz, Detterman, Griscom, & Cirullo, 2008). Taken together, these findings suggest that mechanisms that mediate expert performance do not build on any general innate capacities, and thus individual differences in performance among skilled performers cannot be described by tests of basic abilities. To describe individual differences in skilled performance we need to describe how the individual performance has been constructed by the acquisition of independently derived cognitive structures and physiological adaptations through many years of intense engagement in relevant training activities.

An Approach Based on the Study of Reproducibly Superior Performance

When the goal is to describe the structure of the mechanisms mediating superior performance in a specific domain, it is not useful to simply look for scores on tests of general abilities that might be correlated with individual differences in the attained skilled performance. We need another approach, namely the expert-performance approach, which focuses on the finding and capturing the processes that mediate the expert performance in a target domain. For example, if we are studying expert level of performance in sports, we should decide first which specific event will be studied, then repeatedly observe how a given elite level athlete can perform at a national or international level in the specific event. Sports are particularly attractive to study with this approach, because over millennia—since the original Olympic Games in ancient Greece—athletes and their coaches have designed standardized conditions for each event. For instance, on a sunny day without wind, the conditions for running 100 meters or executing the shot put are almost as controlled as they would be if they were conducted in a scientific laboratory. However, to study the temporal development of forces and the neural transmissions to muscles, it is often necessary to try to reproduce the spontaneous athletic performance in the controlled environment of the laboratory. By recording the speed of running in the laboratory, it is possible to verify that the objectively superior performance has been reproduced in the laboratory in spite of additional electrodes and filming equipment.

For some events, such as the 100 meter sprint and the shot put, the critical performance takes place within 12 seconds and the physical activity is relatively constrained in space; thus, it is relatively easy to reproduce the corresponding conditions in the laboratory. In contrast, how can one study and capture the endurance performance in sports, such as the marathon and long-distance races in skiing and rowing? Researchers have found that elite endurance athletes run at a surprisingly constant speed during most of the race. They have designed various types of stationary exercise machines, such as tread-mills, rowing machines, and skiing machines. The athletes' ability to perform at their preferred speed with lower metabolic costs (higher running efficiency) has been found to be one of the best correlates of actual performance on endurance races (Conley & Krahenbuhl, 1980; Joyner & Coyle, 2008).

Expert performance in many other competitive domains, such as gymnastics, ice-skating, diving, music, and martial arts have a very organized system of education, where various skills and action sequences are ordered in terms of their difficulty. When children are introduced to the domain they are presented with simple skills and techniques, and as they master those they are introduced to increasingly difficult ones until the elite performers aim to perfect the most difficult ones. In these domains it is relatively easy to assess the general skill level by asking the performer to demonstrate proficiency in their most technically advanced set of skills. This general grouping of individuals based on their levels of attained mastery of domain-specific techniques is reliable, because their highest performance will not differ much between tests conducted within a short retest interval.

In many different domains, the encountered tasks and situations vary enormously. For instance, there are virtually no games between two players in chess, tennis, and soccer that are identical to each other. No surgeries are exactly the same and often the disease conditions of the medical patient may differ considerably in their severity and thus probability of full recovery after the surgery. In these domains it is not possible to compare the performance between two performers for the same tasks and conditions. In spite of the lack of direct comparisons, it is possible to infer large individual differences indirectly from a statistical analysis of the long-term outcome of many surgeries and other medical treatments. For example, from studies evaluating the outcomes of a large number of surgeries, it is possible to determine that some surgeons are able to perform surgeries with better survival rates of their patients even after statistical control for the severity of their patients' condition prior to surgery. Similarly, some chess players are more likely to win games at chess tournaments. In a pioneering project, Elo (1978) was able to compute a chess rating that very accurately predicts the outcome of games between two rated chess players. Unfortunately the amount of data necessary to estimate a valid chess rating involves a calculation based on the outcomes of 100–200 hours of tournament playing. Similarly, data on the outcomes of 100–300 hours of surgery is required to measure individual differences among surgeons. If we need such large amounts of data to find statistically significant differences between performers, it would be essentially impossible to identify the specific differences in performance that cause the differences in outcomes.

The critical assumption of the expert performance approach is that an outstanding surgeon's observable behavior will not differ from that of a less skilled individual at all times during a 4-hour surgery. In fact, it is common practice in teaching hospitals that trainees start doing the easiest parts of the surgery; when those are mastered, they are assigned to more difficult parts under the supervision of the teaching surgeon. Eventually, at the end of training and the beginning of independent practice, graduated surgeons should be able to independently perform the entire surgical procedure—at least for typical cases. Individual differences among surgeons and medical doctors are most salient for difficult and rare procedures or in procedures with unexpected complications. Similarly, the first few moves in a chess game (the opening) are not likely to reveal systematic differences in the preferred moves of highly skilled chess players. From the analysis of the chess games, it is possible to identify critical chess positions, where the quality of the selected moves is closely related to the players' ratings of chess skill. Research on expertise in aviation has also shown that expertise in pilots can be differentiated by performance in challenging flight situations rather than total flight hours. Burian (2002) showed that pilots' knowledge about challenging weather conditions is not related to the mere accumulation of flight hours. Guilkey (1997) also suggested that total number of flight hours does not accurately predict pilots' superior performance and problem-solving skills in the face of challenging flight situations. In sum, if we are to understand the differences between experts and less skilled individuals, we must study the differences in behavior and thought processes in challenging situations in which their performance is reliably different.

Finding Representative Tasks and Capturing the Superior Performance of Experts

A crucial advance in the study of expertise was made when investigators successfully identified well-defined tasks in domains of expertise that captured the essence of expert performance (Ericsson & Smith, 1991). These tasks could then be presented under standardized conditions in the laboratory and could be redesigned to study the effects of experimental manipulations. In a pioneering study, de Groot (1946/1978) showed that it was not necessary for chess experts to play complete games of chess to demonstrate their statistically significant superiority in chess. He found that it was possible to display an isolated chess position from unfamiliar games between chess masters and instruct the chess players to find the best next move for those positions while they were thinking aloud (see Figure 7.2 for an illustration).

Subsequent research has shown that this method of presenting representative situations and requiring performers to generate of the most appropriate action provides the best available measure of chess skill that predicts performance in chess tournaments (Ericsson, Patel & Kintsch, 2000; van der Maas & Wagenmakers, 2005). These tasks provide an excellent opportunity to elicit chess experts' thinking under representative, but still controlled, conditions in the laboratory. A test in which individuals select the best move for 10–20 chess positions yields a measure of performance that is very highly correlated with tournament ratings. Hence, it is possible to measure the same or similar performance in a 15-minute test that previously required an analysis of 100 to 200 hours of tournament performance. Any studies attempting to identify the mechanisms mediating the superior performance are much more likely to succeed in analyzing the processes during 15 minutes rather than 6,000 to 12,000 minutes.

Similar types of testing procedures have been developed to study the ability of medical doctors to determine correct diagnoses (Patel, Arocha, & Kaufmann, 1994). Medical doctors are presented with information from previously treated patients. A case consists of descriptions of a given patient's symptoms at time of

Domain	Presented Information	Task
Chess		Select the best chess move for this position
Typing	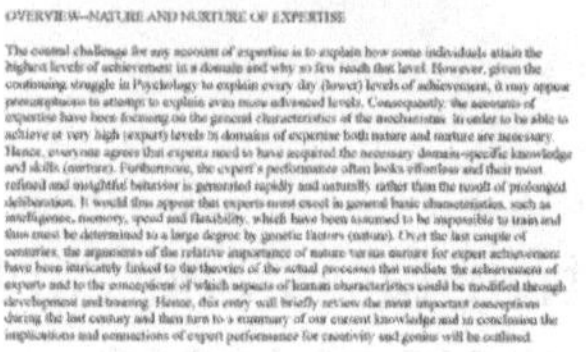	Type as much of the presented text as possible within in one minute
Music		Play the same piece of music twice in same manner

Figure 7.2 Three examples of laboratory tasks that capture the consistently superior performance of domain experts in chess, typing and music. (From "Expertise," by K. A. Ericsson and Andreas C. Lehmann, 1999, *Encyclopedia of Creativity*. Copyright by Academic Press.)

admission along with background information uncovered during the initial interview with the patient. Doctors and medical students are then shown the written documents and test results and asked to think aloud as they generate their proposed diagnosis. Their proposed diagnosis can then be compared with the correct answer, namely the patient's actual disease often only determined after extended treatment and testing. The second example in Figure 7.2 illustrates how scientists have used a similar methodology to measure and reproduce superior typing performance in a controlled situation by instructing every typist to type the same unfamiliar text. The last example, in the bottom panel of Figure 7.2, illustrates an approach to a common problem encountered in the measurement of superior performance by creative artists, such as musicians, who are able to change their interpretation of a piece of music from one occasion to the next. One solution to the problem with intentional variations of successive performances of expert musicians involves instructing the expert musicians to give two identical renditions of the same piece of music (see Ericsson & Lehmann, 1996, for a review). With this type of instruction, the superior ability of expert musicians to control their performance is reflected in reliably higher reproducibility of the subsequent renditions. In contrast, less skilled musicians are technically unable to reproduce their performance even when they are trying to do so.

In the last couple of decades it has been possible to design a number of representative tasks that capture expert performance in many domains and that allow reproduction of the essence of expert performance under controlled laboratory conditions (Ericsson, 2006). For example, expert snooker players are instructed to make a shot for a presented configuration of pool balls (Abernethy, Neal, & Koning, 1994). Similarly, athletes at expert levels make predictions for future events when a video of a soccer game is unexpectedly stopped (Ward, Hodges, Williams, & Starkes, 2004). Scrabble players are presented situations from representative game situations and are asked to select their next move (Tuffiash, Roring, & Ericsson, 2007). In medical domains, experts and less trained individuals are asked to diagnose electrocardiograms (ECG) (Simpson & Gilhooly, 1997) and pictures of microscopic samples of pathological cells (Crowley, Naus, Stewart, & Friedman, 2003). In all of these cases, it is possible to reproduce the superior performance of experts under controlled and standardized conditions within a relatively limited time window, which allows an effective search for the mechanisms and differences that account for the performance advantage of experts over less skilled individuals.

Toward Detailed Accounts of the Development of Expert Performance

The main premise of the expert-performance approach is that the development of an individual's performance occurs gradually—starting with the initial level of acceptable performance, to increasingly higher levels, all the way to expert levels. This assumption implies that it should be possible, at least in principle, to describe the development of each individual's performance as an ordered sequence of stable states with measurable performance as shown in Figure 7.3.

Most of these states represent improvements in performance compared to the immediately prior states, and differences correspond to specific cognitive and physiological changes in the mediating mechanisms that ultimately combine to explain the superior performance. This theoretical framework proposes that the observable reliable increases in performance have definite causes, such as developmental growth and adaptive responses to domain-specific training. There also are substantial interactions between those causes and intensity or duration of training activities. As previously described, specific developmental periods even exist when the body and nervous system can be more easily influenced by training. Based on these theoretical assumptions, each observable change in the performance and the associated structure of the mechanisms illustrated by the transitions in Figure 7.3 needs to be explained and described for each domain of expert performance. Ultimately, a complete theory should account for the development and refinement of all associated biological and cognitive changes that contribute to the acquisition of a stable reproducible expert performance.

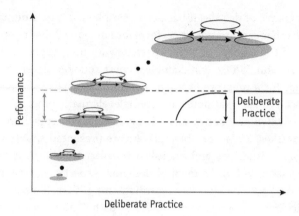

Figure 7.3 A schematic illustration of the acquisition of expert performance as a series of states with mechanisms for monitoring and guiding future improvements of specific aspects of performance. (Adapted from "The scientific study of expert levels of performance can guide training for producing superior achievement in creative domains" by K. A. Ericsson in Proceedings from *International conference on the cultivation and education of creativity and innovation* (p. 14). Beijing, China: Chinese Academy of Sciences. Copyright 2009 by International Research Association for Talent Development and Excellence.)

The detailed processes and practice activities may differ from domain to domain, but the general principle remains that aspiring expert performers need to engage in training activities that are designed to improve particular aspects of performance; once those are mastered, it is necessary to shift their attention to other improvable aspects. For example, in music a teacher listens to an intermediate music student play a piece of music and then helps the student identify mastery goals and subgoals for improving specific aspects, along with practice techniques to achieve these goals (see Figure 7.3). Then the student forms an image of the goal state, tries to find the means to achieve this goal, monitors the sound of the attempt, and makes corrections. This type of practice, with full concentration, immediate feedback, and opportunities to make repetitions with gradual improvements toward the current goals, is referred to as "deliberate practice" by Ericsson et al. (1993). With increased performance, the goals for performance improvements will change, but there are also coincidental improvements in the aspiring expert musician's representations that allow her or him to imagine the desired music experience, to translate the desired image into motor actions, and to monitor the produced sound during performance to identify areas of further improvement. Several recent reviews (Ericsson, 2006, 2007, 2008; Ericsson et al., 2007) have described the particular forms of deliberate practice (and associated representations that are increasingly refined) required to imagine a desired level of performance, direct execution of relevant actions for attaining it, and monitor the produced performance in a wide range of domains, such as chess, medicine, music, dance, sports, games, and professions.

Implications for Video Game–Based Instruction and Training in Schools

Findings from the study of the development of superior skill in various domains of expertise have clear implications for video game–based training. Some might argue that the acquisition of expert performance is qualitatively different from the type of learning involved in K–12 education. We argue that most aspiring experts began the development of their performance as children with limited background knowledge and skills, and as a consequence, knowledge gained from the study of expert performance has direct relevance to K–12 education. As discussed previously, engagement in an activity alone is not sufficient to produce the superior skill of the expert, and this lesson can be directly applied to the use of video game–based education. Just as it is possible to identify the practice activities that contribute to the skilled performance of experts and other activities that seem unrelated to skill level, it is possible to identify educational activities that are most positively associated with positive educational outcomes. Elements strongly related to advanced skill can then be incorporated into educational video games to produce the largest benefit. Some interesting recent studies have begun to assess engagement during early childhood that has relevance to development of academic skills in K–12. For example, experience with board games (Siegler & Ramani, 2009) and with spontaneous encoding of mathematical relations (Hannula & Lehtinen, 2005) is predictive of mastery of mathematics in school. We propose that the same strategy of uncovering specific experiences associated with high levels of skill and then designing structured activities that promote these experiences can be borrowed from the expert performance approach and applied to designing K–12 educational video games.

From the study of expert performance, deliberate practice has been identified as the single most important contributor to the development of high levels of skill. Deliberate activities are guided, provide immediate performance feedback, and allow learners repeated attempts to solve a problem to explore the consequences of different approaches. Particularly, immediate feedback and multiple problem attempts may differ from typical paper and pencil assignments: in this type of assignment, students may have to wait for an assignment to be graded; typically they have completed several intervening problems before receiving feedback, and they may not have the opportunity to attempt failed problems again. Fortunately, the elements of deliberate practice can (and often are) easily incorporated into video games. As one example of how this approach might work, consider an example from the domain of mathematics.

Many school activities in mathematics are motivated by the goal of providing students the skills for real-world behavior involving monetary transactions, price comparisons, and budgeting. With new technology, it is quite possible to test children's performance by presenting them with videos or game-like presentations of such situations with immediate feedback. Some educators might object that such testing ruins the fun of video game playing. However, based on the research on the acquisition of expert performance, we know that engaging in playful (fun) activities in chess (Charness, Tuffiash, Krampe, Reingold, & Vasyukova, 2005), soccer (Ward et al., 2004), darts (Duffy, Baluch, & Ericsson, 2004), Scrabble (Tuffiash et al., 2007), and typing (Keith & Ericsson, 2007) is not as effective as deliberate practice activities in which individuals are focused on improving an aspect of performance in an environment with opportunities for reflection and repeated chances to gradually perfect performance with immediate informative feedback. If engagement in video games is limited to enhancing performance on the particular video game without transfer to the targeted performance, then providing time for video games in school cannot be motivated on educational grounds, except for relaxation and rewards for mastery of the targeted educational goals.

It is rarely recognized that children and other beginners cannot sustain the concentration for deliberate practice for more than 15 to 20 minutes per day. If a parent, teacher, or coach pushes children or beginners beyond that duration they are likely to be unable to maintain concentration and experience failure. Hence, parents, teachers, and coaches should help the child limit the time for deliberate practice to avoid these negative consequences. It would be appropriate to allow the children and beginners to engage in playful interactions once the short deliberate practice session is completed. As learners gain more experience, the duration of deliberate practice can be increased gradually, to a level of around 4 to 5 hours per day for professionals. Even for professionals, the practice is separated into practice blocks of 45–60 minutes with interspersed periods of rest and relaxation (Ericsson et al., 1993). In that regard, the playful aspects of video games might be still beneficial—that is, when playing video games provides an opportunity for rest between intense deliberate practice opportunities and after completed deliberate practice as a reward for successful mastery of some well-defined academic skill.

The question of the effectiveness of providing individuals access to environments like those presented by video games has a long history with rather unequivocal results regarding the types of training that are most effective. Some of the first simulators were created to help future pilots train under safe conditions in an environment that simulated the conditions of flying. Discouragingly, relatively recent reviews of the effectiveness of time spent preparing to fly or flying in flight simulators for the last 50 years have found surprisingly few significant effects of transfer to the targeted performance in the real environment (Roessingh, 2005; Rantanen & Talleur, 2005; Ward, Williams, & Hancock, 2006), especially when one excludes the training of new procedural skills that can be learned in a low fidelity trainer. The interest in simulation training has increased dramatically in the last decade in medicine, where technological advances have allowed surgeons to use advanced tools (including video from inside the body) to complete laparoscopic surgery with a very small opening of the skin. A relatively recent review (Issenberg, McGaghie, Petrusa, Gordon, & Scalese, 2005) found that effective learning was achieved in surgical simulation studies primarily when learning was structured in a particular manner. The most important factors matched those of deliberate practice (Ericsson, 2004, 2008); namely, feedback was provided, and intense, repeated domain-focused practice was required. In a more selective review of studies with deliberate practice-like training, McGaghie, Issenberg, Petrusa, and Scalese (2006) found a strong relationship between the number of hours of simulator training and outcomes on standardized educational outcomes ($\eta^2 = .46$). Recent studies have studied the performance of experienced surgeons in the simulator and established their level of speed and accuracy of performance (Van Sickle et al., 2007). These performance levels have then been used to set criteria for the acceptable performance that medical students need to attain prior to being allowed to participate in surgery of actual patients. Research on simulation based training and deliberate practice in medicine, especially laparoscopic surgery, has emerged as one of the leading ways to develop effective learning environments for students and continuing professional development (McGaghie, Issenberg, Petrusa, & Scalese, 2010). Thus, the domain of training surgical skill can serve as a reference model for developing video game–based learning and training environments for K–12 education.

Recently, some have suggested that unstructured experience with commercially available video games, specifically action video games, can have a variety of perceptual and cognitive benefits (Bavelier, Green, & Dye, 2010; but see also Boot, Blakely, & Simons, 2011). Returning to the training of laparoscopic surgeons, there is also an association between action game experience and skill in performing with surgical simulators, and some (but not all) video game training studies have found an improvement in skill in performing with surgical simulators after action game training (Lynch, Aughwane, & Hammond, 2010). There is currently no evidence that video game experience carries over to more successful surgery with actual patients. What implications does this have for K–12 education? We believe that these apparent demonstrations of broad transfer from action video games to measures of perception, cognition, and complex psychomotor performance are intriguing and certainly worthy of further exploration. However, in terms of training, and specifically K–12 education, structured training that targets specific skills is likely to be a far more fruitful path to the rapid acquisition of advanced levels of skill. All of the work reviewed here is consistent with the necessity of guided deliberate practice within a specific domain to build cognitive structures and induce the physiological adaptations responsible for superior achievement.

As we alluded to previously, video games allow for the portrayal of everyday tasks in which academic skills can be applied with immediate feedback. For example, school children could be asked to work as cashiers in a grocery store to give change for bills, or they could be asked to accept money for deposit in a bank, or they could be asked to buy carpet for rooms in a house. They could be asked to calculate the cost of using various appliances by computing their monthly energy consumption, or asked to budget for a one-week vacation at some attractive resort and then be given feedback by going through the daily activities and see how well their budget worked. These activities might be completed in class, or as homework on either a home PC or tablet. An advantage of completing these activities at home is that students can demonstrate their developing mastery to their family. All the domains of expertise, such as sports, music, and chess, offer beginners opportunities to demonstrate their skills to their parents and other significant adults. Children play music in front of their family and friends, young chess players play and will win against less skilled adults, and young soccer players often play in front of family members. Just imagine how difficult it would be to train musicians and athletes if they were not able to get a sense of mastery by performing in front of supportive parents until they were adults. Furthermore, many young musicians have a lot of support from one or both of their parents, who monitor their training and drive them to practice sessions. It would be interesting and informative to analyze the development of skills of young musicians and young soccer players, and compare their learning environments to the learning environment of schools, in order to identify effective methods to support and encourage continued development and to address common complaints and reasons for dropping out.

In conclusion, we have reviewed evidence from the expertise literature that high levels of skill do not result from innate talent or exceptional genotypes. There is little evidence against the idea that most anyone can reach these levels with practice. However, practice must be of the right type for an individual to reach exceptional levels of performance in domains of sport, music, chess, and medicine. We believe that findings from the expertise literature have direct implications for the use of video games and simulations in K–12 education. Video games have the potential to be greatly beneficial to the extent that they allow opportunities for deliberate practice. These games would target specific skills, would be structured so that they encourage the mastery of subskills required for the performance of these overall skills (Figure 7.3), would provide useful, informative, and immediate feedback, and would allow players multiple opportunities to solve problems, with time and encouragement to reflect on the outcome of each attempt. Deliberate practice activities are not inherently enjoyable, and more enjoyable game components might be incorporated between deliberate practice activities to maintain motivation and allow students periods of rest. Perhaps most exciting is the possibility of generating interesting and motivating everyday situations as a consumer and customer, where the generalizability of these skills can be demonstrated and hopefully convince the students that their academic skills matter and will determine their successful mastery as adults.

References

Abernethy, B., Neal, R. J., & Koning, P. (1994). Visual-perceptual and cognitive differences between expert, intermediate, and novice snooker players. *Applied Cognitive Psychology, 18,* 185–211.

Bavelier, D., Green, C. S., & Dye, M. W. G. (2010). Children—wired, for better or for worse. *Neuron, 67,* 692–701.

Bengtsson, S. L., Nagy, Z., Skare, S., Forsman, L., Forsberg, H., & Ullén, F. (2005). Extensive piano practicing has regionally specific effects on white matter development. *Nature Neuroscience, 8,* 1148–1150.

Boot W. R., Blakely D. P., & Simons, D. J. (2011). Do action video games improve perception and cognition? *Frontiers in Psychology, 2,* 1–5.

Burian, K. B. (2002). General aviation pilot weather knowledge. (Final report #00-G-020). Washington, DC: Federal Aviation Administration.

Bryan, W. L., & Harter, N. (1899). Studies on the telegraphic language: The acquisition of a hierarchy of habits. *Psychological Review, 6,* 345–375.

Charness, N., Tuffiash, M. I., Krampe, R., Reingold, E. & Vasyukova E. (2005). The role of deliberate practice in chess expertise. *Applied Cognitive Psychology, 19,* 151–165.

Conley, D. L., & Krahenbuhl, G. S. (1980). Running economy and distance running performance of highly trained athletes. *Medicine and Science in Sports and Exercise, 12,* 357–360.

Crowley, R. S., Naus, G. J., Stewart, J., & Friedman, C. P. (2003). Development of visual diagnostic expertise in pathology: An information-processing study. *Journal of the American Medical Informatics Association, 10,* 39–51.

de Groot, A. D. (1946/1978). *Thought and choice and chess.* The Hague, The Netherlands: Mouton.

Duffy, L. J., Baluch, B., & Ericsson, K. A. (2004). Dart performance as a function of facets of practice amongst professional and amateur men and women players. *International Journal of Sport Psychology, 35,* 232–245.

Elo, A. E. (1978). *The rating of chess players, past and present.* London, UK: Batsford.

Ericsson, K. A. (2004). Deliberate practice and the acquisition and maintenance of expert performance in medicine and related domains. *Academic Medicine, 79,* S70–S81.

Ericsson, K. A. (2006). The influence of experience and deliberate practice on the development of superior expert performance. In K. A. Ericsson, N. Charness, P. Feltovich, & R. R. Hoffman (Eds.), *Cambridge handbook of expertise and expert performance* (pp. 683–704). Cambridge, UK: Cambridge University Press.

Ericsson, K. A. (2007). Deliberate practice and the modifiability of body and mind: Toward a science of the structure and acquisition of expert and elite performance. *International Journal of Sport Psychology, 38,* 4–34.

Ericsson, K. A. (2008). Deliberate practice and acquisition of expert performance: A general overview. *Academic Emergency Medicine. 15*(11), 988–94.

Ericsson, K. A., Krampe, R. Th., & Tesch-Römer, C. (1993). The role of deliberate practice in the acquisition of expert performance. *Psychological Review, 100,* 363–406.

Ericsson, K. A., & Lehmann, A. C. (1996). Expert and exceptional performance: evidence on maximal adaptations on task constraints. *Annual Review of Psychology, 47,* 273–305.

Ericsson, K. A., & Lehmann, A. C. (1999). Expertise. In M. A. Runco and S. Pritzer (Eds.) *Encyclopedia of Creativity,* Vol. 1 (pp. 695–707). San Diego, CA: Academic Press.

Ericsson, K. A., Patel, V., Kintsch, W. (2000). How experts' adaptations to representative task demands account for the expertise effect in memory recall: Comment on Vicente and Wang (1998). *Psychological Review, 107,* 578–592.

Ericsson, K. A. Roring, R. W., & Nandagopal, K. (2007). Giftedness and evidence for reproducibly superior performance: An account based on the expert-performance framework. *High Ability Studies, 18,* 3–56.

Ericsson, K. A., & Smith, J. (1991). Prospects and limits in the empirical study of expertise: An introduction. In K. A. Ericsson and J. Smith (Eds.), *Toward a general theory of expertise: Prospects and limits* (pp. 1–38). Cambridge, UK: Cambridge University Press.

Gaser, C., & Schlaug, G. (2003). Brain structures differ between musicians and non-musicians. *Journal of Neuroscience, 23,* 9240–9245.

Guilkey, J. E. (1997). *An investigation of aviator problem-solving skills as they relate to amount of total flight time* (Doctoral dissertation). ProQuest Dissertations and Theses. (UMI No. 9731628)

Hannula, M. M., & Lehtinen, E. (2005). Spontaneous focusing on numerosity and mathematical skills in young children. *Learning and Instruction, 15,* 237–256.

Hayes, J. R. (1981). *The complete problem solver.* Philadelphia, PA: Franklin Institute Press.

Hill, N. M., & Schneider, W. (2006). Brain changes in the development of expertise: Neuroanatomical and neurophysiological evidence about skill-based adaptations. In K. A. Ericsson, N. Charness, P. Feltovich, and R. R. Hoffman (Eds.), *Cambridge handbook of expertise and expert performance* (pp. 223–242). Cambridge, UK: Cambridge University Press.

Issenberg, S. B., McGaghie, W. C., Petrusa, E. R., Gordon, D. L., & Scalese, R. J. (2005). Features and uses of high-fidelity medical simulations that lead to effective learning: a BEME systematic review. *Medical Teacher, 27,* 10–28.

Joyner, M. J., & Coyle, E. F., (2008). Endurance exercise performance: The physiology of champions. *Journal of Physiology, 586,* 35–44.

Keith, N., & Ericsson, K. A. (2007). A deliberate practice account of typing proficiency in everyday typists. *Journal of Experimental Psychology: Applied, 13,* 135–145.

Kolb, B., & Whishaw, I. Q. (1998). Brain plasticity and behavior. *Annual Review of Psychology, 49,* 43–64.

Lehmann, H. C. (1953). *Age and achievement.* Princeton, NJ: Princeton University Press.

Lykken, D. T. (1998). The genetics of genius. In A. Steptoe (Ed.), *Genius and the mind: Studies of creativity and temperament in the historical record* (pp. 15–37). New York, NY: Oxford University Press.

Lynch, J., Aughwane, P., & Hammond, T. M. (2010). Video games and surgical ability: A literature review. *Journal of Surgical Education, 67,* 184–189.

Masunaga, H., & Horn, J. (2001). Expertise and age-related changes in components of intelligence. *Psychology and Aging, 16,* 293–311.

McGaghie, W. C., Issenberg, S. B., Petrusa, E. R., & Scalese, R. J. (2006). Effects of practice on standardized learning outcomes in simulation-based medical education. *Medical Education, 40,* 792–797.

McGaghie, W. C., Issenberg, S. B., Petrusa, E. R., & Scalese, R. J. (2010). A critical review of simulation-based medical education research: 2003–2009. *Medical Education, 44,* 50–63.

Patel, W. L., Arocha, J. F., & Kaufmann, D. R. (1994). Diagnostic reasoning and medical expertise. In D. Medin (Ed.), *The psychology of learning and motivation, Vol. 30,* (pp. 187–251). New York, NY: Academic Press.

Polymath. (n.d.). In *Wikipedia.* Retrieved from http://en.wikipedia.org/wiki/Polymath

Rantanen, E. M., & Talleur, D. A. (2005). Incremental transfer and cost effectiveness of ground-based flight trainers in university aviation programs. *Proceedings of the 49th Annual Meeting of the Human Factors and Ergonomics Society* (pp. 764–768).

Roessingh, J. J. M. (2005). Transfer of manual flying skills form PC-based simulation to actual flight—Comparisons of in-flight measured data and instructor ratings. *International Journal of Aviation Psychology, 15,* 67–90.

Ruthsatz, J., Detterman, D., Griscom, W. S., & Cirullo, B. A. (2008). Becoming an expert in the musical domain: It takes more than just practice. *Intelligence, 36,* 330–338.

Schulz, R., & Curnow, C. (1988). Peak performance and age among super athletes: track and field, swimming, baseball, tennis, and golf. *Journal of Gerontology: Psychological Sciences, 43,* 113–120.

Siegler, R. S., & Ramani, G. B. (2009). Playing linear number board games—but not circular ones —improves low-income preschoolers' numerical understanding. *Journal of Educational Psychology, 101*, 545–560.

Simon, H. A., & Chase, W. G. (1973). Skill in chess. *American Scientist, 61*, 394–403.

Simonton, D. K. (1999). Talent and its development: An emergenic and epigenetic model. *Psychological Review, 106*, 435–457.

Simpson, S. A., & Gilhooly, K. J. (1997). Diagnostic thinking processes: Evidence from a constructive interaction study of electrocardiogram (ECG) interpretation. *Applied Cognitive Psychology, 11*, 543–554.

Tuffiash, M., Roring, R. W., & Ericsson, K. A. (2007). Expert word play: Capturing and explaining reproducibly superior verbal task performance. *Journal of Experimental Psychology: Applied, 13*, 124–134.

van der Maas, H. L. J., & Wagenmakers, E. J. (2005). A psychometric analysis of chess expertise. *American Journal of Psychology, 118*, 29–60.

Van Sickle, K. R., Ritter, E. M., McClosky, D. A., Lederman, A., Baghai, M., Gallagher, A. G., & Smith, C. D. (2007). Attempted establishment of proficiency levels for laprascopic performance on a national scale using simulation: The results from the 2004 SAGES Minimally Invasive Surgical Trainer—Virtual reality (MIST_VR) learning center study. *Surgical Endoscopy, 21*, 5–10.

Ward. P., Hodges, N. J., Williams, A. M., & Starkes, J. L. (2004). Deliberate practice and expert performance: Defining the path to excellence. In A. M. Williams & N. J. Hodges (Eds.), *Skill acquisition in sport: Research, theory and practice* (pp. 231–258). London, UK: Routledge.

Ward, P., Williams, A. M., & Hancock, P. A. (2006). Simulation for performance and training. In K. A. Ericsson, N. Charness, P. Feltovich, & R. R. Hoffman (Eds.), *Cambridge handbook of expertise and expert performance* (pp. 243–262). Cambridge, UK: Cambridge University Press.

8

Media Effects, Communication, and Complexity Science Insights on Games for Learning

JOHN L. SHERRY

Introduction

A survey of the research literature on games for learning reveals that most contributions come from game designers, education researchers, and various health researchers. To a lesser extent, the field has been informed by the work of researchers who are primarily associated with communication science. Communication researchers contribute to the larger media effects research, but they approach questions of media effects from a different perspective than social or developmental psychologists do. In fact, literature from these three primary media effects disciplines has long been separate with little cross-citation. As the subfield of games for learning enters into its formal stage, it's helpful to inquire what communication researchers have to offer. Do they have unique perspectives that may enhance our understanding of games for learning? That's the purpose of this chapter: to consider how a communication perspective can contribute to research on games for learning.

Traditions of Media Effects Research

Media effects research has a long tradition; some trace the roots of the field back to early studies of the effects of newspapers on public opinion, while others see the origins of media effects research beginning with the Payne Fund studies of movies in the 1920s (Lowery & DeFleur, 1995). These early studies illustrate certain features that have typified media effects research throughout the twentieth century and into the early twenty-first century:

1. Media effects studies have drawn from multiple academic disciplines for theory and methodology, particularly psychology, sociology, and political science.
2. Media effects studies have typically been in response to popular fears related to new media, from film and radio to comic books to video games (Wartella & Reeves, 1986).
3. These studies have primarily employed static, posttest-only experimental methodology or cross-sectional surveys.
4. Much of media effects research pays little attention to variations within message variables, instead treating an entire film-viewing or game-playing session as a single message (e.g., a message promoting violence, a message promoting the thin ideal), rather than as a stream of varying messages.

The best known and most highly debated studies examine the effects of violent media (typically film, television, and video games) from a social psychological perspective. These researchers posit a connection between violent content and aggression arising from such black-box mechanisms as imitation (Bandura, 1994), priming of associative networks (Berkowitz & Rogers, 1986), transfer of arousal (Zillmann, 1971), habituation (Thomas, Horton, Lippincott, & Drabman, 1977), or some combination of everything (Bushman & Anderson, 2002). More frequently, these studies are conducted by randomly assigning university undergraduates either to a condition featuring the negative content (e.g., a violent game) or to a condition that does not contain the negative content (e.g., a nonviolent game). Nothing is done to manipulate features of the message; the entirety of the content is considered as a single negative message. The dependent variable is assessed immediately post-viewing and typically consists of measures that are theorized as related to possible negative behaviors rather than actual negative behavior (e.g., number of negative adjectives circled rather than behavioral aggression). A significant difference between the treatment and control group is considered evidence that the theorized black-box mechanism occurred as predicted. The emphasis is generally on providing evidence that media exposure can produce negative effects, rather than on investigating the mechanisms by which the effects occurred or determining the strength of such effects.

Social psychology's general effects paradigm has been largely adopted by learning games scholars to establish whether learning has occurred. Typically referred to as "evaluation" research, the designs used most often by educational game researchers are either a single game pretest-posttest design or a posttest only with control group design pitting a learning game against some other control condition (e.g., a different game, a book) to establish evidence of learning immediately after game play (Sherry & Dibble, 2009). Given the general nature of these designs, these studies do not disambiguate the large number of features and interactions found in games that might cause learning. For example, if there is evidence of learning, which formal features (e.g., game mechanics, avatars) conveyed the educational material? How did that conveyance occur? Is there a dose-response curve for learning? Further, there are few take-away lessons from these studies for future game designers. For example, what features of the game did the player attend to? How did the learner allocate attention between game-related material and educational material? What caused these shifts in attention? If you compare games and television programs such as *Sesame Street*, how does the load on limited working memory capacity differ? The general effects paradigm only provides a dichotomous answer: whether or not it is possible that some information was acquired by the gamer, typically in the short run.

Communication Research on Media Use and Media Messages

While much media effects research is done in the social psychology tradition, there is also a robust media literature in the field of communication. Communication research proceeds from a different set of assumptions than social psychology and treats the message variables differently. Insights from this tradition are directly relevant to the unanswered questions from game learning research. Communication science originated as a field of study that was focused on the interactive conveyance of messages (Berlo, 1960). In the case of media effects research, communication researchers, informed by dramatic theory (e.g., Aristotle's *Poetics*) and semiotics (e.g., Metz, 1974), conceive of media messages as a dynamic language that is interpreted by each audience member according to conventions learned across the lifespan. Accordingly, compared with social psychology researchers, communication researchers pay greater attention to the formal features of media, the individual interpretation of those formal features by each audience member, and the reasons why an audience member may choose a particular media message. Thus, communication researchers assume that the audience is an active participant in the media experience rather than a passive entity to be acted upon by the media.

This fundamental difference in focus has important implications for educational games. First, the media user is acknowledged to make choices and be in control of the media experience; individuals use media for their own needs, goals, and satisfaction. The concept of an active audience member is a dual-edged sword for games for learning; the learner is active, but the learner may also choose not to participate in the learning process. Second, emotional and cognitive impact varies within the media experience as formal features change. Formal features pertain to the production techniques used to engage the media user's attention and engagement in content presented on the screen, such as visual special effects or the pace of the action (see Calvert, 1999). Care must be taken to consider the impact of these changes on the learner across time. Third, the varying impact is a function of the interaction between the formal features, the reasons the individual is using the medium, and the individual's processing of the formal features. While media experiences are similar across users, they are not the same.

USER CONTROL

The largest corpus of media effects research in communication is found in the "uses and gratifications" tradition. The uses and gratifications tradition focuses on the reasons people use various media, given a variety of other leisure-time and informational options. Researchers have realized that the media use and effects process extends beyond the moment of viewing/interaction into the contextual factors that gave rise to the use in the first place. For uses and gratifications researchers, media use is one component of each individual's more expansive human system (in the Bronfenbrenner, 2005, or Lerner, 2002, human systems sense), and media use is one of many possible mechanisms to solve perceived problems that arise within that system. Across the lifespan, individuals learn which medium, which genre, and which particular instance of media (e.g., movie, game) is best for each problem via an ongoing dialogue between themselves and the world of media offerings (Rosengren, 1974). For example, Sherry (2001) demonstrated that stable and native temperament traits were strongly related to motivations for using particular types of media as individuals developed preferences for particular media content in response to individual differences. Thus, both the search for and use of media is a dynamic, message-specific process of locating and maintaining goodness-of-fit between an individual's needs and repetitive media content (e.g., genre conventions).

Rosengren's (1974) uses and gratifications model assumes that an audience possesses agency in seeking and using media to solve perceived problems and that the results of that agentic use are what are commonly known as effects. Media effects are a function of the reasons that the individual uses that medium. The interaction between constructs in the human system, basic human needs, individual differences, and societal pressures, create perceived problems for which media is one possible solution (see Figure 8.1). Essentially, basic needs, individual differences, and contextual societal factors culminate in a variety of perceived problems and motivations to which gratifications are sought from the media and elsewhere, leading to differential patterns of media effects at both the individual and societal levels. Media use is individual and contextualized, though broader patterns of use can be found. That is, certain media are better than others for satisfying needs and responding to motivations; across the lifespan, individuals develop a sophisticated understanding of which media, genres, and content work best for

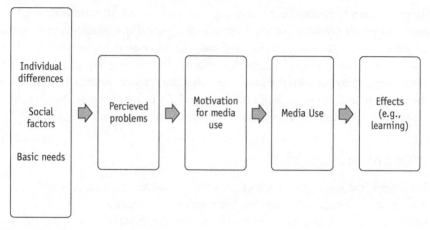

Figure 8.1 The Uses and Gratifications Model.

satisfying perceived needs. Thus, some media are useful when one is bored; other media are useful when one needs companionship. The uses and gratifications tradition provides important insight into how individuals perceive a particular medium; what they expect from that medium and how they relate to and interact with the medium.

This dynamic, message-centered, goodness-of-fit approach to media effects can be applied to games for learning. Such a perspective demands that researchers consider the reasons that individuals play games, which media they prefer to use for learning, and how learning games might solve their perceived learning problems. Next, effects must be considered as part of an ongoing process of interaction between the player/learner and the game. How does the "dialogue" of learning unfold during game play? What is the dynamic process of learning from game play? How do the messages need to change to facilitate individual learning? How do these factors affect the reasons for use? That is, if the learner plays because she perceives a deficit in knowledge, will she continue to play the game after resolving the initial perceived problem?

We can begin by considering the reasons players give for using games. An array of uses and gratifications typologies has emerged in the literature to illuminate the appeal of video games. Selnow (1984) published the first such study in which he surveyed 244 10- to 24-year- olds and isolated five uses and gratifications factors that applied to arcade video game play: such play is preferable to human companions, teaches about people, provides companionship, provides activity/action, and provides solitude/escape. The following year Wigand, Borstelmann, and Boster (1985) published a study revealing a similar set of gratifications for arcade game use: excitement, satisfaction, and tension reduction. A decade later, a survey conducted by Phillips, Rolls, Rouse, and Griffiths (1995) revealed several uses of video game play, including "to pass time," "to avoid doing other things," "to cheer oneself up," and "just for enjoyment." Griffiths's (1991) research on video game addiction included additional uses and gratifications: arousal, social rewards, skill testing, displacement, and stress reduction.

In one of the more comprehensive sets of studies, Sherry and his colleagues (Greenberg, Sherry, Lachlan, Lucas, & Holmstrom, 2010; Lucas & Sherry, 2004; Sherry, Desouza, Greenberg, & Lachlan, 2003; Sherry, Desouza, & Holmstrom, 2003; Sherry, Holmstrom, Binns, Greenberg, & Lachlan, 2003) have enumerated a set of video game uses and gratifications based on focus group research and surveys of more than 1,000 participants ranging in age from 10 to 24 years old. First, the researchers collected reasons for game play from focus groups consisting of a mix of players and nonplayers. These reasons were reduced to a core set that was repeated throughout the focus groups and included:

- competition—to prove to other people who has the best skills and can react or think the fastest;
- challenge—to solve puzzles or to achieve goals, such as getting to the next level or beating the game;
- social interaction—to use video games to interact with friends and learn about the personalities of others;
- diversion—to use games to avoid stress or responsibilities; to fill time, relax, and escape from stress; or because there is nothing else to do;
- fantasy—to do things one would not normally be able to do, such as drive race cars, play professional football, or fly; and
- arousal—to stimulate the emotions as a result of fast action and high quality graphics.

Across all ages, both male and female respondents consistently rated challenge as one of the top motivations for playing games. Corroborating those findings, a Pew Research Center study (Jones, 2003) found that college gamers rated the video game experience as challenging (45%), pleasant (36%), and exciting (34%). Clearly, the appeal of video games results predominantly from the challenge of solving the puzzle presented in the game. Grodal (2000) explained that much of the fascination with video games can be attributed to the ability of players to control the game in terms of outcomes (i.e., deciding how the "plot" will unfold), the speed at which the game progresses, and mastery of the game or mastery over other players. Vorderer, Hartmann, and Klimmt (2003) provided empirical support for the idea that game play was more enjoyable when there were diverse ways to solve a challenge offered in a video game.

Importantly, uses and gratifications research shows that games are not used for learning, or at least for knowledge acquisition or information seeking. During the focus groups by Sherry and colleagues, no respondent reported using games for learning. In fact, other media such as books (Katz, Gurevitch & Haas, 1973; Robinson, 1972), television (Greenberg, 1974; Rubin, 1983) and the Internet

(Ebersole, 2000; Ko, Cho, & Roberts, 2005) are the preferred technology for knowledge and information acquisition (Silk, Sherry, Winn, Keesecker, Horodynski, & Sayir, 2008). The uses and gratification model predicts that an individual who desires to learn will return to the medium for which learning has been most effective in the past. Data suggest that this medium would be books, the Internet, or television (depending on the type of learning). Hence, most individuals would not necessarily think of games as the most likely venue for learning. In fact, learning is not consistent with the motivations and goals of game play. From the perspective of gamers, playing games to learn is like using a hammer to cut wood; it is the wrong choice for the desired job. Despite all the good reasons given for why games offer a powerful learning interface and the ample anecdotal evidence that gamers acquire knowledge of football plays, guns, and other topics from games, games for learning researchers need to come to grips with the fact that individuals simply do not think of games as a primary vehicle for learning.

Dynamic Effects of Formal Features

When the Children's Television Workshop (CTW) set out to invent engaging, educational television for children in 1967, they spent the first year conducting a series of studies examining how children process television messages (Fisch & Truglio, 2001; Palmer, 1969). In particular, they focused on the types of techniques (e.g., sound effects, zooms, animation) and characters (e.g., human, Muppets) that engaged children's attention and facilitated comprehension and retention of educational material. These production techniques or formal features of the program (as described above) were conceived to have varying effects within the program. For example, the formal feature of animated action (e.g., a bouncing letter) was shown to draw and engage children's attention. Within a specific 30-second skit, animated action could be used at several different times to direct children's attention to particular educational content (e.g., the letter the children were learning). Researchers also attempted to determine the threshold of repetitional frequency of formal features to maximize attention during a skit (e.g., not to use animated letters so frequently that they stop drawing attention). Such research-based knowledge about the function of formal features from the CTW has been used subsequently to guide designers of other educational television programs such as *Blue's Clues*, and *Dora the Explorer*.

Unlike the case with educational television, there is little basic scientific literature on how children attend to, process, and learn from games (Sherry & Dibble, 2009). Because video games can have many more formal features than television programs, the need for CTW-type research is even greater. In addition to the audio and visual formal features found in television, games contain mechanics that define and delimit the player's interaction with the game. *Mechanics* is a term used by game designers (e.g., Salen & Zimmerman, 2004) and researchers (e.g., Sellers, 2006; Squire, Barnett, Grant, & Higginbotham, 2004) to denote the game rules, the environmental conditions, and the allowable player actions that can be made in pursuit of play, or the parameters that enable the player to engage the specific challenges provided by digital games (Salen & Zimmerman, 2004). In essence, game mechanics are the rules of the game and character manipulation, including the rules by which phenomena like the forces of gravity, physics, light, time, and other more abstract physical principles operate.

For example, one major category of game mechanics is the physical properties imposed on the structure of the virtual world, such as gravity. In *Super Mario Galaxy*, the player runs, jumps, and explores planets in various planetary systems. The player can physically jump from planet to planet, and the planets are tiny. Planets may be as small as a car (in relation to the avatar) or as large as a football stadium. The gravity mechanics in this game dictate that planetary mass is constant. That is, a player experiences the same gravitational pull of a planet if the planet is 30 yards in diameter and made of clouds or 3 million yards in diameter and made of molten lead. However, the designers of *Super Mario Galaxy* could have chosen to make the gravity mechanics more similar to reality, with gravity proportional to the mass of objects and inversely proportional to the square of the distance between them. Another major category of game mechanics pertains to the abilities afforded the virtual player. Action game mechanics include jumping, running, shooting, and climbing; puzzle games may not have an avatar to control, yet they still provide mechanics for control such as screen rotation, puzzle piece adjustment, or placement as in the case of *Tetris*. How these avatar abilities interact with the properties of the environment establishes a complex set of relationships among the mechanics.

The complex set of relationships among the various types of mechanics can be considered as the fundamental game model. The game model defines the rules and parameters of the game world, including the conditions for winning or losing (Salen & Zimmerman, 2004). Underlying the game model is the precise mathematical language of the software of the game. Ultimately, every game works from a finite set of program rules defining the mechanics and the relationships among those mechanics. The player needs to master these rules to accomplish tasks within the world and ultimately conquer levels or win the game (Boyan & Sherry, 2011). Consistent with uses and gratifications research, this goal is the most essential motivation for playing games; the accomplishment experienced by conquering challenges by learning levels and winning the game (Greenberg, Sherry, Lachlan, Lucas, & Holmstrom, 2010). These challenges can be divided into two types: manifest and intrinsic (Boyan & Sherry, 2011).

Manifest challenges are the challenges presented by the obvious enemies or tasks that the player must overcome to win. For example, in *Tetris* the player is tasked with filling all gaps in horizontal space by matching a series of falling tiles. In *Donkey Kong*, the player must navigate the Mario avatar to the top of the screen to rescue Pauline from a giant gorilla. Intrinsic challenges refer to learning the unique allowances, limits, rules, and strategy of a particular game to be able to control the game environment (its "world") and characters. In *Tetris*, the player must learn how to quickly manipulate falling tiles to fill horizontal space and to plan for future tiles. In *Donkey Kong*, the player must learn how to make Mario move and what threats and rewards are present in the environment. The player must master the intrinsic challenges to overcome the manifest challenge.

Formal feature research on learning games needs to determine how the variety of challenges affect learning so as to address certain questions, such as whether it matters what the manifest challenge is. Should it be apparent that the manifest challenge is to learn, or should that outcome be hidden? How would revealing or hiding learning in the manifest challenge affect the player's motivation to engage in the game? What are the demands placed by various intrinsic challenges? Might these demands vary by age group or individual? For example, Sherry, Rosaen, Bowman and Huh (2006) have shown that individual differences in cognitive skill affect player success with and enjoyment of games. Can a child with poor 3-D mental rotation skill learn from a game environment that is presented in 3-D?

Dynamical Systems

If we think about an educational game as a series of interactions with a game model via game mechanics over time, rather than as a single message, and we bear in mind that each individual learner is making sense of a series of messages according to her own needs, motivations, educational history, and social context (e.g., Bronfenbrenner, 2005; Lerner, 2002), it is apparent that the process of learning from games is a quite complex. Recently, greater interest has been focused on research about these types of dynamical systems (e.g., Miller & Page, 2007; Mitchell, 2011). These systems are quite common in natural science (e.g., the weather, fluid turbulence, guitar distortion in rock music) and they display behavior that is generally more sophisticated than would be predicted by simple analytic systems used in social science research and theory. Rather than simple binary on-off/present–not present behavior of commonly used statistical models such as ANOVA, complex systems can display a variety of regular or random-appearing behavioral patterns, particularly when iterated across time. The introduction of time adds complexity that is consistent with the reality of game play as a self-directed series of interactions unique to each player.

Traditional statistical concepts commonly used in social science most often describe a relationship among variables plotted at a single moment in time (e.g., a snapshot of behavior from a survey or after an experimental manipulation). Statistics used in social science typically specify "variance explained," which is an estimate of the degree to which data map perfectly on a linear function (e.g., least squares regression) in the static snapshot. When social scientists consider time, they frequently create a series of snapshots that are separated by large chunks of time within which many things may occur (e.g., as in a longitudinal survey with two measurements six months apart). In other words, they don't examine the nature of the change, but simply the difference between states at different points in time. However, dynamical systems researchers attempt to analyze the nature of the change by plotting near-continuous time. Unfortunately, nonlinear dynamics are difficult to understand because the math informing them is significantly more difficult than linear mathematics.

Nonlinear systems do not create output that directly proportional to the input to the system. That is, small changes in the predictor variables do not necessarily lead to small changes in the output and large changes in the predictor variables do not necessarily lead to large changes in the output. This situation is odd for social scientists, because we deal almost exclusively with proportional systems. For example, a small change in the value of a predictor variable in simple linear regression will lead to a small change in the criterion variable, and a large change in the value of a predictor variable in simple linear regression will lead to a large change in the criterion variable. Instead, nonlinear dynamic systems are often presented as patterns of solutions over time mapped onto phase space, (a space where each output value of the system across time is plotted) such as attractors. Attractors are subsets of phase space across time resulting from the deterministic rules of a nonlinear system that behave differently as a result of small changes in variable parameters.

To illustrate, we can examine a dynamic system called a logistic difference equation (May, 1976). The logistic difference equation models simple population dynamics, assuming that the population is limited to what the environment can sustain (Vogels, Zoeckler, Stasiw, & Cerny, 1976). That is, some population P (e.g., fish in a lake, squirrels in a field) will increase at a certain rate r until the demands of the population exceed the resources in the environment (referred to as the carrying capacity K). When carrying capacity is reached, population growth must end because the environment cannot sustain further growth. The logistic equation is given as

$$P' = rP(1 - P/K)$$

The rate of population growth is slowed by the number of inhabitants placing demands on the environment, with a maximum at the carrying capacity.

The nonlinear nature of the equation can be seen by making small changes in r or the rate of change. In dynamics parlance, r is the driving parameter in this system that determines whether the series of points in phase space is a fixed point attractor, limit cycle attractor, and strange attractor. A driving parameter from $0 < r < 3.00$ will result in a fixed point attractor, which is a system that tends to settle to a single point. Imagine a child on a swing. After the swing is released from a high point, it will move down to the bottom and then continue swinging up at a distance relative to the speed the child is moving and other factors (gravity,

$$P_{k+1} = 2.75 * P_k * (1 - P_k)$$

Starting at the value $P_0 = 0.25$

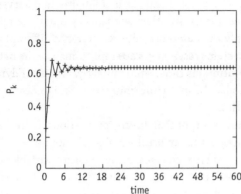

Time	P
0	0.250000
1	0.515625
2	0.686829
3	0.591511
4	0.664471
5	0.652316
6	0.645421
7	0.623699
...	...
44	0.636364
45	0.636364
46	0.636364

Figure 8.2 Fixed Point Attractor.

friction), at which point it stops and gravity draws the child back down. The swing continues to move, losing energy on each cycle, until it eventually settles to a stop at the bottom. The fixed point where the swing eventually stops is the fixed point attractor for that system. Using $r = 2.75$ as the driving parameter in the logistic equation (see Figure 8.2) will result in a fixed point attractor in which $P = .6363$ after the 43rd iteration.

A different attractor emerges if we increase the initial driving parameter from $3.0 < r < 3.57$. This second type of attractor is a limit cycle attractor (in the case of $r = 3.4$, a two-point limit cycle; see Figure 8.3). In a limit cycle attractor, the system settles to a pattern in which the points on phase space repeatedly cycle through the

$$P_{k+1} = 3.4 * P_k * (1 - P_k)$$

Starting at the value $P_0 = 0.25$

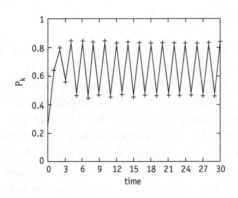

Time	P
0	0.250000
1	0.637500
2	0.785719
3	0.572440
4	0.832158
5	0.474881
6	0.847855
....	....
87	0.451963
88	0.842154
89	0.451963
90	0.842154

Figure 8.3 Limit Cycle Attractor.

Time	P
0	0.250000
1	0.693750
2	0.786105
3	0.622132
4	0.869810
5	0.418989
6	0.900718
7	0.330874
8	0.819166
9	0.548092
10	0.916442
11	0.283330
12	0.751300
13	0.691339
14	0.789541
15	0.614814
...	...
45	0.256716
46	0.706007
47	0.767976
48	0.659300
49	0.831107
50	0.519361

$$P_{k+1} = 3.7 * P_k * (1 - P_k)$$

Starting at the value $P_0 = 0.25$

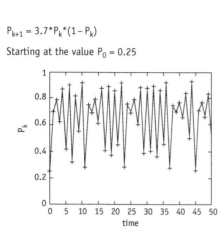

Figure 8.4 Strange Attractor.

same points (e.g., in a two-point limit cycle the system cycles between two points; in a three-point limit cycle the system cycles through three points, etc.). Changing the driving parameter to $r = 3.4$ results in a system that settles into an alternating cycle between $P = 0.451963$ and $P = 0.842154$ beginning after the 86th iteration.

Pushing the driving parameter past $r = 3.57$ results in the third type of attractor, called a strange attractor (see Figure 8.4). Strange attractors display random-appearing behavior because the phase space is never repeated, meaning there is no fixed point or cycle. However, the behavior is not truly random because it is driven by deterministic rules (the logistic equation in this case). As the system iterates, it does not settle to a fixed point or to a limit cycle; instead, the system continues to change without ever overlapping. May (1976) has shown that increasing a driving parameter to $3.57 < r < 4.0$ produces strange attractor behavior with the logistic equation. Strange attractors are often, although not necessarily, chaotic.

It is important to note that three distinct patterns of behavior emerge from relatively small changes in the driving parameter r as the system changes over time. Although the relationship among all the variables remains the same (the proportions in the equation), initial conditions in the driving parameter result in very different patterns of behavior in the system ranging from a kind of equilibrium (fixed point) to a variety of cycles to random-appearing behavior.

Let's reconsider the posttest-only static design used in much of the media effects research in light of nonlinear dynamics. While participants view a stimulus film, their brain systems iterate through a large number of states involved in cognitive and emotional processing of the message. The viewer may be happy when the film begins, evidence fear when the main character is threatened, experience warmth when the main character falls in love, feel excited as the main character fights for his life. At the end of the film, the researcher measures the current brain state of the subjects, never considering all the emotions and cognitions during the film viewing. Aren't these also important effects of the film? Post-stimulus measurement of the "effect" of the film assumes that the brain processing system stops and locks into one point when the movie ends. It is more likely that the dynamics of processing the film continue after viewing. This situation remains the case, unless the film has driven the viewers' processing system into a limit point cycle: the exact time at which the researcher measures the brain state can make a great difference. That is, if a particular system were driven into a four-point limit cycle, mustn't all subjects be measured at the same point in that cycle to be comparable? What are we really comparing in these static designs?

It Isn't as Easy as It Looks

Given the variety of motivations that each student brings to the playing of educational games, the variety of formal features and challenges in games, and the dynamics of neural systems, it would appear that designing effective educational games is a nearly impossible challenge. Certainly, the results coming from static media effects research provide little reason to believe that educational game designers have mastered that complexity. Nonetheless, we know that people of varying motivations attend school with a broad array of teachers who provide them with a variety of challenges and that these people emerge from the school system having acquired a great deal of knowledge. Systematic educational interventions do work. The challenge is how to make systematic educational games work.

LET SCIENCE INFORM DESIGN

One of the great ironies in educational game design is that designers rarely use science to create games designed to teach science. Most funding and effort has gone into creating games based on experience or intuition, and then the resulting games are tested using static media effects research strategies. Scant attention has been given to the basic problem of how people learn from games (despite many journal articles and books that claim to do so). Working from science to design will dramatically shorten the time it takes to understand how to design effective educational games.

STUDY GAMING DYNAMICALLY

It is obvious that game interaction happens across time, yet gaming research continues to use static designs. Consideration needs to be given to learning across time. Games are uniquely positioned for this type of research because the medium can also be used to collect data dynamically, through keystroke tracking. Careful research design can reveal common dynamics associated with decision-making, discovery strategies, attention allocation, and other key dynamical processes. What are the driving parameters that we need to understand and what types of behavior do they engender?

STUDY GAME USE MOTIVATION

More research has been done in this area than any other mentioned in this section. However, game motivation research has rarely examined educational games in the larger ecology of entertainment. Is it realistic to imagine an educational game generating enough interest to draw players away from media that is designed only for entertainment? Or will educational gaming work primarily as a formal, graded school activity, where the primary motivation is supplied by grades?

LEARNING AS A GAME CHALLENGE

What types of challenges are effective in educational games? Specifically, can we assume that all learners will have adequate mastery of game mechanics to overcome the intrinsic challenges of a learning game? One game I played assumed a knowledge of first-person shooter mechanics that I didn't have; my potential learning was defeated before I started. If a child spends two hours of his homework time trying to figure out how to simply navigate the game world, how much education content is being learned?

Conclusion

The simple linear and static general effects paradigm that dominates learning games research fails to account for the levels of complexity implicit in the real-world process. A fully realized theory of game learning must account for the complex interaction among the formal features of the game (entertainment content, learning content, and game model), the reasons the individual is using the medium (uses and gratifications), and the manner in which the individual processes the formal features as a dynamic function of cognitive processing resources. The absence of a fully realized theory is evidenced by the dramatic crash of the educational software industry in the early 2000s (Richtel, 2005) and the lack of a sterling example of educational games equivalent to television's *Sesame Street* and *Blue's Clues*. Given the amount of resources poured into games for learning, where are the success stories?

Considering the problem from a communication perspective increases the complexity of the research, but also increases the likelihood of learning from games by acknowledging player agency and the dynamics of brain/game interaction. First, uses and gratifications theory teaches us that we must consider the player's active role in engaging the game. Does this game conform to the reasons gamers play or is the medium a mismatch for the use? Second, games must be considered a dynamic language system consisting of formal features that change over time, each carrying their own meanings and efficacy. How does the presence of a particular formal feature influence the player? Does it conform to the player's assumptions about that feature? Finally, researchers need to understand that time dynamics in nonlinear systems can have unintended effects. The demands present in the game itself can make it more difficult for the learner to process by setting off chaotic dynamics. How does one tune the processing demand parameters to put the learning into a high-level fixed-point dynamic? Certainly, better understanding of player motivations and formal feature demands is required to tune the parameter.

Educational game designers often labor under an understandable, but false logic. They assume that because games are highly immersive and intrinsically motivating experiences (Sherry, 2002) in which players acquire information to play the game better, using games for education will necessarily result in the same types of immersion and learning. It's easy to forget that for every *Halo* there are thousands of games that failed to find that balance and fulfill gamer motivations and expectations. Games are not inherently motivating, but result when designers have precariously balanced a variety of cognitive demands in an attractive challenging medium that is consistent with players' experiences and expectations.

References

Bandura, A. (1994). The social cognitive theory of mass communication. In J. Bryant & D. Zillmann (Eds.), *Media effects: Advances in theory and research* (pp. 121–154). Hillsdale, NJ: Lawrence Erlbaum Associates.

Berkowitz, L., & Rogers, K. H. (1986). A priming effect analysis of media influences. In J. Bryant & D. Zillmann (Eds.), *Perspectives on media effects* (pp. 57–81). Hillsdale, NJ: Lawrence Erlbaum Associates.

Berlo, D. (1960). *The process of communication*. New York, NY: Holt, Rinehart, and Winston.

Boyan, A., & Sherry, J. L. (2011). The challenge in creating games for education: Aligning mental models with game models. *Child Development Perspectives, 5*, 82–87.

Bronfenbrenner, U. (Ed.). (2005). *Making human beings human: Bioecological perspectives on human development*. Thousand Oaks, CA: Sage.

Bushman, B. J., & Anderson, C. A. (2002). Violent video games and hostile expectations: A test of the general aggression model. *Personality and Social Psychology Bulletin, 28,* 1679–1686.

Calvert, S. (1999). The form of thought. In I. E. Sigel (Ed.), *Development of mental representation* (pp.453–470). Mahwah, NJ: Lawrence Erlbaum Associates.

Ebersole, S. (2000). Uses and gratifications of the web among students. *Journal of Computer Mediated Communication, 6,* 0. doi: 10.1111/j.1083-6101.2000.tb00111.x

Fisch, S. M., & Truglio, R. T. (2001). Why children learn from Sesame Street. In S. M. Fisch & R. T. Truglio (Eds.), *"G" is for growing: Thirty years of research on children and Sesame Street* (pp. 233–244). Mahwah, NJ: Lawrence Erlbaum Associates.

Greenberg, B. S. (1974). Gratifications of television viewing and their correlates for British children. In J. G. Blumler & E. Katz (Eds.), *The uses of mass communication* (Vol. 1, pp. 71–92). Beverly Hills, CA: Sage.

Greenberg, B. S., Sherry, J. L., Lachlan, K., Lucas, K., & Holmstrom, A. (2010). Orientations to video games among gender and age groups. *Simulation & Gaming, 41,* 238–259.

Griffiths, M. D. (1991). The observational analysis of adolescent gambling in U.K. amusement arcades. *Journal of Community and Applied Social Psychology, 1,* 309–320.

Grodal, T. (2000). Video games and the pleasures of control. In D. Zillmann & P. Vorderer (Eds.), *Media entertainment: The psychology of its appeal* (pp. 197–214). Mahwah, NJ: Lawrence Erlbaum Associates.

Jones, S. (2003). *Let the games begin: Gaming technology and entertainment among college students.* Pew Internet and American Life Project. Downloaded from http://www.pewinternet.org/Reports/2003/Let-the-games-begin-Gaming-technology-and-college-students.aspx

Katz, E., Gurevitch, M., & Haas, H. (1973). On the use of mass media for important things. *American Sociological Review, 38,* 164–181.

Ko, H., Cho, C.-H., & Roberts, M. S. (2005). Internet uses and gratifications: A structural equation model of interactive advertising. *Journal of Advertising, 34,* 57–70.

Lerner, R. M. (2002). *Concepts and theories of human development* (3rd ed.). Mahwah, NJ: Lawrence Erlbaum Associates.

Lowery, S. A., & DeFleur, M. L. (1995). *Milestones in mass communication research: Media effects.* White Plains, NY: Longman.

Lucas, K., & Sherry, J. L. (2004). Sex differences in video game play: A communication-based explanation. *Communication Research, 31,* 499–523.

May, R. M. (1976). Simple mathematical models with very complicated dynamics. *Nature, 261,* 459–467.

Metz, C. (1974). *Film language: A semiotics of the cinema.* New York, NY: Oxford University Press.

Miller, J. H., & Page, S. (2007). *Complex adaptive systems.* Princeton, NJ: Princeton University Press.

Mitchell, M. (2011). *Complexity: A guided tour.* Oxford: Oxford University Press.

Palmer, E. (1969). Research at the Children's Television Workshop. *Educational Broadcasting Review, 3*(5), 43–48.

Phillips, C. A., Rolls, S., Rouse, A., & Griffiths, M. D. (1995). Home video game playing in schoolchildren: A study of incidence and patterns of play. *Journal of Adolescence, 18,* 687–691.

Richtel, M. (2005, Aug. 22). Once a booming market, educational software for the PC takes a nose dive. *The New York Times,* p. C-1.

Robinson, J. P. (1972). Toward defining the functions of television. In E. A. Rubinstein, G. A. Comstock, & J. P. Murray (Eds.), *Television and social behavior: Vol.4* (pp. 568–603). Washington, DC: Government Printing Office..

Rosengren, K. E. (1974). Uses and gratifications: A paradigm outlined. In J. G. Blumler & E. Katz (Eds.), *The uses of mass communications: Current perspectives of gratifications research* (pp. 269–286). Beverly Hills, CA: Sage.

Rubin, A. M. (1983). Television uses and gratifications: The interactions of viewing patterns and motivations. *Journal of Broadcasting, 27,* 37–51.

Salen, K., & Zimmerman, E. (2004). *Rules of play: Game design fundamentals.* Cambridge, MA: MIT Press.

Sellers, M. (2006). Designing the experience of interactive play. In P. Vorderer & J. Bryant (Eds.), *Playing video games: Motives, responses, and consequences* (pp. 9–24). Mahwah, NJ: Lawrence Erlbaum Associates.

Selnow, G. W. (1984). Playing videogames: The electronic friend. *Journal of Communication, 34,* 148–156.

Sherry, J. L. (2001). Toward an etiology of media use motivations: The role of temperament in media use. *Communication Monographs, 68,* 274–288.

Sherry, J. L., & Dibble, J. L. (2009). The impact of serious games on childhood development. In U. Ritterfeld, M. Cody, & P. Vorderer (Eds.), *Serious games: Mechanisms and effects* (pp. 143–164). New York, NY: Routledge.

Sherry, J., Desouza, R., & Holmstrom, A. (2003, April). *The appeal of violent video games in children.* Paper presented at the Broadcast Education Association Annual Convention, Las Vegas, NV.

Sherry, J., Desouza, R., Greenberg, B., & Lachlan, K. (2003, May). *Relationship between developmental stages and video game uses and gratifications, game preference and amount of time spent in play.* Paper presented at the International Communication Association Annual Convention, San Diego, CA.

Sherry, J., Holmstrom, A., Binns, R., Greenberg, B., & Lachlan, K. (2003, November). *Gender differences in video game use and preferences.* Paper presented at the National Communication Association Annual Convention, Miami, FL.

Sherry, J. L., Lucas, K., Greenberg, B. S., & Lachlan, K. (2006). Video game uses and gratifications as predictors of use and game preferences. In P. Vorderer & J. Bryant (Eds.), *Playing video games: Motives, responses, consequences* (pp. 213–224). Mahwah, NJ: Lawrence Erlbaum Associates.

Sherry, J. L., Rosaen, S., Bowman, N. D., & Huh, S. (2006, June). *Cognitive skill predicts video game ability.* Paper presented at the annual meeting of the International Communication Association, Dresden, Germany.

Silk, K., Sherry, J. L., Winn, B., Keesecker, N., Horodynski, M. A., & Sayir, A. (2008). Increasing nutrition literacy: Testing the effectiveness of print, web site, and game modalities. *Journal of Nutrition Education and Behavior, 40*(1), 3–10.

Squire, K., Barnett, M., Grant, J. M., & Higginbotham, T. (2004). Electromagnetism supercharged! Learning physics with digital simulation games. In Y. Kafai (Ed.), *Proceedings of the Sixth International Conference of the Learning Sciences: June 22–26* (pp. 513–552). Mahwah, NJ: Erlbaum.

Thomas, M. H., Horton, R. W., Lippincott, E. C., & Drabman, R. S. (1977). Desensitization to portrayals of real life aggression as a function of television violence. *Journal of Personality and Social Psychology, 35,* 450–458.

Vogels, M., Zoeckler, R., Stasiw, D. M., & Cerny, L. C. (1976). P. F. Verhulst's "Notice sur la loique la populations suit dans son accroissement" from Correspondence Mathematique et Physique. Ghent. Vol. X 1838. *Journal of Biological Physics, 3,* 183–192.

Vorderer, P., Hartmann, T., & Klimmt, C. (2003). Explaining the enjoyment of playing video games: The role of competition. In D. Marinelli (Ed.), *Proceedings of the Second International Conference on Computer Games* (pp. 1–9). Pittsburgh, PA: Carnegie Mellon.

Wartella, E., & Reeves, B. (1985). Historical trends in research on children and the media:1900–1960. *Journal of Communication, 35*(2), 118–133.

Wigand, R. T., Borstelmann, S. E., & Boster, F. J. (1985). Electronic leisure: Video game usage and the communication climate of video arcades. In M. McLaughlin (Ed.), *Communication yearbook 9* (pp. 275–293). Beverly Hills, CA: Sage.

Zillmann, D. (1971). Excitation transfer in communication mediated aggressive behavior. *Journal of Experimental Social Psychology, 7,* 419–434.

9

The General Learning Model: Unveiling the Teaching Potential of Video Games

DOUGLAS A. GENTILE, CHRISTOPHER L. GROVES,
AND J. RONALD GENTILE

Introduction

Video games are unlike other media. Traditional forms of media such as television, movies, music, and radio require that media consumers simply listen to or watch provided content. Every consumer hears and sees the same show each time (although individuals can certainly take away different meanings). In contrast, video games involve a unique level of interaction with media content. Every consumer co-creates the story in a game, making each playing somewhat unique. Thus, video game playing is a form of media in which viewers act and those actions have consequences.

This interactive nature has positioned video games at the front line of many research projects designed to tap into the superiority of interactive media as a learning tool. Research regarding the potential for video games to foster learning has focused on a range of academic and nonacademic topics, including reading and math skills (Murphy, Penuel, Means, Korbak, Whaley, & Allen, 2002), aggression (Anderson & Bushman, 2002), health (Papastergiou, 2009), prosocial behavior (Gentile et al., 2009), and cognitive functions such as visuospatial performance (Green & Bavalier, 2003; Sanchez, 2012). The range of areas covered by this research illustrates the flexibility of video games as teaching tools, which may reflect that the interactive nature of video games engages diverse learning mechanisms.

Our understanding of how humans learn has developed dramatically over the past century. Numerous domain-specific learning theories have each contributed to our understanding of how learning occurs. Advances in neuroscience have similarly been largely domain-specific. Each theory tends to describe its learning mechanism in isolation from other learning mechanisms, which allows for targeted study design. This approach, however, can limit our understanding of the bigger picture. No single mechanism or set of processes can explain human learning in its entirety (nor are they designed to).

At a neurological level, understanding how different areas of the brain are specialized for specific learning tasks is beneficial, but it does not address how the brain is integrated. That is, a collection of biological structures or cognitive mechanisms may be responsible for one type of learning (e.g., the association of an outcome with a reward) but these often work in conjunction with other learning mechanisms that work in parallel (e.g., the generalization required to understand how similar behaviors may lead to the same reward). Some learning mechanisms occur serially, others in parallel, and they likely interact with each other. An integrated model may provide a clearer, more holistic picture of how humans learn. The general learning model (GLM; Buckley & Anderson, 2006; Maier & Gentile, 2012) is designed to incorporate each of the domain-specific theories into a meta theoretical model. The GLM may help to generate new hypotheses by developing links between the levels of analysis described by each domain-specific theory. Although the basic aspects have been described elsewhere (e.g., Maier & Gentile, 2012), this chapter provides additional details. First, however, we briefly describe several of the specific learning mechanisms, after which we describe how they may be integrated into the general model.

Domain-Specific Learning Theories

HABITUATION AND DISCRIMINATION

When a stimulus is first presented, it elicits an orienting response and attention to that stimulus. That is, after it is perceived, it influences internal states, such as arousal—leading the actor to attend to its source. Continue repeating exposure to that stimulus, however, and arousal decreases, lowering the time spent attending. *Habituation* has occurred, which implies familiarity with the stimulus—an elementary but important type of learning. All that is needed for habituation learning is single or repeated exposure to a stimulus. In fact, even a single exposure that is too fast to be consciously noticed can be learned and can change behavior (e.g., Bridger, 1961; Colombo & Mitchell, 2009).

Habituation also accounts for our ability to learn to tolerate noxious or threatening situations. Enter a noisy space and it will immediately be noticeable, even jarring. Remain there for some time and you will accommodate to that level of noise. The noise level could even be gradually increased over time and we would habituate to it and show greater tolerance of it. Tolerance to spousal abuse, media violence, and noxious smells can all be at least partly explained by habituation (see Sidman, 1960, for other interesting examples). For example, frequent consumers of violent video game content, those who have habituated to scenes of violence, display lessened physiological arousal to real-life violence (Carnagey, Anderson,

& Bushman, 2007) and exhibit lower activation of event-related potentials associated with aversive motivations when exposed to violent images (Bartholow, Bushman, & Sestir, 2006).

A related learning process is discrimination; learning to distinguish two or more things that are not the same. Discrimination learning only requires repeated exposures for learning to occur. It usually helps if the repeated exposures provide an opportunity for comparison. Discrimination learning also does not need any type of reinforcement, although reinforcement can sometimes speed up learning. These types of learning often need to occur prior to other types, such as associative learning. Only after you can recognize something (habituation) or discriminate it as being different from other things can you learn to associate it with different things and consequences.

CLASSICAL (RESPONDENT) CONDITIONING

When a biological reflex (such as salivation to food) becomes associated with a previously neutral stimulus (such as a tone), that stimulus comes to elicit a similar reflexive response. Pavlov's classic (1927) experiments demonstrated that dogs could learn to associate a tone (conditioned stimulus) with food (unconditioned stimulus), and salivate to the tone alone (unconditioned response to food, but conditioned response to tone). A more mnemonic term for this kind of learning is respondent conditioning (after Skinner, 1938), because it emphasizes that behavior occurs in response or reaction to an eliciting stimulus in an involuntary manner (as contrasted with operant conditioning as discussed below).

Pavlov's contemporary, J. B. Watson (1913; 1919) also studied the condition ability of reflexes and aimed to catalogue which habits or reflexes could be considered "natural" and which "learned." As part of that research program, he provided the classic demonstration of conditioned fear in Little Albert by introducing a previously neutral white rat into a room and following that with a loud noise, inevitably leading to the presence of the rat alone being sufficient to elicit fear.

Despite the apparent ease with which respondent conditioning can occur, there are significant limits. Generalization to other stimuli goes only so far. Fear of a white rat generalized to other furry objects, but not to a wooden duck (Bregman, 1934). Animals made nauseous by a blue liquid will avoid other liquids with the same taste or odor, but they will not associate the nausea with blueness (Garcia & Ervin, 1968). The ostensible principle here is that we are biologically prepared to associate tastes or odors to food and fears to sounds or appearances (see also Seligman's 1971, p. 312, description of phobias). Still, conditioned emotions are one important level of learning, which interacts with behavioral and cognitive acts (as discussed more fully below).

OPERANT CONDITIONING

Whereas respondent conditioning concerns involuntary behavior, operant or instrumental conditioning is concerned with voluntary or purposeful behavior. This behavior is emitted by an organism exploring its environment, often to achieve some desired consequence or goal (Skinner, 1938). Achieving a desired consequence increases the future likelihood of that behavior because it is instrumental in achieving the goal (Thorndike, 1911). Specifically, the organism is learning to control its environment while simultaneously being shaped by the environmental consequences (Skinner, 1974). Here, we say that the behavior has been reinforced: the word *reinforcement* refers to the fact that the behavior is more likely to appear—or to appear more often—in similar future situations.

Reinforcement can occur in two ways. Positive reinforcement occurs by gaining something desirable, as when working earns money, or when one clears a level of a video game and gets access to new levels or skills in the game. Negative reinforcement occurs by escaping or avoiding some negative outcome or noxious stimulus, as when a dog jumps a barrier to escape shock, or a student studies hard (or maybe cheats) to escape a failing grade. Here, positive and negative do not necessarily refer to good or bad behavior.

Voluntary behavior can also be modified via extinction and punishment. Extinction is the process of nonreinforcement, which teaches the learner that responding in previously rewarded ways is no longer effective. Thus, the behavior eventually decreases in frequency, although not in a smooth pattern, because nonreinforcement is frustrating and the behavioral response has not been forgotten. Punishment, in contrast, provides an aversive consequence to a behavior, with the usual effect of suppressing the behavior, at least momentarily and in the presence of the punisher (consider how people tend to obey posted speed limits when highway patrols are present).

Many complexities and side effects accompany extinction and punishment, including frustration effects (e.g., Amsel, 1962), learned helplessness (e.g., Seligman, 1975), and masochistic behaviors (e.g., Church, 1963, 1969; see also Hulse, Egeth, & Deese, 1980, for greater consideration of these effects).

As Skinner (1971) noted, operant conditioning is analogous to Darwin's natural selection: behaviors survive and are maintained because the consequences selected them. The consequences, therefore, are primary in accounting for behavior and their frequencies. Nevertheless, behaviors occur in a situation or context that provides cues (discriminative stimuli) for appropriate behavior. Stated in terms of behavior modification's ABCs, such cues are the *antecedents*, in the presence of which *behaviors* occur and the *consequences* select for future outcomes. Red and green traffic lights cue our stop-and-go behaviors; they do not make us stop (as in respondent conditioning). Rather, we learn to discriminate when it is appropriate to stop or go, presumably because of the consequences associated with those behaviors (or their converse). Once learned, the cue signals the appropriate behavior, which can become habitual, thus requiring little conscious control and promoting multitasking.

As one might expect, the more reinforcement (whether in number or amount) a behavior receives, the faster or better the learning occurs at first. But each new reinforcement follows the law of diminishing returns, thus producing a variation of the well-known S-shaped learning curve (e.g., Hovland, 1937). Even more important than the amount of reinforcement is the schedule of reinforcement, in which intermittent and variable reinforcement (such as that provided by slot machines and their unpredictable rewards) produces more consistent behaviors across time (i.e., if you don't win on one try, you tend to keep trying) than continuous or entirely predictable reinforcement (such as that provided by vending machines) (see Ferster & Skinner, 1957). When a behavior is constantly reinforced, the learner comes to expect and rely on that reinforcement. When reinforcement is withdrawn (e.g., the vending machine swallows your coins but does not deliver your purchase), the learner may become emotionally frustrated. In the case of the vending machine, the learner is unlikely to continue to put more coins in that machine. When a behavior has been intermittently and variably reinforced, however, we learn to tolerate frustration and to persist (resist extinction) despite nonreinforcement: witness gamblers at the slot machines who may persist despite continued losses, or the video game player who may spend hours searching for a rare item.

OBSERVATIONAL LEARNING

While the previously reported research was establishing that reinforcement could be effective in teaching and maintaining new behaviors, research on latent learning (e.g., Tolman, 1932, 1959) demonstrated that learning could occur in the absence of consequences. By simply observing where food could be obtained, for example, organisms could later use this information to negotiate a maze much faster than those who were unable to observe it. Succinctly stated, reinforcement was sufficient, but not necessary, for learning. Thus, reinforcements and other consequences select and shape behaviors, and they regulate the frequency of probability with which they occur. Nonetheless, learning can occur without them and without being immediately observable in behavior.

Bandura and colleagues demonstrated this situation in a series of studies on modeling aggressive acts. Kindergarten children, after being given art materials to work with, were exposed to a model who performed novel aggressive acts, and made comments (e.g., "Pow!") directed toward an inflated Bobo doll. These actions were performed either by an adult in the room, in a TV movie by the same adult; or on the TV by a cartoon character. Then, the children were led to another room full of attractive toys but told they could not play with the toys. This treatment was introduced to produce frustration which, following Dollard, Miller, Doo'b and Mowrer's (1939) frustration-aggression hypothesis, was likely to induce aggression. Children in a control group did everything the three experimental groups did except that they witnessed no modeled aggression. In a third room, the children were allowed to play with any of the available toys, including the Bobo doll, while being observed and scored every five seconds for various aggressive behaviors and comments. Across all conditions (including male versus female models), the experimental treatments produced approximately equal amounts of aggression in the child observers, which was about twice as much as induced by the control treatment (Bandura, Ross, & Ross, 1963).

In follow-up studies (e.g., Bandura & Kupers, 1964), models were praised or reprimanded for aggressive behaviors. As expected, child observers did not spontaneously imitate the punished acts; they did imitate the rewarded acts. The punished behaviors had been learned however, because the children were able to demonstrate them later when asked. Thus, as noted above, reinforcing or punishing consequences primarily affects performance, not learning. The distinction between learning and performance is important in any learning theory.

COGNITIVE LEARNING

Human symbolic communication allows for learning that is devoid of the need to act. Thus, humans can learn by associating cognitive concepts together, by creating new mental representations of concepts, and by creating cognitive maps of spatial arrangements. These conceptualizations do not need to be reinforced to be learned, although reinforcement can make learning occur more quickly.

Declarative conceptual information is often described as being linked into associative neural networks of related concepts. Thus, the concept of bird is probably closely related to the concept of sparrow, but less closely related to the concept of ostrich, and even less to the concept of dinosaur. As we learn, however, that birds are the modern descendants of dinosaurs, we can reorganize our associations between different concepts. Although neural networks are generally assumed to be semantic in nature, concepts can also be linked with feelings related to those concepts.

EMOTIONAL LEARNING

Emotional learning and memory is related to cognitive learning and memory, albeit a distinct form (Eichenbaum, 2008). The brain has circuits, such as in the amygdala, designed specifically to attend to the emotional aspects of situations. These brain circuits support our feelings and expressions of emotions, as well as our learning about the emotional aspects of experiences; they also can change what is learned. There are three major outputs of the amygdala. In response to seeing something (a violent image, for example), one neural response pathway travels to the cerebral cortex to support our conscious awareness of our feelings.

A second pathway travels to other memory systems (e.g., in the striatum and hippocampus), which can influence attention and therefore what is learned. A third pathway controls our bodily responses, such as hormone release and the autonomic nervous system (e.g., the "fight or flight" response). One important implication is that emotion plays an important role in attention and motivation to attend. Specifically, it moderates attention and memories, and facilitates remembering emotional aspects of experiences and concepts.

Also, when we experience an emotional response (especially when the hormones epinephrine and cortisol are released), memory is enhanced. For example, in a study where participants viewed either emotionally arousing or emotionally neutral film clips, the amygdala and related areas were more active during the arousing film clips, and the memory for those clips was better three weeks later than for the neutral film clips (Cahill et al., 1996). Memory performance was significantly related to the amount of amygdala activation for the emotionally arousing film clips, but not for the neutral film clips.

The General Learning Model (GLM)

The general learning model (GLM) includes both short-term and long-term models of learning, as detailed below.

SHORT-TERM LEARNING PROCESSES: OVERVIEW AND DETAILED VIEWS

The basic overview of the short-term model is shown in Figure 9.1. The timing of this figure is intentionally vague—all parts could be completed within a second or two or extend over a couple of minutes. Figures 9.2a and 9.2b display how the learning process can occur within the first few seconds.

Inputs

The GLM starts from the assumption that actors exist within an environment, and that both the person and the environment influence the learning opportunity. The *person factors* include all aspects of the person at that moment in time, including all prior learning, genetic predisposition, personality traits, beliefs and attitudes, mood, sex, short- and long-term goals, motivation, and attentional resources. That is, at any given second, you are a combination of immediate states, primed concepts, long-term traits, and your biological and learned history. You may (or may not) have a set of specific goals in any encounter, and you may direct your attention to focus on particular aspects of your environment. The *situation factors* include all of the information and affordances available in the environment at any given moment. These include all of the physical environment, other

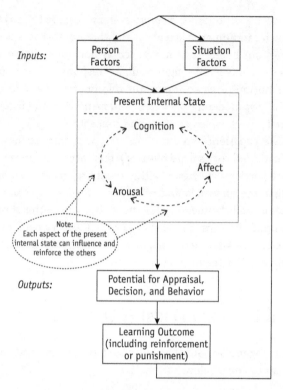

Figure 9.1 Short-term process overview in the General Learning Model.

potential actors in the environment (along with their current states, traits, and motivations), the history of the situation to that point, and all of the information that exists to be detected by an organism in the environment.

The short-term overview model (Figure 9.1) notes that aspects of the person and the environmental situation interact to influence the person's present internal state. Figures 9.2a and 9.2b display the processes that can occur serially and in parallel within the first few seconds of any learning encounter.

Sensation and Perception

Organisms have evolved sensory organs to detect information in the environment relevant to that organism. The first stage of informational input is *sensation*, defined as stimulation of one or more of our senses (e.g., auditory, visual, tactile): this is a neurological act that is precursor to a cognitive act, but probably not yet recognizable as such. *Perception* serves as an immediate product of the situation and the person, which, in contrast to sensation, is usually defined as an active cognitive process of making sense of sensations or making meaning of them (e.g., Neisser, 1967). We can perceive many things directly (e.g., E. J. Gibson, 1967; J. J. Gibson, 1979), sometimes called perceiving to learn, but we also learn to perceive. Perception can benefit from prior knowledge or experience.

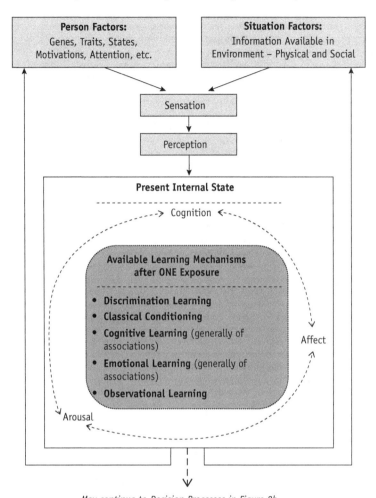

May continue to Decision Processes in Figure 2b

Figure 9.2a Detailed GLM single short-term processes prior to behavioral response.

We therefore perceive using both bottom-up and top-down processes. In the GLM, this top-down aspect is represented by the input from the person in a given situation. In a learning situation, individuals gather information in the environment and summon relevant knowledge structures to help process and operate upon that information.

Several types of learning can occur immediately at this stage (Figure 9.2a). A single perception of an object, event, or stimulus (external or internal) could result in

- Discrimination, if the features salient to the learner at that moment are detectably different from the features of anything to which it might be compared, or if the features are made to be salient.

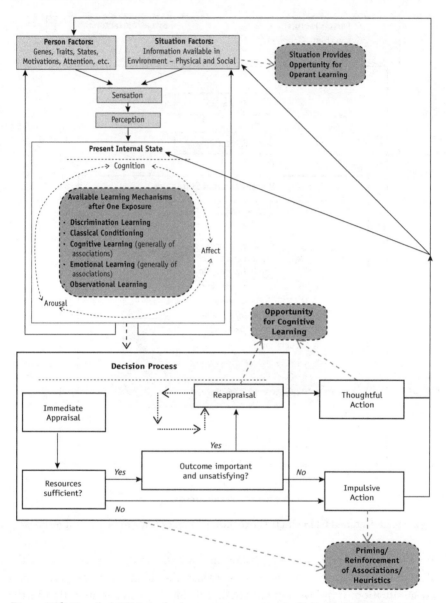

Figure 9.2b Detailed GLM single short-term processes including behavioral response.

- Classical conditioning, if some reflex was triggered at the same time that the learner was perceiving something to which the reflexive behavior could be associated (e.g., seeing a white rat while simultaneously being scared by a loud noise).
- Cognitive learning of associations, if two percepts or concepts are perceived to go together. Advertising often relies on this form of learning, especially since people often only glance at an advertisement for a second or two (e.g.,

seeing the words "Microsoft works" or "M&Ms melt in your mouth, not in your hands").

- Emotional learning of associations, whereby a percept/concept can be connected to an emotion. Advertising uses this approach even more than cognitive learning of associations, as when the tag line "A diamond is forever" is paired with a romantic and warm picture of attractive people in love.
- Observational learning, if some behavior in the environment is attended to. For example, seeing someone eat with chopsticks immediately teaches that it can be done, even if it isn't clear exactly how.

All types of learning can happen very quickly within what Figure 9.1 displays simply as the present internal state—the set of cognitions, feelings, and physiological arousal that may be primed by the interaction of the person and the situation. There is no necessity for anything to be learned. Individuals may engage in the ongoing activity through automatic responding, or they may pay no attention, or they may be so engaged in their own thoughts that the learning opportunity is missed. The detailed view shown in Figure 9.2a, however, helps to demonstrate what can be learned in a very brief period of time. Any changes to thoughts, feelings, or arousal, however, can immediately feed back into the set of person and environmental variables. For example, if I insult you, your heart rate increases, and you may feel hurt and think angry thoughts. You might associate negative feelings with the sight of me (classical conditioning), or you might learn a new insult (observational and cognitive learning). The changes to your thoughts, feelings, and arousal modify your attention, motivations, and alter which concepts are primed, which might in turn influence how future events are perceived. Your face may flush and your body language may change, which provides new information in the environment for others to react to, beginning a new cycle.

After the present internal state has been influenced, the person may have an opportunity to appraise the situation and respond (Figure 9.2b). Depending on both the situational variables that are present and on the person's motivations and available resources, the initial appraisal may be automatic or thoughtful. If the situation demands a fast response or the outcome is not sufficiently important to warrant careful consideration, the appraisal is likely to be made hastily (e.g., via an impulsive behavioral response) or automatically, based on heuristics (e.g., how easily a response comes to mind, which will be influenced by priming, chronic accessibility, and judgments such as the availability heuristic or hostile attribution biases). If the individual has the cognitive resources and time to reappraise the situation and possible actions, a thoughtful action (which could still be based on heuristic biases, and is not necessarily a "better" response) will result. Within this decision process are additional opportunities for learning.

If the actor has the time, motivation, and the cognitive resources necessary to reappraise, the reappraisal process itself may lead to cognitive learning (Figure 9.2b), as the actor considers the connections between ideas and likely operant outcomes of each option. If the actor takes a thoughtful action based on the reappraisal, the thoughts can reinforce the cognitive concepts that led to that action. Any associations and heuristics (which may have been learned previously or in the immediately prior present internal state) may be primed or reinforced by the decision process, especially if an impulsive action is taken based on heuristic processing. For example, if I insult you, a cognitive script could be activated whereby when provoked you should retaliate. If you do, it serves as a practice trial reinforcing the script.

Once an action is taken (including no response, which itself is an action), the action feeds back into the person factors, the situational factors, and the actor's present internal state (Figure 9.2b). Both the situation and the present internal state provide opportunities for operant learning. Others in the environment may respond in a way that is reinforcing or punishing, by which the behaviors chosen by the actor may be shaped. Similarly, the actor may have a response to his or her own behavior, such as feeling happy or guilty about the action taken. These internal feelings and evaluations can act as operant reinforcers or punishments.

All of these opportunities for learning can occur in a single episode, but additional learning opportunities are afforded by multiple exposures to some situation or stimulus. After multiple exposures, the individual may demonstrate habituation to the stimulus. Perhaps more important, however, is the fact that after multiple exposures, discrimination learning becomes much more likely. After repeated experience, people can detect finer and finer differences and similarities between stimuli and categorize them differently. After the differences have been detected, both associative and observational learning mechanisms are enhanced.

Long-Term Processes

Repeated exposure to any experience can also lead to diverse long-term effects. As knowledge structures and emotions are repeatedly primed, associated, and reinforced, they become better developed, more easily accessible, and more interconnected with other knowledge structures. The GLM proposes three categories of long-term effects (Figure 9.3). The first category includes perceptual and cognitive constructs such as the development and reinforcement of beliefs (Huesmann & Guerra, 1997; Fontana & Beckerman, 2004), behavioral scripts (Anderson & Carnagey, 2004), and perceptual or expectancy schemata (Kirsh, 1998). These effects are hypothesized to be learned from repeated exposure to or experience with relevant situations. An example includes experience with media violence, which may increase hostile attribution bias (a perceptual schema by which others' ambiguous actions are perceived to be of hostile intent; Anderson, Gentile, & Buckley, 2007). The second category includes linked cognitive-affective constructs such as attitudes (Anderson et al., 2003) and stereotypes (Dixon & Linz, 2000). An example includes work by Saleem and Anderson (2013), who found that playing a game requiring the fighting of Arab terrorists fostered negative attitudes toward

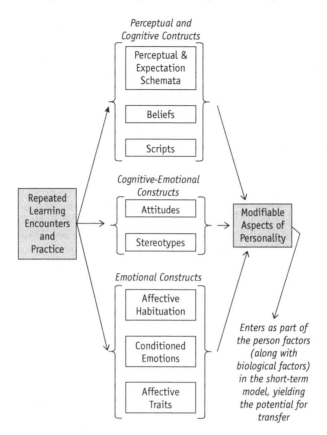

Figure 9.3 Long-term processes in the General Learning Model.

Arabs and Muslims more generally. Third, repeated media exposure can lead to long-term influences on emotional constructs such as affective habituation (e.g., associating media violence with fun and excitement), conditioned emotions (e.g., desensitization to real-life violence following media violence exposure), and affective traits (e.g., the development of trait anger for habitual violent video game players; Bushman & Huesmann, 2006).

A fundamental quality of the GLM is that it recognizes that learning occurs on multiple levels and through a variety of routes, some serially and some in parallel. One simple example of a variety of long-term effects resulting from these processes comes from the design of "loot" systems within many video games, in which killed enemies are looted and players receive a random reward. These rewards are usually of minor consequence (e.g., a piece of jewelry that can be sold for in-game currency) but occasionally reap a large benefit (e.g., a new weapon). By establishing a connection between the cognitive "nodes" of, say "kill the bad guy" and "receive reward," the learning trials develop a knowledge structure associating the two. The most obvious outcome of this linkage is the development of a behavioral script (perceive potential threat, fight and defeat enemy, potentially receive reward, repeat). This reinforcement contingency is closely mirrored by casinos as in the slot machine example. Other long-term effects can also occur concurrently. Learners develop a positive association with merely sitting in front of the video game screen (conditioned emotion) as the space itself is also part of that new knowledge structure. Attitudes toward video game playing (and consequently, aggression) then become more positive (or negative attitudes diminish) and beliefs may change (the belief that aggressive responses to ambiguous scenarios are normative). These processes are continually reinforced with each short-term learning cycle occurring for each enemy killed.

Because the GLM integrates multiple domain-specific theories (such as classical and operant conditioning), the specifics are not novel. Although each specific theory can successfully describe how learning occurs within a given context, it is often the case that multiple learning theories can be applied in any given real-world (or laboratory) context. The GLM may provide novel testable hypotheses, however, by depicting how some types of learning may depend on others occurring first (e.g., associative learning being dependent on discrimination learning), or how multiple learning mechanisms may interact to improve (or hinder) learning.

Transfer

The GLM models presented in Figures 9.1–9.3 imply that highly specific learning occurs first, which then may generalize and transfer. Transfer can be defined as "the ability to use previously learned skills or knowledge in settings or on problems different from the original learning, including the capacity to distinguish when and where these learnings are appropriate" (Gentile, 2000, p. 13). Although transfer is valued by educators (and students), a century of research does not provide much evidence for learners' ability to spontaneously transfer what they have learned. In perhaps the first systematic studies, Thorndike and Woodworth (1901; Thorndike, 1923) found that "formal disciplines" like math and Latin did not discipline the mind and improve thinking in general, thus refuting the dominant educational theory of that period. They proposed identical elements theory instead, which posited that the amount of transfer is a function of the number of common (identical or similar) elements between the original learning and target tasks or settings. Thus fluency in Latin might facilitate learning Spanish, but not Chinese, and learning to read Chinese characters may not facilitate speaking the language. Identical elements theory did not work in all situations, however. Critics such as Judd (1908) and the Gestalt psychologists showed that understanding principles (such as light refraction) could facilitate transfer (such as shooting at an underwater target).

By the 1960s, most of these ideas were incorporated into interference theory, which allowed a more complex study of transfer and memory processes in its proactive and retroactive interference (or facilitation) research designs. All learning occurs in the context of previous learning (a proactive effect where A influences B) and subsequent learning (a retroactive effect where B influences recall of A). The effects can be positive or negative; that is, they can facilitate or interfere with transfer or recall. Hundreds of studies were conducted in this paradigm (Deese & Hulse, 1967, and Ellis, 1965, provide excellent summaries) with concomitant recommendations for properly sequencing curricula to increase the probability of transfer.

By the 1980s, the cognitive revolution was in full force, emphasizing an active, socially mediated construction of meaning. From this conception came situated cognition theory (e.g., Brown, Collins, & Duguid, 1989; Brown & Duguid, 1993), which argued that what comes to be known is context-specific and largely determined by how it is learned. In this view, learning is so contextualized that "authentic" on-the-job training (as in apprenticeships) is necessary for positive transfer to occur. In addition, Singley and Anderson (1989) postulated identical productions theory, which predicts transfer based in part on whether the training-to-transfer tasks are both declarative ("knowing that") or procedural ("knowing how").

More recently, Barnett and Ceci (2002) provided a taxonomy for predicting transfer, with content and context as the major dimensions. Content includes the to-be-learned skill (procedure or principle), the required performance (speed, accuracy), and the memory demands. Context includes the domains of knowledge, as well as the physical, temporal, functional, social, and testing situations. Transfer can thus be considered to be "near" or "far" depending on how similar the transferred content and context are to the original.

Transfer is often cited as rare, although counterexamples are available (e.g., Pressley & Yokai's 1994 review of Detterman & Sternberg, 1993). It is one thing, however, to find counterexamples and another to prove transfer. Nevertheless, finding counterexamples, discovering logical fallacies, and using the scientific method are themselves examples of thinking that are difficult to tie to specific contexts. Perkins and Salomon (1989) summarized the research and suggested two roads to transfer: the *low road,* which requires "much practice in a large variety of situations, leading to a high level of mastery and automaticity," and the *high road,* which requires "deliberate mindful abstraction of a principle" (p. 22).

Given the paucity of strong evidence of transfer from classroom settings to other settings, it is surprising that a great deal of the research on video game effects can be interpreted as demonstrating "far" transfer. For example, meta-analyses demonstrate that violent video games predict (which could be reinterpreted as "train") aggressive ways of thinking, aggressive feelings, and aggressive behaviors in the real world (e.g., Anderson et al., 2010; Ferguson, 2007). Similarly, repeated playing of prosocial video games seems to generalize and transfer to greater helpful and cooperative behaviors in the real world—that is, to situations that share almost no characteristics that are similar to those in the video games (e.g., Gentile et al., 2009). Games, therefore, deserve additional consideration as teaching tools.

Exemplary Dimensions of Video Games

Video games provide a unique context through which the GLM can be applied in order to foster learning. Games have become increasingly complex and have incorporated a number of mechanisms relevant to learning, such as varying difficulty levels, reinforcement schedules, paired associations, and specific training modules. Gentile and Gentile (2008) listed seven exemplary dimensions of video game play that illustrate the use of educational principles and learning theories to effectively teach players, which we abridge here.

Pace Matching

Some evidence suggests that for students at the top third of their class, the average learning rate is at least three times that of students in the bottom third (Gentile & Lalley, 2003; Gentile, Voelkl, Mt. Pleasant, & Monaco, 1995). Video games are carefully crafted by developers to ensure that players coming from a spectrum of expertise are able to engage with the game. The flexibility of a digitally crafted universe provides a context through which developers have a capacity to ensure a matching of objective and pace to the individual differences of each learner. This task is arguably a more difficult task in real-world contexts, in which teachers frequently must design course curricula for "batches" of students with varying needs for instructional pace.

The Melding of Instruction, Practice, and Feedback

Video games require that content and procedural learning are nearly always coupled with practice. Contrary to stand-alone instruction, the immediate opportunity to engage with and use concepts *in vivo* immediately communicates the usefulness of a given concept. Further, learners are provided with instant feedback regarding their practice. Practice and feedback are interlaced throughout many video game experiences—players practice a task, receive feedback, and practice again until they reach a point of mastery. Practicing to the point of mastery is predictive both of how much one remembers and how long it will take to relearn something at a later time (Gentile & Lalley, 2003). Traditional class instruction instead must include wide gaps of days or even weeks between the time when students receive instruction, practice the learned concepts and skills, and receive feedback. More important, class instruction rarely provides everyone with the practice time they need to master the material.

Overlearning and Sequenced Difficulty

When knowledge and skills have developed to the point of mastery, continued practice provides the opportunity for overlearning. Overlearning allows knowledge and skills to become automatized and solidified in memory so that cognitive resources can be freed for a learner to draw upon and apply new concepts and information. For example, when students learn to read, they first must sound out letter by letter until a word forms. As this process is repeatedly practiced, the processing of words becomes automatized and now the meanings of the passages come into focus (Bloom, 1986). Most video games are designed with mastery and automaticity in mind. Early levels train basic game skills; later levels are only solvable if the basic skills have been automatized so that more complex skills can be learned and used.

The difficulty and complexity of game play is carefully sequenced so that players are never overwhelmed by the task at hand, but that they master necessary skills for future game success. At the beginning of many games, for example, there are "training modes" in which players are slowly exposed to each of the controls used in the game. If players are not yet able to continue on to the next stage in a game, they are often allowed to continue playing at a lower difficulty (e.g., replaying a level) until the necessary skills have been mastered.

Motivation for Learning

Mastery in video game contexts is reinforced both extrinsically and intrinsically. Players are rewarded with higher scores, higher character levels, points, better weapons and gear, in-game currency, improvements in character status such as in health or ammo capacity, new abilities, and access to new components of a story line. Further, players are constantly reaching goals and earning access to new levels of complexity, essentially teaching self-efficacy and providing self-esteem that accompanies the recognition of their competence. A number of theorists have stated that self-efficacy arises from competence (Bandura, 1977), and that lack of competence can lead to learned helplessness (Seligman, 1975). Furthermore, intrinsic motivation is highly related to how well a given task fills needs for autonomy, relatedness, and competence (Ryan & Deci, 2000). Games are excellent at giving gamers a sense of control (autonomy) and competence. Many games also fill relatedness needs, both within the game (e.g., in the case of multiplayer games) or outside of the game (e.g., by having friends who also like the same game and share information about it). In contrast, many classroom settings do a poor job with regard to meeting students' needs to feel in control, competent, or connected.

Optimized Massed and Distributed Practice

The motivational and feedback processes discussed previously provide a learning environment in which learners, when encountering failure, often try and retry until they show progress. When a new skill set is introduced (e.g., relating to a new character ability, weapon, or new control schemes) players are typically required to exercise this skill over many trials. As players continue to progress through the game, those same skills are periodically called upon, which distributes practice of that skill. The initial massed practice coupled with subsequent distributed practice builds mastery and continually reinforces the skill, allowing learners to relearn what was forgotten, provide new cues for memory, interpret information in new contexts so that memories can be organized to promote generalization (Gentile & Gentile, 2008), and assist in automatization of relevant knowledge structures (Anderson & Bushman, 2002).

GENERALIZATION AND TRANSFER

Video games allow players to exercise skills, techniques, and knowledge in several different contexts under a range of conditions with a variety of methods. This situation leads players to transfer such skills between contexts much more effectively compared with practice in a single setting. When practicing in a variety of contexts, learners are able to identify and abstract the most relevant features of a skill as it becomes increasingly clear that these features are the most important (Bransford, Brown, & Cocking, 1999). Further, such varying practice allows learners to associate the learned concept with a variety of cues that would be unavailable if practice occurred in a single setting (Brown, Collins, & Duguid, 1989). As noted earlier, given the research on the difficulty of teaching for transfer, it is striking that video games seem to effect far transfer so easily.

GAMES, LEARNING, AND EDUCATION

Learning occurs on numerous levels using a variety of processes, some serially and some in parallel, not unlike how the brain works at the neurological level. No single portion of the brain is responsible for learning. Instead, multiple areas process different levels of information that leads to a holistic learning process. The GLM attempts to describe how these seemingly disconnected processes work together at one point in time and across time to effect specific learning, generalization, and transfer. Gamers learn from games using every learning mechanism (e.g., habituation, operant learning), and games use many of the best practices that exemplary teachers use (Gentile & Gentile, 2008). Furthermore, gamers seem motivated to practice beyond the point of mastery to automaticity. For these reasons, games appear able to effect far transfer almost effortlessly and should be seriously considered for classroom use.

This idea is clearly not new—the 1980s saw a tremendous push in the United States to include computers in the classroom. Unfortunately, the research on their effectiveness in schools has proved to be disappointing (Fouts, 2000). There are several reasons why, including a lack of teacher training and a lack of integration with existing curricula. One might also argue that there has been a surprising lack of investment—the amount of money spent developing entertainment games is likely at least 50 times the amount spent to develop educational games. Although development costs are usually not public information, the 1997 game *Final Fantasy VII* is reported to have had a development budget of $45 million and a marketing budget of $100 million (Most expensive video games, n.d.), with average development costs for entertainment games now about $28 million (Crossley,

2010). We have heard informally from game developers that most educational games are made for substantially under $500,000. With such lower resources, educational games will never be as compelling or use all of the educational techniques of which they are capable. The conclusion to be drawn is that educational games have tremendous promise but cannot live up to their full potential until we invest in them in a significant way.

The research on the effects of games has too often fallen into dichotomies of examining potential benefits or harms (e.g., improvements on perceptual speed or increases in aggressive behavior). In our opinion, this has had the effect of obfuscating the more important underlying issue—games are natural teachers, and gamers are natural learners. Most of the empirically identified effects of video games are evidence of learning, generalization, and transfer. The same learning processes are likely involved in the development of both positive and negative outcomes following video game play. Yet this possibility is often overlooked in contemporary research endeavors. We propose that examining these effects within a single theoretical framework fosters an understanding of how each works individually and how they make work in conjunction to produce various effects. For example, little research has examined the influence of varying amounts of prosocial and violent content within the same video game (e.g., saving a group of merchants by killing bandits). Unfortunately, the discussion about research on games usually focuses on "debates," rather than on the common ground demonstrated by most of the studies. It is our hope that future research can focus on understanding the learning mechanisms underlying game effects and the game features that make learning and transfer easier. Such research would be valuable for improvements in game design, educational use of game technology, and for both gamers and the game industry.

References

Amsel, A. (1962). Frustrative nonreward in partial reinforcement and discrimination learning: Some recent history and a theoretical extension. *Psychological Review, 69*, 306–328.

Anderson, C. A., & Bushman, B. J. (2002). Human aggression. *Annual Review of Psychology, 53*, 27–51.

Anderson, C. A., & Carnagey, N. L. (2004). Violent evil and the general aggression model. In A. Miller (Ed.), *The social psychology of good and evil* (pp. 168–192). New York, NY: Guilford Publications.

Anderson, C. A., Shibuya, A., Ihori, N., Swing, E. L., Bushman, B. J., Sakamoto, A., Rothstein, H. R., & Saleem, M. (2010). Violent video game effects on aggression, empathy, and prosocial behavior in Eastern and Western countries: A meta-analytic review. *Psychological Bulletin, 136*, 151–173.

Bandura, A. (1977). Self-efficacy: Toward a unifying theory of behavior change. *Psychological Review, 84*, 191–215.

Bandura, A., & Kupers, C. J. (1964). Transmission of patterns of self-reinforcement through modeling. *Journal of Abnormal and Social Psychology, 69*, 1–9.

Bandura, A., Ross, D., & Ross, S. A. (1963). Imitation of film-mediated aggressive models. *Journal of Abnormal and Social Psychology, 66*, 3–11.

Barnett, S. M., & Ceci, S. J. (2002). When and where do we apply what we learn? A taxonomy for far transfer. *Psychological Bulletin, 128*, 612–637.

Bartholow, B., Bushman, B., & Sestir, M. (2006). Chronic violent video game exposure and desensitization to violence: Behavioral and event-related brain potential data. *Journal of Experimental Social Psychology, 42*, 532–539.

Bloom, B. S. (1986). Automaticity: The hands and feet of genius. *Educational Leadership, 43*(5), 70–77.

Bransford, J. D., Brown, A. L., & Cocking, R. R. (Eds.). (1999). *How people learn: Brain, mind, experience, and school*. Washington, DC: National Academy Press.

Bregman, E. (1934). An attempt to modify the emotional attitude of infants by the conditioned response technique. *Journal of Genetic Psychology, 45*, 169–198.

Bridger, W. H. (1961). Sensory habituation and discrimination in the human neonate. *The American Journal of Psychiatry, 117*, 991–996.

Brown, J. S., Collins, A., & Duguid, P. (1989). Situated cognition and the culture of learning. *Educational Researcher, 8*, 32–42.

Brown, J. S., Duguid, P. (1993). Stolen knowledge. *Educational Technology, 33*(3), 10–15.

Buckley, K. E., & Anderson, C. A. (2006). A Theoretical Model of the Effects and Consequences of Playing Video Games. Chapter in P. Vorderer & J. Bryant (Eds.), *Playing Video Games - Motives, Responses, and Consequences* (pp. 363–378). Mahwah, NJ: LEA.

Bushman, B. J., & Huesmann, L. R. (2006). Short-term and long-term effects of violent media on aggression in children and adults. *Archives of Pediatrics & Adolescent Medicine, 160*, 348–352.

Cahill, L., Haier, R. J., Fallons, J., Alkire, M. T., Tang, C., Keator, D., Wu, J., & McGaugh, J. L. (1996). Amygdala activity at encoding correlated with long-term free recall of emotional information. *Proceedings of the National Academy of Science, 93*, 273–313.

Carnagey, N., Anderson, C. A., & Bushman, B. (2007). The effect of video game violence on physiological desensitization to real-life violence. *Journal of Experimental Social Psychology, 43*, 489–496.

Church, R. M. (1963). The varied effects of punishment on behavior. *Psychological Review, 70*, 369–402.

Church, R. M. (1969). Response suppression in B. A. Campbell and R. M. Church, (Eds.) *Punishment and aversive behavior*, New York, NY: Appleton-Century-Crofts.

Colombo, J., & Mitchell, D. W. (2009). Infant visual habituation. *Neurobiology of Learning and Memory, 92*, 225–234.

Crossley, R. (2010). Study: Average dev costs as high as $28m. *Develop*. Retrieved at http://www.develop-online.net/news/33625/Study-Average-dev-cost-as-high-as-28m

Deese, J., & Hulse, S. H. (1967). *The psychology of learning*. New York: McGraw-Hill.

Dollard, J., Miller, N. E., Doob, L. W., Mowrer, O. H., & Sears, R. R. (1939). *Frustration and aggression*. New Haven, CT: Yale University Press.

Eichenbaum, H. (2008). *Learning & memory*. New York, NY: W. W. Norton Company.

Ellis, H. C. (1965) *Transfer of learning*. New York, NY: Macmillan.

Ferguson, C. J. (2007). Evidence for publication bias in video game violence effects literature: A meta-analytic review. *Aggression and Violent Behavior, 12*, 470–82.

Ferster, C. B., & Skinner, B. F. (1957). *Schedules of reinforcement*. New York, NY: Appleton-Century-Crofts.

Fontana, L., & Beckerman, A. (2004). Childhood violence prevention education using video games. *Information Technology in Childhood Education Annual, 16*, 49–62.

Fouts, J. T. (2000). *Research on computers and education: Past, present, and future*. Seattle, WA: Bill and Melinda Gates Foundation.

Garcia, J., & Ervin, F. R. (1968). Gustatory-visual and telereceptor-cutaneous conditioning-adaptation in internal and external milieus. *Communications in Behavioral Biology Part A, 1*, 389–415.

Gentile, D. A., Anderson, C. A., Yukawa, N., Saleem, M., Lim, K. M., Shibuya, A.,...Sakamoto, A. (2009). The effects of prosocial video games on prosocial behaviors: International evidence from correlational, longitudinal, and experimental studies. *Personality and Social Psychology Bulletin*, 35, 752–763.

Gentile, D. A., & Gentile, J. R. (2008). Violent video games as exemplary teachers: A conceptual analysis. *Youth Adolescence*, 37, 127–141.

Gentile, J. R. (2000). Then and now: A brief view of Hope College today. In M. P. Doyle (Ed.), *Academic excellence*. Tucson, AZ: Research Corporation.

Gentile, J. R., & Lalley, J. (2003). *Standards and mastery learning: Aligning teaching and assessment so all children can learn*. Thousand Oaks, CA: Corwin.

Gentile, J. R., Voelkl, K. E., Mt. Pleasant, J., & Monaco, N. M. (1995). Recall after relearning by fast and slow learners. *Journal of Experimental Education*, 63, 185–197.

Gibson E. J. (1967). *Principles of perceptual learning and development*. New York, NY: Appleton-Century-Crofts.

Gibson, J. J. (1979). *The Ecological Approach to Visual Perception*. Boston, MA: Houghton Mifflin.

Green, C. S., & Bavelier, D. (2003). Action video games modify visual selective attention. *Nature*, 423, 534–537.

Hovland, C. I. The generalization of conditioned responses: I. The sensory generalization of conditioned responses with varying frequencies of tone. *Journal of General Psychology*, 17, 125–148.

Huesmann, L. R., & Guerra, N. G. (1997). Normative beliefs and the development of aggressive behavior. *Journal of Personality and Social Psychology*, 72, 1–12.

Hulse, S. H., Egeth, H., & Deese, J. (1980). *The psychology of learning*. New York, NY: McGraw-Hill.

Judd, C. H. (1908). The relation of special training to general intelligence. *Educational Review*, 36, 28–42.

Kirsh, S. (1998). Seeing the world through Mortal Kombat–colored glasses: Violent video games and the development of a short-term hostile attribution bias. *Childhood: A Global Journal of Child Research*, 5(2), 177–184.

Maier, J. A., & Gentile, D. A. (2012). Learning aggression through the media: Comparing psychological and communication approaches. In L. J. Shrum (Ed.), *The psychology of entertainment media: Blurring the lines between entertainment and persuasion*, 2nd ed. (pp. 271–303). New York, NY: Routledge/Taylor & Francis Group.

Most expensive video games. (n.d.). Retrieved September 26, 2011, from the Video Game Sales Wiki: http://vgsales.wikia.com/wiki/Most_expensive_games

Murphy, R. F., Penuel, W. R., Means, B., Korbak, C., Whaley, A., & Allen, J. E. (2002). *A review of recent evidence on the effectiveness of discrete educational software*. Washington, DC: Planning and Evaluation Service, U.S. Department of Education.

Neisser, U. (1967). *Cognitive psychology*. New York, NY: Appleton-Century-Crofts.

Papastergiou, M. (2009). Exploring the potential of computer and video games for health and physical education: A literature review. *Computers and Education*, 53, 603–622.

Pavlov, I. P. (1927). *Conditioned reflexes* (G. V. Anrep, Trans.). London, UK: Oxford University Press.

Perkins, D. N., & Salomon, G. (1989). Are cognitive skills context bound? *Educational Researcher*, 18(1), 16–25.

Pressley, M., & Yokoi, L. (1994). Motion for a new trial on transfer. *Educational Researcher*, 25(5), 36–38.

Ryan, R. M., & Deci, E. L. (2000). Self-determination theory and the facilitation of intrinsic motivation, social development, and well-being. *American Psychologist*, 55(1), 68–78.

Saleem, M., & Anderson, C. A. (2013). Arabs as terrorists: Effects of stereotypes within violent contexts on attitudes, perceptions and affect. *Psychology of Violence*, 3, 84–99.

Sanchez, C. A. (2012). Enhancing visuospatial performance through video game training to increase learning in visuospatial science domains. *Psychonomic Bulletin & Review*, 19, 58–65.

Seligman, M. E. P. (1971). Phobias and preparedness. *Behavior Therapy*, 2, 307–320.

Seligman, M. E. P. (1975). *Helplessness: On depression, development, and death*. San Francisco, CA: Freeman.

Sidman, M. (1960). Normal sources of pathological behavior. *Science*, 132, 61–68.

Singley, M. K., & Anderson, J. R. (1989). *The transfer of cognitive skill.* (Vol. 9). Cambridge, MA: Harvard University Press.

Skinner, B. F. (1938). *The behavior of organisms.* New York, NY: Appleton-Century-Crofts.

Skinner, B. F. (1971). *Beyond freedom and dignity.* New York, NY: Knopf.

Skinner, B. F. (1974). *About behaviorism.* New York, NY: Knopf.

Thorndike, E. L., & Woodworth, R. S. (1901). The influence of improvement in one mental function upon the efficiency of other functions. *Psychological Review, 8,* 247–267, 384–395, 553–564.

Thorndike, E. L. (1911). *Animal intelligence.* New York, NY: Macmillan.

Thorndike, E. L. (1923). The influence of first-year Latin upon the ability to read English. *School and Society, 17,* 165–168.

Tolman, E. C. (1932). *Purposive behavior in animals and men.* New York, NY: Appleton-Century-Crofts.

Tolman, E. C. (1959). Principles of purposive behavior. In S. Koch (Ed.), *Psychology: A study of a science* (Vol. 2) (pp. 92–157). New York, NY: McGraw-Hill.

Watson, J. B. (1913). Psychology as the behaviorist views it. *Psychological Review, 20,* 158–177.

Watson, J. B. (1919). *Psychology from the standpoint of a behaviorist.* Philadelphia, PA: J. B. Lippincott.

Part Three

GAME DESIGN PERSPECTIVES: HOW SHOULD WE DESIGN EDUCATIONAL VIDEO GAMES?

10

Toward a Playful and Usable Education

CÉLIA HODENT[1]

To Play is to Learn

Humans are the most playful creatures of the animal kingdom. They watch movies, read novels, view paintings, listen to music, dance, play games, and have an entire industry devoted to art and entertainment. Yet we don't always fully measure the importance of play in the development and sustainability of our affective, cognitive, and social abilities. Play is one of the necessary elements in building a culture (Huizinga, 1938). The action of playing allows the brain to experiment with new and usually more complex situations than in real life. Thus, we could say, "When we stop playing, we start dying" (Brown & Vaughan, 2009), because we stop adapting our neuron networks to our ever-changing environment.

During infancy and childhood—when the brain is much more malleable than later in life—play is critical for healthy development (see Pellegrini, Dupuis, & Smith, 2007, for a review). Play allows the child to assimilate reality (Piaget & Inhelder, 1969) and remains the leading source of development for preschoolers (Vygotsky, 1967; Duncan & Tarulli, 2003). For example, in the game of peekaboo, the baby learns a certain temporal structure: the mother makes initial contact, then hides, only to later reappear and renew contact, usually accompanied by the baby's joyful vocalizations. This structure is thought to serve as a foundation for developing more complex social interactions, such as language (Bruner & Sherwood, 1976). Even innocent and naive games like peekaboo can have an unsuspected learning power.

Play is undoubtedly a crucial actor in education, and as such should be encouraged in school at all grade levels. However, what about the playing of video and computer games? Do such games enhance the value of play? We commonly agree that school and the educational system are meant to prepare children for the future. For example, it is important to learn how to read because written language is often used to communicate. Surely, if schools want to educate minds for the future, they should use tools from the present. In a world where technology, computers, and interactive electronic devices are widely used, including at work, it becomes relevant and advisable to use video games as an educational medium. Not only are video games modern and attractive to children; they are focused on the user's actions, just like any other game, and unlike other media such as most books or videos. They also give immediate feedback on the user's actions. Further, compared to reading a book or listening to a lecture, learning through one's actions is often considered a more efficient way to construct knowledge.

The developmental psychologist Jean Piaget is one of the most well-known pioneers of the constructivist theory and new ideas of how children construct knowledge (Piaget, 1937). According to Piaget, knowledge is not a mere reflection of the environment, nor the projection of innate structures onto the reality. Rather, it is built through the actions of an individual in the world (Houdé, 2004). The environment has to be shaped and assimilated. Building on Piaget's research, psychologists have discovered that infants, in fact, begin to understand many aspects of their environment through perception, before they can efficiently act on the world, as in the case of object permanence (Baillargeon, Spelke, & Wasserman, 1985) or addition and subtraction (Wynn, 1992; Hodent, Bryant, & Houdé, 2005). It also appears that manipulating their environment helps children think. For example, between 4 and 6 years of age, children show more difficulty solving verbal calculation problems (such as "Paul has 2 marbles. His mother offers him 3 more. How many marbles does Paul now have?"), than problems involving physical referents in which children need to construct an array containing the correct number of elements (Levine, Jordan, & Huttenlocher, 1992). Moreover, it has been established that familiar and meaningful information is easier to retain (see Banikowski & Mehring, 1999), and that the deeper the level of information processing, the better the retention of that information (Craik & Lockhart, 1972; Craik & Tulving, 1975). Students also benefit even when incorrectly answering questions while mastering a new topic (Richland, Kornell, & Kao, 2009). Thus, unsuccessful retrieval attempts, followed by feedback, seem more effective than spending the same amount of time simply studying the correct answer (Kornell, Hays, & Bjork, 2009).

We could then argue that video games, as a highly interactive and meaningful medium for children of all ages, which usually provides immediate and adequate feedback, should be explored as an educational tool. Games also offer a wider array of possibilities. Pretty much everything can be virtualized and allow children to experiment with elements that one cannot manipulate in reality, such as time (*Braid* is one such puzzle video game created by Jonathan Blow in 2008, in which one manipulates the flow of time to progress in the game), or space (e.g., *Portal*, developed by Valve Corporation in 2007, in which one creates portals to solve puzzles in a three-dimensional space).

Are Video Games Always Playful?

Video games as a medium have the power to attract and motivate children. However, pleasure only results if children have fun playing them. It's a common misconception that the medium itself—because it's attractive, fashionable, and relatively new—is enough to bring a playful experience. For example, disguising some mathematics exercises in the shape of a video game will not be very helpful to children who are not motivated by mathematics in general. If video games are used as an educational medium, they cannot keep the same traditional content that school provides; instead they have to offer a new experience (Squire, 2006). The basis for the misconception about educational video games probably stems from the fact that some video games with "serious" content have been widely successful, especially with adults on the Nintendo DS handheld platform. Games like *Brain Age™: Train Your Brain in Minutes a Day* (Nintendo, 2006), *Professor Layton and the Curious Village* (Level 5 & Nintendo, 2007), or the Ubisoft *My Coach²* series were commercial successes. However, players who are thriving on these games are usually already motivated by exercising their logical, mathematical, or language skills. People who love doing crosswords or Sudoku can embrace these games, because they offer a more interactive and flexible interface than their paper counterparts. In this case, the video game's main challenge is not really to attract but to sustain players' engagement, usually by giving them immediate feedback and by recording their achievements and progression.

For example, in the Nintendo DS game *Classic Word Games* (Ubisoft, 2009), all the mini-games are designed to enhance the player's vocabulary. The player has to link words that are synonyms or antonyms, complete quotes or phrases, or find a word by its definition. The promise of this video game is to refresh and develop the player's vocabulary "while having fun." It is designed in a way that the words with which the players are less familiar are reintroduced at spaced intervals to enhance their retention, based on the principle that the repetition of a stimulus improves its retention if the learning episodes are spaced apart in time (Paivio, 1974; Toppino, Kasserman, & Mracek, 1991; Greene, 2008). By tracking the time it takes the player to answer and by tracking his or her mistakes, the game can dynamically adjust the content displayed to enable the spacing effect in repetition. Also, with meaningful associative learning (for example, in the game where the player has to link two words with the same meaning) and sentence completion games, *Classic Word Games* are designed to enhance retention with deeper content processing. The game also provides charts showing the player's progression and an individual profile to motivate regular gaming sessions. For people who are already having fun playing with words, *Classic Word Games* can help improve the retention of the newly learned words or less frequently used words. Similarly, video games can effectively enhance the learning-by-doing effects by using algorithms to adapt the learning content to the player. Video games are also usually more attractive than paper games because of the customization, flexibility, and adaptability they offer. However, those types of games (which bring classic word or mathematics games to an interactive medium) fail to motivate people who are not interested in mind games in the first place, and they fail to bring meaning to the content learned. Play is an autotelic activity in essence; games are pursued for their own sake. According to Katie Salen and Eric Zimmerman (2004), "Although there are always some extrinsic reasons for play, there are always intrinsic motivations as well. In playing a game, part of the incentive is simply to play—and often, it is the prime motivator" (p. 332). We play because we find pleasure in doing the activity itself, not for an extrinsic incentive only. That is the reason why if the game itself is not fun and attractive to the population for which it is designed, it cannot be defined as an activity of play and therefore cannot reach the learning power of play. To achieve this goal with children who are not motivated by school activities in the first place, whole gameplay mechanics warrant rethinking.

Enabling the Child to Teach the Computer Instead of Having the Computer Teach the Child

Seymour Papert, mathematician and educator, spotted the educational potential of computer games as early as the 1960s. Inspired by Jean Piaget's constructivist theory, Papert holds a constructionist approach to learning, by which learning is more efficient when experiencing material in concrete and meaningful situations. In that regard, Papert (1980) saw in the computer a powerful machine that children could use to create and manipulate any content. Instead of having the computer program the child, Papert wanted the child to program the computer. Along with a group of colleagues and students at MIT, he created the Logo computer language that allowed children to control a virtual turtle in a playful approach. While engaged in a digital drawing activity, the children had to teach the turtle to do certain things, such as to draw a square shape. In the process, the children were learning, without being taught, through their mistakes and successes, the inherent characteristics of a square. Geometry was then made accessible to the child, in a way that the "knowledge is acquired for a recognizable personal purpose" because the "child does something with it" (Papert, 1980, p. 21). Papert also made children use computers to generate sentences; they had to teach grammar to the program to make it produce meaningful sentences. By teaching the computer, the children presumably understood what grammar entailed (Papert, 1980).

Papert understood early on the importance of letting children manipulate computers in a playful way to enhance learning at school and allowed children to learn through an iterative process, which is commonly recognized today as the successful process in engineering design. For David Kelley, founder of IDEO Product Development (America's largest independent product design and development firm, behind Apple's first mouse), "enlightened trial and error" (Kelley, 2001) is a critical process in design. "Fail faster, succeed sooner" (attributed to David Kelley) is a well-known adage in innovation design and in technology industries. Further, we now have evidence that unsuccessful trials when completing a task do not impair subsequent learning, but seem to enhance it (Kornell et al., 2009).

Following in Papert's footsteps, a growing number of researchers and educators believe that video games are the future of learning. Video games have the potential to offer a meaningful, social, and epistemological experience that children can control at their own pace (Shaffer, Squire, Halverson, & Gee, 2005). But if we take a look at the majority of the so-called educational games that have been created, they have merely transposed paper school exercises into an interactive medium, wrapped in an attractive yet sometimes deceptive promise of making learning fun.

As a species, humans have survived and evolved not because of their strength, but because of their incredible ability to adapt to their environment, to learn about it and swiftly change their behavior accordingly. It is because children are born immature that they can adapt by learning about their physical and social environment: "Nature ensures that we do something that will be good for us (or at least our genes) in the long run, by making it fun (or at least compelling) in the short-run" (Gopnik, 2000, p. 309). This situation explains why babies are so compelled to explore their environment, and young children are driven to play and to eagerly ask so many questions. Discovery brings pleasure, and pleasure is what evolution has found to motivate humans in choosing an efficient behavior (Cabanac, 1992; Anselme, 2010). Hence, it is regrettable that formal education somehow fails to keep learning pleasurable, potentially given its emphasis on extrinsic rewards, such as grades, which may have negative consequences on children; undermining their own intrinsic interest in learning and motivation to learn (Ryan & Deci, 2000a).

EMOTIONAL DESIGN, USABILITY, AND GAME FLOW

If technological gadgets and games are so popular nowadays, it is most likely because they are designed to trigger emotions in the user. For Donald Norman (2005), "The emotional side of design may be more critical to a product's success than its practical elements" (p. 5). Norman describes three aspects of design: visceral, behavioral, and reflective. The visceral level concerns the appearance of the object and its appeal to our senses. The behavioral level is linked with the pleasure and effectiveness of the object's use. The reflective aspect of design concerns the intellectualization of a product; the story it tells to the user, the symbolism behind it, its meaning and how this meaning relates to the user's self-image. All these levels affect humans' cognition and emotion.

Relatively recently, we did not have many choices among products. There were not many shapes, colors, or textures to choose from. When we needed a new gadget or tool, we would choose the one with adequate functionality. However, now we can choose among products of the same functionality and price range, according to our preferences. Successful high-tech objects are not the ones that are simply functional, but those that are beautiful, meaningful to us, emotionally resonant, and easy to use (usable). Not all smartphones create excitement and long waiting lines at their launch, despite their similarities in function. Emotions and affect greatly influence our thinking and our decision-making (Damasio, 1994; Ariely, 2008). Because we are not the rational creatures we believe we are, a product must also appeal to the user at an emotional level if it is to be successful. Children are also sensitive to emotional design and probably to a greater extent than their elders because appealing pieces of technology have always been part of their everyday lives. As they grew up with computers, the Internet, high-tech gadgets, and video games, these "digital natives" (Prensky, 2006) might expect their environment to be usable, to elicit an emotional experience, and to give immediate feedback. If school wants to become the exciting and stimulating place it once was or could be, it has to embrace technology that is usable and engaging. Offering an emotional experience is not only useful for engaging children with an educational medium; it also influences cognitive processes, such as memory, perception, and attention (Phelps, 2006; Pessoa, 2008) (for an overview see LeDoux, 1996; and Fellous & Arbib, 2005).

There is a whole new field dedicated to improving human-computer interaction (such as with a website or a video game): the user experience field (UX). The purpose of this field is to create a user-centered design: the object, website, game, or software is designed by taking into account the final user's perspective, needs, and emotions. For example, when designing a car, placing the radio controller next to the steering wheel reflects user-centered design, whereby the end user's perspective (the driver's) is taken into account by placing within easy reach an object likely to be used often. Therefore, the user will not need to let go of the steering wheel to reach it (thus enhancing security) and can maintain full control of his or her driving while changing channels or adjusting volume on the radio (thus enhancing comfort). The UX field considers diverse concepts such as usability (ease and agreeability of use), engagement (of emotion and motivation), or flow (immersion in usage; Bernhaupt, 2010). Caring about the usability part is what should come first. If an interactive product is not usable, there is very little chance that it will be engaging, let alone fun and immersive. The term *usability* as applied to games refers to accessibility and ease of use. Thus, making a game usable entails making it easy and intuitive to use and "paying attention to human limits in memory, perception, and attention" (Isbister & Schaffer, 2008, p. 4). Playing a video game is a learning experience; the player has to discover the game mechanics, solve problems, and constantly acquire new skills and tools as the game progresses. For example, one may need to learn how to jump in a game. A usable way to teach the player how to do so is to teach this aspect of game mechanics in meaningful context and by letting the player acquire the skill while playing. One usable level design solution would be to place a shiny and attractive object right after a hole, such that the player has to jump over the hole to get the interesting object. When close to the hole, a pop-up text could indicate to the player which button to press to jump (and this text would only be displayed if players did not press the appropriate button on their own). A nonusable way to teach this mechanic would be to give the player the controller mapping image before the game starts, as with instructions to read before playing.

Video game editors have begun to use findings in psychology and cognitive neuroscience to ensure that their games provide a fun and enjoyable learning experience. There are numerous video games released each year and players have to commit time and money to them in order to play them. A game in which basic mechanics and codifications cannot be easily and immediately understood has a greater chance of being abandoned by frustrated players. The key to a successful game for a broad audience today is for it to be "easy to learn and difficult to master" (attributed to Atari founder Nolan Bushnell). Thus, basic concepts should be easily accessible, and the game should be challenging enough so that the player is never bored. A list of usability heuristics has been developed by Jakob Nielson (1994) to improve UX in websites and software. These heuristics have been adapted to video games to serve as guidelines for game and level designers (Desurvire, Caplan & Toth, 2004; Pinelle, Wong, & Stach, 2008). Some video game developers now also use UX labs, conduct usability assessments, and even have human-computer interaction experts, cognitive ergonomics experts, or cognitive and experimental psychologists helping them throughout the stages of video game development. To simplify what usability is about, it mainly concerns all the "signs and feedback" that the game provides, such as the specific shape of a nonplayable character (as in the principle that "form follows function"), iconography, sound effects, or visual effects. These elements shape the experience of the game and guide the players through it. If they are not carefully designed, the exciting journey can turn into a frustrating wrestle with the system (which is not that distinct from what some children may experience in the formal educational system, except that a player has, hopefully, greater freedom in deciding when to quit a video game).

Although usability is a steppingstone toward a rewarding user experience, it is not sufficient to promote fun. Another element is needed, which can be called "game flow" (Sweetser & Wyeth, 2005). The game flow model is inspired by psychologist Mihaly Csikszentmihalyi's theory of flow (1990). Flow is the optimal experience whereby "a person's body or mind is stretched to its limits in a voluntary effort to accomplish something difficult and worthwhile" (Csikszentmihalyi, 1990, p. 3). To stay inside the "flow channel," an activity must not be too easy, or one feels boredom. Similarly, if the activity is too hard, anxiety rises. This not-too-easy-not-too-hard concept interestingly resembles another concept in child development: Lev Vygotsky's zone of proximal development (ZPD) concept (Vygotsky, 1978). For Vygotsky, the ZPD is the zone between that which the child can already do (too easy) and that which she or he cannot yet accomplish (too hard). Within this zone, the child can develop new abilities with the help of an adult or a more advanced learner. In this theory, play becomes a means by which to extend the ZPD. By combining both Csikszentmihalyi's and Vygotsky's theories, we can argue that children (and adults) learn better when they exercise their skills in playful challenges that are not too easy nor too hard, if a more advanced mentor—or a system—helps them master these new skills. The ultimate purpose of Csikszentmihalyi's theory of flow is to better understand how to reach happiness in life. The purpose of the game flow model, by comparison, is to determine which elements of flow can be conveyed in video games and how to efficiently use them to improve players' enjoyment (Sweetser & Wyeth, 2005).

Game usability heuristics and the game flow model both allow the evaluation of player enjoyment, using UX expertise and tools such as playtests, whereby the player's behavior is analyzed while playing a game in development. The game flow model consists of eight elements; some of them have already been examined by usability heuristics: concentration, challenge, skills, control, clear goals, feedback, immersion, and social interaction. To be enjoyable and allow a playful and learning experience, an educational video game has to be usable and "flow-able." The problem is that this state is difficult to achieve. Video game companies increasingly invest time and money in UX labs and expertise to ensure that their games are usable and fun, and even then the end result is not guaranteed. Educational video game creators usually have much less money to invest, which makes usability even harder for them to reach. However, by answering the following questions, the developers of an educational game can help to enable usability and game flow in their games:

- Is the game introducing its mechanics through a learning-by-doing practice instead of requiring players to read instructions first, before doing?
- Is the game conforming to usability heuristics (see Laitinen, 2008)? For example, the user interface must be consistent; the menus and icons must always function in a similar way; and every action of the player must provide immediate, adequate, and understandable feedback.
- Is the game motivating? To answer this tricky question, the self-determination theory (SDT) developed by Ryan and Deci (2000b) is often used. This theory places autonomy as the core concept of intrinsic motivation, which results in high-quality learning and creativity. Thus, the activity (here, the video game) must have the appeal of novelty, challenge, and aesthetic value for the children. It should also be connected to the children's reality and tackle an issue or content of interest to the player. For example, instead of overtly teaching geometry rules, does the game allow the children to experiment with those concepts freely to do something meaningful, such as create drawings?
- Does the game offer challenges with increasing difficulty following the children's skills development? The best way to maintain an appropriate difficulty level in a video game is by using a dynamic difficulty adjustment (DDA) system.

In this system, the difficulty of a game should change dynamically based on the player's performance. This approach was formulated by game designer Jenova Chen in his thesis about flow in games (Chen, 2007). Just as all children do not learn at the same speed, different players have different flow zones (i.e., experts need more challenge than novices). Therefore, Chen proposed that players should progress in the game at their own pace and stay in their specific flow zone (not too easy, not too hard) by offering them different difficulties, challenges, and choices. Chen applied this concept in the video game called *Flow* (published by Sony Computer Entertainment in 2006).

These questions are certainly not exhaustive, but they can provide a useful framework for creating educational video games (and any video games in general). Educational games that are designed to address these questions of usability and game flow will most likely be more engaging to children, and hopefully more playful and fun.

FROM TRANSFER TO PLAYFUL LEARNING EXPERIENCES

The question of transfer is fundamental in education: humans need to recognize elements from their prior knowledge to learn a new concept more quickly, and they need to apply their knowledge and skills to various new situations to solve problems and be creative. As Jean Piaget once stated, "The principle goal of education is to create men who are capable of doing new things, not simply of repeating what other generations have done—men who are creative, inventive, and discoverers" (as cited in Elkins, 1991, p. 97).

One of the first theories of transfer was proposed long before computers and video games were regularly used as educational tools (Thorndike & Woodworth, 1901). However, this question is even more critical in our modern world, with its increase in complexity and pace (Haskell, 2004). If it is clear now that video games can be an invaluable tool to motivate children and allow them to experience and acquire new concepts, whether transfer of the skills learned in the game can occur is more questionable. Motivation is an essential component in transfer (McKeachie, 1987). If what one learns is engaging, interesting, and meaningful, chances are that one will learn it and apply it better than if the learning content is not meaningful or interesting.

Let us take the example of learning a language. Children learn to speak their native language without being formally taught for the most part. Instead, they acquire it "by being immersed in rich, meaningful, and natural communicative settings" (Gee, 1994, p. 332). It is an everyday practice, and mastering this skill is crucial, given that an inability to communicate effectively with our peers compromises our survival. Hence, children master their first language (at least the spoken component of the language) fairly quickly. The way we learn a second language is usually very different. Specifically, it's taught at school, it is practiced much less regularly, and usually in a nonmeaningful way, whereby the learner is not necessarily compelled to communicate in the foreign language. Total immersion in a foreign country is often seen as the best way to learn the language spoken there (Papert, 1980). Conveniently, new technologies and video games can help provide this immersion, whereas books and blackboards cannot. A video game has the potential to immerse the child in any environment, even a foreign language environment.

However, before thinking of using a video game to motivate children to learn a second language, we must ask ourselves what would be the most meaningful way to teach this subject. Mary Gick and Keith Holyoak (1987) advocate that "some of the most spectacular and widely decried failures of transfer—failures to apply knowledge learned in school to practical problems encountered in everyday life—may largely reflect the fact that material taught in school is often disconnected from any clear goal and hence lacks a primary cue for retrieval in potentially relevant problem contexts" (p. 31). To accomplish their educational duty, video games must be playful and meaningful, and should enable collaborative learning as much as possible, as cooperation appears beneficial to learning and transfer (Lambiotte et al., 1987). Schools and educational games could greatly gain from UX practices that are increasingly used by video game companies to engage a player who has to learn how to play and master the game, and to enable fun, or game flow. Two main elements could be considered to improve the educational system. First, schools should use usable and enjoyable video games that allow the children to experiment with new concepts, but also to teach the computer. Instead of learning mathematical formulae, they should be put in situations where they need to use these formulae to play as engineers. With the Logo computer language, Seymour Papert did not try to make geometry rules fun. Instead, he enabled children to discover these rules by themselves, through an iterative trial-and-error process, by allowing them to have fun creating drawings. Students developing strategies in the context of playing Papert's game were able to transfer these strategies to other contexts (Klahr & Carver, 1988). Thus, it seems that games where the child manipulates the computer instead of being taught by it were and remain promising tools to explore.

Many tools can be used to enable meaningful and playful activities that promote learning. The video game is only one of them, and it can be a powerful ally if well-designed. Games that allow the child to assimilate knowledge and use it in a meaningful and creative way are the ones that can enhance learning efficiently (Shaffer, 2006), as long as they are fun. Being playful is the important element to favor, that is, having a spirit of play, although not necessarily "gamifying" each and every activity. The Blackawton Bees project is one striking example of a playful and meaningful educational activity (Blackawton et al., 2011). The purpose of this project was to allow 8- to 10-year-old children to conduct a collaborative scientific study on bumblebees' visuospatial abilities. Through play and real experimentation, children had fun doing science and even published an article about their findings in a scientific journal.

One also may advocate for the position that formal schooling be usable. Teaching should be usable. We could use UX knowledge and tools to enable school usability, enjoyability, and effectiveness. Companies now widely use "A/B testing" to try different versions of an online product and see which one works best with their consumers. A/B testing is an experimental approach to web or game design whereby two versions of a design (A and B) are tested online. For example, users' behavior toward a blue versus a red button can be tested and compared, and ultimately the developer will keep the button color that provoked more clicks. Arguably, school practices also could be tracked to determine via iteration best educational practices. For example, children could take a survey at the beginning of the year about what they like to do, what they are good at, and their favorite center of interest. Then, throughout the year, the performance of the child and the teaching practices of the teacher could be analyzed to help teachers and educators determine optimal learning and teaching patterns. There are also algorithms that promote the best matchmaking in online first-person shooter games. Thus, students could be matched in a similar fashion with the teachers who fit best with their interests, and who could propose customized learning tools.

Although it may sound like science fiction today, just as having one computer per child sounded crazy not so long ago, these new technologies will soon be cheap and efficient enough to spill over from online businesses to education. Also, classes could be level-designed (designed to mimic a good video game learning curve) in a way that the challenges are never too easy nor too hard, such that each child could progress at his or her own pace.

Educational tools would possibly be greatly improved if they were created via collaboration among educators, psychologists, designers, gameplay programmers, UX experts, and data analysts. Strikingly, there are many similarities between the educational system and the video game industry. Both need to be appealing, have usable content, offer good challenges, be engaging, be motivating, be meaningful, and provide a learning curve that will enable game flow, thereby promoting enjoyment and fun. Games are tools to explore and experiment with the world. They represent a space where trial-and-error and iteration are possible at a low cost. They can be used to make learning more real and meaningful. More important, they can be used to sustain curiosity and the pleasure of learning. After all, transfer is the application to a different task of some knowledge or skills previously learned (Gick & Holyoak, 1987). Having this perspective in mind, learning to learn becomes learning to transfer.

Author Notes

1. The reflection developed in this chapter was largely elaborated during my work at Ubisoft as Strategic Innovation Lab manager

2. The *My Coach* series includes multiple games such as *My Word Coach, My Weight Loss Coach, My Spanish Coach*, and *My SAT Coach*. See http://mycoachgames.us.ubi.com/.

References

Anselme, P. (2010). The uncertainty processing theory of motivation. *Behavioural Brain Research, 208*, 291–310.

Ariely, Dan (2008). *Predictably irrational: The hidden forces that shape our decisions.* New York, NY: Harper Collins.

Baillargeon, R., Spelke, E., & Wasserman, S. (1985). Object permanence in five-month-old infants. *Cognition, 20*, 191–208.

Banikowski, A. K., & Mehring, T. A. (1999). Strategies to enhance memory based on brain-research. *Focus on Exceptional Children, 32*, 1–16.

Bernhaupt, R. (2010). User experience evaluation in entertainment. In R. Bernhaupt (Ed.), *Evaluating user experience in games.* London, UK: Springer-Verlag.

Blackawton, P. S., Airzee, S., Allen, A., Baker, S., Berrow, A., Blair, C.,... Lotto, R. B. (2011). Blackawton bees. *Biology Letters, 7*, 168–72.

Brown, S., & Vaughan, C. (2009). *Play: How it shapes the brain, opens the imagination, and invigorates the soul.* New York, NY: Avery.

Bruner, J., & Sherwood, V. (1976). Peekaboo and the learning of rule structures. In J. Bruner, A. Jolly, & K. Sylva (Eds.), *Play: Its role in development and evolution.* Harmondsworth, UK: Penguin.

Cabanac, M. (1992). Pleasure: The common currency. *Journal of Theoretical Biology, 155*, 173–200.

Chen, J. (2007). Flow in games (and everything else). *Communication of the ACM, 50*, 31–34.

Craik, F. I. M., & Lockhart, R. S. (1972). Levels of processing: A framework for memory research. *Journal of Verbal Learning and Verbal Behavior, 11*, 671–684.

Craik, F. I. M., & Tulving, E. (1975). Depth of processing and the retention of words in episodic memory. *Journal of Experimental Psychology: General, 104*, 268–294.

Csikszentmihalyi, M. (1990). *Flow: The psychology of optimal experience.* New York, NY: Harper Perennial.

Damasio, A. R. (1994). *Descartes' error: Emotion, reason, and the human brain.* New York, NY: Avon.

Desurvire, H., Caplan, M., & Toth, J. A. (2004). Using heuristics to evaluate the playability of games. *Extended Abstracts CHI 2004*, 1509–1512.

Duncan, R. M., & Tarulli, D. (2003). Play as the leading activity of the preschool period: Insights fromVygotsky, Leont'ev, and Bakhtin. *Early Education and Development, 14*, 271–292.

Elkins, D. (1991). Developmentally appropriate practice: Philosophical and practical implications. In B. Persky & L. H. Golubchick (Eds.), *Early Childhood Education* (pp. 93–102). Lanham, MD: University Press of America.

Fellous, J.-M., & Arbib, M. A. (2005). *Who needs emotions? The brain meets the robot.* New York: Oxford University Press.

Gee, J. P. (1994). First language acquisition as a guide for theories of learning and pedagogy. *Linguistics and Education, 6*, 331–354.

Gick, M. L., & Holyoak, K. J. (1987). The cognitive basis of knowledge transfer. In S. M. Cormier & J. D. Hagman (Eds.), *Transfer of learning: Contemporary research and applications* (pp. 9–46). Orlando, FL: Academic Press.

Gopnik, A. (2000). Explanation as orgasm and the drive for causal understanding: The evolution, function, and phenomenology of the theory-formation system. In F. Keil & R. Wilson (Eds.), *Cognition and explanation* (pp. 299–323). Cambridge, MA: MIT Press.

Greene, R. L. (2008). Repetition and spacing effects. In J. Byrne (Ed.), *Learning and memory: A comprehensive reference.* Oxford, UK: Elsevier.

Haskell, R. E. (2004). The transfer of learning. *Encyclopedia of Applied Psychology, 3*, 575–586.

Hodent, C., Bryant, P. & Houdé, O. (2005). Language-specific effects on number computation in toddlers. *Developmental Science, 8*, 373–392.

Houdé, O. (2004). Constructivism. In O. Houdé (Ed.), *Dictionary of Cognitive Science*, (pp. 93–94). New York, NY: Routledge/Taylor & Francis (Psychology Press).

Huizinga, J. (1938/1955). *Homo ludens: A study of the play element in culture.* Boston, MA: Beacon Press.

Isbister, K., & Schaffer, N. (2008). What is usability and why should I care? Introduction. In K. Ibister & N. Schaffer (Eds.), *Game Usability.* Burlington, MA: Elsevier.

Kelley, D. (2001). Design as an iterative process. Retrieved from http://ecorner.stanford.edu/authorMaterialInfo.html?mid=686

Klahr, D., & Carver, S. M. (1988). Cognitive objectives in a LOGO debugging curriculum: Instruction, learning, and transfer. *Cognitive Psychology, 20*, 362–404.

Kornell, N., Hays, M. J., & Bjork, R. (2009). Unsuccessful retrieval attempts enhance subsequent learning. *Journal of Experimental Psychology: Learning, Memory, and Cognition, 35*, 989–998.

Laitinen, S. (2008). Usability and playability expert evaluation. In K. Ibister & N. Schaffer (Eds.), *Game Usability*, (pp. 91–111). Burlington, MA: Elsevier.

Lambiotte, J. G., Dansereau, D. F., Rocklin, T. R., Fletcher, B., Hythecker, V. I., Larson, C. O. & O'Donnell, A. M. (1987). Cooperative learning and test taking: Transfer of skills. *Contemporary Educational Psychology, 12*, 52–61.

LeDoux, J. E. (1996). *The Emotional Brain.* New York: Simon & Schuster.

Levine, S. C., Jordan, N. C., & Huttenlocher, J. (1992). Development of calculation abilities in young children. *Journal of Experimental Child Psychology, 53*, 72–103.

McKeachie, W. J. (1987). Cognitive skills and their transfer: Discussion. *International Journal of Educational Research, 11*, 707–712.

Nielsen, J. (1994). Heuristic evaluation. In J. Nielsen & R. L. Molich (Eds.), *Usability Inspection Methods*, (pp. 25–62). New York, NY: John Wiley & Sons.

Norman, D. A. (2005). *Emotional design: Why we love (or hate) everyday things.* New York, NY: Basic Books.

Paivio, A. (1974). Spacing of repetitions in the incidental and intentional free recall of pictures and words. *Journal of Verbal Learning and Verbal Behavior, 13*, 497–511.

Papert, S. (1980). *Mindstorms: Children, computers, and powerful ideas.* New York, NY: Basic Books.

Pellegrini, A. D., Dupuis, D., & Smith, P. K. (2007). Play in evolution and development. *Developmental Review, 27*, 261–276.

Pessoa, L. (2008). On the Relationship Between Emotion and Cognition. *Nature Reviews Neuroscience, 9*, 148–158

Phelps, E. A. (2006). Emotion and Cognition: Insights from Studies of the Human Amygdala. *Annual Review of Psychology, 57*, 27–53

Piaget, J. (1937). *La construction du reel chez l'enfant.* Neuchâtel, France: Delachaux & Niestlé.

Piaget, J., & Inhelder, B. (1969). *The psychology of the child.* New York, NY: Basic Books.

Pinelle, D., Wong, N., & Stach, T. (2008). Heuristic evaluation for games: Usability principles for video game design. In *Proceedings of the ACM Conference on Human Factors in Computing Systems (CHI 2008)*, 1453–1462.

Prensky, M. (2006). *"Don't bother me Mom—I'm learning!".* Minneapolis, MN: Paragon House Publishers.

Richland, L. E., Kornell, N., & Kao, L. S. (2009). The pretesting effect: Do unsuccessful retrieval attempts enhance learning? *Journal of Experimental Psychology: Applied, 15*, 243–257.

Ryan, R. M., & Deci, E. L. (2000a). When rewards compete with nature: The undermining of intrinsic motivation and self-regulation. In C. Sansone & J. M. Harackiewicz (Eds.), *Intrinsic and extrinsic motivation: The search for optimal motivation and performance* (pp. 13–54). New York, NY: Academic Press.

Ryan, R. M., & Deci, E. L. (2000b). Self-determination theory and the facilitation of intrinsic motivation, social development, and well-being. *American Psychologist, 55*, 141–166.

Salen, K., & Zimmerman, E. (2004). *Rules of play: Game design fundamentals*, Vol. 1. London, UK: MIT.

Shaffer, D. W. (2006). *How computer games help children learn.* New York, NY: Palgrave Macmillan.

Shaffer, D. W., Squire, K. R., Halverson, R., & Gee, J. P. (2005). Video games and the future of learning. *Phi Delta Kappan, 87,* 104–111.

Squire, K. (2006). From content to context: videogames as designed experience. *Educational Researcher, 35,* 19–29.

Sweetser, P. & Wyeth, P. (2005). GameFlow: A model for evaluating player enjoyment in games. *ACM Computers in Entertainment, 3,* 1–24.

Toppino, T. C., Kasserman, J. E., & Mracek, W. A. (1991). The effect of spacing repetitions on the recognition memory of young children and adults. *Journal of Experimental Child Psychology, 51,* 123–138.

Thorndike, E. L. & Woodworth, R. S. (1901). The influence of improvement in one mental function upon the efficiency of other functions. *Psychological Review, 8,* 247–261.

Vygotsky, L. S. (1967). Play and its role in the mental development of the child. *Soviet Psychology, 5,* 6–18.

Vygotsky, L. S. (1978). Interaction between learning and development. In M. Cole, V. John-Steiner, S. Scribner, & E. Souberman (Eds.), *Mind in society: The development of higher psychological processes* (pp. 79–91). Cambridge, MA: Harvard University Press.

Wynn, K. (1992). Addition and subtraction by human infants. *Nature, 358,* 749–750.

11

Educational Video Games: Two Tools for Research and Development

MATTHEW GAYDOS

Introduction

In his 2011 presentation at the annual Video Game Developer's Conference, long-time video game designer Brian Moriarty defended long-time movie critic Roger Ebert's stance that video games are not art. "I am prepared to believe," Ebert wrote and Moriarty quoted, "that video games can be elegant, subtle, sophisticated, challenging and visually wonderful. But I believe the nature of the medium prevents it from moving beyond craftsmanship to the stature of art" (Moriarty, 2011). Expanding on Ebert's position, Moriarty (2011) argued that, because games force players to make decisions, they continually remove contingency and deny the player the opportunity to remain contemplative. Real art, or sublime art, evokes the inexpressible and embraces the mystery of choice, whereas video games, by requiring their players to reduce contingency through action, remove this mystery. Because video games inherently center on meaningful choices, they are not likely to achieve the sublime, and instead should be content with their position. After all, kitsch and craft can still be entertaining.

While the outcome of the arguments regarding the artfulness of games by these two luminaries is largely inconsequential to the academic study of video games, their writing is presented to underscore their position and the position of many others with regard to video games. That is to say, while researchers consider games predominantly in terms of their function as research tools and potential to achieve fine-grained control over parameters of user experience (e.g., Donchin, 1995), critics have taken to comparing *Pac-Man* and Picasso. Games are useful models that can be useful interventions to affect cognition (Honey & Hilton, 2011). They are also a growing cultural phenomenon, which has begun to push boundaries of technology, art, and entertainment. They are an active culture that grows and is redefined with every new game produced.

Researchers engaging with video games for learning or education are inherently participating in a complex environment of production and consumption with which most young people (often research participants) will likely already have had some experience—sometimes much more than the researcher. Players can have lofty expectations for their games, and some might side against Ebert and Moriarty, considering games on par with the works of other great artists working in music, visual art, or sculpture. Conducting video game research, design, and development means working at the intersection of player expectations and those of the academic community. Work at this intersection of disciplines has the opportunity to contribute simultaneously to academic fields as well as video games as an artistic medium. Because research and commercial game consumers maintain diverse and strict standards, meeting their expectations can mean relying on interdisciplinary teams, with researchers looking to game designers for their expertise in shaping player experience and game designers to academics for theories or content.

The diversity of theoretical and practical approaches currently being applied to research and development on video games and learning makes interdisciplinary work challenging, however. Researchers understand games through different theories and perspectives including approaches from psychology, education, learning sciences, sociology, and anthropology. Commercial developers, however, are less likely to be familiar with the academic approaches and more likely to be familiar with the work of notable video game designers such as Chris Crawford (*Balance of Power*), Will Wright (*Sims*), Sid Meier (*Civilization*), Warren Spector (*Deus Ex*), or Peter Molyneux (*Populous*). Because of their different approaches, researchers and developers, when brought together around video games, may understandably find collaborative projects difficult, given the different definitions of games and learning that they maintain.

In this chapter, a brief overview of the different approaches to video games and learning is presented. Then, two tools that may be useful for addressing these different approaches are discussed. The goal for this chapter is to promote the integration of different learning theories and game design to better create games that appeal to both communities.

Video Games for Learning

Good video games, academics have argued, can be adapted and adopted to improve and study formal and informal learning (Honey & Hilton, 2011). *Space Fortress* (SF), one of the first games to do so, was developed in the early '80s by researchers at the University of Illinois at Urbana-Champaign (Mane & Donchin, 1989). In SF, players control a spaceship and try to destroy an on-screen space fortress while shooting missiles and avoiding counterattacks. By manipulating in-game parameters, such as the feedback received by players, researchers could test hypotheses, such as the effects of practice on attention in the context of a complex, game-based task (Gopher, Weil, & Bareket, 1994).

More recently, sociocultural approaches to learning and education have also begun to examine the potential for games and learning. Rather than framing games as investigative devices that allow researchers to collect better data by controlling conditions more acutely, sociocultural theories approach games as potentially powerful educational and cultural *artifacts* (Gee, 2003; Squire, 2004, 2006). For example, Squire (2004, 2006), drawing on Wertsch (1998), considers video games as artifacts that mediate player activity, some of which is educationally valuable. For Squire, learning in games is based on the way that games privilege certain actions over others. They are ideological virtual worlds that provide their players with *designed experiences* through which players come to learn new ways of doing and being. From his perspective, video games are tools to be used to introduce educationally valued material (e.g., information, values) to players within purposefully designed contexts that align the values of the world with educationally desirable outcomes.

Pyschological approaches like Mane & Donchin's (1989) and sociocultural approaches like Squire's (2005), are just two examples of the theories currently being applied to the study of video games. Assessment researchers, for example, have begun to explore video games as potential assessment devices that can seamlessly combine student activity and testing (Behrens, Frezzo, Mislevy, Kroopnick, & Wise, 2006; Shute, 2011). Public policy and science education perspectives suggest that games can be used to improve access to and interest in science, technology, engineering, and mathematics learning (Honey & Hilton, 2011; Mayo, 2009). Computer scientists have begun to use games to crowd source difficult computation (Cooper et al., 2010; Kawrykow et al., 2012). As researchers and designers explore new ways that educational games can be used or develop new games themselves, they must also find new ways to work through already-existing differences between theories (Anderson, Greeno, Reder, & Simon, 2000).

Because newcomers to education and learning theory may find navigating the nuances of different theoretical approaches frustrating, what follows are examples of three major paradigms for learning as applied to video games. Generally, the examples can be categorized according to what Collins, Greeno, and Resnick (1992) denote as *behaviorist/empiricist, cognitivist/rationalist,* and *situative/pragmatist-sociohistoric.* To highlight the differences among the approaches, the examples focus on what changes as a result of learning: an individual's behavior, an individual's biology, or the social interactions and relationships between agents (i.e., the individual and the game).

Three Approaches to Games and Learning: Behavior, Biology, and Social Interactions

Some of the most notable investigations into learning and video games have stemmed from psychology studies, including work on motivation (Lepper

& Malone, 1987; Malone, 1981), attention (Gopher et al., 1994; Green & Bavelier, 2003), and aggression (Anderson & Bushman, 2001). More recently, psychology-based studies of video games have expanded and diversified to include, for example, neuroscientific approaches (Mathiak & Weber, 2006) and to investigate the role of games in therapy (Jameson, Trevena, & Swain, 2011). Though psychology, broadly, has been a leader in the study of video games for learning, different lines of research apply different assumptions of learning and levels of analysis. Further diversification of games studies can be found in education where a variety of sociocultural approaches have been applied to interpret the learning that video games afford. A complete review of games and learning literature is beyond the scope of this chapter, but a brief review of three lines of research is sufficient to highlight some of the differences that games researchers hold, particularly with regard to their definitions of learning.

In a series of studies of video game player populations and controlled interventions, Green and Bavelier (2003, 2006a, 2006b) suggested that action video games may improve participants' visual-attention processes, both in terms of spatial and temporal capacity. Using neurological models, Green, Pouget, and Bavelier (2010) further suggested that improved learning may be attributed to an increased capability for video game players to make use of information available. Learning, to the authors, is understood as an improved ability to integrate evidence in pursuit of a decision. To show this learning, Green, Pouget, and Bavelier (2010) manipulated the amount of information that was available to participants in a series of movement discrimination tasks (are the dots in this scene moving left or right?) and auditory discrimination tasks (is a tone present among white noise in your left or right ear?). When presented with the same amount of information as nonplayers, video game players made faster but not more accurate decisions. Neurological models that vary the strength of the connection between evidence and integration can account for this selective improvement, and the authors concluded that the mechanism behind improved visual attention tasks may be an improved capacity for probabilistic inference. Green and colleagues' work characterizes an approach to learning that focuses on biological and specifically neurological change, rather than on symbolic structures in the mind or social interactions.

Alternatively, Anderson and colleagues theorize about learning in video games in terms of the general aggression model, and focus on mental representations rather than biological change (Anderson & Bushman, 2001). Anderson and colleagues' model supposes that an individual maintains particular knowledge structures such as perceptual and person schemata, or knowledge about sensed objects and beliefs about people, and behavioral scripts, or knowledge of how people behave. From this perspective, learning is considered the process of acquiring, rehearsing, and reinforcing these knowledge structures through direct experiences and observations. To gain an understanding of their approach, consider Anderson et al.'s (2004) study: participants were presented with two games that were matched along dimensions of difficulty, enjoyment, action, and frustration but that differed in violent content. Using a modified version of the competitive reaction time task (CRT) (Anderson & Bushman, 1997), participants were asked to compete with an opponent in responding quickly to the presentation of a tone and to adjust the volume of a noise that would be used to punish the slower competitor. In the first phase of the task, punishment was set by the participant's opponents (who were actually and secretly computers), and participants received tones that were either randomly ordered or that increased in loudness. When the punishments were randomly ordered, participants who had played the violent video game for twenty minutes prior to the CRT task punished their opponents with louder tones on average than did the participants who had played the nonviolent game. Anderson et al. (2004) concluded that aggressive responses by these participants could be attributed to the violent video game content. Thus, by rewarding and supporting the practice of aggressive action, video games may be seen as teaching players to be more aggressive outside of the game environment.

Anderson and colleagues' focus on the representations (especially of violent or aggressive action) found within games privileges an information-based approach to learning that is distinct both from the biological focus of Green and colleagues, and the sociocultural or situated approach as adapted by James Paul Gee (2003). Drawing on a broad range of social theorists that includes, for example, Art Glenberg, Jerome Bruner, Yrjo Engstrom, Jean Lave, Etienne Wenger, James Wertsch, and Lev Vygotstky, Gee and colleagues have tended to focus on social elements and interactions that are associated with video games and play, including the identity of the players (Fields & Kafai, 2012; Gee, 2003), the role of the game with respect to individual and cultural narratives (Barab et al., 2010), and the practices in which game communities engage (Steinkuehler & Duncan, 2008). Gee (2005) argues that good video games and their communities may serve as a basis for much-needed education reform.

His argument goes something like this. The current U.S. public education system is largely inadequate with regard to educating its students, particularly for an increasingly competitive and global society, and much of the knowledge, skills, and practices that are supported by informal learning environments (i.e., games, fan communities) are more helpful to students than are those taught and valued by formal schooling. The issue is not that teachers cannot teach, but that policy makers and the educational system's preoccupation and emphasis on accountability through high-stakes, standardized testing has prevented teachers from doing their jobs and has devalued deep learning in favor of superficial but testable content retention (Gee, 2004, 2005). Gee does not present a body of empirical evidence backing his claim that video games can be used to address these educational issues and acknowledges that such evidence does not yet exist. Nevertheless, for Gee, the learning that happens in and around good video games is a self-evident social process, given that successful game play and participation in game communities depends on player learning. Learning occurs regularly in the context of video game play, though it is infrequently applicable to formal learning contexts. It is up to video game researchers to find new ways to leverage video games' potential for educational and other prosocial goals.

The three characterizations of learning theories presented here are generalizations. None of the authors claim that learning in video games occurs solely through the mechanism they describe; it's likely that they would acknowledge that there are multiple ways and theories with which to interpret video game–based learning. Gee (2011) for example, explicitly claims that his "own view of learning is a sociocultural-situated-embodied-extended mind type of theory" (p. 227). Nevertheless, the approaches to games taken by Green, Anderson, and Gee can be differentiated based on their assumptions of learning and emphasis on the biological, symbolic, or social changes that are assumed to be pertinent under each approach. Identifying the different learning theories throughout the process of developing an educational game allows designers to make pragmatic choices about which theory most appropriately achieves a game development project's goals.

That is, theories of learning can be reframed from a design approach, where design is defined as a process of exploring and meeting constraints (Gross, 1985). From the commercial development perspective, examples of essential constraints that must be considered during the game development process include the game's scope, theme, and mechanics. What counts as learning can similarly be considered a design constraint, and learning may be framed in terms of neurological change, information acquisition, or identity construction.

Because developing good educational games involves working at the intersection of fields such as commercial game development and learning, connecting tools and theories like definitions of learning and design constraints will be likely be useful. Two tools are presented here. The first tool presented here is an assessment framework that provides a theoretical basis for bringing together disparate disciplinary approaches (e.g., theories of learning). The second tool is a design activity, or a game jam, which provides a shared experience that researchers and developers could use to spur innovation and collaboration. The theories and methods presented here offer two methods for games and learning researchers and developers to confront the goals and assumptions that might otherwise conflict.

Integrating Game Development and Education

One reason that video games have become a popular and diverse medium is the increasing ease of game development, specifically in terms of new tools, education programs, and social structures. New tools that streamline the production process include, for example, *Unity, Game Maker, Scratch,* and *Kodu,* which are development environments that allow for games to be developed more easily. Whether streamlining the process (e.g., by allowing art to be more easily integrated) or providing intuitive and graphical scripting languages, these new development environments and game engines mean that video games can be made with fewer resources (people and budgets), and in less time while maintaining relatively high production value and polish. In terms of education programs, a few schools or programs have, for some time, focused exclusively on video games such as DigiPen, which was founded in 1988, and the Entertainment Technology Center, which was founded in 1999. These older programs have been more recently joined by games-oriented curricula at more mainstream institutions across the country, including programs at the Indiana University Bloomington (2008), University of Washington-Seattle (2013), University of Wisconsin–Madison (Games Learning Society, 2013), Rensselaer Polytechnic Institute (2013), DePaul University (2013), Michigan State University (2013), and New York University (2013).

Communities of professional and amateur game developers and consumers have also grown substantially, empowered by social and technological structures. Contests and awards such as the Gamer's Choice Awards and Independent Games Festival (IGF) are annually held to honor industry-select titles. Games that receive these awards are generally held in high regard for their contributions to the medium. Smaller events, such as Indiecade, the Games for Health Challenge, and the Serious Games Showcase similarly honor well-made games, though they address smaller, more niche categories. Even the U.S. government has begun to award development using competition structures. With the passing and reauthorization of the America Competes Act, some federal agencies can and have taken the opportunity to spur innovation and job creation through competitions, some of which have been specifically oriented toward video game or digital application development. The Equal Pay App Challenge (Solis & Chopra, 2012) and the Occupational Employment Statistics challenge (Department of Labor, 2011), for example, both launched by the Department of Labor, have awarded thousands of dollars in prizes to U.S.-based developers for application development. Unlike traditional grants or contracts (such as work with military simulations), these new competitions result in multiple products being made by the community and awarding the prize only to the best. The scale and type of their prizes suggest that they are aimed at smaller commercial independent developers rather than larger established companies, as prizes were on the order of thousands of USD or access to business assistance programs (e.g., accelerators, mentorship).

Finally, it should be noted that new, low-cost methods for publishing games have helped independent developers see a project completed and in the hands of players. Publishing games on smartphones and tablets is relatively low-cost, and developer kits can cost as little as $100. Websites such as TIGSource and Kongregate, which hold competitions, host games, and support online discussion forums, have helped to connect players and developers and have grown large communities (some games on Kongregate have received millions of plays). The Kickstarter website allows funders to pledge varying amounts of money, ranging from tens to millions of dollars, to see a project come to fruition, usually in return for some project-related merchandise or other acknowledgments. If the funding goal set forth by the funder is met, the money is dispersed and the project proceeds. Project Greenlight, a submission and voting system run by the game company Valve, is a similarly low-cost and community-centered approach to publishing games.

These new tools, education programs, and social structures have helped game developers produce, release, and distribute their games. It is easier now for small teams of developers to reach global audiences, and arguably some of these teams can and should include psychologists and other learning experts who are interested in taking their research from the laboratory to the market. However, as new applications for video games are explored, from learning mathematics to meditation, psychologists and game developers will likely see differences in opinion over theoretical and design issues. At the NSF-funded conference Academic Lessons from Video Game Learning, held at Fordham University in 2010, leading psychologists and game designers were brought together to discuss the learning research associated with video games, especially with regard to translating the work into the classroom. During discussions, when asked whether skills learned in-game could transfer to other contexts, one designer responded, "I'm not sure that we believe in transfer." This perspective is not representative of commercial or educational game designers generally, but suggests a misalignment between views. Working with developers may require that psychologists and other learning researchers establish common theoretical ground and explore theories that are not only supported by empirical evidence but are also useful for a game's design. In cases in which a game's learning goals and in-game goals are not aligned, game elements may interfere with learning and result in poorer outcomes than in cases where traditional methods or no game has been used (Lepper & Malone, 1987).

Evidence-Centered Design: Assessment as a Theoretical Frame

The first tool that may be helpful in coordinating designers and researchers is theoretical. The assessment framework known as evidence-centered design (ECD) frames assessment as akin to constructing a scientific argument: the primary goal of the process is to generate empirically supported claims about an individual's knowledge, skills, or competencies (Mislevy, Almond, & Lukas, 2006). Assessment, from an ECD perspective, is a process of defining and then gathering evidence that would support some initial claim. Specifically, this process can be understood in two primary parts: a conceptual assessment framework (CAF) and the four-process delivery architecture. The conceptual assessment framework generally includes models of the student, the task, evidence, assembly, and presentation. The student model is an estimate (typically Bayesian) of student knowledge or proficiency. The task model includes the products that are used to generate evidence and an explanation of variables that must be considered with respect to the gathering of that evidence, or a general outline of the class of tasks. The task model may include variables related to the environment (e.g., time constraints), and the tools available (e.g., scaffolding systems). The evidence model links the task to claims about the individual, specifying how task observations will result in the generation of evidence and defining the statistical properties of the evidence associated with the individual. The assembly model defines the tasks that will be specifically used within the assessment; the presentation model defines how the assessment will look within a specific environment. Combined, these models comprise the conceptual assessment framework. In practice, they are implemented in accordance with the delivery architecture, which defines (1) processing and scoring results, (2) selecting new assessment activities or deciding to stop the assessment, and (3) a task/evidence library that houses all of the materials to be used in the assessment (Mislevy & Riconscente, 2005; Mislevy, Steinberg, & Almond, 2003).

Suggesting an assessment framework like ECD for games research may seem odd at first, given that at its core ECD is fundamentally a process of scientific argumentation. However, ECD offers a structured assessment framework that can guide the construction of a valid assessment device in which evidence—whether neurological, symbolic, or social—can be counted in support of claims made about student knowledge and skills. Its theory-agnosticism allows different learning approaches to be integrated or to coexist across the same game or project.

Further, Behrens et al. (2006) point out that video games maintain structural, functional, and semiotic similarities to evidence-centered design. For example, both games and assessments are artificial systems with which players engage, and through which quantifiable outcomes are produced (e.g., a player's score) (Behrens et al., 2006). Additionally, many video games, especially those that rely heavily on simulation to generate game play, maintain game models (tasks) that are updated with player activity (student) and that respond accordingly, both by changing the task model (evidence) and presenting new information to the player (assembly and presentation). Finally, meaning constructed through game play or while taking an examination is context-dependent, and individuals may interpret the game or test differently (e.g., playfully). The utility of ECD derives from its correspondence with elements of game design, and flexibility in defining what counts as evidence for learning.

Game Jams: Beyond Design Education

The second tool that may be useful for interdisciplinary work is an organized event, a *game jam,* which can be a useful way to prototype new and academic video games. Game jams are structured design events that are frequently used by the game development education community to teach and reinforce design practices. At the annual Ludum Dare game jam, for example, small teams of students and independent developers work to create a playable game that meets particular thematic constraints within 48 hours. For Ludum Dare 2013, more than 2,300 games were created over the course of the weekend, 1,715 of which were submitted to the main event (Rose, 2013). Granted, most of these games will probably not become the next million-dollar commercial success, rather (like many academic papers), they will probably remain insulated within their social networks played mostly by peers. Still, these games matter. As designers bring to screen their video game concepts, their games, like all games, contribute to the process of redefining and shaping the character of the medium. At events like Ludum Dare or other game development jams, this just happens to occur en masse, in a short amount of time, and (often) by small groups of students. As events that are often run cheaply and with large groups of participants working together to make game prototypes, jams can be useful for coordinating the efforts of designers and researchers.

The format of a jam can vary. They can range from small weekend gatherings among friends or professionals, such as the Indie Game Jam, to large-scale and highly coordinated events such as the Global Game Jam, a global event that includes thousands of participants, most of whom are students. What distinguishes jams, regardless of their size or participants, are their constraints, including time, theme, and goal. That is, in a game jam participants must, by the end of some allotted time period, produce a playable game that addresses some predetermined theme. The games created can be digital or nondigital and are not expected to be complete by the end of the session. However, all games created by a jam are expected to be playable, and ideally should have been played by the designers at least once before the end of the allotted time (Gray, Gabler, Shodhan, & Kucic, 2005). Table 11.1 lists some general guidelines for starting a game jam.

Game jams are typically oriented toward the game development industry, and help achieve two important goals. First, they provide participants with the opportunity to make a game with others. Completing this process can be difficult, especially when working with strangers under tight time constraints. It can also motivating, however, as the production of a playable prototype may result in a portfolio piece that students could show off to future employers. By participating in a didactic production process, students can refine important production skills, such as accurately estimating a project's size and difficulty.

Second, jams are events sometimes used by experienced game developers to increase their productivity and creativity and can take on many names and formats. The 0h Game Jam, for example, takes place during the hour when clocks get turned back for daylight savings time so that participants start at 2:00 a.m. and end at 2:00 a.m. (0hgame.eu). The Seven-Day Rogue like Challenge (7drl. org) lasts seven days and requires participants to make a game in the rogue-like genre (e.g., *NetHack*). While the jam format is sometimes used by individuals to

Table 11.1 **General Guidelines for Running a Game Jam**

Supplies	To get started running a game jam, a set of polyhedral dice, a deck of cards, paper, pencils and some tokens may be sufficient. Many of the supplies listed in Raph Koster's (2005) game design prototype kit (without the dremel tool) are also inexpensive and available online. Board games from local thrift stores are easy ways to acquire cheap miscellaneous parts, such as timers, game boards, and trivia cards.
Format	Though some commercial jams allot just one hour for design, accounting for initial content explanation and time to reflect has pushed our jams to approximately two hours, with 10 to 15 minutes for introductions and a presentation of expert content (e.g., meditation), one hour for design, and the remaining time for playing the just-made games. Groups of two to five with adequate space to work are encouraged, as singletons miss out on the group experience and overly large groups struggle with determining who works on what. Additional useful design activities can be found in *Challenges for Game Designers* (Brathwaite & Schreiber, 2008).
Administrators/ Participants	It is sometimes helpful for jam administrators to have experience with game design or classroom management experience, especially when running a jam for a captive audience. Participants who are unfamiliar with design or uninterested in participating may struggle with project scope, diagnosing the changes that their game needs, and may request direct instruction on what to do next. In some cases, the audience may be more suited to working through rule changes to pre-existing games, rather than game construction from scratch. When jams include professional researchers and game designers, purposeful selection of teams is recommended, in order to evenly distribute research scientists, content experts, and game designers.

challenge themselves (e.g., make a playable game during a plane flight) jams are also used to produce innovation in the industry. The Independent Game Jam and the Experimental Game Play Project, for example, are explicitly directed toward producing new, compelling, and innovative player experiences.

Similar to their use as educational interventions for aspiring game developers, jams can also be used as interventions for other educational topics by constraining a jam's theme to an educational content area. Though not focused on game jams specifically, previous research has explored the use of game design as a way to introduce students to other topics such as mathematics (Kafai, Franke, Ching, & Shih, 1998) and programming (Maloney, Peppler, Kafai, Resnick, &

Rusk, 2008). Limited-time game design events like jams are special cases of this paradigm that could easily be integrated into larger curricula that explore game design for content areas.

Notably, however, there are few game jams that parallel the Indie Game Jam or Ludum Dare in the context of games for education, and none that match the scale of the larger jam events. Some groups have begun to use small game jams to innovate around games for education or other prosocial purposes (Alhadeff, 2013). Occasionally, industry-oriented events take up the banner of creating games for social good. For example, Eric Zimmerman's annual game design challenge in 2012 asked select designers to create a game that could improve the world in a measurable way and that could be played in 60 seconds or less. Nevertheless, the scale, popularity, and regularity of commercial and hobbyist game jams is currently unmatched by serious games or education researchers despite the potential that jams offer to encourage creativity among content experts, learning theorists, and game designers.

Applications to Education

Assessment theories and game jams are useful for development because they allow individuals from different theoretical backgrounds and practices to work toward shared, achievable goals. Additionally, challenging participants' definitions of what games *are* is helpful in exploring what games *could be*, especially given new collaborations between scientists and designers. Though some commercial games, such as *Pong, Tetris*, and *Mario*, have been around long enough to become widely recognized cultural references, and others, such as *Call of Duty, The Sims,* and *World of Warcraft* have recently become household names, video games are rapidly becoming a diverse and sophisticated medium.

There are a growing number of video games that address unconventional topics, including for example, alcoholism (*Papo & Yo*), industrial farming practices (*McDonald's Video Game*), the U.S. Constitution (*Do I Have a Right?*), and gender-identity (*Dys4ia*). Along with their popular-media counterparts, these games and their developers contribute to a growing diversity both in terms of the games being made and the cultures developed and are carving out new possible models for successful game development. Leveraging the popularity of mainstream games provides one avenue for improving education; research can also look to smaller studios and independently made games to innovate around particular content or issues that are important to address.

Consider for example, the success of *Minecraft,* a game produced by Mojang, a small studio that began with limited resources (one part-time developer) that has sold more than 21 million copies worldwide across platforms (Seitz, 2012). In *Minecraft,* the player deconstructs a simple three-dimensional world to gather resources, which are then pieced back together to create new objects and environments. Even though the resources used to create *Minecraft* were vastly different than, for example, *Call of Duty*, which wielded a $200 million production and distribution budget (Fritz, 2009), units sold were still comparable—*Call of Duty: Modern Warfare 2* sold around 15 million copies. Despite larger game studios' move toward big-budget Hollywood films, one- and two-person studios have still managed to find commercial success. More importantly, *Minecraft*, and supporting sites like minecraftteacher.tumblr.com, have expanded into formal education settings, offering supporting curriculum, custom versions of the game, discounts to educators, and professional training sessions. As researchers are unlikely to have access to the budgets, resources, or developers akin to those used in *Call of Duty*, partnerships with small studios or independent developers provide potentially practical and more approachable way to collaborate. Additionally, games produced by smaller studios, games with niche audiences in mind, and games that address unconventional topics may help lead researchers to explore new ways that games can be leveraged for learning.

In addition to examining more unconventional video game–based learning opportunities, jams and assessment may be helpful in catching up to already-existing uses of games in educational settings: currently, the will to use video games for education far exceeds the research available to support its use. For example, two charter schools whose curricula are based on game mechanics have been founded, one in New York City (Quest to Learn) and one in Chicago (ChicagoQuest). In these schools, students gain points, level up, and defeat "boss" challenges as they work through content (Torres & Wolozin, 2011). Researchers and education staff at the University of Wisconsin–Madison have regularly used augmented reality games to tell stories about the campus and Wisconsin's history (Brooks, 2011; Mathews & Holden, 2012; Squire & Jan, 2007). Teachers in all 50 states have begun to use the iCivics curriculum, including custom video games designed to teach players about the branches of government, the constitution, and budgetary process (*iCivics Annual Report,* 2011, 2012). *Minecraft* may be exceptional in its sales and adoption, but these examples of video game use are showing up increasingly in formal and informal education environments, as researchers, designers, and teachers begin not only exploring currently existing games for learning, but making their own. Games for research and learning are no longer just the object of study within laboratories or commercial entertainment technologies, but are now used in settings ranging from classrooms to federal contests.

From a video game design perspective, the different emphases that learning theories place on game-based activity reveal the multiple ways that content can be integrated into game play. For example, information-centric approaches might suggest that in-game representations and activity may need to accurately depict real-world phenomena. Biologically based theories may suggest that, regardless of the representations used, game play should be fast-paced and attention-demanding. Because video games, like other education technology, continue to face challenges of adoption, especially in schools (Van Eck, 2006), understanding the tradeoffs and appropriate uses of the different learning theories may lead to designs that better fit the intended use and goals of the game and facilitate transfer across game play and classroom learning.

From a research perspective, collaborative work with designers means finding new ways to apply and interpret theories given the messiness of real-world contexts (e.g., classrooms). Theories of motivation (Lepper & Malone, 1987) and aggression (Anderson & Bushman, 1997) have seen some crossover from laboratory studies to the real world, but issues in education are large and systemic, including problems such as unequal access (Moss, Pullin, Gee, Haertel, & Young, 2008) and skewed dropout rates (Bridgeland, DiIulio, & Morison, 2006). Because current evidence for effective game-based learning is drawn from different domains with different assumptions about the games themselves, the contexts in which they are used, and the learning that occurs, academics must work closely with developers to sort through current research to help translate theory into practical solutions.

References

Alhadeff, E. (2013, January 14). The Global Serious Games Jam. Retrieved from http://serious-gamesmarket.blogspot.com/2013/01/the-global-serious-games-jam.html

Anderson, C. A. (2004). An update on the effects of playing violent video games. *Journal of Adolescence, 27*, 113–122.

Anderson, C. A., & Bushman, B. J. (1997). External validity of "trivial" experiments: The case of laboratory aggression. *Review of General Psychology, 1*(1), 19–41. doi:10.1037//1089-2680.1.1.19

Anderson, C. A., & Bushman, B. J. (2001). Effects of violent video games on aggressive behavior, aggressive cognition, aggressive affect, physiological arousal, and prosocial behavior: A meta-analytic review of the scientific literature. *Psychological Science, 12*, 353–359.

Anderson, C. A., Carnagey, N., Flanagan, M., Benjamin, A., Eubanks, J., & Valentine, J. (2004). Violent video games: Specific effects of violent content on aggressive thoughts and behavior. *Advances in Experimental Social Psychology, 36*, 199–249.

Anderson, J. R., Greeno, J. G., Reder, L. M., & Simon, H. A. (2000). Perspectives on learning, thinking, and activity. *Educational Researcher, 29*(4), 11–13.

Barab, S., Dodge, T., Ingram-Goble, A., Pettyjohn, P., Peppler, K., Volk, C., & Solomou, M. (2010). Pedagogical dramas and transformational play: Narratively rich games for learning. *Mind, Culture, and Activity, 17*, 235–264.

Behrens, J. T., Frezzo, D., Mislevy, R., Kroopnick, M., & Wise, D. (2006). Structural, functional and semiotic symmetries in simulation-based games and assessments. In E. Dickieson, W. Wulfeck, & H. F. O'Neil (Eds.), *Assessment of problem solving using simulations,* (pp. 59–80). New York, NY: Erlbaum.

Brathwaite, B., & Schreiber, I. (2008). Challenges for game designers (1st ed.). Boston, MA: Charles River Media.

Bridgeland, J. M., DiIulio, J. J., & Morison, K. B. (2006). The silent epidemic: Perspectives of high school dropouts. Washington, DC: Civic Enterprises.

Brooks, S. (2011, Oct. 11). "Stories on the Hill" uses app to tell tales. Retrieved from http://www.news.wisc.edu/19883

Collins, A., Greeno, J., & Resnick, L. B. (1992). Cognition and learning. In B. Berliner & R. Calfee (Eds.), *Handbook of Educational Psychology*, (pp. 15–46). New York, NY: Simon & Shuster MacMillan.

Cooper, S., Khatib, F., Treuille, A., Barbero, J., Lee, J., Beenen, M.,...Popović, Z. (2010). Predicting protein structures with a multiplayer online game. *Nature, 466*(7307), 756–760.

Department of Labor. (2011). Occupational Employment Statistics Challenge. Retrieved from http://employment.challenge.gov/

DePaul University (2013). DePaul Game Dev. Retrieved from http://gamedev.depaul.edu/

Donchin, E. (1995). Video games as research tools: The space fortress game. *Science, 27*(2), 217–223.

Fields, D., & Kafai, Y. (2012). Navigating life as an avatar: The shifting identities-in-practice of a girl player in a tween virtual world. In C. C. Ching & B. Foley (Eds.) *Constructing the self in a digital world*, (pp. 222–250). Cambridge, UK: Cambridge University Press.

Filament Games. (2009). *Do I Have A Right?* Retrieved from http://www.icivics.org/games/do-i-have-right

Fritz, B. (2009, November 18). Video game borrows page from Hollywood playbook. *Los Angeles Times*. Retrieved from http://articles.latimes.com/2009/nov/18/business/fi-ct-duty18

Games Learning Society. (2013). Retrieved from http://www.gameslearningsociety.org/

Gee, J. P. (2003). *What video games have to teach us about learning and literacy*. Palgrave Macmillan.

Gee, J. P. (2004). *Situated language and learning: A critique of traditional schooling*. Routledge.

Gee, J. P. (2005). What would a state of the art instructional video game look like? *Innovate, 1*(6).

Gee, J. P. (2011). Reflections on empirical evidence on games and learning. In S. Tobias & J. D. Fletcher (Eds.), *Computer games and instruction*. Charlotte, NC: Information Age Publishing.

Gopher, D., Weil, M., & Bareket, T. (1994). Transfer of skill from a computer game trainer to flight. *Human Factors: The Journal of the Human Factors and Ergonomics Society, 36*, 387–405.

Gray, K., Gabler, K., Shodhan, S., & Kucic, M. (2005). How to prototype a game in under 7 days. *Gamasutra*. Retrieved from http://www.gamasutra.com/view/feature/2438/how_to_prototype_a_game_in_under_7_.php

Green, C. S., & Bavelier, D. (2003). Action video game modifies visual selective attention. *Nature, 423*(6939), 534–537.

Green, C. S., & Bavelier, D. (2006a). Enumeration versus multiple object tracking: the case of action video game players. *Cognition, 101*(1), 217–245. doi:10.1016/j.cognition.2005.10.004

Green, C. S., & Bavelier, D. (2006b). Effect of action video games on the spatial distribution of visuospatial attention. *Journal of Experimental Psychology. Human Perception and Performance, 32*(6), 1465–1478. doi:10.1037/0096-1523.32.6.1465

Green, C. S., Pouget, A., & Bavelier, D. (2010). Improved probabilistic inference as a general learning mechanism with action video games. *Current Biology : CB, 20*, 1573–1579. doi:10.1016/j.cub.2010.07.040

Gross, M. (1985). Design as exploring constraints. (Unpublished doctoral dissertation). Massachussetts Institute of Technology, Cambridge, MA.

Honey, M., & Hilton, M. (Eds.). (2011). *Learning science through computer games and simulations*. Washington, DC: National Academies Press.

iCivics Annual Report 2011. (2012). Retrieved from http://static.icivics.org/sites/default/files/iCivicsFY2011AnnualReport.pdf

Indiana University Bloomington. (2008). Certificate in game studies. Retrieved from http://www.indiana.edu/~telecom/undergraduate/certificate_game.shtml

Jameson, E., Trevena, J., & Swain, N. (2011). Electronic gaming as pain distraction. *Pain Research & Management : The Journal of the Canadian Pain Society, 16*(1), 27–32.

Kafai, Y. B., Franke, M. L., Ching, C. C., & Shih, J. C. (1998). Game design as an interactive learning environment for fostering students' and teachers' mathematical inquiry. *International Journal of Computers for Mathematical Learning, 3*(2), 149–184.

Kawrykow, A., Roumanis, G., Kam, A., Kwak, D., Leung, C., Wu, C.,...Waldispuhl, J. (2012). Phylo: A citizen science approach for improving multiple sequence alignment. *PLoS ONE, 7*(3). doi:10.1371/journal.pone.0031362

Koster, R. (2005). How to prototype a game in under 7 days. Retrieved from http://www.raphkoster.com/2005/11/01/how-to-prototype-a-game-in-under-7-days/

Lepper, M., & Malone, T. (1987). Intrinsic motivation and instructional effectiveness in computer-based education. In *Aptitude, learning and instruction: Cognitive and affective process analysis* (Vol. 3) (pp. 255–286). Hilldale, NJ: Lawrence Erlbaum.

Malone, T. (1981). Toward a theory of intrinsically motivating instruction. *Cognitive Science*, 5(4), 333–369.

Maloney, J. H., Peppler, K., Kafai, Y., Resnick, M., & Rusk, N. (2008). Programming by choice: urban youth learning programming with scratch. *ACM SIGCSE Bulletin*, 40(1), 367–371.

Mane, A., & Donchin, A. (1989). The space fortress game. *Acta Psychologica*, 71, 17–22.

Mathews, J., & Holden, J. (2012). Place-based design for civic participation. In S. Dikkers, J. Martin, & B. Coulter (Eds.), Mobile media learning. (pp. 131–148). Berlin, Heidelberg, Germany: Springer-Verlag. Retrieved from http://dl.acm.org/citation.cfm?id=2331562.2331570

Mathiak, K., & Weber, R. (2006). Toward brain correlates of natural behavior: fMRI during violent video games. *Human Brain Mapping*, 27(12), 948–956. doi:10.1002/hbm.20234

Mayo, M. J. (2009). Video games: A route to large-scale STEM education. *Science*, 323(5910), 79–82.

Michigan State University. (2013). Games and Meaningful Play. Retrieved from http://serious-games.msu.edu/

Minority. (2013). *Papo & Yo*. Retrieved from http://www.weareminority.com/papo-yo/

Mislevy, R. J., Almond, R., & Lukas, J. (2006). *A brief introduction to evidence-centered design*. (Technical No. 632). Los Angeles, CA: The National Center for Research on Evaluation Standards and Student Testing.

Mislevy, R. J., & Riconscente, M. M. (2005). *Evidence-centered assessment design: Layers, structures, and terminology*. Menlo Park, CA: SRI International.

Mislevy, R. J., Steinberg, L. S., & Almond, R. G. (2003). Focus article: On the structure of educational assessments. *Measurement: Interdisciplinary Research & Perspective*, 1(1), 3–62. doi:10.1207/S15366359MEA0101_02

Molleindustria. (2006). *McDonalds Video Game*. Retrieved from http://www.molleindustria.org/

Moriarty, B. (2011, March 24). *An apology for Roger Ebert*. Presented at the Game Developer's Conference, San Francisco, CA. Retrieved from http://www.ludix.com/moriarty/apology.html

Moss, P. A., Pullin, D. C., Gee, J. P., Haertel, E. H., & Young, L. J. (Eds.). (2008). *Assessment, Equity, and Opportunity to Learn* (1st ed.). Cambridge University Press.

National Science Foundation. (2012). *Advancing informal STEM learning* (Program solicitation no. NSF 12–560). Washington, DC: National Science Foundation.

New York University. (2013). NYU Game Center. Retrieved from http://gamecenter.nyu.edu/

Rensselaer Polytechnic Institute (2013). Games and Simulations Arts and Sciences. Retrieved from http://www.hass.rpi.edu/pl/gaming

Rose, M. (2013). Here's what makes Ludum Dare so special. *Gamasutra*. Retrieved from http://www.gamasutra.com/view/news/191460/Heres_what_makes_Ludum_Dare_so_special.php

Seitz, D. (2012, October 2). After 11 million in sales, Minecraft heads to retail Retrieved from http://www.gametrailers.com/side-mission/31109/after-11-million-in-sales-minecraft-heads-to-retail

Shute, V. J. (2011). Stealth assessment in computer-based games to support learning. In S Tobias & J. D. Fletcher (Eds.), *Computer games and instruction*. Charlotte, NC: Information Age Publishers.

Solis, H., & Chopra, A. (2012). Equal pay app challenge. *The Office of Science and Technology Blog*. Retrieved from http://equalpay.challenge.gov/

Squire, K. (2004). Replaying history: Learning world history through playing Civilization III (Unpublished doctoral dissertation). Indiana University Bloomington, Bloomington, IN.

Squire, K. (2006). From content to context: Videogames as designed experience. *Educational Researcher*, 35(8), 19–29.

Squire, K., & Jan, M. (2007). Mad City Mystery: Developing scientific argumentation skills with a place-based augmented reality game on handheld computers. *Journal of Science Education and Technology, 16*(1), 5–29. doi:10.1007/s10956-006-9037-z

Steinkuehler, C., & Duncan, S. (2008). Scientific habits of mind in virtual worlds. *Journal of Science Education and Technology,* 17(6), 530–543. doi:10.1007/s10956-008-9120-8

Torres, R., & Wolozin, L. (2011). *Quest to learn: Developing the school for digital kids.* Cambridge, MA: MIT Press.

University of Washington (2013). Critical Gaming Project. Retrieved from https://depts.washington.edu/critgame/wordpress/

Van Eck, R. (2006). Digital game-based learning: It's not just the digital natives who are restless. *Educause Review, 41*(2), 16–30.

Wertsch, J. V. (1998). *Mind as action.* New York, NY: Oxford University Press.

12

Formative Research for Game Design

JAMES BACHHUBER

Introduction

Educational game designers fight an uphill battle: creating games that encourage students to build new knowledge, as opposed to rehearsing skills they have already mastered, is a daunting challenge. Many students find admitting confusion, or trying and failing at new challenges in an academic context, to be risky and unrewarding (Ames & Archer, 1988; Van Eck, 2006). For these students, attempting an unfamiliar educational game can be totally unappealing. When approaching this challenge, educational game developers often fall into one of two camps. Designers from the commercial world tend to craft their games from hunches and insights gained from personal experience, while academics build their games around accepted psychological or pedagogical theories.

Each approach has its merits but, too often, each approach falls short, producing either entertaining but thinly educational games, or pedagogically sound but dull ones. By focusing on the skills that struggling students need to develop, rather than the skills they have now, educational games can alienate the very population for whom they are designed (Ames & Archer, 1988; Tüzün, 2007). Designing a game for the specific skills and mental habits of struggling students is an incredibly challenging task. This is true in part because little research exists with regard to how children approach academic tasks they do not yet understand, or how they attempt to reason about material they have not yet been taught. This gap in the research presents an opportunity for developmental and educational psychologists to collaborate with game designers and greatly improve the quality of educational games, similar to the very successful process that occurred in the development of educational programming for the Children's Television Workshop (which produced *Sesame Street*; Fisch & Bernstein, 2000).

During our development work at the Center for Children and Technology (CCT), we have found formative research to be an invaluable tool because it allows us to gain insight into how our target audience perceives and responds to learning goals they have not yet achieved. These insights allow us to create designs that meet students where they are and engage them in game play that helps them build new knowledge. By discussing concrete examples from the design process of one of our projects, this chapter is intended to acquaint readers with the practices and benefits of this practical methodology.

What Is Formative Research?

During the game development process, certain design questions have no clear answers. Current psychological theories could support a number of options, and thus without further research these theories have limited predictive power with regard to whether specific design choices will be effective. Formative research is a way to resolve these issues by using appropriate stimuli to probe how children make sense of specific tasks or media (Fisch & Bernstein, 2000).

This type of work is not meant to expand what is known about how students in general understand a given topic or about assessing the knowledge of any specific child. Instead, research participants are viewed as members of a particular subgroup, and psychological theory provides theoretical models against which student responses can be checked. For this reason, research participants must be from the same age group as the one for whom the game is designed. Methodologically similar to clinical interviewing as practiced by Piaget (1929) and more recently by Ginsburg (1997) and others, formative research is fruitful when interviewees feel comfortable speaking honestly without concern for the accuracy of their answers. This situation, however, may generate imprecise comments that the researcher then must clarify without judgment, while listening for issues that warrant further exploration. I have found this process to be very similar to that of interviewing sources for newspaper articles, and my background as a journalist has served me well here. Overall, when practiced well, formative research can be a reliable way of ensuring that the artifact being designed has the best chance to accomplish its purpose.

What the Formative Process Looks Like

Formative research can look slightly different, depending on whether it occurs before or after the creation of a prototype, though the process and goals are fundamentally the same in either instance. Before there is a prototype, evocative objects and activities are used to prompt a child's thinking about a specific topic, and we often create testing materials that don't resemble the eventual final product. Instead, the designed activity is meant to target student thinking about specific subject matter or concepts. Gaining insight into the student's thought process can eventually help us design better games.

Once preliminary testing has established the instructional design, a prototype of the educational media or its current iteration, is used to help designers understand whether it is eliciting the intended type of thinking. Here, existing theory has informed certain design choices but research is required to observe whether children make sense of it as expected, or how the media provokes unintended thinking and what that thinking is.

While formative research does not replace the experience and intuition of designers, it provides useful guidance and constraints. As long as the interviewer has a clear idea of the information he is seeking, and the ability to improvise while staying true to a disciplined methodology, this research can be done with minimal preparation, relying on only small groups of children. Formative research can be planned and implemented within a day or two, answering design questions as they arise, to advance the development process.

Using Formative Research to Guide Game Development

In 2009, EDC | CCT received funding from the Bill & Melinda Gates Foundation for the Portable Wordplay project, a two-year research and development effort with two primary goals. First, the project explored the feasibility of designing instructionally rich digital games that could engage seventh graders in sustained, playful literacy practices relevant to improving their reading comprehension skills. Second, the project was designed to demonstrate that digital reading comprehension games could be integrated with regular classroom instruction in ways that were both logistically manageable for teachers and beneficial to student learning.

The project was intended to respond to the academic needs of students who have basic decoding skills, but lack adequate fluency and comprehension strategies needed to negotiate the more complex texts required of them during middle school. We refer to this subset of struggling readers as struggling comprehenders. A lack of vocabulary knowledge can compound reading comprehension challenges and may inhibit students from engaging with content that they are cognitively ready to handle. Thus, we decided that it would be valuable to make a game focused on vocabulary skills that could improve comprehension.

We also kept in mind that digital games offer a number of unique affordances that we have tried to leverage in our designs. Specifically, they offer unintimidating play spaces in which students can construct and evaluate new conceptual knowledge, adapt to changing rule sets, and experiment with unfamiliar ideas while pursuing motivating goals. In well-designed games, players pay close attention to the environment and their actions within that environment, looking for relationships between their actions and desired outcomes.

With these ideas in mind, we developed and field-tested two related Nintendo DSi games—*Code Invaders* and *Cipher Force*—with supporting materials to help teachers integrate the games with traditional literacy instruction. Based on observations from the field-test and teacher feedback, we translated the games into an asynchronous Web experience and tested them to better pursue our two principal project goals.

Research-Led Development

In spring 2010, we had established broad goals for the Portable Wordplay project and we soon decided to focus on multiple-meaning words. Four principles underlay our design decisions: (1) word play is beneficial to student literacy learning, and a game that motivates students to spend time with words can have positive effects beyond those measured in standardized tests; (2) students with basic, below-grade-level literacy skills may be capable of other complex challenges such as spatial puzzles or memorization, and so the game should capitalize on these challenges to be fun for a wide audience; (3) the game must not privilege skilled readers over struggling readers; and (4) the game need not teach vocabulary, but rather support a teacher's traditional classroom instruction.

We knew that when reading complex texts, students sometimes interpret the wrong definition of a multiple-meaning word, and without the metacognitive habit of monitoring comprehension while reading, they may not notice that they have lost track of a text's logic. A game that incorporated the strategies that strong readers use to disambiguate word meaning seemed like a useful tool for struggling comprehenders.

While we knew of the reading strategies that were taught to seventh graders, we found that the literature generally described what struggling readers should do when reading challenging texts, but offered very little guidance about what struggling readers actually do. This situation is precisely the challenge formative research can address to help bring together the perspectives of designers and academics. We needed to understand the thinking of struggling readers, in order to design a game that they would understand and to help them move toward a richer relationship with text, in which they would understand words not as static blocks of meaning but as flexible tools that serve communication.

STAGE 1: SPEAKERS AND MULTIPLE MEANINGS

One idea we initially considered was a game design involving communities of usage. We knew that in different fields, such as architecture or computer programming, the same words can have different meanings. New words are often brought into usage and used in unique ways to solve shortcomings of existing vocabulary.

When encountering an unknown word, considering the community of usage is one strategy for narrowing down a word's possible meanings. We thought that communities of usage could be a way to make the sometimes subtle differences between word meanings more concrete for students. Perhaps readers could better decipher the meaning of a word in context if we paired statements with images of the people who spoke those statements and who were obviously from different fields. Different looking speakers could create a salient cue signaling that students should consider alternate interpretations of a word in a sentence. To understand whether this was a reasonable approach, we first wanted to hear how students thought about what they knew about words, and how they discerned and interpreted word connotations.

Our initial formative testing activity involved pictures of different speakers, ambiguous phrases such as "I live on a higher plane..." and a number of potential phrases to finish the statement. Students were asked to match a photo of a speaker with the ending phrase that the student thought made the most sense for that speaker. For example, students were shown the phrase "I live on a higher plane..." with a picture of a meditating guru. They were asked to choose an appropriate ending to the sentence from phrases including "now that I have risen above concerns of the flesh," "up on that plateau in the mountains," and "enjoying luxuries I never knew existed." I designed the materials such that the six speakers and their quotes corresponded to six different usage categories of the phrase "higher plane," including status, spiritual, and literal. The different speakers in the exercise corresponded with different communities of usage that would use the phrase in different ways.

While we intended the sentences and images to fit together in a logical way, our interest was not whether the students would match the ending phrases with the speakers as we had. Instead, what was most interesting was their process: how they thought through the different possible meanings of *higher* and *plane*, and what their reasoning was for pairing the meaning of the sentences, as they understood them, with the photos of the speakers, as they understood them.

To conduct the research, I went to an unstructured afterschool program where students have free time to play on computers. I met individually with four students between the ages of 10 and 12, explaining to each that there were no right or wrong answers; I was simply interested in how they thought through the activity. I made efforts to ensure that the students felt that we were considering the activity together from a simple, inconsequential, and unhurried curiosity.

While working on this activity with students, I saw them interpret the content in a wide range of ways, but the processes by which they interpreted the activity shared many commonalities. Part of what I saw was that students were frequently unfamiliar with the speakers used in the exercise, and interpreted them very differently from how we, as developers, had imagined them. For example, one student thought a picture of a pilot was a picture of a bus driver. Thus, this speaker had no clear connection to any of the sentences. The speaker-as-scaffolding approach seemed to be of no help because we found that students interpreted the images of the speakers differently depending on their background knowledge.

Even when students did pair speakers and ending phrases as we had intended, I was not sure their interpretations of "higher plane" were the same as mine. It was entirely possible that a student had completed the activity as I had intended purely by chance, or by using a set of assumptions and decisions that were not the assumptions and decisions I had imagined when designing the activity. In these situations, asking nonjudgmental or nonevaluative questions like, "How do you know that?" or "How did you decide that?" were useful for uncovering how a student was approaching the problem.

Having seen students' efforts to interpret the speakers and sentences, I was interested to see how they would explain alternate pairings. I matched speakers and ending phrases as I understood them, and asked students what they thought "higher plane" might mean as I had arranged the materials. By doing so, they produced very creative, if convoluted, explanations of the sentence meanings. Rather than consider alternate connotations of "higher plane" to fit the speaker identity and ending phrase, they held onto their initial understanding of "higher plane" and bent the sentences to fit it.

For example, another sentence set I used involved the phrase "the draft was chilling." One student was familiar with the definition of draft referring to a breeze through a room, but not with the definition referring to an early piece of writing. I presented him with photos of a scared-looking man and an essay with copywriting marks, along with the sentences "The draft was chilling. I had nightmares from the scary details I read." When asked what the first sentence meant, he explained to me that someone became cold while reading a book in the winter. This situation underscored the need to listen to the students' explanations carefully and to ask thoughtful follow-up questions to best determine how they were understanding the task posed and how best to elicit information pertaining to how they were solving the task.

After asking students to explain their thinking during the exercise, I also asked more general questions about their knowledge of word meanings and what they did when encountering unknown words and phrases while reading. Most of the students I worked with said that they used context clues to determine meaning when they didn't know a word. This commonality seemed to warrant further exploration. I was not sure if students had simply been told so often by their teachers to "use context clues" that they thought that this was the answer I wanted to hear, or whether they did use the strategy, but their poor understanding of word meanings led them to misinterpret the surrounding phrases that could create context. During the "higher plane" activity, struggling readers did not seem to consider that words could have alternate meanings they did not know, and I thought this situation could impair their ability to effectively use context to understand unknown words.

STAGE 2: IMAGES AND MULTIPLE MEANINGS

For the next formative activity, we decided to stop pursuing speakers and communities of usage as scaffolding. Instead, we were interested to see whether images related to word definitions could help students discern the meaning of multiple-meaning words in an ambiguous phrase or sentence. We thought that by having students use image-based context clues instead of textual ones to interpret unknown words, we could better understand their thinking unhindered by their having to decode the words. Again, I returned to the community center after-school program where much of our testing took place.

To begin, we presented the word *complex* in isolation and asked students to talk about anything they knew about that word. Next, we showed the phrase "complex survey" and asked what they thought that phrase might mean. We added two pictures related to the phrase "complex survey"—a complicated-looking subway map and a survey with check boxes—and asked, "What do you think about 'complex survey' when you see these pictures?" After some discussion, we left the pictures in view, but replaced the phrase "complex survey" with "It was a complex survey. There were many parts and sections to fill out," and asked, "What do you think 'complex survey' means here?" Finally, we removed the pictures and sentences and repeated the process with "It was a complex survey. The department of housing wanted to see how many blocks the buildings covered" and pictures of a person surveying land and a building complex.

From this and a testing session that followed, we gained a number of insights and one key question that would determine the game's ultimate focus. Although students struggled to understand unknown words and were hesitant to express ideas about what an unknown word in context might mean, they had no reservations when looking at a picture that was unfamiliar to them and offering interpretations of it. Also, images ostensibly jarred the students, and made them question what they knew about a word, which was particularly exciting for us.

For example, one girl initially explained that complex means difficult, and that a survey is a group of questions. A complex survey, then, was a survey that was difficult to understand. When showed the sentence "It was a complex survey. There were many parts and sections to fill out," she readily explained that the survey was hard to complete because of all the questions. When shown the picture of the survey form and the many interconnected lines of the subway map, however, she was confused. The survey photo fit with her understanding of survey, but she could not connect her understanding of *complex* with the subway map. This confusion provided an opportunity to begin a conversation about the different definitions of *complex*, and how something complex can be hard to understand (as the student understood it to mean) but that this characterization was not synonymous with *complicated*. While the pictures did not provide sufficient scaffolding to help the student understand an unknown word, or unknown usage of a word in a context, the images were helpful in beginning a discussion about word meanings.

If struggling readers have a tendency to use inappropriate or insufficient word meanings that cause them to misinterpret sentences, a cue that makes them reconsider their interpretation of a word might be very useful. Although we had imagined that pictures might be a way to provide context to understand unknown word meanings, what we found was that perhaps the opposite would work better: new word meanings could help students understand confusing pictures and, in the process, come to better understand a word. Because we were designing the game to work in a blended model with traditional instruction, we reasoned that teachers could build on the work students did in the game and relate those interpretation skills to traditional use of in-text context clues.

During this same session of formative testing, we also conducted an activity in which a student saw three versions of a sentence containing a multiple-meaning word, each iteration having more detail than the one before. The first version of the sentence might be "I read a convoluted story," followed by "that I could barely understand" and finally, "because of all the strange plot twists." Each sentence was accompanied by three words, and I explained that one of them was the meaning of the unknown word (*convoluted*, in the prior example). One group of sentences used the word *excruciating*, and one of the options for its meaning was *mild*.

One student read the first sentence, and after reading the word *mild* confidently expressed that it was not the answer because he knew what that meant. When asked to explain, he paused for a moment and said, "I know mild chicken," and explained that mild chicken is close to spicy, but not spicy, so mild means "close to something but not it." He knew the word *mild* from the context of a fast food restaurant and developed his own quite reasonable and functional, though inaccurate, definition.

During instances like this, it was important for us as researchers to look without judging, a perspective that underlies all formative research. At the time, it was not important what the student thought the definition of *mild* was; it was important why he thought it and how he came to think it. After the student explained how he "knew mild chicken," my follow-up questions concerned how he came to know other words, and how, when encountering a word that was unfamiliar or only slightly familiar, he pieced together potential meanings for it. From the mild chicken conversation, and others, we realized that if never checked against dictionary definitions, misconceptions about a word also can be continually reinforced from repeated exposures.

After this round of testing, a key question about student thinking remained. We were still uncertain how students understood word definitions. It was unclear whether students thought of words as having distinct, sometimes unrelated, meanings that could be used in a variety of ways, or whether they thought of words as having "fuzzy" meanings that overlapped and could be used in virtually limitless ways. Continued testing focused on resolving this question.

Building on Formative Feedback

In the two months that followed our initial testing sessions, we tried a range of materials and activities to help us better grasp how students understood word meanings. We came to label the types of word knowledge we were seeing with the very sophisticated terms "mush ball" and "rough hewn." In the first case, the student had likely encountered a number of a word's meanings and was not differentiating among them. A word could have a number of meanings, possibly even contradictory ones, that were all rolled together. This was especially true of words with subtle distinctions, such as *set*. In contrast, a rough-hewn understanding was similar to the dictionary definition of a word, but still quite vague. This type of understanding is more reflective of the student who explained that the word *complex* means "hard" or "difficult." While in many common usages complexity can imply difficulty ("a complex problem"), difficulty is only one part of one definition of *complex*.

From the beginning of the project, we had intended to address vocabulary concepts more than specific vocabulary words, and our formative work seemed to bear out the utility of this approach. Misconceptions about word definitions appeared to be pervasive among struggling readers, and acted as real barriers to literacy proficiency. The months of testing also helped us resolve a question about which level of word understanding our game should prioritize. We had considered three options: language in any community at any register, e.g., a science classroom, a family dinner, the school playground; multiple communities within one register, e.g., different subjects at school; and, finally, just one community in one register, e.g., an English class.

Reflecting on what I saw during our research, our team decided to stop exploring communities of usage as a form of scaffolding because identifying a speaker and using that understanding to decipher a sentence required background knowledge that we could not rely on all students having. We also decided that different word connotations when words were used by different communities was too sophisticated a concept for struggling comprehenders. We had thought that students were more likely to understand a multiple-meaning word's different connotations by seeing it used in different situations than by learning its distinct, formal definitions. Instead, we learned that the differences between how different communities used a word are often subtle, and accurately interpreting them requires understanding the formal definition of a word.

Though different communities may use one of a word's definitions (for example, a band teacher and gym teacher are likely to use different definitions of the word *score*), the disambiguation technique we were investigating in our research did not seem worth including in our game. This realization freed us to focus on helping students better understand word meanings within one register, such as school. We also decided it was important for the game to encourage students to attend to the specific, distinct definitions of multiple-meaning words. One way to do this, we thought, would be for students to use images to communicate word definitions to each other.

From both the literature and our formative work, we understood that adolescents showed increased interest in peer relationships as they moved through the middle and high school years. We also were aware of adolescents' ability to understand the world in increasingly complex ways, to discern contradictions and inconsistencies, to consider alternate points of view, and to imagine the perspectives and thinking of other people (Eccles, Wigfield, & Byrne, 2003). It seemed likely that we could leverage these capabilities in our game design, encouraging players to consider word meaning through a social game with mechanics emphasizing clear communication. Using pictures instead of text to communicate would hopefully put struggling and confident readers on more equal footing.

After brainstorming game ideas, we created a paper prototype in which students alternated playing two roles. The "codemaster" was given a word with three definitions and tried to communicate one of the word's definitions using three images, called an image code. The "guesser" tried to interpret the image code to choose which definition from five possible words was being depicted. We used several early versions of this activity in our test with students.

From testing, we learned three things fairly quickly. First, this activity was kind of fun, and there was real potential to make an engaging game. Using pictures to communicate did help readers with varying proficiencies play together, and they liked trying to figure out each other's thinking. None of the images available to the codemaster depicted her definitions exactly, and often students initially found this situation frustrating. After a few rounds, however, they came to appreciate the opportunity this ambiguity provided for creative play. We felt encouraged to stick with the game's core mechanic of making and guessing codes, and to begin refining the game design.

Second, we saw that showing the codemaster all three definitions and having the guesser guess the word undermined the game's purpose. We wanted the activity to help the codemaster see the distinctions among a word's different definitions. In practice, however, codemasters would often make an image code referencing all three definitions, either picking one image for each definition instead of using three pictures for one meaning, or combining the definitions in their head and making a code for this new amalgam. When presented with the word *feature*, a student used one image that related to a distinctive attribute or aspect of something, one image that related to a newspaper or magazine article on a particular topic, and one for a full-length film.

Guessers also weren't attending to the specific definitions; instead, they were focusing on the words from which they were choosing. We adjusted the game so that the codemaster was shown only one definition, and the guesser had to choose among a minimum of three definitions for one word or a maximum of nine total definitions among three words.

Third, if the players felt that they were competing, they would try to trick each other by creating image codes that associated with the chosen definition only through extremely convoluted or idiosyncratic logic. This situation presented an interesting challenge: how to get students excited about cooperating, while keeping the motivation that they felt from competition. Throughout all our testing, we continued to see indications that our core activity worked pedagogically as we intended, but making it function as a game took a significant amount of research, revision, and work with our production partners.

After two field tests and a number of iterations, we now have a version of the game of which we are very proud. In the current version, play now occurs asynchronously at home instead of together during class. While the current version's gameplay is quite a bit different from our original game design, the dynamic of students making and guessing codes using images has remained, and has been refined to allow easier integration into traditional classrooms, play between students of different abilities, and player focus on understanding and communicating the distinct definitions of multiple-meaning words.

Now teachers also can customize a game for their class by choosing the vocabulary words students will be playing with how many words and definitions the players will be choosing from when they are guessing a teammate's code, and how many points the class is collectively trying to achieve. Once assigned a game, students go online and log into their account on the game site. They then enter the game created by their teacher, and choose from a library of photos to create image codes for different word definitions. Each code consists of three pictures, and can include custom images the students make using geometric shapes. Players also can alter the pictures they choose, using arrows and cropping to draw attention to or away from elements of the picture.

The following night, players log in again and try to guess the image codes created by their classmates. Teachers can view all the students' codes and reference them later while facilitating conversations about a variety of literacy topics.

Future Steps

The field tests that have helped us improve our game design and implementation model also have provided opportunities for us to check whether core features of the game that we focused on in formative testing are in evidence when kids are playing the games alone. As noted earlier in this chapter, three of our four design principles were that (1) word play can help students improve their literacy skills and, therefore, (2) we should make a game that is challenging and fun for students (3) without privileging literacy skills. Having seen students of different reading abilities play together well, we are optimistic that *Cipher Force* is holding true to those principles. We have heard from teachers that students who normally do not participate much in their classes have been eager to contribute, and even take on mentor roles with students less familiar with gaming conventions. We are excited to see that our games seem to encourage struggling readers to enjoy word games.

Our fourth design principle was to make a game that integrated well with current classroom practices and helped teachers. Moving the games from the Nintendo DSi to the Internet has helped with that, and we're now launching our games on the educational media aggregation site Edmodo. With the professional development videos we are offering with the games, we think they will be easier for teachers and students to use.

Conclusion

No matter how beautifully made or engaging an educational game may be, its value as a learning tool comes solely from how well the game's core activity maps to accepted academic practices or content. After playing the game, we can only expect players to remember what they did over and over, and therefore that action must clearly connect with specific learning goals. This is why teachers may be more amenable to trying traditional skill and drill games than to trying flashier learning games with less obvious connections to academic content.

With Portable Wordplay, we chose to create games that have value within a prolonged educational process. While players do not master the specific definitions of the words in our games after just a few rounds of play, they do become more familiar with the words, and this contributes to the iterative process of vocabulary learning. Through formative research and pilot testing, we are confident that both teachers and students understand how play in our games connects to work in the classroom.

As researchers such as Donna Alvermann (2002) have noted, students who perform below accepted norms on tasks related to academic texts often show considerable literacy proficiency when working with other types of texts. The problem is not always with the students and their abilities, but rather with how their abilities in specific areas are prioritized or invalidated. With formative researchers serving as advocates for student abilities, however, perhaps more educational projects can be designed to help students as they are, rather than as we would like them to be.

References

Alvermann, D. E. (2002). Effective literacy instruction for adolescents. *Journal of Literacy Research, 34*, 189–208.
Ames, C., & Archer, J. (1988). Achievement goals in the classroom: Students' learning strategies and motivation processes. *Journal of Educational Psychology, 80*(3), 260.

Eccles, J. S., Wigfield, A., & Byrnes, J. (2003). Cognitive development in adolescence. In R. Lerner, M. A. Easterbrooks, & J. Mistry (Eds.), *Handbook of psychology V*, 6th ed. (Vol. 6.) (pp. 325–350). Hoboken, NJ: Wiley & Sons, Inc.

Fisch, S. M., & Bernstein, L. (2000). Formative research revealed: Methodological and process issues in formative research. In S. Fisch & R. T. Truglio (Eds.), *"G" is for growing* (pp. 39–60). Mahwah, NJ: Lawrence Erlbaum Associates.

Ginsburg, H. P. (1997). *Entering the child's mind: The clinical interview in psychological research and practice.* New York, NY: Cambridge University Press.

Piaget, J. (1929). *The child's conception of the world.* New York, NY: Rowan & Littlefield.

Tüzün, H. (2007). Blending video games with learning: Issues and challenges with classroom implementations in the Turkish context. *British Journal of Educational Technology, 38,* 465–477.

Van Eck, R. V. (2006). Digital game–based learning. *Educause Review*, (March/April), 17–30.

13

Transfer of Learning from Video Game Play to the Classroom

DEBRA A. LIEBERMAN, ERICA BIELY,
CHAN L. THAI, AND SUSANA PEINADO

Introduction

Transfer, also called transfer of learning, occurs when prior knowledge and skills (transfer source) that were learned in one context, are applied to a new but somewhat similar task (transfer target) in a new context (Mayer & Wittrock, 1996; Perkins & Salomon, 1992; Salomon & Perkins, 1989). Essentially, transfer involves using existing knowledge and skills to learn, solve problems, or carry out a new task in a new situation. For example, people who speak Spanish could use their knowledge of that language to learn and speak another Romance language, such as Italian. People who play tennis could use their skills in that sport to learn and play another racquet sport, such as racquetball.

An extensive body of research has defined and examined (1) types of transfer; (2) conditions under which transfer is most likely to occur; (3) cognitive processes that are associated with successful transfer; and (4) methods of instructional design and teaching that can equip learners with the skills and inclinations to transfer their learning to new settings (see Barnett, this volume; Barnett & Ceci, 2002; Mayer, 1999; Mayer & Wittrock, 1996; Perkins & Salomon, 1987, 1992; Schunk, 2004). In this chapter we discuss the fourth area, methods of instructional design and teaching, and we particularly look at instructional design methods that might be used in video games potentially to motivate and support transfer from video game-based learning to academic performance at school. Scholars have identified several types of transfer, and we discuss a few here.

Near transfer happens when the transfer source and target are similar, such as the examples of using prior knowledge of Spanish to learn and speak Italian, and using prior skills in tennis to learn and play racquetball. In these cases, there is obvious overlap between the transfer source and transfer target, and the learning contexts are similar. Far transfer, however, is more difficult to achieve because the source and target do not clearly overlap and the original setting is highly dissimilar to the transfer setting. Explicit coaching and guidance may be necessary to enable far transfer to occur (Barnett & Ceci, 2002; Schunk, 2004). For example, using prior knowledge of tennis to learn how to play baseball instead of racquetball would involve far transfer because tennis and baseball are more dissimilar. People who transfer their tennis skills to baseball must identify basic sports skills and strategies they have learned in tennis that are in some less-obvious ways similar in both games, such as how to keep one's eye on the ball; how to swing effectively even though swing mechanics, equipment, playing fields, and rules are different in each game; how to move in tricky ways that can make the opponent inaccurately anticipate one's next move; and other skills the two games have in common that some individuals may discover on their own and others may recognize only when a coach points them out.

Low-road (or reflexive) transfer involves the use of well-established skills that are so ingrained that they are easily triggered and occur in an automatic way. High-road (or mindful) transfer involves abstracting prior knowledge and applying it to another context, consciously searching for associations between contexts that are hard to recognize. Both low-road and high-road transfer can work together even though their mechanisms are different (Mayer & Wittrock, 1996; Perkins & Salomon, 1992; Salomon & Perkins, 1989).

Positive transfer takes place when knowledge and skills acquired in the source context enhance learning and performance in the target context. Negative transfer occurs when prior learning in the source context hinders or delays learning and performance in the target context, or when prior knowledge is not applied appropriately (Cree & Macaulay, 2000).

There are other types of transfer, such as vertical, horizontal, literal, and figural (Ormrod, 2004; Schunk, 2004) although in many cases the definitions are not entirely distinct from each other and the terms are not always defined consistently. This situation has made it challenging to synthesize research on transfer or to identify trends because it is difficult or impossible to compare research findings when studies have defined and operationalized transfer in different ways (see Barnett & Ceci, 2002). Several taxonomies of transfer have been published (Barnett & Ceci, 2002; Butterfield, 1988; Detterman, 1993; Gagné, 1977; Reeves & Weisberg, 1994; Salomon & Perkins, 1989; Schunk, 2004; Singley & Anderson, 1989). Schunk (2004) notes that the taxonomies tend to focus on describing features of the various types of transfer but they often fail to define the process of transfer in each case or the optimal conditions needed for each type of transfer to occur. As a result, many transfer taxonomies offer an excessive number of labels without describing the underlying processes that would make a clear distinction between each type. However, we can extract from the research some general insights about conditions that foster transfer and align them with features of video games that could be used potentially to create those conditions.

Video Games as Learning Environments

Fundamentally, a video game is a rule-based activity that involves challenge to reach a goal and provides feedback on the player's progress toward the goal (see Lieberman, 2006, 2012). Video games can be played on a variety of technology platforms that enable different kinds of game play and player inputs. For example, mobile phone games appear on a small screen and are networked and mobile, whereas console games that use the Kinect motion-sensing camera-based interface are also networked but are played on a larger screen in a single stationary location. The interfaces, player inputs, displays, and portability of mobile phone games and Kinect games differ, and so different game challenges and game experiences are suitable for each platform. However, both technology platforms are capable of delivering, in their own ways, the rules, challenges, and feedback that are basic features of video games. In addition to mobile phones and video game consoles, other video game technology platforms include computers, tablets, handheld game devices, electronic toys, electronic learning systems, gym equipment games, 3-D virtual displays, and robots, to name a few. In video games played on any of these technology platforms, there are features, interfaces, and affordances that have the potential to support learning (see Bransford, Brown, & Cocking, 2000; Gee, 2009; Lieberman, 2006, 2009; Lieberman, Fisk, & Biely, 2009; Shute & Ke, 2012; Shute, Rieber, & Van Eck, 2011; Vogel, Vogel, Cannon-Bowers, Bowers, Muse, & Wright, 2006). Following are some examples.

Video games are usually highly interactive and they range from pure puzzle games to physically challenging active games to story-based dramatic adventure games, all of which provide immediate feedback on performance as they challenge players to solve compelling problems. Players apply their skills and learn from experience as they focus on achieving the game goal. In story-based games they are immersed in a dramatic, event-filled virtual world where they try to achieve goals and advance the story line by gathering information, making decisions, overcoming obstacles, solving puzzles or mysteries, and using new skills, often interacting with objects, systems, and other characters in simulated environments that support learning-by-doing. When networked, games enable players to access online sources of information or interact with other players or with the characters (avatars) that other players in distant locations are controlling.

Game challenges motivate learning because players want to develop the knowledge and skills needed to win, and so it is typical for players to rehearse essential game skills avidly and repeatedly until they have mastered them and won the game (Gee, 2009; Lieberman, 2006; Ritterfeld, Cody, & Vorderer, 2009; Vogel, Vogel, Cannon-Bowers, Bowers, Muse, & Wright, 2006). For example, games enable players to experiment, fail, and try again until they succeed, receiving help when needed (Gee, 2009; Lieberman 2013; Shaffer, Squire, Halverson, & Gee, 2005). Games are often designed to adapt to players' abilities, keeping the level of difficulty in a range that is highly challenging but not impossible for each individual. Players receive feedback on their progress and they are able to see how their choices have enhanced or hindered the desired outcome. In games that use rewards, players learn what is valued when their decisions and performance cause them to gain or lose points, status, access to resources, or access to new game levels. Players may also see role-model game characters who experience positive or negative consequences for their behaviors, which may cause players to learn through observation and vicarious experience, two of the learning processes featured in social cognitive theory (Bandura, 1997, 1986). Some games involve collaboration in player pairs or teams where players coach and support each other and serve in a teaching role, and some games require players to compete. In collaborative games there is motivation to contribute to the team and not let teammates down, while in competitive games there is motivation to prevail over an opponent or to surpass one's own personal best (Lieberman, 2012, 2013). Games foster learning and cognitive skill development in many other ways. For instance, players may need to use persistence, risk-taking, problem-solving, mindfulness, or attention to detail in order to win.

Following is a list of a few of the video game features that have the potential to motivate and support learning (see Bransford, Brown, & Cocking, 2000; Gee, 2003, 2009; Lieberman, 2006, 2009; Lieberman, Fisk, & Biely, 2009; Pillay, Brownlee, & Wilss, 1999; Pugh & Bergin, 2006; Ritterfeld, Cody, & Vorderer, 2009; Shaffer, Squire, Halverson, & Gee, 2005; Shute, Rieber, & Van Eck, 2011). These interrelated features are organized into the topic areas addressed in this chapter. Examples of advances in video game technology are also included.

LEARNING WITH VIDEO GAMES AND USING VIDEO GAMES TO TEACH TRANSFER

- Knowledge and skills are natural products of game play.
- Video games require interactive problem-solving.
- Active learning in video games is goal-oriented and set in a relevant context, with frameworks that enable experimentation.
- Player control over the choices and actions in a game can promote self-regulated learning.
- Video games can offer help, hints, coaching, and scaffolding to support learning.
- Video games can adapt to the player's changing abilities and can adjust the difficulty level in response to player success or failure, to keep the game highly challenging—at the uppermost boundary of the player's ability—so game play does not become too easy and boring or too difficult and frustrating.

- Visuals, sounds, and kinesthetic experiences can convey abstract concepts in multiple and juxtaposed modalities, such as images, graphs, animations, text, narration, music, sound effects, haptics (tactile feedback), and interactions with virtual characters.
- Role-modeling and observational learning can occur when players observe game characters enacting behaviors and experiencing desirable or undesirable outcomes.
- Self-modeling and observational/experiential learning can occur by seeing and experiencing one's own game character (avatar) in action and seeing the avatar experience desirable or undesirable outcomes for actions the player had chosen to do.
- Video games are highly interactive environments that support processes of experiential learning, learning-by-doing, constructivist learning, problem-based learning, and authentic problem-solving.
- Collaboration, teamwork, or competition in video game play can motivate players to work hard to master the learning challenges in a game.
- Scenario-based learning puts video game players in environments that resemble players' lives and provide rich feedback about players' choices.
- Epistemic learning puts players in the virtual environment of a professional practitioner so they can confront the problems and use the tools and resources the professional would use in a realistic simulation, such as in city planning or emergency medicine or scientific research.
- Game environments put players in interactive simulated worlds they could never visit themselves, such as worlds in the past or future, or that present extreme risks and dangers, or that are at the scale of molecules or galaxies, or that must slow down or speed up time to demonstrate processes that humans cannot ordinarily detect.
- Data from games can be sent to classroom learning management systems so teachers can track each student's progress and skills and so students can track their own progress.

MOTIVATION AND SELF-EFFICACY

- Video games provide rules, challenge to reach a goal, and progress feedback in an environment that can spark interest and involvement.
- Video game challenges are intriguing, compelling, and engaging. Some players will be motivated to learn in a game because the content and skills are inherently interesting to them, while other players will be motivated to learn the content and skills only because learning them is necessary to win the game.
- Video games often raise players' emotional engagement in the subject matter presented within the game.

- Video game–based stories engage players emotionally when they identify with characters and feel empathy for them, which can foster closer attention and greater depth of learning and attitude change.
- Game challenges require effort and persistence.
- In well-designed video games, players have control over the action and a sense of agency and power; player actions are consequential in the game and success can sustain interest and motivation.
- Opportunities to learn while playing a game, apply new skills, fail, and try again an unlimited number of times until successful can lead to improved self-efficacy (self-confidence) for carrying out the newly learned game skills in the player's daily life; self-efficacy increases the likelihood of transfer and behavior change.

MINDFULNESS, SELF-MONITORING, AND METACOGNITION

- Video game challenges require mindful processing of new content to apply it appropriately and successfully.
- Players must track more than one event at a time in a video game, remember details, and use many other cognitive skills for problem solving.
- Video games can coach players to self-monitor their thinking and learning, and their strategies for making decisions and solving problems.
- Video games can teach learners how to learn, and how to approach new learning tasks.
- Images and sounds in video games can help make abstract concepts more memorable and concrete, and they provide opportunities to rehearse transfer in a variety of target tasks and contexts.

ASSESSMENT AND FEEDBACK

- Video games are interactive and responsive to player input; the game state reflects all previous player inputs.
- Immediate performance feedback and cumulative ongoing feedback in video games provide constant assessment that players welcome. Players expect feedback, failure, and eventual success in video games.
- Video games provide unlimited chances to rehearse skills and receive interactive intelligent feedback based on many previous actions, not just the most recent action.
- Games can deliver dynamic assessment, where feedback is not an end-state but an opportunity to reflect on and learn from errors, receive specific and individualized help and coaching, and try again until successful.

ADVANCES IN GAME TECHNOLOGIES

- Active video games offer interfaces that require players to exert themselves or use balance, range of motion, or other motor skills.
- Data from sensors can be integrated into video game play, such as geo-location, heart rate, steps taken, vital signs, brain waves, body movements, and facial expressions that indicate emotional state.
- Information about each player can be gathered from sensors, game play performance, data sources outside the game environment, or the player's answers to questions, and can be used to tailor the game to meet the player's needs, abilities, interests, and intrinsic motivations.
- Beyond screen displays, video games can be delivered in the actions of a robot, in feedback from gym equipment, in signals emitted from electronic toys, and in events that occur in social networks online or in immersive 3-D virtual worlds seen via a headset display.

These examples of video game features give the instructional designer an array of tools and learning environments that can be used to teach concrete hands-on skills and abstract concepts, and to teach metacognitive processes to help students learn how to learn and also learn how to transfer their learning to new contexts.

Research investigating effects of video games on both learning and the transfer of learning is just emerging. Although many of the video game design ideas presented here are based on longstanding theory and research in the fields of instructional design, game design, and multimedia learning, the ideas must be implemented and tested in video games before we can know how poorly or well they support transfer of learning. Theory and research are useful and essential as a basis for designing video games for learning, but designing on a strong foundation of prior theory and research does not eliminate the need to investigate the effectiveness of new video game designs in iterative user testing during production and also in outcome studies after they have been produced.

Designing Video Games to Promote and Support Transfer

LEARNING FROM VIDEO GAME PLAY

It is no surprise that playing video games enhances the skills required for success in playing video games (Gee, 2003, 2009; Lieberman, 2006, 2013; Ritterfeld, Cody, & Vorderer, 2009; Shute, Rieber, & Van Eck, 2011). Studies of brain plasticity and video games have found that playing fast-paced action video games, for example, improves the cognitive and motor skills that help players win, such as learning to learn, spatial and temporal resolution of vision, visual short-term memory, spatial cognition, reaction time and speed-accuracy, selective attention, divided attention, sustained attention, and aspects of executive functioning (see review by Bavelier, Green, Pouget, & Schrater, 2012). Other studies have found substantial gains in knowledge about subject matter presented in well-designed video games (see reviews by Lieberman, 2006, 2009; Vogel, Vogel, Cannon-Bowers, Bowers, Muse, & Wright, 2006)).

Bavelier et al. (2012) found that playing action video games increased players' ability to extract patterns in the environment and players were able to transfer this skill to contexts outside of game play. Other studies have found transfer from video games to applied contexts. For example, flight school cadets who played a flight simulator game outperformed a no-game control group on actual flight performance, which indicated that skills learned in the video game may have transferred to flight performance, especially since the visual displays were not identical in the game and in the actual airplane (see review by Boot, Kramer, Simons, Fabiani, & Gratton, 2008).

TEACHING TRANSFER EXPLICITLY

We can take this automatically occurring transfer a step further and consider how to teach transfer by making the video game player more consciously aware of and involved in the process of learning how to transfer. For example, video games could provide information and lessons in one virtual context and then ask players to use the same skills in a variety of game-based virtual scenarios, to help them rehearse the process of transfer and learn that the set of skills they gained can be applied in various other contexts.

To increase the likelihood of transfer, Perkins and Salomon (1992) recommended deliberately teaching transfer through processes they called *hugging*, for near transfer, which involves using approximations of the original learning context so that learners can see the similarities, and *bridging*, for far transfer, which involves using abstraction to make connections between learning contexts that are not apparently very similar. Strategies for teaching hugging engage learners in tasks in a variety of contexts so that they can see how their source knowledge is applicable in a range of target tasks and environments. Bridging, by comparison, encourages learners to use mindfulness (such as paying close attention, thinking about how to apply new knowledge, consciously looking for common elements among learning contexts) and metacognition (in this case, thinking about how to learn and how to transfer) to search for possible similarities on a more abstract level. In both hugging and bridging, the material is taught in multiple contexts and students are led to see the connections between those contexts, either in concrete ways, with hugging, or in abstract ways, with bridging.

PROBLEM-SOLVING SKILLS

Transfer is important because learners will spend their lives confronting new problems. Thus, they will need the ability and propensity to draw on their existing knowledge and skills in a variety of new contexts. Video games are potentially rich environments for learning problem-solving skills and transfer because players are constantly challenged to tackle difficult problems. They control their learning as they experiment with various approaches to each problem and see the outcomes. Constructivism is a pedagogical approach that involves students in the construction of their own learning, which includes learning new concepts and procedures that can help them put their learning into practice. The goal is to give students applied opportunities to solve complex problems so they can become active, independent learners and problem solvers. Constructivist learning can include collaborative learning activities, interactive models of learning, educational games, and establishing a culture of inquiry and scholarship (Lujan & DiCarlo, 2006). All of these constructivist learning components can take place in video game–based learning. To enhance transfer, video games can prompt and guide transfer and can make transfer of problem-solving skills an explicit game goal.

MOTIVATION

Motivation to learn involves the learner's willingness to engage in learning, exert effort, and persist in learning tasks. Strong motivation can lead to deeper learning, which is important for transfer because students' depth of prior knowledge is a predictor of transfer (Perkins & Salomon, 1992; see Zusho, Anthony, Hashimoto, & Robertson, this volume). To motivate and foster in-depth learning, instructional designers could leverage the inherent appeal of video games. Good teachers introduce new lessons by motivating students and setting up expectations that the subject matter and skills to be taught will be interesting and worth learning. Video games could do this, too, and they often do this, by offering game challenges and story lines that make learning relevant, intensify interest, engage depth of processing, and increase participation (Gee, 2009; Lieberman, 2006; Lieberman & Linn, 1991; Shute & Ke, 2012). Emotion plays an important role in motivation. Research on the role of emotion in learning has found that it can capture attention and enhance memory (Baranowski, Buday, Thompson, & Baranowski, 2008; Pugh & Bergin, 2006). When coupled with appropriate instructional support, video games have the potential to engage, both cognitively and emotionally, even the most reluctant learners (Garris, Ahlers, & Driskell, 2002).

   A video game could be designed to motivate students to learn and it could also show them how the material could be applied usefully in a variety of venues—to prime students with the notion that what they are about to learn will be transferable and applicable in a variety of tasks and settings. A game that is engaging, fun, and emotionally involving, and that lets students experiment with the subject matter in various virtual settings, could potentially enhance their interest and engagement in classroom-based learning and also show them how their knowledge can be transferred to new tasks and environments in and outside the classroom.

SELF-EFFICACY

In addition to believing that the material in a lesson is worth learning and can be used in and transferred to various settings, students should also feel that they are capable of learning it (Pugh & Bergin, 2006). Video games offer experiences that are ideal for building skills and self-confidence because players have repeated and often unlimited chances to try things out, learn from failure, receive tailored coaching and support, and ultimately succeed. A game-based taste of success in the material to be presented later in the class-room could build self-confidence. Many studies of games designed for learning and behavior change have found improvements in players' self-efficacy, which is their level of self-confidence that they could successfully carry out a particu-lar task (Bandura, 1997; Brown et al., 1997; Lieberman, 2006, 2009). A video game designed to enhance students' motivation could also contain elements that boost their self-efficacy by including challenges that they can ultimately achieve. This way, students would arrive at school with the powerful combi-nation of having enthusiasm to learn, belief that their learning will be trans-ferable and useful in a variety of settings, and self-efficacy and confidence as learners.

MINDFULNESS AND SELF-MONITORING

To improve the chance that transfer will occur, learners should attend to relevant information; monitor their own level of comprehension; take action to improve comprehension when needed during learning; consolidate information into mean-ingful and organized concepts; and integrate this knowledge with prior knowl-edge drawn from long-term memory (Mayer, 1999). Ideally learners are conscious of their learning process and engaged in self-monitoring (Perkins & Salomon, 1992; Salomon & Globerson, 1987). When a video game guides the learner's cog-nitive processing and attention explicitly during game play, there is evidence that the learning that occurs in the video game will be more likely to transfer (Mayer, 1999, 2003). To increase these kinds of mindfulness and self-monitoring, Mayer and Johnson (2010) asked learners to do some self-explanation. Specifically, undergraduates were asked to play a video game about electrical circuits and some were asked to select a reason for their choices in the game. This process of self-explanation led to significantly greater improvements and accuracy in the transfer of knowledge from the video game to another context. Moreno and Mayer (2004) found that students retained more and performed better on problem-solving transfer tasks in game-based multimedia lessons if they had on-screen coaches who spoke to them in a personalized style. Collectively, these studies and others (see Mayer 1999, 2003; Mayer & Wittrock, 1996; Singley & Anderson, 1989) demonstrate how video games might be designed to foster the mindfulness, cognitive elaboration, and self-monitoring that could lead to deeper levels of knowledge as well as the inclination to transfer that knowledge outside the original learning setting. Research has shown that these orientations toward learning can be facilitated by prompting learners to engage in deeper cognitive processing, such as using self-explanation and using various forms of game-based coaching that encourage learners to reflect on their own knowledge and processes of learning and transfer while they are taking place.

METACOGNITION

Metacognition is another goal in the pedagogy of transfer. It occurs when learners are aware of what they know and do not know, can monitor their level of understanding, can assess their own readiness to learn, can see that there are multiple viewpoints and multiple ways of knowing about a topic, and have strategies for applying their knowledge appropriately (Bransford, Brown, & Cocking, 2000; Bransford & Schwartz, 2001; Huffaker & Calvert, 2003; Lieberman & Linn, 1991). Research has also found that metacognitive reflection on how one is thinking can promote the transfer of skills. In one early study, teaching children to monitor their own thinking processes led to more successful transfer; metacognition helped them recognize when and how to apply their knowledge in new settings (Belmont, Butterfield, & Ferretti, 1982). Teaching by analogy, such as using similes and metaphors to show how seemingly different situations actually have commonalities, has also improved learners' metacognition and transfer by widening their perspectives (Gick & Holyoak, 1980, 1983; Mayer & Wittrock, 1996; Perkins & Salomon, 1992; Reeves & Weisberg, 1994).

In video games, learners can be taught explicitly to be cognizant of their own thinking and learning processes, including being aware of useful strategies for transfer that involve metacognition. They could learn why their knowledge will be useful, where it could be applied, and how they could transfer it to new environments. Further, a game could provide examples of new environments and could challenge learners to practice their transfer skills in each environment presented in the game and also in the classroom and community. Thus, video games could put successful transfer in the spotlight and make it the game goal. Feedback in the game could assess players' transfer skills and provide explicit guidance to help them improve their transfer performance in the next set of game challenges. Salomon and Perkins (1992) note several conditions that lead to transfer, including thorough and diverse practice, explicit abstraction, active self-monitoring, mindfulness, and using metaphor or analogy. All of these conditions have the potential to be taught, rehearsed, and extended in video game-based learning.

As players' success at transfer improves, video games that teach transfer could wean them off of hints and prompts received during early stages of game play, so they can begin to prompt themselves. Another approach to teaching metacognition in video games aimed at enhancing transfer is to provide "what if" questions about problem-solving strategies and to ask players how they would solve a problem if it changed in certain ways, to give them practice at transfer and to help them see that their skills can be applied more broadly than they might have originally believed (Bransford & Schwartz, 2001; Shute & Ke, 2011).

ASSESSMENT AND FEEDBACK

A special advantage of video games as environments for learning the skills and orientations for transfer is the continuous assessment and feedback that video games provide. Feedback on progress is a key component of video games and players are constantly assessed on a wide range of skills and tasks. Game players expect and welcome ongoing assessment so they can adjust their strategies and learn from errors as they strive to reach the goals of the game (Collins & Halverson, 2009; Gee, 2009). Assessment and feedback are central to motivation (Garris, Ahlers, & Driskell, 2002), especially when there is high goal commitment and confidence in ultimate success, which well-designed games naturally inspire and enhance (Bransford & Schwartz, 2001; Lieberman, 2006; Shute & Ke, 2012; Shute, Rieber, & Van Eck, 2011). It is not surprising that some K-12 classrooms and university courses are beginning to use popular video game elements to structure the coursework, by engaging students in "quests" to learn multidisciplinary content with constructivist approaches to solving compelling problems, and by offering many forms of assessment and feedback that are not used as endpoints to learning and to establish a final grade but instead are used as opportunities to learn and improve (Sheldon, 2011).

Conclusion

This chapter presents features of video games that can potentially support learning and improve the transfer of learning from video games to classroom settings. Video game learning environments can be highly motivating and cognitively engaging, and can prepare students to come to class excited and ready to learn, while also feeling confident as learners. Research has found that video games can be designed to enhance the thinking, learning, and problem-solving skills that lead to transfer and they can teach transfer explicitly. They can also provide opportunities to practice transfer and can enhance skills and self-concepts associated with successful transfer, such as self-efficacy, mindfulness, and metacognition.

Advances in video game technologies are providing new interfaces and data sources that can enrich video game experiences. Sensors, data tracking, avatars, software agents, search engines, virtual worlds, augmented reality, intelligent social characters, big data, motion tracking, mobile technologies, nanotechnologies, health monitoring devices, social networks, recommender systems, and the networked world of everyday objects (the Internet of things) are just a few examples of the tools that can be used to develop creative innovations in the design of video games that can potentially motivate, support, and inspire transfer of learning.

To investigate video game-supported transfer, we need more randomized, controlled studies that test one potential transfer-enhancing component of video game design at a time, while keeping all other components equal (see Mayer, 2003). We also need field studies of video game use in homes, schools, and communities to discover how people normally play them in these everyday settings and to identify the types of learning and transfer that can be supported for various populations of learners. There is much more to learn about designing video games to enhance transfer of learning, and the ideas we have presented here are some promising places to begin.

Authors' Note

Support for this chapter was provided by the Robert Wood Johnson Foundation's Pioneer Portfolio through a grant from its national program, Health Games Research: Advancing Effectiveness of Interactive Games for Health.

References

Bandura, A. (1986). *Social foundations for thought and action: A social cognitive theory*. Englewood Cliffs, NJ: Prentice Hall.

Bandura, A. (1997). *Self-efficacy: The exercise of control*. New York, NY: W. H. Freeman and Company.

Baranowski, T., Buday, R., Thompson, D. I., & Baranowski, J. (2008). Playing for real: Video games and stories for health-related behavior change. *American Journal of Preventive Medicine*, 34(1), 74–82.

Barnett, S. M., & Ceci, S. J. (2002). When and where do we apply what we learn? A taxonomy for far transfer. *Psychological Bulletin*, 128, 612–637.

Bavelier, D., Green, S. C., Pouget, A., & Schrater, P. (2012). Brain plasticity through the life span: Learning to learn and action video games. *The Annual Review of Neuroscience*, 35, 391–416.

Belmont, J. M., Butterfield, E. C., & Ferretti, R. P. (1982). To secure transfer of training: Instruct self-management skills. In D. K. Detterman & R. J. Sternberg (Eds.), *How and how much can intelligence be increased?* (pp. 147–154). Norwood, NJ: Ablex.

Boot, W. R., Kramer, A. F., Simons, D. J., Fabiani, M., & Gratton, G. (2008). The effects of video game playing on attention, memory, and executive control. *Acta Psychologica*, 129, 387–398.

Bransford, J. D., Brown, A. L. & Cocking, R. R. (Eds.). (2000). *How people learn: Brain, mind, experience, and school*. Washington, D.C.: National Academy Press.

Bransford, J. D., & Schwartz, D. L. (2001). Rethinking transfer: A simple proposal with multiple implications. In A. Iran-Nejad & P. D. Pearson (Eds.), *Review of Research in Education*. (pp. 61–100). Washington, DC: American Educational Research Association (AERA).

Brown, S. J., Lieberman, D. A., Gemeny, B. A., Fan, Y. C., Wilson, D. M., & Pasta, D. J. (1997). Educational video game for juvenile diabetes: Results of a controlled trial. *Medical Informatics, 22*(1), 77–89.

Butterfield, E. C. (1988). On solving the problem of transfer. In M. M. Grunesberg, P. E. Morris, & R. N. Skyes (Eds.), *Practical aspects of memory* (Vol. 2, pp. 377–382). London, UK: Academic Press.

Collins, A., & Halverson, R. (2009). *Rethinking education in the age of technology*. New York, NY: Teachers College Press.

Cree, V., & Macaulay, C. (2000). *Transfer of learning in professional and vocational education*. London, UK: Routledge.

Detterman, D. K. (1993). The case for prosecution: Transfer as an epiphenomenon. In D. K. Detterman & R. J. Sternberg (Eds.), *Transfer on trial: Intelligence, cognition, and instruction* (pp. 39–67). Stamford, CT: Ablex Publishing Corp.

Gagné, R. M. (1977). *The conditions of learning*. New York, NY: Holt, Rinehart, and Winston.

Garris, R., Ahlers, R., Driskell, J. E. (2002). Games, motivation, and learning: A research and practice model. *Simulation and Gaming, 33*, 441–467.

Gee, J. P. (2003). *What digital games have to teach us about learning and literacy*. New York, NY: Palgrave Macmillan.

Gee, J. P. (2009). Deep learning properties of good digital games: How far can they go? In U. Ritterfeld, M. Cody, & P. Vorderer (Eds.), *Serious games: Mechanisms and effects* (pp. 65–80). New York, NY: Routledge.

Gick, M. L., & Holyoak, K. J. (1980). Analogical problem solving. *Cognitive Psychology, 12*, 306–365.

Gick, M. L., & Holyoak, K. J. (1983). Schema induction and analogical transfer. *Cognitive Psychology, 15*, 1–38.

Huffaker, D. A., & Calvert, S. L. (2003). The new science of learning: Active learning, metacognition, and transfer of knowledge in e-learning applications. *Journal of Educational Computing Research, 29*, 325–334.

Lieberman, D. A. (2006). What can we learn from playing interactive games? Chapter in P. Vorderer & J. Bryant (Eds.), *Playing video games: Motives, responses, and consequences* (pp. 379–397). Mahwah, NJ: Lawrence Erlbaum Associates.

Lieberman, D. A. (2009). Designing serious games for learning and health in informal and formal settings. In U. Ritterfeld, M. Cody, & P. Vorderer (Eds.), *Serious games: Mechanisms and effects* (pp. 117–130). New York, NY: Routledge.

Lieberman, D. A. (2012). Digital games for health behavior change: Research, design, and future directions. In S. M. Noar & N. G. Harrington (Eds.), *eHealth applications: Promising strategies for behavior change* (pp. 110–127). New York, NY: Routledge.

Lieberman, D. A. (2013). Designing digital games, social networks, and mobile technologies to motivate and support health behavior change. In R. E. Rice & C. K. Atkin (Eds.), *Public communication campaigns*, 4th ed. (pp. 273–287). Thousand Oaks, CA: Sage Publications.

Lieberman, D. A., Fisk, M. C., & Biely, E. (2009). Digital games for young children ages three to six: From research to design. *Computers in the Schools, 26*, 299–313.

Lieberman, D. A., & Linn, M. C. (1991). Learning to learn revisited: Computers and the development of self-directed learning skills. *Journal of Research on Computing in Education, 23*(3), 373–395.

Lujan, H. L., & DiCarlo, S. E. (2006). Too much teaching, not enough learning: What is the solution? *Advanced Physiology Education, 30*, 17–22.

Mayer, R. E. (1999). Multimedia aids to problem solving transfer. *International Journal of Educational Research, 31*, 611–623.

Mayer, R. E. (2003). The promise of multimedia learning: Using the same instructional design methods across different media. *Learning and Instruction, 13*, 125–139.

Mayer, R. E., & Johnson, C. I. (2010). Adding instructional features that promote learning in a game-like environment. *Journal of Educational Computing Research, 42*, 241–265.

Mayer, R. E., & Wittrock, M. C. (1996). Problem-solving transfer. In D. Berliner & R. Calfee (Eds.), *Handbook of educational psychology* (pp. 47–62). New York, NY: Simon & Schuster Macmillan.

Moreno, R., & Mayer, R. E. (2004). Personalized messages that promote science learning in virtual environments. *Journal of Educational Psychology, 96*, 165–173.

Ormrod, J. E. (2004). *Human learning* (4th ed.). Upper Saddle River, NJ: Pearson.

Perkins, D. N., & Salomon, G. (1987). Transfer and teaching thinking. In D. Perkins, J. Lochhead, & J. Bishop (Eds.), *Thinking: The second international conference* (pp. 285–303). Hillsdale, NJ: Erlbaum.

Perkins, D. N., & Salomon, G. (1992). Transfer of learning. In *International encyclopedia of education*, 2nd ed. Oxford, UK: Pergamon Press.

Pillay, H., Brownlee, J., & Wilss, L. (1999). Cognition and recreational computer games: Implications for educational technology. *Journal of Research on Computing in Education, 32*(1), 203–216.

Pugh, K. J., & Bergin, D. A. (2006). Motivational influences on transfer. *Educational Psychologist, 41*(3), 147–160.

Reeves, L. M., & Weisberg, R. W. (1994). The role of content and abstract information in analogical transfer. *Psychological Bulletin, 115*, 381–400.

Ritterfeld, U., Cody, M., & Vorderer, P. (Eds.) (2009). *Serious games: Mechanisms and effects.* New York, NY: Routledge.

Salomon, G., & Globerson, T. (1987). Skill may not be enough: The role of mindfulness in learning and transfer. *International Journal of Educational Research, 11*, 623–637.

Salomon, G., & Perkins, D. N. (1989). Rocky roads to transfer: Rethinking mechanisms of a neglected phenomenon. *Educational Psychologist, 24*(2), 113–142.

Schunk, D. (2004). *Learning theories: An educational perspective*, 4th ed. Upper Saddle River, NJ: Pearson.

Shaffer, D. W., Squire, K. A., Halverson, R., & Gee, J. P. (2005). Digital games and the future of learning. *Phi Delta Kappan, 87*(2), s104–111.

Sheldon, L. (2011). *The multiplayer classroom: Designing coursework as a game.* Independence, KY: Cengage Learning.

Shute, V. J., & Ke, F. (2012). Games, learning, and assessment. In D. Ifenthaler, D. Eseryel, & X. Ge (Eds.), *Assessment in game-based learning: Foundations, innovations, and perspectives* (pp. 43–58). New York, NY: Springer.

Shute, V. J., Rieber, L., & VanEck, R. (2011). Games…and…learning. In R. Reiser & J. Dempsey (Eds.), *Trends and issues in instructional design and technology* (3rd ed., pp. 321–332). Upper Saddle River, NJ: Pearson Education.

Singley, M. K., & Anderson, J. R. (1989). *The transfer of cognitive skill.* Cambridge, MA: Harvard University Press.

Vogel, J. F., Vogel, D. S., Cannon-Bowers, J., Bowers, C. A., Muse, K., & Wright, M. (2006). Computer gaming and interactive simulations for learning: A meta-analysis. *Journal of Educational Computing Research, 34*(3), 229–243.

Part Four

LEARNING IN PRACTICE: HOW SHOULD WE STUDY LEARNING IN VIDEO GAMES FOR TRANSFER TO ACADEMIC TASKS?

14

Cross-Platform Learning: How Do Children Learn from Multiple Media?

SHALOM M. FISCH, RICHARD LESH, ELIZABETH MOTOKI,
SANDRA CRESPO, AND VINCENT MELFI

Numerous research studies have demonstrated that children learn from watching well-designed educational television programs. Viewing of educational television has been found to contribute to children's knowledge, skills, and attitudes regarding subjects such as literacy, mathematics, and science. Other studies have found significant learning from interactive games as well. (For a review of some of this research, see Fisch, 2009.)

Often, however, producers do not create "just" a television series or "just" an interactive game. Amid industry buzzwords such as "multiple platforms" and "transmedia," it is increasingly common for projects to span several media platforms, so that, for example, an educational television series might be accompanied by a related website, hands-on outreach materials, or even a museum exhibit or live show. From an educational standpoint, producers and funders assume this combination of media yields added benefits for children's learning, beyond those that might be provided by one medium alone.

Indeed, educational theory suggests that there might be some basis for this assumption. In particular, consider the theoretical and empirical literature regarding transfer of learning—that is, students' ability to apply concepts or skills acquired in one context to a new problem or context. Several researchers have proposed that transfer can be elicited through varied practice (i.e., providing learners with multiple examples of the same concept or repeated practice of a skill in multiple contexts). Varied practice helps learners create a generalized mental representation of the material that is less context-dependent, and more easily applied to new tasks and situations (e.g., Gick & Holyoak, 1983; Salomon & Perkins, 1989; Singley & Anderson, 1989). Thus, if a child encounters multiple treatments of similar educational content (e.g., a particular mathematical concept) in multiple contexts across different media platforms, the result could be a better grasp of the content, and a greater likelihood that the child will be able to apply the content in new problems.

Still, such arguments are only theoretical. Does learning via multiple media platforms produce added benefits? Past research has focused almost entirely on the impact of one media component, such as a television series or a computer game in isolation, not a group of components that span multiple platforms. The lack of research on learning from multiple media—what we shall refer to as cross-platform learning—leaves open a number of important questions: How do children use multiple media? How does learning from multiple media platforms compare to learning from a single medium? How can cross-platform educational media projects be designed to build on the strengths of each medium, so that the media components best complement and support each other?

To find out, we conducted a two-part study of cross-platform learning that included both a naturalistic study of children's use of related, multiple media platforms, and an experimental study to assess learning from combined use of these platforms. Materials for the study were taken from *Cyberchase*, a multiple-media project that promotes mathematical problem-solving and positive attitudes toward mathematics among 8- to 11-year-olds. Produced by Thirteen/WNET, the components of *Cyberchase* include an animated television series that airs daily in the PBS Kids Go! block, a website that offers interactive games and puzzles (www.pbskids.org/cyberchase), and a variety of hands-on games and activities that teachers or parents can use with children (See Figure 14.1). Other components include family activity books and a traveling *Cyberchase* museum exhibit, among other materials.

A total of 672 children in Michigan and Indiana participated in both the naturalistic and experimental phases of the research. All the children transitioned from third to fourth grade during the study and were fairly evenly divided by gender (52% girls, 48% boys), mathematics ability (31% high, 42% medium, 27% low), and whether mathematics was their favorite school subject before the study (43% yes, 57% no). Approximately 30% were minority children (17% African-American, 6% Latino, 4% Asian, 3% other).

Naturally, unique benefits of cross-platform learning can arise only if children use more than one of the available media platforms. With this in mind, the first phase of the research (the naturalistic phase) investigated children's spontaneous, everyday use of *Cyberchase* media. Specific questions of interest were whether children's use of *Cyberchase* use was primarily a one-shot experience or sustained over time, and whether use of *Cyberchase* spanned multiple media platforms, or was typically limited to one medium.

We tracked children's naturalistic use of *Cyberchase* via a weekly "*Cyberchase* journal." Over a period of three months (half in the spring and half in the fall), children used their journals to record the number of times they used the *Cyberchase* television series and/or website, the amount of time they spent, and

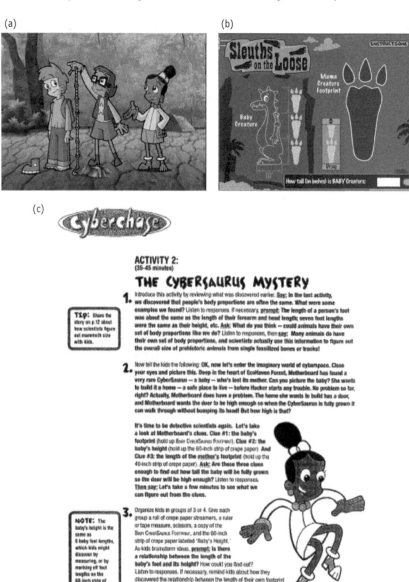

Figure 14.1 Proportional reasoning and "body math" (comparing the sizes of different parts of the body) are dealt with in: (a) the *Cyberchase* television series, (b) an interactive "Sleuths on the Loose" game on the *Cyberchase* Web site, and (c) a "Cybersaurus Mystery" hands-on activity. (Images © THIRTEEN. All rights reserved).

what (if anything) they did on the website. For comparison, we had them do the same for a highly popular, noneducational series, *SpongeBob Squarepants*.

After the naturalistic phase concluded, an experimental phase explored children's learning from *Cyberchase*, and how cross-platform learning compared to learning from a single medium. For eight weeks, children were divided into five groups:

- DVD Only: Each week, this group watched three half-hour episodes of *Cyberchase* in school (a total of 24 episodes).
- Web Only: Each week, this group played a new mathematical game on the *Cyberchase* website (a total of eight games), but were not shown the television series.
- DVD + Web: This group used all of the above video and online materials.
- All Materials: This group used all of the above materials, and also did one hands-on *Cyberchase* outreach activity per week (a total of eight hands-on activities).
- No Exposure: This group did not use any *Cyberchase* materials. Instead, they watched *Liberty's Kids*, a series about American history.

Before and after the eight weeks, we measured problem-solving via rich, meaningful problem-solving tasks similar to those used in mathematics education research (e.g., Lesh, Hoover, Hole, Kelly, & Post, 2000). Some of these were hands-on tasks, and others were pencil-and-paper tasks; every task focused on one of two broad mathematical topics, either measurement or organizing data. For example, in one hands-on task, children pretended to be detectives at a crime scene, and had to infer as much as they could about a thief from clues that indicated shoe size, arm span, and head size (by using proportional reasoning and "body math"). One pencil-and-paper task asked children to organize charts of data to find the most effective method to publicize a food drive.

In addition, we developed an innovative new approach to assessment: online tracking software automatically recorded every click children made while playing three games on the *Cyberchase* website. Detailed coding schemes enabled us to use these data to gain insight into the evolution of children's mathematical thinking over the course of each game (see Fisch, Lesh, Motoki, Crespo, & Melfi, 2011).

Highlights of Results

Because the research design employed multiple methods (with both naturalistic and experimental phases), hundreds of subjects, and multiple measures, a full explication of the results of the study would be prohibitively long. Thus, we present the major findings of the study here. Interested readers can find further details in the full report on the study (see Fisch, Lesh, Motoki, Crespo, & Melfi, 2010).

Use of Multiple Media

As noted earlier, the benefits of cross-platform learning can arise only if children choose to use multiple media platforms in the first place—and the results of the present study suggest they do. Data from the naturalistic phase indicated that children's use of *Cyberchase* was consistent over time and spanned multiple media; in almost every case, path analyses revealed significant relationships between use of *Cyberchase* from month to month, and between use of the *Cyberchase* television series and website ($p < .05$). Those children who chose to use *Cyberchase* typically did not engage in one-time use. Instead, they became "*Cyberchase* fans" whose interest in *Cyberchase* sustained itself over a period of several months and carried across television and the Web.

Certainly, we must be careful in generalizing from *Cyberchase* to children's use of other educational media projects. Every project is different and may be used differently. However, there are good reasons to believe that the patterns of use observed for *Cyberchase* may be typical of children's media use as a whole. First, although use of *SpongeBob Squarepants* was higher than *Cyberchase* overall (a finding consistent with Nielsen ratings), data from children's use of *SpongeBob Squarepants* during the naturalistic phase followed similar patterns to those found for *Cyberchase*; it was consistent from month to month, and significant relationships were found between use of the *SpongeBob Squarepants* television series and website. Second, other research on children's Web use (unrelated to *Cyberchase*) also supports the relationship between television and the Web. For example, approximately one-half of 2009's ten most popular children's websites were associated with television programs or characters (Kido'z, 2009).

Benefits for Learning

Effects on children's learning were approached in two ways. First, we evaluated learning from *Cyberchase* in general, by comparing growth among users of *Cyberchase* to the No Exposure (control) group. Second, we addressed the unique benefits of cross-platform learning by comparing growth among the groups that used various combinations of *Cyberchase* media.

Like past research (e.g., Clements, 2002; Fisch, 2003, 2004; Rockman Et Al., 2002), this study attests to the educational power of television and computer games to help children learn mathematics. Model-fitting analyses (primarily GLM) revealed that users of *Cyberchase* media demonstrated significantly greater gains in problems-solving performance than nonusers. Among the paper-and-pencil tasks, the organizing data task revealed that all of the *Cyberchase* groups produced more sophisticated solutions in the posttest while the control group declined, and the DVD Only and DVD + Web groups significantly outperformed the control

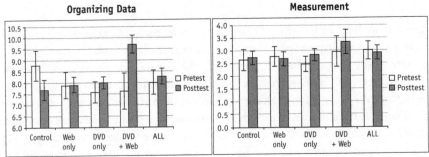

Figure 14.2 Pretest-posttest trends in the sophistication of children's solutions to pencil-and-paper problem-solving tasks.

group in the other posttest task as well (See Figure 14.2). In the measurement task, the DVD Only and DVD + Web groups both scored significantly higher than the No Exposure group in the posttest, and also improved significantly more than the All Materials group. The DVD Only group also improved marginally more than the Web Only group.

The hands-on tasks showed that learning from *Cyberchase* was not manifest in children's simply doing a greater number of things while working on the tasks, but rather in their using a greater variety of strategies and heuristics to solve the problems. From pretest to posttest, the DVD Only and DVD + Web groups both increased significantly more than the No Exposure group in the variety of problem-solving heuristics that they applied to organizing data tasks. Perhaps for this reason, the DVD Only group also improved significantly more than the No Exposure group in terms of the sophistication of the solutions they produced. Similarly, in the measurement/body mathematics task, the DVD + Web group was the only group that showed significant gains in the variety of heuristics they used and the sophistication of their solutions; the DVD Only and All Materials groups also produced marginally more sophisticated solutions than the No Exposure group in the posttest. (See Figures 14.3 and 14.4.)

Observations revealed that, while working on problem-solving tasks, *Cyberchase* users employed a wider variety of strategies and heuristics, applied them more effectively, worked well in groups, demonstrated persistence, and engaged in top-down planning. Indeed, approximately one-third of the children who used *Cyberchase* spontaneously mentioned *Cyberchase* explicitly (without any prompting from either researchers or classroom teachers) while working on one of the tasks.

Many of the effects in the pretest-posttest tasks appeared to be driven more by the *Cyberchase* television series than by the website. Perhaps this situation is to

Hands-on Tasks: Unique Heuristics

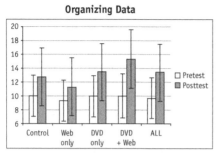

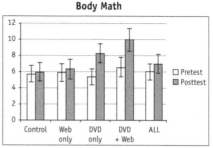

DVD + Web and DVD Only > other groups
($p < .01$ or greater)

Only DVD + Web group used significantly greater
variety of heuristics in posttest ($p < .05$)

Figure 14.3 Mean number of unique heuristics produced by each treatment group in the pretest and posttest.

be expected, since television is the central component of the *Cyberchase* project. Indeed, we found that the children in the present study spent more time with the television series than the website (because our experimental treatment was designed to simulate real-world use, in which the television series is used more often). Notably, the *Cyberchase* television series carries far more explanation of embedded mathematics concepts than the online games do. The story-based format of the *Cyberchase* television series also may have played a role, by presenting models of successful problem-solving in the context of compelling stories. As one of our participating teachers indicated, "I think kids remember things longer

Hand-on Tasks: Solution

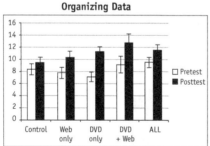

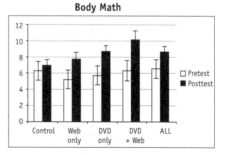

DVD Only and Web Only improved significantly
($p < .05$ or greater); marginal gain for All
Materials group ($p < .10$)

DVD + Web group improved
significantly ($p < .05$)
DVD + Web ($p < .05$), DVD Only ($p < .10$), and
All Materials ($p < .10$) outperformed No
Exposure in posttest

Figure 14.4 Mathematical sophistication of solutions produced by each treatment group in the pretest and posttest.

when they associate things with stories. They sometimes say, 'This is like when [the Cyberchase characters did something]'."

Because all of the materials in this study were taken from *Cyberchase*, the present data are not intended as evidence that television necessarily has greater educational potential than digital games. It is quite possible that another project, designed with online games as its centerpiece, might find stronger effects for its games than for its video component. Indeed, we also found that, in the course of playing a given *Cyberchase* online game, children often engaged in cycles of increasingly sophisticated mathematical reasoning, just as in classroom learning (see Fisch et al., 2011). Further, the present study was not intended to discover which medium was "best," but rather, to explore how different media might interact to yield cumulative effects, as we discuss below.

Cross-Platform Learning

As detailed above, gains in problem-solving were found more consistently among children who used multiple media. Many effects were stronger among the DVD + Web group than among either the DVD Only or (especially) the Web Only group, supporting the idea of greater benefits from cross-platform learning. Surprisingly, these benefits did not hold up as strongly for the All Materials group, although the All Materials group used all of the same materials plus hands-on classroom activities. We cannot be certain, but we believe that the less consistent performance of the All Materials group may have been influenced by the demands of their teachers' having to make time for so many *Cyberchase* materials within the demands of an already-full school schedule.

The benefits of cross-platform learning were even more apparent in our online tracking data. As Figures 14.5a and 14.5b indicate, children who used multiple media employed significantly more sophisticated strategies to play the three

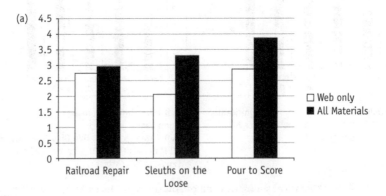

Figure 14.5a Strategy scores produced by Web Only and All Materials groups.

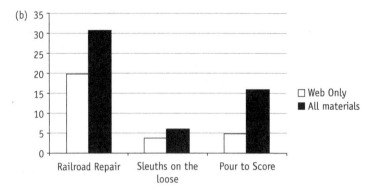

Figure 14.5b Correct Answers produced by Web Only and All Materials groups.

online games, and produced significantly more correct responses while playing two of the three games. It appears that children took the educational content they encountered in one medium (television and/or hands-on activities) and applied it while engaging with mathematics content in another medium (online games). This transfer of learning supported their interaction with the second medium, allowing children to apply more sophisticated approaches and producing a richer, more successful engagement with the games. We return to this point below.

Cross-Platform Learning and the Role of Transfer

Together, the above data point to two types of transfer of learning that can operate in cross-platform learning: (1) applying content acquired from educational media to yield greater performance in posttest assessment tasks and (2) applying content acquired from one form of educational media to produce richer engagement with a second educational media platform. The first type of transfer is not unique to cross-platform learning. It is often found in research on learning from a single media platform, where (for example) exposure to a television series results in significantly more sophisticated performance in novel posttest tasks (Fisch, 2004). However, the present data demonstrate that such transfer effects may be stronger when children are exposed to multiple treatments of educational content in related media platforms. In the present study, many pretest-posttest effects were stronger among the DVD + Web group than among either the DVD Only or the Web Only group.

Notably, contrary to our expectations, the same was not true of the All Materials group, which used all of the same materials as the DVD + Web group plus teacher-led hands-on materials. We cannot be certain why the All Materials group did not perform at the same level as the DVD + Web group, but we hypothesize that it may be because the All Materials group was the only one that used *Cyberchase* materials every day; perhaps this schedule was excessive in light of the other constraints on teachers' schedules, and was simply too much for participants to integrate effectively. Further research is necessary to determine whether an "optimal level" of media use exists. Nevertheless, data from the DVD + Web group suggest that cross-platform learning can hold added benefits for transfer of learning.

The second type of learning transfer—transfer from one educational medium to another—is unique to cross-platform learning. In the present study, online tracking data revealed that children who used multiple media employed more sophisticated strategies while playing three online games, and produced more correct responses while playing two of the three games. Just as in the posttest tasks, it appears that children took the educational content they encountered in one medium (television and/or hands-on activities) and applied it while engaging with mathematics content in another medium (online games). This transfer of learning supported their interaction with the second medium, allowing children to apply more sophisticated approaches and producing a richer, more successful engagement with the material.

How, then, did cross-platform learning contribute toward transfer of learning—and toward greater transfer to posttest tasks? One possible explanation is simply that children who used multiple *Cyberchase* media spent more time engaging with their embedded mathematics content. To some degree, this explanation is probably at least partially correct. Indeed, one of the chief purposes of informal education is precisely that—to encourage children to spend more time with educational content than they would otherwise. However, time clearly cannot explain the present findings by itself, because the benefits found for the DVD + Web group were not equaled by the All Materials group, which devoted even more time to *Cyberchase* activities. If time were the sole explanation, the gains shown by the All Materials group would have been at least as large as those of the DVD + Web group, if not larger.

A more promising explanation may lie in the concept of varied practice discussed in the educational research literature on transfer of learning (e.g., Gick & Holyoak, 1983; Salomon & Perkins, 1989; Singley & Anderson, 1989). As noted earlier, in varied practice, learners are provided with multiple examples of the same concept or repeated practice of a skill in multiple contexts, which increases the likelihood that the learner will apply the material in new tasks or situations. When children in the present study encountered mathematics and problem-solving content in multiple *Cyberchase* media, they were clearly engaged in varied practice, especially in those instances where there was close alignment among the content of a related television episode, hands-on activity, and online game. Effects within the online tracking data attest to children's connecting the content of the different media, and even applying the content learned from one medium while they were learning from the other. Not only did children gain additional, varied practice by using multiple media, but their engagement with the latter medium was richer and more sophisticated. In this way, cross-platform learning has the potential to support learning by contributing to two types of transfer: transfer across educational media platforms (resulting in richer engagement and understanding), and transfer from educational media to new problems or situations encountered subsequently (such as our posttest assessments).

Moreover, it is quite possible that transfer may even be facilitated by the presence of the same characters and contexts across media. Past research on transfer of learning has shown that transfer is more likely to occur when two situations appear similar on their face (surface structure similarity) than when they are dissimilar on their surface but rest on similar underlying principles (deep structure similarity; e.g., Bassok & Holyoak, 1993; Gentner & Forbus, 1991). Thus, for example, encountering *Cyberchase* characters in an online game might lead children to think of other times when they saw the same characters (e.g., on television). This situation could facilitate the transfer of information and skills from one medium to another, in a way that seeing different characters on television and in a game might not. (For an extended discussion of these issues that draws on data from several contemporaneous studies as well, see Fisch, 2013).

Implications for the Design of Educational Media

Apart from the contribution that this research makes to our understanding of children's learning from media, the data also hold practical implications for the design of future educational media projects. Perhaps the broadest moral for future multiple-media projects is that there are benefits to cross-platform learning, but "more media" may not always be better. Further research is needed to determine whether there may be an optimal level of educational media use—and, if so, what that level might be. In the meantime, the data also suggest ways in which media can be designed to maximize their educational power:

- *Explanation and scaffolding:* One reason that effects were often driven by the *Cyberchase* TV series may be that it presented explanations of the relevant mathematical concepts, and it used characters and narrative to model successful problem-solving. If so, this situation argues for the need for educational media (in any medium) to provide, not only opportunities for children to exercise their emerging skills, but also explanatory support and scaffolding when needed.
- *Narrative:* Researchers such as Schank and Abelson (1995) have theorized that narrative can serve as a powerful means for conveying information, and for organizing and storing information in memory. This view is consistent with our finding that effects were often strongest among children who viewed the *Cyberchase* television series, and that many children explicitly referred to *Cyberchase* stories and characters as they worked on problems. This is not to say, of course, that non-narrative formats (e.g., games, live demonstrations) cannot also convey educational content effectively. However, our findings are

a useful reminder of the power of narrative as an educational tool—even in subjects not typically associated with stories, such as mathematics.

- *Complementary media:* Conveying the same educational content in several different media opens opportunities for children to build connections among the concepts presented in these media. In *Cyberchase*, television supplies explanations of content and models of successful problem-solving, whereas interactive and hands-on media provide opportunities for children to exercise these skills themselves. The use of a common world and characters can encourage children to connect content from one medium to another. The appeal of children's experience in one medium also can enhance their motivation to engage with other educational media that employ the same characters.

- *Convergent media:* These points suggest intriguing possibilities for convergent media, in which the narrative and explanatory power of video, the participatory strength of interactive games, and the in-person support provided via hands-on media can be combined in a single experience. For example, consider an interactive game in which the "hint" button pulls up an explanatory video clip, or imagine a video with an embedded interactive game that allows the viewer to use mathematics to help the protagonist achieve her goal in the video.

In these ways, we can build on the lessons learned from past and current research, both to stimulate future research and—even more important—to build projects that will take even better advantage of the power of educational media to help children learn.

Authors' Note

This research was funded by a grant from the National Science Foundation (DRL-0723829). We gratefully acknowledge the support of the entire *Cyberchase* production team at Thirteen/WNET (especially Sandra Sheppard, Frances Nankin, Michael Templeton, Rekha Menon, and Cathy Cevoli), and online producers David Hirmes and Brian Lee for building the tracking software used here. We also thank the dozens of researchers who helped collect and analyze the data, our board of advisors, and—most of all—the staff, teachers, and students of the participating schools for their cooperation and patience throughout a long and intensive study. Without them, the research would have been impossible.

Note

1. A demographic mix was important, because research in mathematics education often finds that mathematics performance differs as a function of children's gender, ethnicity, mathematics ability, and interest (e.g., National Council of Teachers of Mathematics, 2000). In this study, however, none of these factors influenced children's learning from *Cyberchase*.

Boys and girls of different ethnicities and different levels of ability all benefited from using *Cyberchase*, suggesting that the series is successful in its mission to reach a diverse audience of children. As such, nonsignificant effects of gender and ethnicity are not reported here.

2. The amount of exposure to each *Cyberchase* medium was based on statistics regarding real-world use, as reflected in indicators such as Nielsen ratings and Web analytics.

References

Bassok, M., & Holyoak, K. J. (1993). Pragmatic knowledge and conceptual structure: Determinants of transfer across quantitative domains. In D. K. Detterman & R. J. Sternberg (Eds.), *Transfer on trial: Intelligence, cognition, and instruction* (pp. 68–98). Norwood, NJ: Ablex.

Clements, D. H. (2002). Computers in early childhood mathematics. *Contemporary Issues in Early Childhood, 3*, 160–181.

Fisch, S. M. (2003). *The impact of Cyberchase on children's mathematical problem solving: Cyberchase season 2 summative study.* Teaneck, NJ: MediaKidz Research & Consulting. Executive summary available online: http://www.pbs.org/parents/cyberchase/show/philosophy.html.

Fisch, S. M. (2004). *Children's learning from educational television: Sesame Street and beyond.* Mahwah, NJ: Lawrence Erlbaum Associates.

Fisch, S. M. (2009). Educational television and interactive media for children: Effects on academic knowledge, skills, and attitudes. In J. Bryant & M. B. Oliver (Eds.), *Media effects: Advances in theory and research* (3rd ed., pp. 402–435). New York, NY: Routledge.

Fisch, S. M. (2013). Cross-platform learning: On the nature of children's learning from multiple media platforms. *New Directions for Child and Adolescent Development, 139*, 59–70.

Fisch, S. M., Lesh, R., Motoki, E., Crespo, S., & Melfi, V. (2010). *Children's learning from multiple media in informal mathematics education.* Teaneck, NJ: MediaKidz Research & Consulting (with Indiana University/PRISM Learning and Michigan State University). Retrieved from http://www.pbs.org/parents/cyberchase/show/philosophy.html

Fisch, S. M., Lesh, R., Motoki, E., Crespo, S., & Melfi, V. (2011). Children's mathematical reasoning in online games: Can data mining reveal strategic thinking? *Child Development Perspectives, 5*, 88–92.

Gentner, D., & Forbus, K. D. (1991). MAC/FAC: A model of similarity-based retrieval. *Cognitive Science, 19*, 141–205.

Gick, M. L., & Holyoak, K. J. (1983). Schema induction and analogical transfer. *Cognitive Psychology, 15*, 1–38.

Kido'z. (2009). 10 most popular Websites for kids. Retrieved from http://kidoz.net/blog/10-most-popular-websites-for-kids/

Lesh, R. A., Hoover, M., Hole, B., Kelly, A., & Post, T. (2000). Principles for developing thought-revealing activities for students and teachers. In A. E. Kelly & R. A. Lesh (Eds.), *Handbook of research design in mathematics and science education* (pp. 591–646). Mahwah, NJ: Lawrence Erlbaum Associates.

National Council of Teachers of Mathematics. (2000). *Principles and standards for school mathematics.* Reston, VA: National Council of Teachers of Mathematics.

Rockman Et Al. (2002). *Evaluation of Cyberchase phase one pilot study: Vol. 1, executive summary.* San Francisco, CA: Rockman Et Al.

Salomon, G., & Perkins, D. N. (1989). Rocky roads to transfer: Rethinking mechanisms of a neglected phenomenon. *Educational Psychologist, 24*, 113–142.

Schank, R. C., & Abelson, R. P. (1995). Knowledge and memory: The real story. In R. S. Wyer (Ed.), Knowledge and memory: The real story (pp. 1–85). Hillsdale, NJ: Lawrence Erlbaum Associates.

Singley, M. K., & Anderson, J. R. (1989). *The transfer of cognitive skill.* Cambridge, MA: Harvard University Press.

15

Electronic Game Changers
for the Obesity Crisis

SANDRA L. CALVERT, BRADLEY J. BOND, AND AMANDA E. STAIANO

Introduction

Learning through game play has been recognized as an important and enduring way to teach by scholars as eminent as Plato. Children have always enjoyed and learned through game play, and technological advances have added electronic games to their recreational options. Attitudes by scholars and parents toward contemporary electronic games, however, have been mixed (e.g., Rideout & Hamel, 2006; Greenfield, 1993). A case in point is the role of electronic gaming in the obesity crisis, in which U.S. obesity rates have tripled over the past 30 years (McGinnis, Gootman & Kraak, 2006). On the one hand, gaming has generally been viewed as a negative factor in the childhood obesity epidemic, due to the plausible contribution of gaming to increased sedentary behaviors and poor eating habits (Vandewater & Cummings, 2008). On the other hand, gaming can also offer the potential for healthy weight outcomes (e.g., Calvert, Staiano & Bond, 2013).

In this chapter, we explore the negative and the positive effects of electronic games in relation to the childhood obesity crisis. We focus on the role of electronic games in terms of energy balance, the concept that calories consumed must be equal to the calories expended in order to maintain weight (Koplan, Liverman & Kraak, 2005). Time spent playing electronic games may, in fact, contribute to both sides of the energy balance equation.

We begin with a discussion of the properties of electronic gaming that enhance young players' motivations and interests, and then we focus on obesity as a specific topic of concern for gaming. Next we turn to the theories that describe and explain how game play can disrupt or improve child and adolescent health. We describe research investigating how healthy messages in games can be transferred from the virtual world to the actual world and then how electronic game play can result in energy expenditure. We end with conclusions about the skills learned during video game play and how those skills may transfer to academic settings, and we lay out recommendations for a future research agenda to explore this potential.

The Motivational Elements of Gaming

Malone (1981) argued that electronic games create an intrinsically interesting learning environment in which children become engaged in the activities that they are doing. Three motivational properties of play make electronic games important venues for learning: challenge, curiosity, and fantasy.

Challenge entails the goals of the game. To be challenging, a game should have a goal with an uncertain outcome. Uncertainty is created through variable levels of difficulty, multiple levels of goals, randomness that requires quick responses, and hidden information that must be strategically uncovered (Malone, 1981).

Curiosity involves exploration and investigation. Curiosity consists of two areas: sensory curiosity and cognitive curiosity. Sensory curiosity focuses on the attention-getting properties of the game, such as visual and audio special effects (e.g., bursting bombs and loud noises that accompany on-screen actions). Sensory curiosity is similar to Berlyne's (1960) concept of perceptual salience, which posits that environmental features such as movement, contrast, complexity, and surprise are likely to elicit the attention of young children. Cognitive curiosity involves an optimal level of informational complexity; that is, one that is neither too easy nor too difficult (Malone, 1981). In short, enough information must be given to make the game clear, but the game still has to involve an element of unpredictability to sustain interest over time.

Fantasy involves representation, evoking mental images of objects or social situations that are not actually present. According to Malone (1981), some fantasies are intrinsic to the game, where the skill relies on the fantasy and the fantasy relies on the skill. For example, playing darts in a video game uses the real-life skill of estimating distances to hit a target on-screen. Intrinsic fantasies help the player transfer knowledge acquired from prior game play to new situations. Fantasies also involve emotional dimensions that can help satisfy the needs of gamers such as achieving power, success, and fame that might be unattainable in real life (Malone & Lepper, 1987).

An additional motivational property of gaming involves the avatar, defined as the character that players choose to represent themselves in the gaming environment (Byrne et al., 2012). Avatars can become proxies for players' own identity: players become embedded in the game as the characters, using the avatars to represent their own actions. The ability to customize an avatar can affect both children's objective feelings of presence in a game and their levels of emotion during play, which may make learning from the gaming experience more likely (Bailey, Wise, & Bolls, 2009). Children can also interact with and relate to the other avatars that are present in the gaming environment. Interactions with other avatars could perhaps lead to the formation of parasocial relationships, in which children take other characters to be people and may treat them as such (Lauricella, Gola, & Calvert, 2011; Gola, Richards, Lauricella & Calvert, 2013), even when they are only computer-generated images.

In summary, to cultivate an engaging learning environment, electronic games must be complex but not too difficult, such that the player can eventually win. This requires the game to evoke fantasies that are appealing to the player and have varying levels of difficulty so that it can be played repeatedly without becoming boring. The outcome also needs to be somewhat surprising and unknown. Unlike redundant drill and practice activities, gaming can foster curiosity through challenging play embedded within a fantasy context. Avatars may increase the feeling of being present in these fantasy contexts. The motivational elements of gaming likely increase game play, which, in turn, may improve children's learning from the game (Calvert, 2004).

Theories to Describe Behavioral Changes and Information Transfer

Digital gaming may influence a player's weight by encouraging information transfer so that the player makes healthier choices related to energy intake and by promoting behavioral change that could influence energy expenditure both within and outside of the gaming environment. Social cognitive theory describes the activities that a player must engage in for behavioral change to occur through imitation of observed models (Bandura, 1986). The subprocesses of social cognitive theory that are needed for a child to translate observed behavior into his or her own behavioral repertoire involve a chain of events. More specifically, the child must (1) attend to the model's behavior; (2) retain the actions observed; (3) produce the observed behavior; and (4) be motivated to perform that activity in the future (Bandura, 1986). As an example related to game play, the *WiiFit* exergame employs a virtual fitness trainer that executes yoga poses as a model for the player. To imitate this behavior, the player (1) attends to the visual and auditory stimuli of the virtual trainer engaging in the yoga poses; (2) remembers the leg and arm placement required of the pose; (3) actually produces the pose; and (4) is motivated to continue performing this behavior to earn points in the game.

Modeled behavior that is learned is not necessarily executed. Self-efficacy, the belief that one can control one's actions in ways that produce desired outcomes, is a key aspect of success in executing these subprocesses (Bandura, 1986). Inhibition and response facilitation also influence the performance of the observed behaviors. Inhibition occurs when punishment of the model's behavior decreases the likelihood that the observer will perform that behavior. In response facilitation, observing a model's behavior reinforced increases the likelihood that similar kinds of behaviors will be performed by the observer (Bandura, 1986).

Another useful theory in understanding behavioral change is learning theory, which involves both classical and operant conditioning (Ferster & Skinner, 1957). Classical conditioning involves the "mere exposure" effect: that is, repeated exposure to content may lead to positive associations (i.e., feelings) about that content without a person's conscious knowledge of why he or she feels that way. Positive associations can thereby influence behavior. In operant conditioning, the consequences of behavior act as guides for future behavior: if an individual is reinforced for performing certain activities, that behavior is more likely to occur in the future.

For learning to be truly effective, it must extend beyond the immediate learning context; that is, there must be transfer in learning (Bransford, Brown, & Cocking, 1999). Conditions that improve the likelihood of information transfer from one context to others include knowledge of *when* learning can be transferred; the use of generalized principles when applying any learning to new contexts; conceptual knowledge that helps learners understand how a problem is similar and different from what has previously been learned; and awareness of oneself as a learner (Bransford et al., 1999).

Transfer of learning is important when considering how children learn from digital games. For example, if a child repeatedly plays a video game where the avatar is rewarded for consuming low-nutrient foods, that child may be more likely to transfer the positive association with low-nutrient foods in the game to the child's food choices in real life.

The Obesity Crisis: The Risks of Gaming

Pediatric obesity rates in the United States have skyrocketed in recent decades, portending less healthy and shorter lives for children than for their parents (Olshansky et al., 2005). Although children naturally gain weight as they reach their adult stature, many now gain excessive amounts of fat rather than lean muscle mass, which places them at elevated risk for serious health problems (Maffeis, 2000). Healthy weight maintenance involves a deceptively simple energy-balance formula that is in reality difficult to achieve: children must expend as many calories as they consume to maintain a constant weight. To lose weight, children must expend more calories than they consume, an even more difficult accomplishment.

Children's passion for playing electronic games has often been blamed for the obesity epidemic. In particular, the sedentary behavior involved in gaming can potentially lead to inadequate caloric expenditure, thereby leading to unhealthy weight gain (Vandewater & Cummings, 2008). Moreover, the content children see during gaming typically involves exposure to advertisements for foods and beverages that are high in calories and low in nutritional value, another risk factor for consuming increased quantities of these products, thereby leading to weight gain (Harris, Speers, Schwartz & Brownell, 2012).

According to a Kaiser Family Foundation study (Rideout, Foehr, & Roberts, 2010), 8- to 18-year-old youth are immersed in electronic media, including gaming experiences. Of the 7 hours and 38 minutes that youth spend with media each day, 1 hour and 13 minutes is spent playing video games. Presumably, time spent with electronic media could be spent pursuing more physically active pursuits that could lead to weight maintenance or even to weight loss. Data supporting the premise that playing videogames leads to increases in weight, however, are in short supply (see Vandewater & Cummings, 2008). That is, it is not at all clear that playing fewer electronic games would lead to more physically active pursuits.

Marketers heavily rely on media to sell products to children and adolescents. The products targeted to youth are often foods and beverages that are high in calories and low in nutrients (McGinnis et al., 2006). In a comprehensive review of the extant empirical literature, a team of scholars concluded that food and beverage marketing was causally linked to increased preferences, requests, and short-term consumption of the advertised foods, and was consistent with the prediction that consuming the advertised foods would lead to obesity (McGinnis et al., 2006). The data linking exposure to food advertising and obesity, however, was correlational, not causal, because researchers cannot ethically conduct studies that intentionally cause children to become overweight or obese.

While most of the empirical research involves television advertising, the marketing influences of newer media are now being examined as well. Advergames— video games designed to sell products (Calvert, 2008)—are one example. Advergames rely on stealth marketing in which the advertised foods are placed in the game and become associated with a fun experience (Calvert, 2008). For example, in the Boulder Coaster advergame sponsored by Post Foods, the player selects a branded Flintstones avatar to ride a roller coaster in order to virtually consume Fruity Pebbles cereal.

Moore (2008) conducted a content analysis of popular food websites sponsored by food manufacturers. Ninety-seven percent of the advergames found on food websites contained references to the brand. Unlike television advertisements, however, which provide limited periods of exposure, children can play advergames for an unlimited amount of time. The creation of "sticky" websites that keep children involved for long periods of time is a major goal of this marketing technique. Motivational incentives include options that allow children to control how challenging the advergame is with multiple levels of play, and players being allowed to track their own game progress. Most products that appear in online marketing at popular children's websites, including the advergames on these websites, are high in calories and low in nutrients (Alvy & Calvert, 2008).

Harris and colleagues (2012) found that more than 1.2 million children are exposed to food company websites each month, many of which feature advergames.

The foods marketed on these sites (e.g., sugared cereals, fast food, and candy) were low in nutritional value and high in calories. Only one website had advergames that promoted healthy foods (i.e., fruit). Children also played advergames from these food company websites. Those who played advergames that promoted unhealthy foods subsequently consumed those foods, whereas those who played advergames that promoted healthy foods subsequently consumed healthier foods. These findings implicate advergames as an effective approach for influencing children's consumption of healthy or unhealthy foods.

Gaming as a Tool to Combat the Obesity Crisis

Gaming could be a tool to combat the obesity crisis. On the energy intake side of the equation, media diets can include exposure to high-nutrient food advergames (Calvert, 2008) and mobile games (Byrne et al., 2012) as ways to foster children's interest, motivation, and consumption of healthy foods and beverages. On the energy expenditure side of the equation, exergames—video games that require gross motor movement—can increase energy expenditure and result in weight loss (Staiano & Calvert, 2011a; Staiano, Abraham, & Calvert, 2013).

Games for Healthy Eating

The literature investigating advergames as a way to combat obesity is limited at present. Therefore, we present one study in detail as an example of how this approach could work. Pempek and Calvert (2009) used a *Pac-Man* advergame to alter the food and drink choices and consumption patterns of children. Low-income third- and fourth-grade African American children individually played *Pac-Man* in one of three conditions. In one condition, children gained points for "eating" healthier foods like bananas and carrots and "drinking" a healthier beverage like orange juice. They lost points for "eating" less healthy foods like chips and candy bars, and for "drinking" a soda. In a second condition, children gained points for consuming the less healthy foods and beverages, and they lost points for consuming the healthier products. The game had two levels; children advanced from the simpler level with fewer foods and beverages to the more difficult level with more foods and beverages after accumulating enough points to win the first level. On average, children took about 10 minutes to play both levels of the game.

After game play ended, children selected a snack consisting of a banana or a bag of chips, and a bottle of orange juice or a soda. Those who played the healthier version of the *Pac-Man* game were more likely to select and consume the healthier products in a real setting, compared to those who played the less healthy version.

Thus, playing advergames can easily sway the children's preferences and snack consumption.

These results indicate that transfer effects from game play to the real world can occur even after a brief treatment. One reason for effective transfer may be that the game was played and the snack choices were made and then consumed in the same school environment, which indicates a close rather than a distal transfer effect. Persuading children to eat healthier snacks at home or during the lunch hour may be more challenging. In addition, even though there was a delay between playing the game and subsequent snack choices and consumption, the delay was a matter of minutes rather than days, weeks, or months. Future research should investigate if playing the game in multiple settings numerous times will maximize effective transfer.

Children also enjoyed the advergame. About 93% of the children reported that they really liked the game, and 7% said that they liked it. About 66% said that the game was the right level of difficulty, with about 17% saying that the game was too easy and another 17% saying that the game was too hard. We also discovered that more African American girls than African American boys visited food websites and played games there, making advergames an important approach for targeting African American girls (Pempek & Calvert, 2009), who are at particularly high risk for being overweight and obese (Ogden, Carroll, Curtin, Lamb & Flegal, 2010).

Overall, the design elements found in this very simple *Pac-Man* game were enjoyable for children and offered a valuable resource for them to learn healthy eating habits from gaming. The intrinsic value of the game, which is documented in the success of *Pac-Man* games overall, suggests that variable levels of game challenge coupled with an attractive character can create an effective pathway for food intake interventions with minority children. Future research is needed to disentangle the specific features of the *Pac-Man* game that make it such an engaging and effective approach for children.

Mobile games can also improve children's eating habits. For example, Byrne and colleagues (2012) investigated the role that virtual pets play in breakfast consumption. In their study, a sample of adolescents was given iPhones for nine days and some were told to play with a virtual pet app on the phone. Participants were told to take and send pictures of their breakfasts in one of three conditions: (1) they sent a photo of their breakfast to their pets, whose "responses" to the photo ranged from very positive (very happy expressions) to very negative (very sad expressions); (2) they sent a photo of their breakfast to their pets, whose "responses" to the photo ranged from very positive (very happy expressions) to neutral (neutral expressions); and (3) youth simply took pictures of their breakfast (control) and sent them to a generic email address rather than to a pet.

Adolescents who sent pictures of their breakfast to a virtual pet who gave them a full range of positive and negative feedback were significantly more likely to eat breakfast than those who only received the positive and neutral feedback or those in the control group. There were no treatment differences, however, in how healthy the breakfast foods consumed were.

Games for Energy Expenditure

A second way that electronic games can combat the obesity crisis is through energy expenditure. Exergames are a highly popular activity for youth; 61% of children in one survey reported playing exergames, just one year after the release of the highly popular Nintendo Wii console (Lenhart, 2008). Exergames require a player to engage in gross motor movement in order to control the on-screen avatar (Staiano & Calvert, 2011a). Playing exergames yields caloric expenditure in children that is comparable to moderate to vigorous levels of exercise and may be an alternative to traditional sports activities (Bailey & McInnis, 2011).

Social variables in the external environment play an important role in the efficacy of exergames as a tool to combat the obesity crisis. For instance, adolescents who played a tennis exergame on the Nintendo Wii against a peer expended more calories than adolescents who played the same game alone (Staiano & Calvert, 2011a). Cooperation with a peer is an even better way to improve energy expenditure. In particular, Staiano and colleagues (2013) conducted an intervention study in which overweight and obese youth played Nintendo Wii *EA Sports Active*, which involves a series of activity promoting games, over a six-month intervention period. Adolescents played the games in one of three conditions: a cooperative condition in which youth played with a peer as a team to expend the most calories on a daily basis; a competitive condition in which youth played against a peer to see who could expend the most calories individually on a daily basis; and a control group who went about their typical daily activities. When compared to their original baseline scores, youth who played together cooperatively as a team lost significantly more weight over the six-month intervention period than those who went about their daily routines. However, there was no difference between the competitive and the control conditions in terms of weight loss.

Because many exergames involve sports activities, exergames also have rich potential to teach or to reinforce movements that could then improve players' skills in actual sports activities. The potential for this positive transfer effect is probably dependent on how well the skill that is practiced in the game maps onto the behavior needed to play the real sport (i.e., its physical fidelity) and the extent to which accurate kinesthetic and tactual cues are provided (i.e., its functional fidelity; Fery & Ponserre, 2001). For instance, in Nintendo Wii *Sports*, the player hits forehands and backhands with similar swinging motions that lead to effective tennis play (unless, of course, the player uses shortcut, abbreviated motions). By contrast, the game sensor often loses track of the ball during the execution of an effective serving motion that is used in an actual game of tennis. This tracking problem can result in potential player frustration for those who really know how to serve, and also reinforce poor serving motions in order to win the exergame, thereby disrupting the learning and potential transfer of effective motions for a tennis serve.

Bowling is a game where the Nintendo Wii movements are similar to those needed for successful play in a real game of bowling. Dorrfub and colleagues (2008) examined transfer effects between Wii bowling and real bowling at an alley. One group of college students played Wii bowling; a control group did not. Then all participants went to a bowling alley and played an actual game. Those who had participated in Wii bowling performed better on actual bowling when compared to the control group. By contrast, very few transfer effects were found from real-world experience of real bowling to the world of Wii bowling, but the sample size was small (Peters, 2009).

Positive transfer to real-life activities has been found for putting golf balls during video games, though these were not exergames. Fery and Ponserre (2001) had young adult novice male golfers play a golf video game in which they controlled an animated character with a mouse. An analogue group learned how to execute putting by examining the virtual player's swing and remembering its timing and amplitude. A symbolic group could see a gauge that provided feedback about how hard they needed to swing the club to achieve the correct timing and amplitude. There was also a control group. All groups were pretested on putting skills on a real golf course green. Then the treatment groups played 10 golf video game sessions. After treatment, groups again putted on the golf course. Results revealed positive transfer from playing the video game to actual putting, but only for players in the symbolic group.

The results of this video game study are of interest, in part, because exergames can allow the player to gain the feel of putting by using a virtual golf club. Swings then make the golf ball go varying lengths, depending on how hard the ball is struck. Thus, getting the ball in the hole in the analogue group may improve when the "gauge" is integrated into game movements. This kind of study is one for future research.

Games that require little technical skill might be best for weight loss, as these games may appeal to a wide range of youth. For example, exergames that require dancing, such as *Dance Dance Revolution*, are relatively easy for players to imitate and are very popular. In one study, physical education teachers reported that participation in *Dance Dance Revolution* might increase their students' self-efficacy (Zhang & Linn, 2011). Thus, dance-based exergames may show considerable promise as a way to transfer electronic game movements to real-life settings.

Conclusions and Future Research Agenda

Although advergames, mobile games, and exergames can encourage more nutritious food and beverage consumption and greater energy expenditure by children, the extant literature is somewhat sparse at this time. In the advergame and mobile area, transfer effects have been found for eating foods that are consumed in the game or for engaging in activities that are reinforced by the virtual game characters. These interventions have been relatively short in duration. Longer exposure would provide more conclusive evidence, as would investigations of more general transfer outcomes on food and beverage consumption beyond the immediate game setting. Examining the role of the characters in the game is another fruitful research direction. For example, are children more likely to mimic eating behaviors of electronic game characters to whom they have high levels of attachment and close parasocial relationships than those to whom they have low levels of attachment and low levels of parasocial relationships?

In the exergame arena, transfer studies could examine how closely the gaming activities are to the real-life skills that they might facilitate, as there is potential for gaming to motivate children to play sports. Those efforts ideally would lead to positive experiences if the game cultivates the correct motions for success in real-life activities. Which electronic games lead to closer mapping of the skills that are needed to win real-life games? Do children learn to play sports better when the mapping is closer to the actual game movements? Advergames and exergames could also be integrated into school classrooms. Advergames, for instance, could be part of nutrition courses and exergames could be part of physical education courses (Staiano & Calvert, 2011b).

In conclusion, the obesity crisis is consuming children and adolescents. Possible solutions to this health-care problem may reside in an electronic world filled with games that are intrinsically interesting to youth. To the degree that we are successful in making electronic games a healthy and engaging experience for children, we may also be successful in curbing the obesity epidemic.

References

Alvy, E., & Calvert, S. L. (2008). Food marketing on popular children's websites: A content analysis. *Journal of the American Dietetic Association, 108*, 710–713.

Bailey, B. W., & McInnis, K. (2011). Energy cost of exergaming: A comparison of the energy cost of 6 forms of exergaming. *Archives of Pediatric & Adolescent Medicine, 165*, 597–602.

Bailey, R., Wise, K., & Bolls, P. (2009). How avatar customizability affects children's arousal and subjective presence during junk food-sponsored online video games. *Cyberpsychology & Behavior, 12*, 277–283.

Bandura, A. (1986). *Social foundations of thought and action: A social cognitive theory.* Englewood Cliffs, NJ: Prentice Hall.

Berlyne, D. E. (1960). *Conflict, arousal, and curiosity.* New York, NY: McGraw Hill.

Bransford, J., Brown, A., & Cocking, R. R. (1999). *How people learn: Brain, mind, experience, and school.* Washington, DC: National Academy Press.

Byrne, S., Gay, G. K., Pollak, J. P., Retelny, D., Gonzales, A. L., Lee, T., & Wansink, B. (2012). Caring for mobile phone based avatars can influence youth eating behaviors. *Journal of Children and Media, 6*, 83–89.

Calvert, S. L. (2004). Cognitive effects of video games. In J. Goldstein & J. Raessens (Eds.), *Handbook of computer game studies* (pp. 125–131). Cambridge, MA: MIT Press.

Calvert, S. L. (2008). Growing consumers: Media marketing and advertising. In J. Brooks-Gunn & E. Donahue, (Eds.) *The future of children: Children, media and technology*. Princeton, NJ: Princeton/Brookings.

Calvert S. L., Staiano, A. E., & Bond B. J. (2013). Electronic gaming and the obesity crisis. *New Directions for Child and Adolescent Development, 139*, 51–57.

Dorrfub, K., Bader, F., Wegener, R., Siemon, A., Schwake, J. U., Hofman, F., . . . Schmid, U. (2008). *Video games can improve performance in sports—an empirical study with Wii sports bowling*. Unpublished manuscript.

Ferster, C. B., & Skinner, B. F. (1957). *Schedules of reinforcement*. New York: Appleton-Century-Crofts.

Fery, Y., & Ponserre, S. (2001). Enhancing the control of force in putting by video game training. *Ergonomics, 44*, 1025–1037.

Gola, A. A., Richards, M., Lauricella, A., & Calvert, S. L. (2013). Building meaningful relationships between toddlers and media characters to teach early mathematical skills. *Media Psychology, 16*, 390–411. doi:10.1080/15213269.2013.783774

Greenfield, P. M. (1993). Representational competence in shared symbol systems. Electronic media from radio to games. In R. R. Cocking & K. A. Renninger (Eds.), *The development and meaning of psychological distance* (pp. 161–83). Hillsdale, NJ: Erlbaum.

Harris, J., Speers, S., Schwartz, M., & Brownell, K. (2012). Food company branded advergames on the Internet: Children's exposure and effects on snack consumption. *Journal of Children and the Media, 6*, 51–56.

Koplan, J., Liverman, C., & Kraak, V. (Eds.). (2005). *Preventing childhood obesity: Health in the balance*. Washington, DC: The National Academies Press.

Lauricella, A., Gola, A. A. H., & Calvert, S. L. (2011). Meaningful characters for toddlers learning from video. *Media Psychology, 14*, 216–232.

Lenhart, A. (2008). *Teens, video games, and civics*. Washington, DC: Pew Internet & American Life Project.

Maffeis, C. (2000). Aetiology of overweight and obesity in children and adolescents. *European Journal of Pediatrics, 159*, s35–s44.

Malone, T. W. (1981). Toward a theory of intrinsically motivating instruction. *Cognitive Science, 4*, 333–369.

Malone, T. W., & Lepper, M. R. (1987). Making learning fun: A taxonomy of intrinsic motivations for learning. In R. E. Snow & M. J. Farr (Eds.), *Aptitude learning and instruction: Conative and affective process analysis* (pp. 223–253). Hillsdale, NJ: Lawrence Erlbaum.

McGinnis, J. M., Gootman, J. A., & Kraak, V. I. (Eds.) (2006). *Food marketing to children and youth: Threat or opportunity?* Washington, DC: The National Academies Press.

Moore, E. S. (2008). Food marketing goes online: a content analysis of web sites for children. In H. Fizgerald & H. Mousouli (Eds.), *Obesity in childhood and adolescence: Volume 2: Understanding development and prevention* (pp. 93–110). Westport, CT: Praeger.

Ogden, C. L., Carroll, M. D., Curtin, L. R., Lamb, M. M., & Flegal, K. M. (2010). Prevalence of high body mass index in US children and adolescents, 2007–2008. *Journal of the American Medical Association, 303*, 242–249.

Olshansky, S. J., Passaro, D. J., Hershow, R. C., Layden, J., Carnes, B. A., Brody, J., . . . Ludwig, D. S. (2005). A potential decline in life expectancy in the United States in the 21st century. *The New England Journal of Medicine, 352*, 1138–1145.

Pempek, T., & Calvert, S. L. (2009). Use of advergames to promote consumption of nutritious foods and beverages by low-income African American children. *Archives of Pediatrics & Adolescent Medicine, 163*, 633–637.

Peters, K. A. (2009). Influence of real-world ten-pin bowling experience performance during first-time Nintendo Wii bowling practice. *Human-Computer Interaction, 5613*, 396–405.

Rideout, V., & Hamel, E. (2006). *The media family: Electronic media in the lives of infants, toddlers, and preschoolers*. Menlo Park: CA: Kaiser Family Foundation.

Rideout, V., Foehr, U., & Roberts, D. (2010). *Generation M2: Media in the lives of 8–18 year-olds*. Menlo Park, CA: The Henry J. Kaiser Family Foundation.

Staiano, A. E., & Calvert, S. L. (2011a). Wii tennis play for low-income African American adolescents' energy expenditure. *Cyberpsychology.* Retrieved from http://cyberpsychology.eu/
view.php?cisloclanku=2011060801&article=1

Staiano, A. E., & Calvert, S. L. (2011b). Exergames for physical education courses: Physical,
social, and cognitive benefits. *Child Development Perspectives, 5,* 93–98.

Staiano, A. E., Abraham, A. A., & Calvert, S. L. (2013). Adolescent exergame play for weight loss
and psychological improvement: A controlled physical activity intervention. *Obesity, 21*(3),
598–601.

Vandewater, E., & Cummings, H. (2008). Media use and childhood obesity. In S. L. Calvert &
B. J. Wilson (Eds.), *Handbook of children, media, and development* (pp. 355–380). Boston,
MA: Wiley-Blackwell.

Zhang, T., & Lin, L. (2011). Benefits and challenges of using Dance Revolution in teaching: physical education teachers' perspectives. In M. Koehler & P. Mishra (Eds.), *Proceedings of Society
for Information Technology & Teacher Education International Conference 2011* (pp. 2287–
2291). Chesapeake, VA: AACE.

16

Tug-of-War: Seeking Help while Playing an Educational Card Game

OSVALDO JIMÉNEZ, UGOCHI ACHOLONU, AND DYLAN ARENA

Many researchers have noted that video games are motivating (e.g., Bogost, 2007; Gee, 2003; Prensky, 2007; Reeves & Read, 2009). However, this characterization may not hold for educational video games. To date, few educational video games have empirical evidence to support their claims of effectiveness in supporting learning (Honey & Hilton, 2011; Barlett, Anderson, & Swing, 2009). Authors in this book have begun to fill this gap by demonstrating, for example, that video games can enhance visual cognitive abilities (Green & Bavelier, 2003) and persuade children to engage in healthier eating practices (Pempek & Calvert, 2009). Educational video games can also have positive effects on the classroom experience. In the ideal case, these positive effects go beyond engagement to actually support learning the material.

The goal of this chapter is threefold. The first goal is to discuss motivational aspects that we believe cause students to play educational games and learn the content featured. The second goal is to introduce *Tug-of-War*, a card game developed by the authors that has been shown to produce significant learning gains on traditional academic measures. Our third goal is to propose an initial way to measure motivation to learn: by discussing the type and amount of help students seek from others in the classroom while playing the game. For example, if a student looks for help with regard to how to solve a fractions problem in the game, that act of help-seeking demonstrates the student's motivation to learn about fractions. As part of our discussion of this final goal, we report on an initial study that found both more types and more instances of help-seeking in a card-game environment than in traditional classroom exercises, which provides initial evidence of students' desire to learn the material when playing an educational game.

Help-Seeking in Technical Environments

In less than four decades, video games have become a powerhouse medium for entertainment, with consumers spending almost as much on video games as they do on movies and TV shows (The NPD Group, 2013). Video games are an important part of children's lives. On average, boys spend 11.32 hours per week playing video games, while girls spend 5.6 hours per week (Rideout, Foehr, & Roberts, 2010). Children are clearly willing to play games: the trick is getting them to either learn material that is outside the game, or leave the game to learn. For example, the physics-puzzle game *Portal 2* is currently one of the most highly rated PC games of all time (CBS Interactive, n.d.; Metacritic, n.d.). How do we capitalize on this demonstrated appeal to inspire players to learn more about physics? Some commercial video games have had success in getting children and others to learn about the game by devoting time outside of the game in what Gee (2003) has called the game's affinity space. For example, researchers have noted the deep learning and research inquiry that occurs in online forums of popular massively multiplayer online games like *Lineage* and *World of Warcraft* (Steinkuehler & Duncan, 2008; Steinkuehler, 2006). The discussions that occur in these forums demonstrate that games can motivate players to have rich learning experiences about the game outside the context of playing the game.

Educational games have not had as much luck as commercial games in being viewed as positive models for education (Kirriemuir & McFarlane, 2004). There seem to be few instances of educational games that have been able to get students to switch, at the appropriate time, from playing the game to learning about material that is associated with it. For example, if students are playing a mathematics game and struggling with the mathematics content, does the software in some way help students switch out of the game to learn that necessary content before they move back to playing the game? This problem affects educational software beyond educational games, as with cognitive tutor software, which is at the forefront of educational technology. Cognitive-tutor researchers Aleven and Koedinger (2000) have bemoaned their users' lackadaisical efforts to access the help resources when solving problems. This lack of effort is troubling because seeking help is so vital to learning. According to these researchers, "Recognizing the need for help is a (metacognitive) skill in its own right. It requires that students monitor their own progress and understanding" (2000, p. 293). The fact that children who used Aleven and Koedinger's software did not seek certain types of help inside their technology ecosystem clearly represents a missed opportunity for students.

Usability experts have reached similar conclusions to Aleven and Koedinger (2000) about software and their in-help systems. For example, Hoekman (2010) wrote that users rarely use the help resources in any computer application. Other researchers provided even more depressing statements in their usability reports: "What we did not expect were the extreme lengths to which our test subjects would go to avoid using the Help menu" (Grayling, 1998, p. 170). In commercial games, avoiding help seems inconsequential if users can determine what they want to do. Since the goal is for users to have fun, it seems to be of less interest to commercial game designers whether players use their software as intended. However, in educational software in general and in educational games in particular, users must learn the software and the content associated with that software.

When people interact with new software, they often use trial-and-error to learn how to interact with it (Grayling, 1998). However, trial-and-error is not always the best strategy for children who have trouble learning difficult material. Children can become confused and stuck for a variety of reasons, but the opportunities for them to become confused are especially numerous in educational games, because they have to learn both the game's rules and the knowledge that the game is designed to teach. Outside of software, other researchers have also noted the disheartening link between low-achieving students and their reluctance to seek help (Newman & Goldin, 1990; Ryan, Gheen, & Midgley, 1998). For this reason, the educational games community needs to ensure that students feel comfortable seeking help. Regardless of whether educational game designers guide users to find help resources inside the game (e.g., via a built-in help module) or outside it (e.g., in forums or from other people), more needs to be done to support students in learning the curricular content of educational games. This support should extend to students' decisions to stop playing the game so they can search for help from available resources, to make a conscious decision in the game to learn the material, or to seek help.

Although there is not a large literature on help-seeking specifically in video games, there is literature on general help-seeking and learning, as well as about the help-seeking that occurs in interactive learning environments. In a widely cited review on help-seeking and learning, Nelson-Le Gall (1985) discusses how early research focused on the frequency with which people asked for help, with researchers hoping to relate that frequency to help-seekers' self-esteem and/or cultural norms. Rather than focusing on these frameworks, Nelson-Le Gall provides an alternative framework, by examining whether students sought help given their personal learning goals. Nelson-Le Gall highlights two types of learning goals: performance and mastery learning goals. Students labeled as having performance learning goals are motivated by receiving approval, comparing their ability to others' abilities, getting good grades, or other extrinsic goals (Aleven, Stahl, Schworm, Fischer, & Wallace, 2003). By contrast, students labeled as having mastery learning goals would complete a goal for the sake of mastering the content. This framework is important because multiple researchers have found that when students have performance learning goals, they avoid or are reluctant to seek help (Ryan & Pintrich, 1997). (See Zusho et al., this volume, for further discussion of mastery and performance goals.) One notable reason for students avoiding help is that they do not want to appear dumb to either their teachers or peers (Ryan et al., 1998). Performance-oriented students also have a greater tendency to simply seek the answer when asking for help (Arbreton, 1998), whereas mastery-oriented students want to learn the material. Thus, if seeking help would promote that learning, mastery-oriented students would be expected to seek hints that would allow them to learn and eventually master the material (Nelson-Le Gall, 1985; Newman, 1994).

In addition to general help-seeking, it is important to discuss help-seeking behaviors as they pertain to software. For example, Aleven et al. (2003) states that software environments have a different set of challenges when providing help to students: software programs may not have the resources to understand the help that a child might need, but they may be able to help children determine when they need help by providing them with clear feedback about their performance, which is a problem in collaborative situations (Aleven et al., 2003). Another difference is how the help is used. Because students do not have to worry about looking dumb for the computer, researchers have noted student's misuse of help systems as mere answer dispensers (Aleven et al., 2003; Wood & Wood, 1999); thus, two goals for software development are (1) to make sure that students understand when they need to use help; and (2) to encourage students to go beyond so-called "executive" help-seeking (Nelson-Le Gall, 1985), in which students just use the help system to get the answer.

One possible way of countering executive help-seeking and having students use a more adaptive type of help is by piquing students' interest. According to Aleven et al. (2003), "If it is possible to arouse interest in a domain, students may not only try harder to understand the domain, they might also try to use the help in a more adaptive way" (p. 299). Other researchers have also discussed the role that related factors such as affect (Newman, 1994) and attitude (Ryan & Pintrich, 1997) have had on ameliorating students' reluctance to seek help. This particular point is important for video games because games have a tendency to be associated with positive interest, affect, and attitudes, as indicated by the amount of time that children have spent playing such games (Rideout, Foehr, & Roberts, 2010). If we can create a positive experience in a game, that positivity can be a vehicle for students to seek help—and to seek it in ways that would be more productive than simply seeking the right answer. This is a strong benefit that educational video games can provide for learning.

To give this discussion a concrete footing, we will describe our game, *Tug-of-War*, which has been shown to produce learning gains in fourth-graders. We then turn our attention to insight gained form an initial study of one way to help motivate children to seek help when they need it.

Designing *Tug-of-War*

When we started our design of *Tug-of-War*, we agreed on three ideas. The first was that we were going to begin with a simple, physical, nondigital prototype (Rick, Francois, Fields, Fleck, Yuill, & Carr, 2010; Sefelin, Tscheligi, & Giller, 2003). Like the *Envisioning Machine*, which was a small program designed to help students understand velocity and acceleration (Roschelle, 1986), our simple yet functional prototype enabled us to refine game play without contending with the complexities of writing software. Second, we chose to support learning about fractions, because this content area is one of the most difficult concepts for children in elementary education (Petit, Laird, & Marsden, 2010); it is one of the first topics that cause children to avoid STEM careers (Nunes, 2006); and it requires extensive practice to build fluency, which we thought made it a great context for a game involving repeated opportunities to solve simple problems. Finally, to help ensure that the game was enjoyable, we wanted to build our game using an existing and popular style of game: the card game (Parlett, 1991). Specifically, our goal was to leverage the rules and game play of certain games like *Yu-Gi-Oh!* and *Pokemon*, which have been studied by educational researchers and found to be both entertaining and complex (Buckingham & Sefton-Green, 2003; Ito, 2005; Vasquez, 2003). Game play in this card genre involves marshaling "troops" and choosing cards from one's hand to attack an opponent's troops or defend one's own troops. In *Tug-of-War*, the "troops" are groups of teammates on either side of a tug-of-war line, and the "attacks" and "defenses" are pranks (e.g., Stink Bombs) or fibs (e.g., "I hear the ice cream truck!") and their countermeasures (e.g., air fresheners and radios).

Once we settled on the game genre, we embedded the curricular objective of learning how to take fractional operations of whole numbers within the game's narrative and mechanical structure. This technique, described by Malone (1981) as intrinsic fantasy, has been more fully explored by Habgood and colleagues (Habgood, Ainsworth, & Benford, 2005), who expressed it in terms of flow, core mechanics, and representations. The basic notion is that the game elements that are essential to learning should be incorporated into the narrative structure of game play, linked to the core mechanical operations players undertake in the game, and enacted using pedagogically sound representations to anchor thinking about the learning objectives.

Consistent with this notion, the cards for attack and defense in *Tug-of-War* (Stink Bombs, air fresheners) fit into the narrative of a playground tug-of-war. Mechanically, each card contains a rational number (represented as a fraction, decimal, partially filled meter, or ratio) that is applied to one of the whole-number teammate groups, weaving our two learning objectives seamlessly into the basic game mechanic. An example shows how the game represents fractional operations on whole numbers. Figure 16.1 shows a group of eight teammates (the Johnson

Figure 16.1 Examples of two types of cards, a Teammate Card (left) and a Trick Card (right).

Family), and an attack card (a Stink Bomb) with the value 3/4. If this attack card were to be placed on the Johnson Family, 3/4 of that set of teammates would no longer be able to play, leaving only two Johnson Family teammates available for the tug-of-war match.

To play the Stink Bomb on the Johnson Family, players would first decide how to split the Johnson Family into four equal groups (because four is the denominator of the Stink Bomb fraction); once those groups were formed, players would symbolically choose three of those groups (the numerator of the Stink Bomb fraction) to be scared away from the tug-of-war by the Stink Bomb. This process of forming and choosing subsets of whole-number quantities is our main representation for fractional operations on whole numbers in *Tug-of-War*. It is also part of the part-whole representation researchers have identified as a critical component missing in fractions knowledge among mid- to late-elementary-aged children (Confrey, Maloney, Nguyen, Mojica, & Myers, 2009; Kerslake, 1986; Petit et al., 2010). *Tug-of-War* uses the "set model" to discuss fractions by having students deal with fractions using a set of figures (Petit et al., 2010).

In addition to the pedagogical research literature, we leveraged several psychological findings to motivate players to play the card game. We gave players a limited set of choices to ensure they were not overwhelmed or unsatisfied (Iyengar

& Lepper, 2000) with their game play options. We also introduced a card that would initiate a chip-drawing mechanic (selecting a poker chip at random from an opaque bag), which has several benefits: it gives players the illusion of control (Langer, 1975) while also serving as a scapegoat for when players perform poorly (e.g., "We lost because we had bad luck with the chips"), which is an ego-protective step that builds on locus-of-control research (Weiner, 1985); and finally, the randomness introduces enough variability in game play to keep players who are behind in a game feeling as if they are still "in the running" (Strickland & Grote, 1967; Cote et al., 2003). We have found these features to be especially helpful for lower-performing students, possibly because they help those students avoid adopting a performance-oriented mindset with respect to game play (Elliott & Dweck, 1988), in which students might decide that they lose a game primarily because they were "bad at fractions" and therefore be less likely to re-engage in the activity.

Once our basic design was in place, we tested it internally with colleagues and then with sixth- and seventh-grade students (who were older than our target audience), to find problems and refine the game so that it would work well for fourth-graders. During each round of user study, we made modifications and interviewed users about the problems experienced with the game. This iterative process helped shape the game into an understandable and playable one within a short amount of time. After this initial period, we conducted user studies with children who were closer to the target age, introducing them to the game for one- or two-hour sessions while checking for enjoyment and understanding of the game (we also involved parents in some of these sessions). Finally, we recorded and analyzed extended play sessions with participants from local after-school clubs to resolve any problems with boredom, understanding of the rules, or unsatisfying game play characterized by verbalizations and actions children could make while playing the game.

After confirming the overall game design, we conducted multiple studies to test the effectiveness of the game. The studies all used a crossover experimental paradigm to compare student performance on fractions before and after the introduction of *Tug-of-War*. After a few final refinements to the game, we were able to demonstrate that children who had been randomly assigned to play the game scored significantly higher on paper-and-pencil fractions tests than did their classmates who had been randomly assigned to participate in unrelated mathematics research (Jimenez, Arena, & Acholonu, 2011). Our results demonstrated that children's average scores more than doubled after playing the game, which was a significant difference.

Our results support the claim that educational games can impart valuable academic lessons. Beyond that, however, in our experiences as moderators in the classroom, we noticed that children were finding ways of getting themselves "unstuck" while playing the game. To investigate this behavior, we conducted a study to examine how children sought help in different learning environments.

The pilot study was run with a small sample, and the experimenters were not blind to condition. Nonetheless, the results were striking. Children used the environment's resources more in our game context than they did in a traditional classroom environment. More work needs to be done in this area, but our preliminary results suggest that games can be designed to encourage students to learn challenging academic content, in part by fostering greater help-seeking behavior, as we discuss below.

Tug-of-War and How Children Help Each Other

In addition to the research that informed our decisions for making the game engaging for children, we also built upon research about helping them learn. For example, we designed many fractional-operation opportunities in *Tug-of-War* so that players could watch, help, and correct their peers' mathematics solutions. This type of monitoring and correcting has been shown to be easier than monitoring one's own performance (Gelman & Meck, 1983; Okita, 2008; Siegler, 1995). To ensure that there are many opportunities to monitor another's performance, the game consists of many rounds of play, and students are encouraged to play in groups of four (two versus two) when feasible. Mechanics also are in place whereby students can challenge and correct their opponents' operations. In our classroom work, we also arranged players into mixed-ability groups, which have been shown to be more effective for learning than pairing students in groups of similar ability (Guberman & Saxe, 2000). Our overall goal has been to create an informal learning environment with numerous social, emotional, and cognitive supports for the task of learning about rational numbers.

The help-seeking study reported below is an analysis of these supports, with an initial test of the game's design, mechanics, and appeal that focused specifically on help-seeking behaviors. Thirty fourth-grade students (fifteen boys and fifteen girls) from one class participated in the study. Eighty-three percent of students were categorized as economically disadvantaged, and 73% were categorized as English language learners. The class was divided into two samples of 15 students each, using stratified random sampling to balance gender and mathematics achievement.

In the first one-hour session, researchers explained the game and divided students into single-gender, mixed-ability groups of three or four students each. (We chose to have single-gender groups because the teacher had notified us that mixed-gender groups in their classroom were not yet as cooperative as single-gender groups.) One researcher acted as the "dealer" for each group, which involved structuring the game session, dividing the group into two teams, assigning tasks (e.g., dealing cards, organizing custom-designed plastic manipulatives that are part of the game materials, and keeping score) to individual students, helping clarify rules, and adjudicating conflicts. Across the next two weeks, students played for another one-hour session in the same groups (possibly changing teammates). The researchers continued to moderate game activity for each group but made a conscious effort to slowly withdraw to more peripheral roles as students became familiar with the game.

The fourth session was slightly different. Researchers shuffled students into new single-gender, mixed-ability groups and explained that this time, rather than moderating, the researchers would watch to see how well students could run the game sessions by themselves. During a specified 15-minute window within that session, each researcher cataloged help-seeking behaviors in one group of students using a checklist consisting of the codes shown in Table 16.1 below. This checklist was developed beforehand from field notes generated from previous game sessions and separate classroom observations. After generating the codes, we then grouped them into three overall categories based on our observation of student behavior: help-seeking behaviors whereby one relies on someone else

Table 16.1 **Help-Seeking Codes by Category**

Help-Seeking Codes	*Category*
Ask grown-up (teacher/instructor/researcher)	Rely on Others
Ask classmate (e.g., "What did she just say?" or "What's ½ of 8?")	Rely on Others
Look at classmate's notes/work/actions	Rely on Others
Let someone else answer in one's place (e.g., when asked a question one doesn't know)	Rely on Others
Answer for someone else (e.g., interrupting someone, blurting out the answer, correcting someone else)	Work with Others
Collaborate with fellow group member (e.g., working together to find solution)	Work with Others
Collaborate with classmate outside of group (e.g., clarifying)	Work with Others
Perform partial action (e.g., answering question quietly without raising hand, or partially playing a card)	Work with Others
Make a guess (e.g., shouting an answer or playing a card incorrectly "as a joke")	Work with Others
Rely on resource (textbook, handout, card rules text or surface features, etc.)	Work with Environment
Rely on manipulatives (miniature figures, etc.)	Work with Environment
Rely on analogy or anchoring representation (e.g., "1/2 is like $.50, and 3/4 is like $.75, so...")	Work with Environment
Change environment to avoid situation (e.g., crawling on floor, cheating at cards)	Work with Environment

for the information, behaviors whereby one works instead with another person, and finally behaviors in which one works with the environment or nonhuman resources that are available.

Using this checklist, researchers identified all instances of help-seeking that occurred during the observation window and kept a tally of the occurrences for each code. If researchers observed an instance of help-seeking that did not clearly correspond to any of the codes, they wrote down a description of the event; all such descriptions were later discussed and categorized by the research team into one of the existing codes. For the traditional classroom lesson, a team of four researchers used the same checklist (which had been specifically designed to be appropriate for observation in both the game and lesson contexts) to observe 15 minutes of a normal mathematics lecture plus 15 minutes of subsequent seat work in the same classroom with the same students.

The primary result, shown in Figure 16.2, is that researchers observed significantly more instances of help-seeking behaviors in the card-game environment than in the traditional school environment, labeled as "Class." Our first analysis confirmed that there were significantly more instances of help-seeking in the game environment than in the class environment. Because the researchers who observed the two game sessions, the lesson, and the seat work period were not the same four people in every case (and thus might have different standards for identifying help-seeking behaviors), we then confirmed the difference using only data from the two observers who participated in all four observation sessions, and we still found significant results.

Another interesting result was that girls exhibited significantly more help-seeking behaviors than boys in the collaborative game environment, but not in the class environment. This result is important in light of previous research showing that girls are more hesitant to seek help in mathematics contexts (Newman & Goldin, 1990), because it suggests that more collaborative

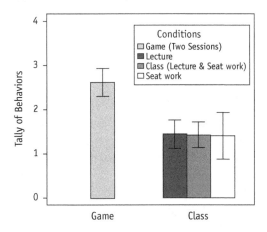

Figure 16.2 Difference in Help-Seeking Behaviors by Occasion ($p < .0005$).

informal game environments such as ours might be useful in supporting girls' math achievement.

When we examined the codes by category ("rely on others," "work with others," and "work with environment"), we noticed that, on average, each student demonstrated more instances of help-seeking in all three categories, although only the "work with others" category reached a level of significance between the two contexts. That is, students worked with others significantly more in the game environment than in the class environment. Among the individual codes, there were some unsurprising differences between environments. For example, students asked adults for help marginally more often in the game environment, in which the ratio of students to adults was never more than four to one, than in the class environment with 30 students and a single teacher. Students also collaborated significantly more across groups in the game environment than in the class environment.

Other differences were unanticipated, such as the finding that students were significantly more likely to answer for one another in the game environment and marginally more likely to copy from one another in the class environment. One possible explanation for this pattern of results is that in our game environment students are eager to contribute to the problem-solving process to keep the game going, whereas in the more formal environment of traditional classroom instruction students are more willing to rely on the work of their peers.

The fact that children exhibited both more help-seeking behaviors and more types of help-seeking behaviors that were task-goal oriented provides evidence of their being more motivated to learn the content (Newman, 1994; Ryan & Pintrich, 1997). Although our methodology cannot pinpoint the exact causes for the increase in help-seeking behaviors, we believe that the game format and the social structure of our game play provide good first candidates for further investigation. Specifically, our finding that students helped one another much more in the game than in the classroom environment provides evidence for the importance of the social structure, but more research needs to be done.

Conclusion

We hope that the discussion in this chapter contributes to the conversation about how academic skills acquired during game play transfer to academic settings. While we did not report on it extensively here, we have referred to research demonstrating that students who played *Tug-of-War* displayed gains in fractions knowledge on traditional paper-and-pencil tests taken in a classroom setting, which supports the claim that academic learning that occurs in games can transfer to school settings (Jimenez, Arena, & Acholonu, 2013). In this chapter we claimed that one way to measure motivation to learn is to measure help-seeking behavior and that game contexts tend to support richer and more productive help-seeking behavior than do traditional classroom contexts. Of course, curricula in traditional classroom environments could also be structured to provide more opportunities for students to seek help and learn the material. More work is needed, however, to investigate the specific mechanisms that can help students become motivated enough to seek help in productive ways, such as obtaining hints and mastering the material (rather than just fishing for answers).

There is also an additional question in this book about the types of research, goals, and plans that can help us, the educational games community, to succeed in our efforts of creating effective video games that help children learn. Our suggestions are to build on existing mechanics (as we did with our card game), which provide enough "familiar ground" for players to let them focus on and master the novel features of the game, and to begin the design process with technologies that are easily modified (such as simple paper-based prototypes). If the educational game community can figure out how to get students to learn difficult material in a game, it can then hopefully help them to learn difficult material in the classroom as well.

References

Aleven, V., & Koedinger, K. (2000). Limitations of student control: Do students know when they need help? In G. Gauthier, C. Frasson, & K. VanLehn (Eds.), *Intelligent tutoring systems* (Vol. 1839, pp. 292–303). Berlin / Heidelberg, Germany: Springer. Retrieved from http://www.springerlink.com/content/7d68kj9nwc7jetqe/abstract/

Aleven, V., Stahl, E., Schworm, S., Fischer, F., & Wallace, R. (2003). Help seeking and help design in interactive learning environments. *Review of Educational Research, 73*, 277–320.

Arbreton, A. (1998). Student goal orientation and help-seeking strategy use. In S. A. Karabenick (Ed.), *Strategic help seeking: implications for learning and teaching* (pp. 95–116). Mahwah, NJ: L. Erlbaum Associates.

Barlett, C. P., Anderson, C. A., & Swing, E. L. (2009). Video game effects—Confirmed, suspected, and speculative. *Simulation & Gaming, 40*, 377–403.

Bogost, I. (2007). The rhetoric of video games. In K. Salen (Ed.), *The ecology of games: Connecting youth, games, and learning.* (pp. 117–139).

Buckingham, D., & Sefton-Green, J. (2003). Gotta catch'em all: Structure, agency and pedagogy in children's media culture. *Media, Culture & Society, 25*, 379–399.

CBS Interactive. (n.d.). Portal 2 for PC - GameRankings. Retrieved from http://www.gamerankings.com/pc/991073-portal-2/index.html

Confrey, J., Maloney, A., Nguyen, K., Mojica, G., & Myers, M. (2009). Equipartitioning/splitting as a foundation of rational number reasoning using learning trajectories. *Proceedings of the 33rd Conference of the International Group for the Psychology of Mathematics Education, 1*(1998), 1–8.

Côté, D., Caron, A., Aubert, J., Desrochers, V., & Ladouceur, R. (2003). Near wins prolong gambling on a video lottery terminal. *Journal of Gambling Studies, 19*(4), 433–438.

Elliott, E. S., & Dweck, C. S. (1988). Goals: an approach to motivation and achievement. *Journal of Personality and Social Psychology, 54*(1), 5–12.

Gee, J. P. (2003). *What video games have to teach us about learning and literacy.* New York: Palgrave Macmillan.

Gelman, R., & Meck, E. (1983). Preschoolers' counting: Principles before skill. *Cognition*, *13*, 343–359.

Grayling, T. (1998). Fear and loathing of the help menu: A usability test of online help. *Technical Communication*, *45*, 168–79.

Green, C. S., & Bavelier, D. (2003). Action video game modifies visual selective attention. *Nature*, *423*(6939), 534–537.

Guberman, S. R., & Saxe, G. B. (2000). Mathematical problems and goals in children's play of an educational game. *Mind, Culture, and Activity*, *7*, 201–216.

Habgood, M. P. J., Ainsworth, S. E., & Benford, S. (2005). Endogenous fantasy and learning in digital games. *Simulation & Gaming*, *36*, 483–498.

Hoekman, R. (2010). *Designing the obvious: A common sense approach to Web and mobile application design*. Berkeley, CA: New Riders.

Honey, M., & Hilton, M. (2011). *Learning Science: Computer Games, Simulations, and Education*. Washington, D.C.: National Academies Press.

Ito, M. (2005). Intertextual Enterprises: Writing Alternative Places and Meanings in the Media Mixed Networks of Yugioh. In D. Battaglia (Ed.), *E.T. Culture: Anthropology in Outerspaces* (pp. 180–199). Durham, NC: Duke University Press.

Iyengar, S. S., & Lepper, M. (2000). When choice is demotivating: Can one desire too much of a good thing? *Journal of Personality and Social Psychology*, *79*, 995–1006.

Jimenez, O., Arena, D. A., & Acholonu, U. (2011). *Tug-of-War*: A card game for pulling students to fractions fluency. In Constance Steinkuehler, C. Martin, & A. Ochsner (Eds.), *Proceedings of the Games, Learning, & Society Conference 7.0*. Madison, WI: ETC Press.

Jimenez, O., Arena, D., & Acholonu, U. (2013). Educational video games: The devil is in the details. Presented at the American Educational Research Association, San Francisco, CA.

Kerslake, D. (1986). Fractions: Children's strategies and errors: a report of the Strategies and Errors in Secondary Mathematics Project. Windsor, Berkshire: NFER-NELSON.

Kirriemuir, J., & McFarlane, A. (2004). *Literature review in games and learning* (No. 8). Bristol, UK: Futurelab. Retrieved from www.futurelab.org.uk/research/lit_reviews.htm

Langer, E. J. (1975). The illusion of control. *Journal of Personality and Social Psychology*, *32*, 311–328.

Malone, T. W. (1981). Towards a theory of intrinsic motivation. *Cognitive Science*, *4*, 333–369.

Metacritic. (n.d.). Portal 2. *Metacritic*. Retrieved from http://www.metacritic.com/game/pc/portal-2

Nelson-Le Gall, S. (1985). Help-seeking behavior in learning. *Review of Research in Education*, *12*, 55–90. doi:10.2307/1167146

Newman, R. S. (1994). Adaptive help seeking: A strategy of self-regulated learning. In D. H. Schunk & B. J. Zimmerman (Eds.), *Self-regulation of learning and performance : issues and educational applications* (pp. 283–301). Hillsdale, NJ: Lawrence Erlbaum Associates.

Newman, R. S., & Goldin, L. (1990). Children's reluctance to seek help with schoolwork. *Journal of Educational Psychology*, *82*(1), 92–100. doi:10.1037/0022-0663.82.1.92

Nunes, T. (2006). Fractions: difficult but crucial in mathematics learning. Teaching and Learning Research Programme (TLRP) research briefing. Retrieved from www.tlrp.org/pub/documents/no13_nunes.pdf

Okita, S. Y. (2008, August). Learn wisdom by the folly of others: Children learning to self correct by monitoring the reasoning of projective pedagogical agents. Retrieved from http://gradworks.umi.com/33/13/3313635.html

Parlett, D. (1991). *A history of card games*. New York: Oxford University Press.

Pempek, T. A., & Calvert, S. L. (2009). Tipping the balance: Use of advergames to promote consumption of nutritious foods and beverages by low-income African American children. *Archives of Pediatrics & Adolescent Medicine*, *163*, 633–637. doi:10.1001/archpediatrics.2009.71

Petit, M. M., Laird, R. E., & Marsden, E. L. (2010). *A focus on fractions: Bringing research to the classroom*. New York: Routledge.

Prensky, M. (2007). *Digital game-based learning*. St. Paul, MN: Paragon House.

Reeves, B., & Read, J. L. (2009). *Total engagement: using games and virtual worlds to change the way people work and businesses compete.* Boston, MA: Harvard Business School Press.

Rick, J., Francois, P., Fields, B., Fleck, R., Yuill, N., & Carr, A. (2010). Lo-fi prototyping to design interactive-tabletop applications for children. In *Proceedings of the 9th International Conference on Interaction Design and Children* (pp. 138–146).

Rideout, V. J., Foehr, U. G., & Roberts, D. F. (2010). *Generation M [superscript 2]: Media in the Lives of 8-to 18-Year-Olds.* The Henry J. Kaiser Family Foundation. Retrieved from http://kaiser-familyfoundation.files.wordpress.com/2013/01/8010.pdf

Roschelle, J. (1986). The Envisioning Machine: Facilitating students' reconceptualization of motion. *Xerox Palo Alto Research Center Working Paper.*

Ryan, A. M., Gheen, M. H., & Midgley, C. (1998). Why do some students avoid asking for help? An examination of the interplay among students' academic efficacy, teachers' social-emotional role, and the classroom goal structure. *Journal of Educational Psychology*, *90*, 528–535. doi:10.1037/0022-0663.90.3.528

Ryan, A. M., & Pintrich, P. R. (1997). "Should I ask for help?" The role of motivation and attitudes in adolescents' help seeking in math class. *Journal of Educational Psychology*, *89*, 329–341. doi:10.1037/0022-0663.89.2.329

Sefelin, R., Tscheligi, M., & Giller, V. (2003). Paper prototyping—What is it good for?: A comparison of paper- and computer-based low-fidelity prototyping. In *Proceedings of CHI '03 Extended Abstracts on Human Factors in Computing Systems* (pp. 778–779). New York, NY: ACM. doi:10.1145/765891.765986

Siegler, R. S. (1995). How does change occur: A microgenetic study of number conservation. *Cognitive Psychology*, *28*, 225–273.

Steinkuehler, C., & Duncan, S. (2008). Scientific Habits of Mind in Virtual Worlds. *Journal of Science Education & Technology*, *17*(6), 530–543.

Steinkuehler, Constance. (2006). Massively multiplayer online video gaming as participation in a discourse. *Mind, Culture, and Activity*, *13*(1), 38–52.

Strickland, L. H., & Grote, F. W. (1967). Temporal presentation of winning symbols and slot-machine playing. *Journal of Experimental Psychology*, *74*(1), 10–13.

The NPD Group. (2013). *Entertainment Trends in America.* Retrieved from https://www.npd.com/lps/EntertainmentTrends2013/

Vasquez, V. (2003). What Pokemon can teach us about learning and literacy. *Language Arts*, *81*(2), 118–125.

Weiner, B. (1985). An attributional theory of achievement motivation and emotion. *Psychological Review*, *92*, 548–573. doi:10.1037/0033-295X.92.4.548

Wood, H., & Wood, D. (1999). Help seeking, learning and contingent tutoring. *Computers & Education*, *33*(2), 153–169.

17

Scientific Inquiry in Digital Games

JODI ASBELL-CLARKE AND ELIZABETH ROWE

> In a good computer or video game you're always playing on the
> very edge of your skill level, always on the brink of falling off.
> When you do fall off, you feel the urge to climb back on. That's
> because there is virtually nothing as engaging as this state of
> working at the very limits of your ability.
> —(McGonigal, 2011, p. 24)

Jane McGonigal describes a state of "blissful productivity" of gamers (2011). Others refer to this state of complete immersion and engagement as "flow"—the feeling people get when they are so involved in an activity that they lose all track of time (Csikszentmihalyi, 1990; Lemay, 2008). Flow is characterized by intense concentration, merging of action and awareness, loss of self-consciousness, altered sense of time, and the paradox of being both in control and pleasantly out of control at the same time. Unfortunately, classroom science teachers rarely see this state of engagement in their learners. Students might go through the motions in classes, but are rarely driven to flow by the science learning offered there. The claim has been made that the U.S. educational system is not fostering the creativity, innovation, and love for learning that is needed for a successful workforce or even a scientifically literate public (U.S. Department of Labor, 2007).

Digital games are among the free-choice Internet environments that account for the major part of U.S. adults' science learning and factor significantly in youth and adult attitudes and knowledge in science (Falk & Dierking, 2010), a trend that is only increasing (Klopfer, Osterweil, & Salen, 2009). Specifically, free-choice Internet-based learning experiences initiate a child's long-term interest in science, and they can also significantly improve science understanding among populations underrepresented in science (National Research Council, 2009). Reaching out to a gaming audience and infusing public games with rich opportunities for scientific inquiry may open the doors for educators to challenge learners where they are already spending huge amounts of time and potentially, experiencing flow. Social digital games, in particular, may offer potential for fostering innovation and knowledge-building skills with a broad audience (Gee, 2003; Klopfer et al., 2009), many of whom do not consider themselves science-oriented (Asbell-Clarke, Edwards, Larsen, Rowe, Sylvan, & Hewitt, 2011; Ketelhut, 2007).

This chapter examines how social digital gaming environments are fostering communities of public scientific inquiry and how that inquiry might be measured for educational purposes. The goal of our research is to understand how social digital games may be an important component to ubiquitous learning environments that engage a diverse public in productive scientific inquiry, scientific knowledge building, and citizen science activities.

Gaming: A Force to be Reckoned With... or a Door to Walk Through?

Nearly all U.S. youth (boys and girls) play digital games, many supported by social networking or massively multiplayer online (MMOs) games (Lenhart, 2008; Ito et al., 2008). In 2010, already 67% of heads of households had played electronic games (Entertainment Software Association, 2011). Although the typical video gamer is often reported as a 37-year-old white male, in 2012 47% of all players were women and women over 18 years of age are now one of the industry's fastest growing demographics (Entertainment Software Association, 2013).

People play many different types of digital games, each with different affordances. Casual games resemble arcade video games and often involve repetitive short tasks that may promote rote and spatial learning but are unlikely to foster sustained inquiry. In contrast, social games provide inherent community goals, bringing people together to solve problems and build knowledge. In a social game, players typically can accomplish initial tasks alone, but as challenges get harder players must work collaboratively for success. Social and casual games can be of many genres including word and puzzle games (e.g., *WordGrid, Tetris*); alternate reality games (e.g., *World Without Oil, Evoke*); first-person shooters (e.g., *Call of Duty, Portal*); MMO games (e.g., *World of Warcraft, Martian Boneyards*); and social networking (e.g., *Mafia Wars, Farmville*). The EdGE at TERC team is starting to design transmedia games, which have several elements using a mix of various genres and media (e.g., web, MMO, smartphone apps) that work together to create a rich, multifaceted experience for players.

A growing body of research is examining how different types of digital games can provide complex learning experiences and potentially transform learning (Asbell-Clarke et al., 2011; Barab, Arcici, & Jackson, 2005; de Freitas, Rebolledo-Mendez, Liarokapis, Magoulas, & Poulovassilis, 2010; Ketelhut, 2007). To seize this potential opportunity, educators must learn what can be exploited from games and how to infuse them with high-quality content learning and real world connections. Gee (2003, 2004) argues that in game playing, people model how they need to learn in stark contrast to the way learning activities are implemented in traditional learning environments. Social games, where players collaborate with others to build knowledge and/or resources in a community, have many parallels with recent research in science education and may be an important part of preparing people for today's workforce (Steinkeuhler & Duncan, 2008; Thomas & Brown, 2011).

Social Games as Collaborative Learning Environments

Today the workplace involves technological tools and social interaction mediated by digital devices (Davidson, 2011; Partnership for 21st Century Skills, 2009). Learners need to be facile with evolving computational environments, and those environments must foster innovation and collaboration where people generate, share, and critique work (National Research Council, 2011). They must be able to connect information and skills learned in different settings and contexts (Colardyn & Bjornavold, 2004; Jenkins, 2006). This type of learning is consistent with the prevalent theories in learning sciences and also with emergent principles of game design. Vygotsky (1978) recognized the inextricability of environment and community, as both mediate the child's learning process. He defined the zone of proximal development (ZPD) as the range of activities a learner can do with assistance from others. Interestingly, a similar tenet in game design is to craft tasks that lie just outside the current grasp of a player—doable, yet challenging—and often requiring the assistance of other players and/or tools within the game (McGonigal, 2011).

Social learning theorists often describe learning in a community of practice, where experts model the norms and accepted behaviors while novices have their own peripheral roles of legitimate participation as they learn (Lave, 1988; Lave & Wenger, 1991). The idea of experts and novices can become muddled in a formal learning experience. For example, in a science class the teacher may be closer to the students on the novice-expert continuum than to a professional scientist. Barab and Duffy (2000) introduce the idea of practice fields as learning environments where students come together as novices to prepare for the kinds of activities they will encounter outside the learning environment (Senge, Kleiner, Roberts, Ross, & Smith, 2004). In sports, practice fields are used for training for competition—these fields are where athletes can take risks, make mistakes, and hone skills. Using this analogy, one can consider a cognitive practice field where learners try new ideas and revise their thinking as they understand how their ideas fit with the collective wisdom of the community. Games may provide a unique opportunity to create practice fields among novices within a scientific domain. In a social game, players work together in a domain or context-based investigation. Game designers initiate the problems and storyline, but the games have the potential to be very player-driven with ongoing open-ended inquiry triggering new investigations. In fact, the game industry is turning more and more to games without instructions, relying on users to figure nearly everything out on their own (McGonigal, 2011).

When these practices are carefully used with content learning goals, designers can create what Barab and colleagues call conceptual play spaces (Barab, Warren, & Ingram-Goble, 2008). Gameplay can immerse learners in rich networks of interactions and unfolding storylines embedding problem-solving and reflective activities. Gaming communities often establish common habits, language, and cultural rules of engagement. In some popular role-playing games (e.g., *World of Warcraft*), players' practices involve peer review, collaboration, sharing and analysis of data, and evidence-based reasoning (Steinkuehler & Duncan, 2008) —similar to the habits of practicing scientists in professional communities (Dunbar, 2000).

Well-crafted advancement structures in games allow players abundant practice and application of what they have learned earlier both in similar situations (within a level) and then require transfer to less similar situations (across levels). Advancement structures that offer useful and immediate feedback to learners about their progress and require demonstration of knowledge and skills for players to advance provide a rich resource in games that educators may be able to leverage for pedagogical and assessment purposes.

Designing Games for Learning Communities

When creating educational games as opposed to curriculum, there is a shift from designing prescribed learning tasks to choreographing learning experiences (deFreitas et al., 2010). Designers prepare the initial framework, scaffolds, and narrative for the environment but at some point the activity in a social game becomes dictated by the player community as much as the designers. A social game requires a community to bring in their own information and resources, their passion, and their innovations.

Several games are emerging as exemplars that provide lessons for educators. Some are designed for the classroom and some are commercial games. Some are single-player and others are multiplayer. With their variety and common trends, they each offer a unique lesson.

Classroom Games

In the past decade, design research projects such as Harvard University's *River City* and Indiana University-Bloomington's *Quest Atlantis* have used situated social gaming with an educational goal to support classroom learning (Barab, Thomas, Didge, Carteaux, & Tuzun, 2005; Barab, Sadler, Heiselt, Hickey, & Zuiker, 2007; Barab et al., 2008; Ketelhut, 2007). By deploying gaming environments to supplement curriculum in formal educational settings, these projects show one example of games for use in formal learning environments.

Quest Atlantis embeds a framework for transformational play within a learning environment designed for middle-school classrooms, where learners become protagonists who use the knowledge, skills, and concepts of the educational content to make sense of a situation and to learn while they transform the play space. In a 10-hour classroom implementation of *Quest Atlantis*, Barab and colleagues (2007) found a significant change on close-level science learning outcomes (using independent, rubric-based scoring of student work) and proximal-level outcomes (using open-ended performance assessments). On distal-level outcomes (18 standardized test items), however, there was no significant change.

In another game developed for formal learning environments, *River City* (Galas & Ketelhut, 2006; Ketelhut, 2007), middle-school students collaborated with classmates to solve problems critical to the health of a community in a possible medical crisis. Researchers used variants on the instructional design. They used virtual and physical lab notebooks and in-class interpretive sessions with a situated pedagogy based on expert modeling and coaching in which students interacted with expert avatars (played by college science majors) and computer-based agents embedded in the virtual environment. *River City* has proven successful in engaging traditionally underserved students, although significant changes in science learning have varied depending on the assessment method used (Ketelhut, Nelson, Clarke, & Dede, 2010). The *River City* project has evolved into EcoMUVE; an ecology oriented multiuser virtual environment) where nonplayer characters (NPCs) guide students through quests with data collection and problem-solving (Metcalf, 2011). In this environment, the inquiry is highly structured and the answers are provided by the NPCs on a need-to-know basis.

Quest Atlantis and *River City* have made major strides in understanding game usage in formal learning environments. They also point to the need for different types of assessments to understand and measure the learning that may be happening in games. Recent research suggests, however, that science learning and educational achievement may be predicted by out-of-school time experiences as much or more than in-school learning (Falk & Dierking, 2010). People are increasingly seeking "hard fun" activities on the Internet—activities that are fun *because* they are hard rather than *in spite* of being hard (Papert, 2002).

This situation raises interesting questions about what educators should look for in terms of transfer of learning between formal and informal learning environments. Many educators look for transfer from informal or game settings to learning that can take place in the classroom. This comparison could imply that classroom learning is what is to be strived for. Research suggests however, that activities take place in games that can go beyond the types of inquiry and investigation that take place in typical classrooms (Asbell-Clarke, Edwards, Larsen, Rowe, Sylvan, & Hewitt, 2012; Steinheuhler & Duncan, 2008).

Free-Choice Games

One of the most popular public gaming environments in the past decade has been the MMO role-playing game, *World of Warcraft* (*WoW*). An estimated 6 million years of people's time have already been spent playing the game (McGonigal, 2011). Researchers have also found that within this remarkably large and popular online community, there is evidence of scientific inquiry that is aligned with American Association for the Advancement of Science (AAAS) standards for scientific inquiry (Steinkeuhler & Duncan, 2008). These researchers also found that it is not unusual for *WoW* players to gather data in spreadsheets, create models of the data in the form of simple mathematical equations, and then argue about whose model was "better" in terms of prediction and explanatory scope. Thus, users from all backgrounds have worked together to build situated understandings of important phenomena (e.g., physical laws) that are embedded in the virtual world.

Another intriguing form of public game on the Internet is alternate reality games (ARGs), where the game is based in the real world and occurs in real time, but the narrative is fictionalized. In an ARG, game designers lay out the premise and environment for the game, but often the storyline and content are mutually expanded over time by the designers and players. Games like *I Love Bees,* have engaged hundreds of thousands of players in knowledge building—gathering and analyzing data to create claims and predictions about fictional or real-world phenomena (McGonigal, 2007). In 2007, over 1800 players convened online for a month to collectively play out and document a fictional oil crisis in *World Without Oil* (McGonigal, 2011). Some players report to have transformed their real lives as a result. McGonigal claims that the reason that they all came to participate is this:

> By turning a real problem into a voluntary obstacle, we activated more genuine interest, curiosity, motivation, effort, and optimism than we would have otherwise. We can change our real-life behaviors in the context of a fictional game precisely because there isn't any negative pressure surrounding the decision to change. (McGonigal, 2011; p. 311)

In our own work, EdGE exploited the immersive features of an MMO in *Martian Boneyards*. EdGE designers worked with professional game developers to build an environment in a new high-definition MMO called *Blue Mars*. The MMO was still in open beta and had a small community of about 50–100 regular adult visitors when EdGE implemented a four-month game of scientific mystery in May to September 2010. The designers of *Martian Boneyards* placed evidence for a murder mystery in the environment and then played characters (using avatars) to facilitate the game. The designers used an open storyline and provided a dynamic design through their characters. This strategy allowed designers and researchers to interact frequently and directly with players, providing unique insight into players' activities. Designers were then able to be responsive to players, putting their ideas at the center of the storyline.

The mystery of *Martian Boneyards* required players to identify and distinguish various skeletons using comparative anatomy (Asbell-Clarke et al., 2011). Players (mostly not science-oriented) used Internet resources to correctly identify and distinguish human, Neanderthal, and chimpanzee skeletons. The game designers did not provide any of the data or methods. Thus, the players needed to gather information on various Internet sites (e.g., the eSkeletons and Smithsonian sites).

EdGE designed game tools for *Martian Boneyards* that scaffold and measure stages of scientific inquiry framed by theories of argumentation or knowledge building (Scardamalia & Bereiter, 1996; Toulmin, 1958; Kuhn, 2005). Players gathered data using their virtual PDAs in the MMO game, used virtual collaborative workstations to analyze the data to generate evidence, and posted their claims and evidence on the community theory-building area, where evidence is coordinated with players' claims building toward explanatory, peer-reviewed theories. Researchers used the clicks on each of these tools to measure the extent of scientific inquiry contributed by each player. These digital activity logs were used with surveys, interviews, participant observations, and expert review of artifacts to describe the nature of scientific inquiry within the player community.

A panel of three scientists in related areas read all science-related player postings to the theory-building area, the *Blue Mars* Web-based discussion board, and a small convenience sample of chat. The majority of players' postings were included in the sample. Reviewers examined over 200 text entries in total. The panel used a rubric and process modified from previous research to review the quality of materials from online science courses (see Rowe & Asbell-Clarke, 2008). Reviewers rated the quality of inquiry along four dimensions on a 5-point scale (ranging from 1 = poor to 5 = excellent). The dimensions included the extent of scientific inquiry; sophistication of the scientific inquiry; accuracy of core ideas in comparative anatomy; and depth of core ideas in comparative anatomy. The panel rated the quality of the inquiry as very good along each dimension when comparing the inquiry in the game to a typical group project conducted in an introductory undergraduate science class for nonscience majors.

The science reviewers also judged that the player community engaged in sustained scientific inquiry—posing questions, making claims, substantiating claims with evidence—to an extent that would be considered very good (rating of 4 out of 5) in an undergraduate introductory science course (Asbell-Clarke et al., 2011). The content generated in comparative anatomy was rated very good (4) on accuracy and good (3) on depth. Reviewers also noted that nearly all Internet resources used by players were from reasonable scientific websites, including accredited sites from universities, national labs, and museums. They also said the game appeared to motivate a level of inquiry among some players that was similar to the very top students in a class.

When reflecting on the learning that took place in *Martian Boneyards*, to ask how the learning will transfer from the game to the real world feels like a backwards question. The players in the game were challenged by the game to go to the real world to apply what they learned. Players in *Martian Boneyards* moved fluidly back and forth between the game environment and the Internet while they were solving the scientific mystery. They were not isolating the science to the game. They asked themselves how scientists would identify the bones and used the resources available on sites such as the Smithsonian and eSkeletons to gather methods and data (Asbell-Clarke et al., 2012).

The players were involved in very real acts of prolonged scientific inquiry, in a state that the science reviewers agreed they strive for in their classes. This finding raises the question of how we can invoke that type of inquiry in classrooms. It may not be in the best interest of learning to ask how we can measure game-based learning using school-like metrics (multiple choice or other traditional exams). It may be more interesting to understand how we can measure the learning that takes place naturally in games, and then understand how to leverage that type of learning to make classroom learning and assessment more relevant to the ways students are learning today.

Leveling Up: The Next Steps in Game-Based Learning Research

It is difficult to initiate and maintain social games with the intensity our team expended during *Martian Boneyards*. To advance our research and understand how games could be used for innovative new assessments in STEM education, we decided to focus on mobile app games because mobile apps are the fastest growing game platform (Entertainment Software Association, 2013) and relatively easy to develop, revise, and study. We also see mobile devices, with their affordances of augmented reality, as having potential for connections between game-based and real-world learning.

Researchers have long advocated for learning assessments designed as tools that both measure and foster deep inquiry and collaboration, and provide strong feedback and recognition of students' progress (Clark, Englert, Frazee, Shebby, & Randel, 2009; Lee, Chan, & van Aalst, 2006). Some researchers use game assessments that build from the evidence-centered approach to assessment design (Mislevy, Steinberg, & Almond, 2003) and create Bayesian networks or other methods to predict learners' paths through a game (Koenig, Lee, Iseli, & Wainess,

2010; Shute, 2011). These assessments are typically studied in the current model of schools.

In many typical mobile games, mechanics often rely on intuitive knowledge of a simple game mechanic that is then applied in increasingly difficult or complex situations. In a well-crafted game, learners are able to cohere their various game experiences into a larger understanding and begin to appreciate how their cumulative game experiences build a systemic picture of the properties and behaviors of the mechanic and the environment. This knowledge may be implicit and players may be unable to articulate explicitly their conceptual understanding. However, players may use these intuitive understandings to predict and navigate their way through the environment. These actions in the game may provide measurable evidence of their implicit knowledge.

EdGE's research framework to study the development of implicit knowledge in games stems from the philosophy of scientist Michael Polanyi (1966) and has been suggested by Thomas and Brown (2011) for educators and researchers to consider when studying twenty-first century learning environments. Our research strives to describe how this measurement of emergent implicit learning takes place in games and what it offers for the development of innovative learning assessments for a new generation of learners.

Within this framework the question of transfer becomes more about how implicit knowledge can be leveraged to help explicit learning. First the implicit knowledge building that can be fostered within a game must be identified; then the connections between the emergent game-based learning and real-life phenomena can be explored.

Impulse: A Game for Implicit Learning about Forces and Motion

An example of a game we designed to measure implicit learning about forces and motion is *Impulse*, which can be played on most mobile devices (see Figure 17.1). In *Impulse*, particles have different masses and thus behave differently under the corresponding gravitational forces. Players use an impulse (upon a touch or click) to apply a force to particles, moving their particle to the goal while avoiding the ambient particles. If the player's particle collides with any ambient particle, she loses that round. In terms of the science, the player is immersed inside an N-body simulation with accurate gravitational interactions and elastic collisions among up to 30 ambient particles.

As players reach higher levels, they require cognitive strategies to predict the motion of the particles so that they can get to the goal, not run out of energy, and avoid collision with other particles. While navigating a sea of (elastically) colliding particles that are attracted to each other (through gravity), players need to "study" the particles' behavior to win. They also need to predict ambient particles'

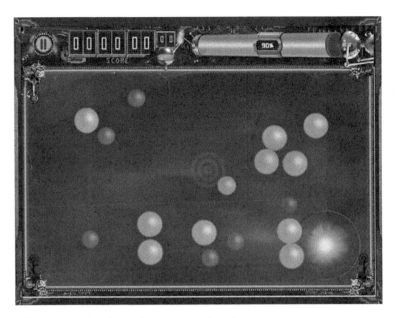

Figure 17.1 Screenshot from physics game, *Impulse*.

motion and interactions with each other to avoid them as they guide their own particle to the goal.

Studying Implicit Learning in *Impulse*

Since there is no known best way for learners to build intuitive understanding of these physics phenomena in games, our research captures the myriad of strategies players develop during gameplay that may reveal tacit knowledge. As a first step of this work, we have identified an initial set of strategic moves that we observe players making in the game *Impulse*. We use video-recorded play-testing data with dozens of players to code strategic game play moves. With coded clicks as "ground truth," we then use educational data mining techniques to detect those strategic moves and describe how strategies evolve as players advance in the game.

While the video data allow us to observe and describe the strategic moves that players make during play-testing, these techniques are limited to the samples we can observe directly. To detect these cognitive strategies without video, our first step is to accurately identify their component parts—the strategic moves—from the game log data. Each "click" or touch from the player is recorded, along with a time stamp, anonymous player ID, and the features of the state of the game conditions that may be salient to determining the intent of players' actions.

We use these data to develop models to detect players' strategic moves in the data, from which we can look for sequences of those moves as evidence of cognitive strategies players use to succeed in the game that we hypothesize reflect a tacit understanding of Newtonian motion. We can further mine the data to examine the sets of strategies that apply to players who advance farther or more rapidly in the game (expert players), using regression models to identify the combinations of strategies that are characteristic of greater and lesser degrees of advancement.

The EdGE research team plans to build such models and use them in a comparative assessment study with hundreds of high school students. Students will be invited to play the games outside of school time. Some of their teachers will use bridge activities in class, curriculum activities that use examples from the games to illustrate principles of Newtonian motion. A variety of learning outcomes indicating their conceptual understanding of Newton's first and second laws of motion will be measured and compared among four groups:

- Students who play the game and are in a class where teachers use bridge activities
- Students who play the game and are in a class where teachers do not use bridge activities
- Students who do not play the game and are in a class where teachers use bridge activities
- Students who do not play the game and are not in a class where teachers use bridge activities (control group)

We hypothesize that students who play the game extensively (throughout most of the 70 levels) before having bridge activities in class will have better learning outcomes than any of the other groups.

Our hypothesis is that implicit learning in games is a powerful precursor to formal learning and that the connections between implicit and explicit learning cannot be guaranteed. Designers must create conditions in which learners can dwell in the phenomena of interest, establishing tacit understandings, which may go unexpressed. We believe that if game designers can craft games to foster implicit learning, educators can leverage that implicit learning through bridge activities that establish visual and conceptual linkages from game to classroom. We believe this framework provides additional avenues for bridging learning across many settings, building more ubiquitous learning environments that may transcend school, home, game environments, the natural world, and all facets of learners' lives.

Conclusion

Games are showing potential to support creative problem-solving in ways our current educational instruments are not well equipped to measure. Game-based educators are seeking ways to assess the development of knowledge and skills within games, using the innovative affordances these new environments may offer. Every study that measures learning within a game environment will face this question: How does the game-based learning transfer to real-world settings?

The EdGE team is working with a framework that employs the implicit learning that takes place by virtue of engagement and investigation that occurs naturally when a player is immersed in a well-crafted game. This framing requires a different approach to the question of transfer. First of all, the learning that we are seeking to identify is often unexpressed or sometimes even recognized explicitly by the learner. This situation makes the measurement more difficult and needs innovative methods. Implicit learning, however, may be foundational to explicit knowledge development (Polanyi, 1966; Thomas & Brown, 2011). Thus, by understanding how to shape these implicit learning experiences, we may be able to improve the very core of conceptual understanding.

In addition, as games and other digital activities become increasingly prevalent in our society, the question of transfer becomes more one of connectivity. The lines are blurring between the digital and what we call the "real world" in the lives and likely the minds of future learners. It behooves educators to look at how learning in one modality might be leveraged to foster learning in another venue— how learning becomes more distributed across settings—rather than focusing on whether or not one can replicate the same type of learning in different settings. Expanding this notion from transfer to connectivity might be better suited to the ubiquitous learning environments that span home, school, and community in the twenty-first century.

Authors' Note

TERC is a not-for-profit organization in Cambridge, MA, focusing on innovations in math and science education. The Educational Gaming Environments group (EdGE) at TERC was founded in 2009. EdGE research is supported by the National Science Foundation's DRL programs.

References

Asbell-Clarke, J., Edwards, T., Larsen, J., Rowe, E., Sylvan, E., & Hewitt, J. (2011, April). Collaborative scientific inquiry in Arcadia: An MMO gaming environment on Blue Mars. Paper presented at the American Education Research Association Annual Meeting, New Orleans, LA. *Winner of AERA ARVEL-SIG Emergent Scholar Award.

Asbell-Clarke, J., Edwards, T., Larsen, J., Rowe, E., Sylvan, E., & Hewitt, J. (2012). Martian Boneyards: Scientific inquiry in an MMO Game. *International Journal of Game-Based Learning*, 2(1),52–76. doi:10.4018/ijgbl.2012010104

Barab, S., Arcici, A., & Jackson, C. (2005). Eat your vegetables and do your home-work: A design-based investigation of enjoyment and meaning in learning. *Educational Technology*, 45(1), 15–21.

Barab, S., & Duffy, T. (2000). From practice fields to communities of practice. In D. Jonassen & L. Lands (Eds.), *Theoretical foundations of learning environments*. Mahwah, NJ: Lawrence Erlbaum Associates.

Barab, S. A., Sadler, T., Heiselt, C., Hickey, D., & Zuiker, S. (2007). Relating narrative, inquiry, and inscriptions: Aframework for socio-scientific inquiry. *Journal of Science Education and Technology*, 16(1), 59–82.

Barab, S., Thomas, M., Dodge, T., Carteaux, R., & Tuzun, H. (2005). Making learning fun: *Quest Atlantis*, agame without guns. *Educational Technology Research and Development*, 53(1), 86–107.

Barab, S., Warren, S., & Ingram-Goble, A. (2008). Conceptual playspaces. In R. Ferdig (Ed.), *Handbook of research on effective electronic gaming in education* (pp. 1–20). Hershey, PA: IGI Global Publications.

Clark, T., Englert, K., Frazee, D., Shebby, S., & Randel, B. (2009). McREL report prepared for Stupski Foundation's learning system: assessment. Retrieved from http://www.mcrel.org/pdf/SchoolImprovementReform/McREL.

Colardyn, D., & Bjornavold, J. (2004). Validation of formal, non-formal and informal learning: Policy and practices in EU member states. *European Journal of Education*, 39(1), 69–89.

Csikszentmihalyi, M. (1990). *Flow: The psychology of optimal experience*. New York, NY: Harper and Row.

Davidson, C. (2011). *Now you see it: How the brain science of attention will transform the way we live, work, and learn*. New York, NY: Viking Press.

deFreitas, S., Rebolledo-Mendez, G., Liarokapis, F., Magoulas, G., & Poulovassilis, A. (2010). Learning as immersive experiences: Using the four-dimensional framework for designing and evaluating immersive learning experiences in a virtual world. *British Journal of Educational Technology*, 41(1),69–85.

Dunbar, K. (2000). How scientists think in the world: Implications for science education. *Journal of Applied Developmental Psychology*, 21(1),49–58.

Entertainment Software Association (2011). Essential facts about the computer and video game industry. Retrieved from http://www.theesa.com/facts/pdfs/ESA_EF_2011.pdf

Entertainment Software Association. (2013). Game player data. *ESA Industry Facts*. Retrieved from http://www.theesa.com/facts/gameplayer.asp

Falk, J. H. & Dierking, L. D. (2010). The 95 percent solution: School is not where most Americans learn most of their science. *American Scientist*, 98(6), 486–493.

Galas, C., & Ketelhut, D. J. (2006). River City, the MUVE. *Learning and Leading with Technology*, 33(7), 31–32.

Gee, J. P. (2003). *What video games have to teach us about learning and literacy*. New York, NY: Palgrave/St. Martin's.

Gee, J. P. (2004). *Situated language and learning: A critique of traditional schooling*. London, UK: Routledge.

Ito, M., Horst, H., Bittanti, M., Boyd, D., Herr-Stephenson, B., Lange, P. G.,...Robinson, R. (2008). *Living and learning with new media: Summary of findings from the Digital Youth Project*. Chicago, IL: John D. and Catherine T. MacArthur Foundation Reports on Digital Media and Learning.

Jenkins, H. (2006). *Convergence culture: Where old and new media collide*. New York, NY: NYU Press.

Ketelhut, D. J. (2007). The impact of student self-efficacy on scientific inquiry skills: An exploratory investigation in River City, a multi-user virtual environment. *The Journal of Science Education and Technology*, 16(1), 99–111.

Ketelhut, D. J., Nelson, B. C., Clarke, J., & Dede, C. (2010). A multi-user virtual environment for building and assessing higher order inquiry skills in science. *British Journal of Educational Technology*, 41(1), 56–68.

Klopfer, E., Osterweil, S., & Salen, K. (2009). *Moving learning games forward: Obstacles, opportunities & openness.* Cambridge, MA: The Education Arcade, Massachusetts Institute of Technology. Retrieved from education.mit.edu/papers/MovingLearningGamesForward_EdArcade.pdf

Koenig, A. D., Lee, J. J., Iseli, M., & Wainess, R. (2010). *A conceptual framework for assessing performance in games and simulations.* Los Angeles, CA: National Center for Research on Evaluation, Standards, and Student Testing. Retrieved from http://www.cse.ucla.edu/products/reports/R771.pdf

Kuhn, D. (2005). *Education for thinking.* Cambridge, MA: Harvard University Press.

Lave, J. (1988). *Cognition in practice.* New York, NY: Cambridge University Press.

Lave, J., & Wenger, E. (1991). *Situated learning: Legitimate peripheral participation.* Cambridge, UK: Cambridge University Press.

Lee, E. Y. C., Chan, C. K. K., & van Aalst, J. (2006). Students assessing their own collaborative knowledge building. *International Journal of Computer-Supported Collaborative Learning, 1,* 277–307. Retrieved from http://www.springerlink.com/content/j82660523x82271154/

Lemay, P. (2008). Game and flow concepts for learning: some considerations. In K. McFerrin et al. (Eds.), *Proceedings of Society for Information Technology & Teacher Education International Conference 2008* (pp. 510–515). Chesapeake, VA: AACE.

Lenhart, A., Kahne, J., Middaugh, E., MacGill, A. R., Evans, C., & Vitak, J. (2008). *Teens, video games, and civics: Teens' gaming experiences are diverse and include significant social interaction and civic engagement.* Washington, DC: Pew Internet & American Life Project.

McGonigal, J. (2007). Why I love bees: A casestudy in collective intelligence gaming. Retrieved from www.avantgame.com/McGonigal_WhyILoveBees_Feb2007.pdf

McGonigal, J. (2011). *Reality is broken: Why games make us better and how they can change the world.* New York, NY: Penguin Press.

Metcalf, S. (2011, March). *EcoMUVE: Immersive virtual worlds for collaborative learning about complex causality in ecosystems.* Paper presented at the 2011Cyberlearning Tools for STEM Education Conference, Monterey, CA.

Mislevy, R., Steinberg, L., & Almond, R. (2003). On the structure of educational assessments. *Measurement: Interdisciplinary Research and Perspectives, 1,* 3–67

National Research Council. (2009). *Learning science in informal environments: People, places, and pursuits.* P. Bell, B. Lewenstein, A. W. Shouse, & M. A. Feder (Eds.) Washington, DC: National Academies Press.

National Research Council (2011). *Learning science through computer games and simulations.* Margaret A. Honey & Margaret L. Hilton (Eds.), Board on Science Education, Division of Behavioral and Social Sciences and Education. Washington, DC: National Academies Press. Retrieved from http://www.nap.edu/catalog/13078.html

Papert, S. (2002). Hard fun. *Bangor Daily News.* Bangor, ME. Retrieved from http://www.papert.org/articles/HardFun.html

Partnership for 21st Century Skills (2009). Framework for 21st century learning. Retrieved from http://www.p21.org/documents/P21_Framework.pdf

Polanyi, M. (1966). *The tacit dimension.* London, UK:Routledge.

Rowe, E., & Asbell-Clarke, J. (2008). Learning science online: What matters for science teachers? *Journal of Interactive Online Learning, 7*(2), 75–104.

Scardamalia, M., & Bereiter, C. (1996). Computer support for knowledge-building communities. In T. Koschmann (Ed.), *CSCL: Theory and practice of an emerging paradigm* (pp. 249–268). Mahwah, NJ: Lawrence Erlbaum Associates, Inc.

Senge, P., Kleiner, A., Roberts, C., Ross, R., & Smith, B. (2004). *The fifth discipline fieldbook: Strategies and tools for building a learning organization.* New York, NY: Doubleday Currency.

Shute, V. J. (2011). Stealth assessment in computer-based games to support learning. In S. Tobias & J. D. Fletcher (Eds.), *Computer games and instruction.* Charlotte, NC: Information Age Publishers.

Steinkuehler, C., & Duncan, S. (2008). Scientific habits of mind in virtual worlds. *Journal of Science Education and Technology*, 17(6), 530–543.

Thomas, D., & Brown, J. S. (2011). *A New Culture of Learning: Cultivating the Imagination for a World of Constant Change*: Printed by CreateSpace.

Toulmin, S. (1958). *The uses of argument*. Cambridge, UK: Cambridge University Press.

U.S. Department of Labor (2007). The STEM workforce challenge: The role of the public workforce system in a national solution for a competitive science, technology, engineering, and mathematics (STEM) workforce. Retrieved from www.doleta.gov/youth_services/pdf/STEM_Report_4%2007.pdf

Vygotsky, L. S. (1978). *Mind in society: The development of higher psychological processes*. Cambridge, MA: Harvard University Press.

18

Computer Games and Education: A Multidimensional Relationship

KEITH ROE AND ANNE DICKMEIS

Introduction

As in many countries, the Flemish government has for some time been facilitating the integration of information communication technology into primary education by providing funds to purchase equipment and train teachers. However, in terms of content, schools are uncertain how and to what degree to employ these tools. In 2004, the Flemish Ministry of Education published a best-practices document (Dienst voor Onderwijsontwikkeling, 2004) containing examples of how to integrate educational software into regular school instruction. In these examples, much of the software consisted of video games, such as memory and labyrinth games. However, no coherent strategy for the integration of games into the curriculum was proposed. More recently, however, there have been indications of a more targeted approach. For example, in 2011, in response to concerns about bullying, the Minister of Education launched a government-sponsored antibullying video game for use in classrooms, entitled "Poverty Is Not a Game" (PING). At the same time, he incorporated the game into the specifications of targeted final attainment levels for media literacy, stating that this was "the first attempt to introduce and stimulate the potential of video games as an educational tool" (Smet, 2011, p. 30).

In a wider European context, in 2009 the European Schoolnet published a report based on six case studies in different European countries, commissioned by the Interactive Software Federation of Europe, on the pedagogical possibilities of using video games in European schools (Wastiau, Kearney, & Van den Berghe, 2009). The results indicated that most of the surveyed teachers (n = 528) were already using both educational and entertainment-oriented commercial video games in their classes, mostly in the context of mother-tongue and foreign language teaching. Further, teachers reported heightened motivation and advancement in a wide range of general skills among their pupils (cf. Pivec & Pivec, 2009).

However, the report also noted that the surveyed teachers were tentative with regard to the impact of video games on specific course skills. The report further cited the educational context and the amount and quality of teacher guidance as important mediating variables.

In a wider international context, Gee (2003) found that video games can provide an inherently motivating context for learning and there is a considerable body of empirical evidence (e.g., Rosas et al., 2003; Castel, Pratt, & Drummond, 2005; Green & Bavelier, 2007; Blumberg, Altschuler, Almonte, & Mileaf, 2013) supporting the view that such games can have a positive impact on specific skills and forms of learning. However, far less research has situated game playing within the broader context of adolescents' orientation to and experience of schooling. It is this aspect which forms the focus of this chapter.

Education and Media Use

The general influence of education on the ways in which people relate to culture and cultural activities has been demonstrated many times (e.g., Bourdieu, 1984; DiMaggio & Mukhtar, 2004; Alderson, Junisbai, & Heacock, 2007). In addition, numerous studies from different countries have investigated the ways in which education structures the audiences for specific media. For example, with regard to the print media, Kraaykamp and Dijkstra (1999) stressed the importance of educational level with regard to social group differences in book reading preferences in the Netherlands, a finding echoed by van Rees, Vermunt and Verboord (1999) and, in Hungary, by Bukodi (2007). Similarly, Torche (2007) reported that education is "highly relevant" to newspaper and magazine reading in Chile.

If education is a main determinant of reading practices, it follows that it may also play a major role in structuring all media practices. Furthermore, there is an accumulated body of evidence supporting this hypothesis. For example, in the 1960s and 1970s, British and American research showed that involvement in adolescent subcultures (such as rockers, hippies, and punks) was negatively related to school achievement, and that many of these subcultures were found to express a strong attachment to some form of music (for an overview see Roe, 1995). In the 1980s and 1990s, Swedish research (Roe, 1985; 1992; 1993; 1994) demonstrated that adolescents' school commitment and school achievement had independent effects on their music preferences, even when controlling for social background. Similar effects have been also reported with regard to adolescents' VCR use (Roe, 1989), television use (Roe, 2000), and computer game play (Roe & Muijs, 1998).

In terms of the relationship between education and media use, extant research also stresses the importance of distinguishing between medium types and content preferences. For example, Kraaykamp (2001; cf. Kraaykamp, 2003) found that content similarities (e.g., action and fast-pacing) were more evident than medium similarities (e.g., television and film) in predicting media preferences. Moreover, he noted that researchers have mainly regarded audiovisual and the print media as opposites, whereas cultivation theory implies that we may also expect social differentiation between heavy and light users of all media; a proposition supported by Roe, Eggermont, and Minnebo's (2001) finding that, while school achievement among secondary school students was positively related to use of print media and negatively related to use of audiovisual media, there was also a rather strong positive relationship between the time adolescents spent using the two types of media. This finding indicated that heavy users of one media type tended to be heavy users of the other.

Differentiating Student Groups in Terms of Education and Media Use

While research such as that described above has frequently differentiated the media audience in terms of uses and preferences, education has typically been operationalized one-dimensionally in terms of some kind of achieved level. There is evidence, however, (see Rosengren & Windahl, 1989; Roe, 1992; Muijs, 1997) that factors such as commitment to school, parental involvement, perceptions of the future, and academic self-concept are also important in relation to media use. Further, time spent doing, and attitude toward homework could also be hypothesized as mediating both educational achievement and media use. Dissecting different elements of education in this way would provide a denser map of the ways in which educational factors are interwoven with the fabric of media segmentation and thereby enhance our understanding of the dynamics of the education-media interface. Exploration of this possibility is the purpose of our discussion below.

In a study of Flemish adolescents, Roe, Van den Bulck, De Cock, and Dusart (2001) found that the relationship between education and the media use of young adolescents was more intricate than had been assumed, involving complex interactions across at least six major dimensions: school commitment, school achievement, media segmentation, socioeconomic status background (SES), age, and gender. On the basis of these interactions, the authors identified four distinct groups of students: one positive and three negative toward school.

The first group, labeled "The Positive to School High Achievers" (43.4% of respondents), combined the highest mean SES with a very high commitment to school and the highest mean level of school achievement. These students also showed the lowest levels of orientation to digital media and the highest levels of orientation to the print media. Although there was a small majority of females in this group, gender did not appear to be a defining factor in its composition. Thus, a taste for the print media, combined with a relative distaste for the electronic media, appeared to be characteristic of individuals from higher status backgrounds who were committed to school and high achievement (i.e., those possessing the highest mean levels of cultural and academic capital). This finding supports previous research and can easily be explained by reference to the theories of Bourdieu (Bourdieu & Passeron, 1979; Bourdieu, 1984) and others concerning the pivotal role that schools continue to play in reproducing the structure of these forms of capital. Perhaps the only surprise is that, with the exception of seeking information for schoolwork, relatively speaking, this group did not appear to have embraced the digital media, preferring to remain loyal to print.

The second group was labeled "The Negative to School Low Achievers" (37% of respondents) and constituted the majority of those who were negative in attitude toward school. This group was comprised of low SES, low-achieving, predominantly male students who, comparatively speaking, were not oriented to the media. In terms of cultural and academic capital, their profile situated them at the opposite end of the pole from the first group. The relatively low levels of overall media use of this group, combined with the fact that they watched the least television at weekends, suggested that these adolescents diverted their energies to activities other than school work or media use.

The third group was "The Negative to School, Media Oriented Low Achievers" (6.8% of respondents). This group was the smallest and most negative to school and consisted of low-SES, low-achieving, predominantly male students who were strongly oriented to film, computer games, and other digital applications, while most negative to the print media. The fact that this group combined very negative attitudes toward school and very low achievement with the highest need to achieve of any group, suggests that their heavy investment in digital media use constituted an alternative source of gratification and status to that provided by the traditional academic reward system.

The fourth group was "The Negative to School, Media Oriented High Achievers" (13% of respondents). This group was almost two-thirds female and performed the juggling act of combining a low commitment to school with relatively high achievement, a feat which could be connected to the unusual fact that their mothers had higher mean levels of educational and occupational status than their fathers. In terms of media use, this group shunned the digital media in favor of a heavy preference for television.

In summary, in terms of explaining young adolescents' media use, a number of significant conclusions can be drawn from these results. First, orientation to the print media continued to be associated with a high status background, positive attitudes toward school, and high achievement. Second, greater orientation to digital media, in general, was associated with neither a low commitment to school or low achievement. Here the picture becomes more complex. Relatively speaking, the majority of negative to school, low achieving adolescents were not media oriented. They appear to have been mainly interested in other things. The minority of negative to school adolescents who were media oriented fell into two groups distinguished by different interactions between level of school achievement, gender, and type of media preferred. Thus, a heavy involvement with digital media was most characteristic of very negative toward school, very low achieving males; a heavy involvement with television was most characteristic of negative to school, above average achieving females. Gender would appear to be the decisive differentiating factor involved here, since existing research suggests that, on average, females tend to score higher on overall school achievement than do males, and also seem less attracted to digital media. Nevertheless, even given this mediation, on the basis of this study, it could be concluded that, if there is a negative relationship between school achievement and any form of media use, it is with computer game playing and the Internet rather than television, a finding which is to some extent antithetical to conventional wisdom. Finally, given that some adolescents managed to combine higher achievement with comparatively heavy use of some media, it follows that, in this study, the best predictor of media use at this age was not school achievement but school commitment.

Education and Computer Game Playing

The authors also conducted a study in 2012 of 1,250 Flemish adolescents aged 12–19 years (M = 15.2 years; SD = 1.81); 46.2% of whom were male and 53.8% female. Respondents were administered a written questionnaire during school hours containing items designed to measure the amount of time they spent playing computer games in general, and playing various game genres (both online and offline) in particular, and their perceived relative school achievement ("How good are your grades compared to the others in your class?"). They also were asked about various aspects of their school performance and attitudes, and of personality variables such as self-concept, impulsivity, and sensation seeking.

Findings showed that males and younger adolescents were found to have home access to more computer and game applications than females and older adolescents. Not surprisingly, such access was strongly related to higher amounts of both online and offline playing of all categories of games. Greater access to games was also weakly associated with having more quarrels with teachers but, interestingly, with slightly less difficulty in completing homework. Finally, there were weak significant correlations between greater access to games and higher levels of impulsivity, sensation seeking, and having a positive, but not a negative, self-concept.

Total amount of computer game playing was measured by adding the amount of time spent playing various game genres (online and offline). The results indicated a strong relationship with gender, whereby males played much more than females (especially online). On average, younger adolescents played more than older adolescents. There were also weak negative correlations between total amount and total amount of offline playing and both fathers' occupational and mothers' educational status. In terms of school, those playing more online games had slightly more quarrels and other problems with teachers and a negative perception of their school atmosphere. There was no relationship between game playing and being happy or unhappy at school. Conversely, more offline playing did not correlate with problems with teachers, but was positively associated with being unhappy at school. Online playing correlated with higher levels of impulsivity and sensation seeking, while offline playing was only associated with impulsivity. A positive self-concept was associated with total time spent playing computer games and amount of online playing, but not with offline playing. Conversely, a negative self-concept was associated with playing less, both in total and online.

In terms of specific genres, on the basis of an exploratory factor analysis, three factors were extracted: action (fighting, racing, and sports games), puzzle (puzzle, platform, and simulation games), and strategy (strategy and role-playing games). Males were more likely than females to play action and strategy games; females were more likely than males to play puzzle games. Younger adolescents played more of all three genres than did older adolescents. Action and strategy games, but not puzzle games, were associated with impulsivity and sensation seeking; having a positive self-concept correlated with playing action and strategy games more, and puzzle games less often. However, having a negative self-concept was associated with playing less with action and strategy games and more with puzzle games. Quarrels and friction with teachers were associated with more action and strategy game playing and a negative school atmosphere, while being unhappier at school was associated with strategy game playing. Conversely, playing more puzzle games was associated with fewer problems with teachers, although there was a weak correlation with having problems with other students. Interestingly, there was a weak positive correlation between perceived relative school achievement and amount of action game playing.

As noted above, the personality traits of impulsivity, sensation seeking, and self-concept were related to a number of computer game variables. Moreover, impulsivity and sensation seeking were strongly correlated with each other. Having a negative self-concept was weakly related to sensation seeking but not impulsivity. However, it is also important to note that these traits were also associated with a number of other relevant variables. First, males scored higher on impulsivity and sensation seeking and had appreciably more positive self-concepts than did females. Second, younger adolescents tend to be more impulsive than older adolescents, although there was no association between age and sensation seeking or self-concept. In terms of the school variables, greater impulsivity and sensation seeking were related to lower perceived school achievement, quarrels and other problems with teachers, defiant behavior, and a negative school atmosphere. In addition, sensation seeking was also significantly related to problems in completing homework. A more positive self-concept was associated with higher perceived achievement, being happier at school, having fewer problems with teachers, and having fewer problems completing homework. Having a more negative self-concept was associated with lower perceived achievement, being unhappier at school, having more quarrels and other problems with teachers, and having more problems completing homework.

Given the number of significant correlations that were found in the data involving gender and age, we split the sample into four subgroups: 12- to 14-year-old males, 12- to 14-year-old females, 15- to 17-year-old males, and 15- to 17-year-old females. The number of respondents who were 18 years or more was too small to allow meaningful analysis on the basis of this subdivision. Among 12- to 14-year-old males, there was a positive relationship between total amount of online game playing and having a positive self-concept. There were also positive relationships between amount of playing action games and perceived school achievement, impulsivity, sensation seeking, and having a positive self-concept. There also was a negative relationship with mothers' educational status (basic compulsory through university). Playing puzzle games was associated with fewer problems with teachers; playing strategy games failed to correlate significantly with any of these variables. Among 12- to 14-year-old females, playing action games correlated with having a lower occupational status mother and a lower educational status among both parents, and with greater sensation seeking and a negative school atmosphere. Playing puzzle and strategy games correlated only with greater sensation seeking. In this group having a positive self-concept correlated negatively with amount of online, offline, and total amount of game playing, as did amount of playing puzzle and strategy games.

Among 15- to 17-year-old males, there was a positive relationship between playing action games and sensation seeking, and with a lower occupational and educational status of the mother, but no significant relationships with the school variables. However, having a positive self-concept was associated with playing puzzle games less; a negative self-concept was associated with playing more with puzzle and strategy games. Among and 15- to 17-year-old females, total game playing time was associated with a negative self-concept, while playing more action games was associated with greater impulsivity and sensation seeking, and with more quarrels with teachers. Similarly, playing more strategy games was associated with more quarrels and other problems with teachers and with greater impulsivity and sensation seeking. Finally, playing more puzzle games was associated with a negative self-concept.

Computer Games and the Transfer of Learning

As noted above, there is a significant amount of published research indicating that the use of computer games in the school context can have positive effects on student motivation and skills. While we certainly do not reject these findings, in this chapter we have employed a more macro-level approach to the relationship between the school and channels of learning based on media of communication, and it is from this perspective that we approach the issue of learning transfer.

Schools are complex social institutions providing opportunities for learning that also involve enforced attendance, labels and identities of success and failure, interaction with authority figures and, for some, social and cultural alienation. In this context, communication media and their contents can be employed not only to enhance learning but also by some students, as expressions and symbols of resistance. Consequently, while employing such media in the curriculum in some respects can be seen as a positive stratagem, the question needs to be raised as to whether the outcomes will be positive for all groups of students.

The results of the first study reported here (Roe et al., 2001) indicated that the relationship between education and the media use of young adolescents involves complex interactions between age, gender, socioeconomic background, media segmentation, school achievement, and school commitment. Moreover, a heavy involvement with digital media, such as computer game playing, was most characteristic of very low achieving males with very negative attitudes toward school. This situation raises the question of why some low achieving, negative to school students become more media oriented than others. As indicated by this study, one promising line of inquiry with regard to the very negative to school, digital media group, would be to focus on the fact that, while they have a very high need to achieve, for some reason they are unable or unwilling to do so in the conventional academic setting of the school. One explanation might be that they divert their commitment and effort to computer game playing and Internet use, possibly in an attempt to find alternative sources of competence, status, and self-esteem. From this perspective, incorporating the digital competences of this group within the school curriculum would appear to offer excellent opportunities for engaging their motivation and achievement.

However, as this study also demonstrated, the overall picture with regard to the relationship between education and media is somewhat more complex. For example, the highest achievers manifested the lowest levels of orientation to digital media and the highest orientation to print. Forcing them into game-playing activities may consequently have had a negative impact on their motivation and academic achievement. Secondly, the members of the largest group of negative to school, low achievers were not particularly oriented to the media, suggesting that these adolescents spent much of their time in activities unrelated to both school work and media use. Consequently, it could be argued that their learning was unlikely to be especially enhanced by greater use of digital applications in the school context.

The results of the second study reported here blur the overall picture further, since they indicate that computer game playing is embedded in a complex and variable network of interactions involving age, gender, socioeconomic background, academic achievement, being happy/unhappy at school, relationships with teachers, impulsivity, self-concept, and sensation seeking. The implication of these findings is that any implementation of game playing into the curriculum would have to be carefully targeted at specific groups if it is to have a positive overall effect on learning transfer and general educational outcomes.

Perhaps the most consistent finding in these and other studies is that full account must be taken of gender. Males had more home access to computer games and on average they played far more than females, especially online. Further, they played action and strategy games far more than did females, while the latter were drawn more to puzzle games. It follows that designing games for the curriculum has to take account of these differences to maximize potential learning transfer outcomes. Females are less likely to respond positively to action and strategy games than are males, whereas most males do not seem to find puzzle games very appealing. Secondly, there are clear and consistent relationships between game playing and age. On average, younger adolescents played more than did older adolescents, and more of all types of genres studied, implying that the efficacy of game based learning transfer may also vary with age. The subgroup analyses also indicated that age and gender interacted to produce sometimes highly variable, not to say sometimes inconsistent, results. Perhaps the main lesson to be learned from these studies is that, in terms of game types and learning transfer, what may be appropriate for males and females at one age may not be appropriate for males and females in another age group. Third, the socioeconomic status (SES) background of the students was also related to game playing, with higher SES students, on average, playing games less than lower SES students. While this factor is difficult to accommodate in the school curriculum, it is an added question with regard to any across-the-board integration of computer games into the curriculum. While not dealt with here, the same question could be asked with regard to students from different ethnic and cultural backgrounds.

The results reported here also clearly indicate that not only socio-demographic factors are involved in this web of interaction, but also personality characteristics. In addition to strongly correlating with each other, impulsivity, sensation seeking, and self-concept also interact with gender and age, as well as manifesting clear and sometimes strong relationships with certain aspects of computer game playing. It follows that while students who are high in impulsivity and sensation seeking may respond positively in terms of learning to computer games (especially those with fast pace and action), students scoring lower on these traits may have little interest, or simply be turned off by such material.

School based factors, too, were found to be related to variations in game playing. In some respects, game playing was related to having more quarrels and other problems with teachers, experiencing the school atmosphere as negative, and being unhappy at school. Preference for game genres was also associated with school factors: more action and strategy game playing was associated with more quarrels and friction with teachers and strategy game playing was related to being unhappier at school. However, the fact that playing more with puzzle games was associated with fewer problems with teachers suggests that these relationships may, at least in part, be spurious as a result of the mediation of gender. Moreover, school experience was also clearly related to variations in levels of impulsivity, sensation seeking, and self-concept. Finally, it should be noted that there were few relationships between game playing and perceived relative school achievement, although this may have resulted from the subjective measure of school achievement employed.

In summary, from the perspective of the work presented in this chapter, the issue of the nature and extent of learning transfer that can be expected from systematic use of computer games in the curriculum depends on how one interprets the relationships between the school context and computer game playing reported by this and other studies. From our results it appears that, in the Flemish context at least, (1) not all groups of students manifest much interest in computer game playing in their leisure time; and (2) a high level of computer game playing, especially of certain genres, is strongly associated among some adolescents with school problems and (especially in the case of the first study) even school rejection. In terms of potential learning transfer, therefore, we may ask whether incorporating more computer game playing into the curriculum would interest or stimulate the first group; or induce the members of the second group back into more active and motivated participation in the educational project, or merely alienate them still further by encroaching on their symbols of resistance.

Clearly, more research directed at this question is needed. Based on the results of our studies, we are tempted to answer the question regarding positive learning transfer from computer game use by paraphrasing the conclusion of Joseph Klapper's (1960) seminal work on media effects: for some groups of students under some circumstances, "yes"; for other groups of students, under other circumstances, "no." In other words, any strategy for systematically incorporating computer game playing into the curriculum needs to be carefully designed, and tailored and targeted to specific groups, since it is highly unlikely that a one-size-fits-all stratagem will accommodate the complex set of interactions and variations that we have reported here.

Finally, it is worth remembering that, in different forms, the discussion as to whether to incorporate media of communication into the school curriculum is a very old one, having been conducted with regard to popular literature, film, television, and rock music. Moreover, historically, this debate can be located within the larger context of the relationship between education and popular culture. The lessons of these previous experiences teach us that while incorporating popular cultural forms into the curriculum may make the school experience more relevant to some contemporary students, to the extent that the flaunting of elements of popular culture is employed as a symbolic act of resistance by school-alienated and -rejecting students, it is highly unlikely to result in positive achievement outcomes.

References

Alderson, A. S., Junisbai, I., & Heacock, I. (2007). Social status and cultural consumption in the United States. *Poetics: Journal of Empirical Research on Culture, the Media and the Arts, 35,* 191–212.

Blumberg, F. C., Altschuler, E. A., Almonte, D. E., & Mileaf, M. I. (2013). The impact of recreational video game play on children and adolescents' cognition. In F. C. Blumberg & S. M. Fisch (Eds.), *New Directions for Child and Adolescent Development, 139,* 41–50.

Bourdieu, P. (1984). *Distinction: A social critique of the judgment of taste.* London, UK: Routledge.

Bourdieu, P.,& Passeron, J.-C. (1979). *The inheritors: French students and their relation to culture.* London, UK: University of Chicago Press.

Bukodi, E. (2007). Social stratification and cultural consumption in Hungary: Book readership. *Poetics: Journal of Empirical Research on Culture, the Media and the Arts, 35,* 112–131.

Castel, A. D., Pratt, J., & Drummond, E. (2005). The effects of action video game experience on the time course of inhibition of return and efficiency of visual search. *Acta Psychologica, 119,* 217–230.

Dienst voor Onderwijsontwikkeling, Ministerie van de Vlaamse Gemeenschap: Departement Onderwijs. (2004). *ICT-Competenties in het Basisonderwijs: Via ICT-Integratie naar ICT-Competentie.* Retrieved from http://www.vlaanderen.be/nl/publicaties/detail/ict-competenties-in-het-basisonderwijs-via-ict-integratie-naar-ict-competenties

DiMaggio, P., & Mukhtar, T. (2004). Arts participation as cultural capital in the United States, 1982–2002. *Poetics: Journal of Empirical Research on Culture, the Media and The Arts, 32,* 169–194.

Gee, J. P. (2003). *What video games have to teach us about learning and literacy.* New York, NY: Palgrave.

Green, C. S., & Bavelier, D. (2007). Action-Video-Game Experience Alters the Spatial Resolution of Vision. *Psychological Science, 18*(1), 88–94.

Klapper, J. (1960). *The Effects of Mass Communication.* New York, NY: Free Press.

Kraaykamp, G. (2001). Parents, personality, and media preferences. *Communications: The European Journal of Communication Research, 26,* 15–37.

Kraaykamp, G. (2003). Literary socialization and reading preferences: Effects of parents the library and the school. *Poetics: Journal of Empirical Research on Culture, the Media and the Arts, 31,* 235–257.

Kraaykamp, G., & Dijkstra, K. (1999). Preferences in leisure time book reading: A study on the social differentiation in book reading for the Netherlands. *Poetics: Journal of Empirical Research on Culture, the Media and the Arts, 26,* 203–234.

Muijs, R. D. (1997). *Self, school and media.* Leuven, Belgium: Department of Communication KU Leuven.

Pivec, M., & Pivec, P. (2009). What do we know from research about the use of games in education? In, P. Wastiau., C. Kearney, & W. Van den Berghe. *How are digital games used in schools?* Brussels, Belgium: European Schoolnet.

Roe, K. (1985). Swedish youth and music: Listening patterns and motivations. *Communication Research, 12,* 353–362.

Roe, K. (1989). School achievement, self-esteem and adolescents' video use. In M. R. Levy (Ed.), *The VCR Age: Home video and mass communication*. Newbury Park, CA: Sage.

Roe, K. (1992). Different destinies—different melodies: School achievement, anticipated status and adolescents' tastes in music. *European Journal of Communication, 7*, 335–358.

Roe, K. (1993). Academic capital and music tastes among Swedish adolescents. *Young: Nordic Journal of Youth Research, 1*, 40–55.

Roe, K. (1994). Media use and social mobility. In K. E. Rosengren (Ed.), *Media effects and beyond: Culture, socialization and lifestyles*. London, UK: Routledge.

Roe, K. (1995). Adolescents' use of socially disvalued media: Towards a theory of media delinquency. *Journal of Youth and Adolescence, 24*, 617–631.

Roe, K. (2000). Socio-economic status and children's television use. *Communications: The European Journal of Communication Research, 25*(1), 3–18.

Roe, K., Eggermont, S., & Minnebo, J. (2001). Media use and academic achievement: Which effects? *Communications: The European Journal of Communication, 26*, 39–58.

Roe, K., & Muijs, D. (1998). Children and computer games: A portrait of the heavy user. *European Journal of Communication, 13*(2), 181–200.

Roe, K.,Van den Bulck, J. De Cock, K., & Dusart, C. (2001). *Het onderwijs in een Concurrentiestrijd: Een studie naar de positie van formele leerkanalen in een informele kennismaatschappij*. Leuven, Belgium: Department of Communication KU Leuven.

Rosas, R., Nussbaum, M., Cumsille, P., Marianov, V., Correa, M., Flores, P.,... Salinas, M. (2003). Beyond Nintendo: Design and assessment of educational games for first and second grade students. *Computers and Education, 40*, 71–94.

Rosengren, K. E., & Windahl, S. (1989). *Media matter: TV use in childhood and adolescence*. Norwood, NJ: Ablex.

Smet, P. (2011). *Beleidsprioriteiten Onderwijs 2011–2012*. Retrieved from http://docs.vlaamsparlement.be/docs/stukken/2011-2012/g1317-1.pdf

Torche, F. (2007). Social status and cultural consumption: The case of reading in Chile. *Poetics: Journal of Empirical Research on Culture, the Media and the Arts, 35*, 70–92.

VanRees, K.,Vermunt, J., & Verboord, M. (1999). Cultural classifications under discussion: Latent class analysis of highbrow and lowbrow reading. *Poetics: Journal of Empirical Research on Culture, the Media and the Arts, 26*, 349–365.

Wastiau, P., Kearney, C., & Van denBerghe, W. (2009). *How are digital games used in schools?* Brussels, Belgium: European Schoolnet.

19

Video Games, Motivation, and Learning

MICHAEL A. EVANS, BRETT D. JONES,
AND JENNIFER BIEDLER

Introduction

Since the 1961 creation of *Spacewar*, recreational video games have become a cultural phenomenon that readily competes with the movie and music industries for consumer dollars. Video game revenue has more than doubled since 1996, reaching $7 billion in 2005 (Nielsen, Smith, & Tosca, 2008). Video games attract players of all ages and genders: the Kaiser Family Foundation has reported that males and females between the ages 8 and 18 spend an average of 8 hours and 33 minutes a day interacting with digital media, including video games (Rideout, Foehr, & Roberts, 2010). Further, people of all ages spend 3 billion hours a week playing online games and teenagers spend as much time, if not more, playing video games as they do on their homework (Jackson, 2011). With such a high level of engagement exhibited by youth in various media platforms, giving particular attention to video games, it was only a matter of time before academics noticed the potential for educational interventions (Nielsen, Smith, & Tosca, 2008).

The high-level of engagement experienced by students via video games led to the development of "edutainment," which combines education and entertainment to create educational games (Khine, 2011). As reflected in the early titles such as *Math Blasters*, and now several titles available on the Apple App Store such as *Pearl Diver*, many educational games are based on drill and practice methods in which students repeat a task until the knowledge or skill has been mastered. These titles should not be labeled as games per se, but more as entertaining media that allow users to master and increase fluency of previously learned material. Nevertheless, these titles may have successfully incorporated basic game mechanics such as achievement points for hitting a succession of targets within narrow tolerances. For example, in one game, *Typing of the Dead*, players killed zombies while practicing their typing skills (Green & McNeese, 2011). Simulations also have been used for educational purposes (Collins & Halverson, 2009). Experiential simulations are designed to model real-life situations that are seen as too dangerous or expensive for actual experimentation and failure. Simulations such as *Crystal Island* and *Quest Atlantis* have been cited as particularly effective in educational settings that focus on science (Honey & Hilton, 2011; Evans, 2009).

Among the greatest liabilities of edutainment games are their failure to fully meet the standards of high quality set by the game industry, primarily because of problematic design choices and an inability to engage the learner in purposeful and intentional ways (see Jackson, 2011; Khine, 2011; Tüzün, 2007). Recreational video games, by comparison, contain well-tested elements that contribute to learning (van Staalduinen & de Freitas, 2011); and thereby, have the potential to operate as a medium for inquiry-driven instruction (Squire, 2011). For example, children who play recreational video games have been shown to develop sophisticated skills such as problem solving, strategic thinking, increased hand-eye coordination, and communication (Blumberg & Randall, 2013; Collins & Halverson, 2009; Green & McNeese, 2011). This behavioral and cognitive learning might reflect that video games adopt (by design and best practice) many pedagogical techniques that are commonly used in the classroom, such as teamwork (Green & McNeese, 2011), problem-based or design-based learning (Jackson, 2011), and basing of tasks in a real-world context (Collins & Halverson, 2009). In fact, many students are sufficiently motivated to play video games, as illustrated by the spending of over 10,000 hours of play by age 21 (McGonigal, 2010). Further, well-designed video games might facilitate "flow" (Csikszentmihalyi, 1990), a concept that refers to a state of complete absorption and engagement in a task, which serves to motivate players to play for extended periods of time (van Staalduinen & de Freitas, 2011). Overall, well-designed recreational video games can be portrayed as desirable "learning machines" that incorporate sound instructional design principles such as calibrating challenges to match player ability as reflected in specific design attributes such as dynamic difficulty adjustment. Moreover, leader boards serve as healthy forms of competition that drive players to persist to achieve a high score relevant to game performance (Gee & Hayes, 2011).

Our research program has entailed examining what constitutes well-designed games and how they can be used to teach and motivate students in STEM (science, technology, engineering, and mathematics) content in real-world environments. As part of our research, we have examined recreational video game attributes and design principles that contribute to student motivation and learning in the context of informal design-based science teaching and learning. In this chapter, we share a review of our findings from our *Mission: Evolution* project, funded by the MacArthur Foundation (#2010–2453), as a working example to demonstrate how recreational video games can be appropriated as learning platforms for middle and high school students.

Mission: Evolution—Using Video Games to Enhance Informal Science Education

The question that inspired our project, *Mission: Evolution,* was this: How can recreational video games be integrated into a free-choice, afterschool environment in ways that motivate high school students to engage in science? This project has unfolded in three phases since its inception in 2009. During the initial stage, multiple class sections of middle school students individually played *Spore Origins* on an iPod Touch during regularly scheduled class time. Individual play on the iPods was enhanced by whole-class discussion of the game using an interactive whiteboard. A detailed account of this phase of the project can be found in Evans (2010). In phase two (Fall, 2010), high school students played the title *Spore* during class time to explore concepts such as speciation and mutation, as depicted in the game. The students were required to keep an expert log that noted consistencies and inconsistencies while also justifying the imposed functional evolution of their own creatures during game play. In the final phase (Spring, 2011), small groups of high school students developed scientifically sound learning games using *Spore Galactic Adventures* in an afterschool setting. A detailed account of these phases can be found in Evans and Biedler (2012). Given that the same teacher was involved in all three phases (and is co-author on this chapter), the development of her views for adopting recreational video games matured along with the sophistication of the games. The role of learners also progressed from consumers of prebuilt titles to designers and developers of their own titles. The extant literature highlights the value of adopting video game technology with a variety of teaching strategies and learning approaches dependent on the goals of instruction (Honey & Hilton, 2011; Stenkuehler & Duncan, 2009).

The story of *Mission: Evolution* begins from the perspective of a middle-school teacher, determined to make a seventh-grade science classroom interesting because early adolescent students often find traditional methods of instruction mundane compared to recreational video games. Given this challenge, the science teacher was inspired to integrate recreational video games, specifically the *Spore* series of titles for multiple platforms (iPod Touches and PC laptops), into the science curriculum during coverage of the topic of evolutionary biology. The overall purpose of such integration was to provide learners an engaging mediated experience to facilitate learning that could be evidenced via traditional and alternative assessment protocols. The specific curricular goal was to teach biological evolution with regard to natural selection and speciation as required by state and national standards. A noted challenge of this phase of the project was to balance the constraints of the curriculum with the opportunities for engagement provided by recreational video games.

The start of the intervention process began with collaboration between the classroom science teacher and university professors from the fields of the learning sciences and educational psychology (author and co-author), with the intent of making learning meaningful to students while closely aligning with existing course curricula and state standards. Understandably, the district science advisor and school principal were concerned about deviating too far from established and standardized instructional and assessment protocols to the detriment of student achievement. After much iterative refinement and collaboration among the authors, the results were inspiring as students immersed themselves in critical inquiry motivated by player-invoked evolution of their creatures in *Spore Origins*, and in thinking about how the video game was deficient in its portrayal of the biology curriculum they had learned. These deficiencies have been documented elsewhere (Bohannon, 2008; Evans, Holbrook, Blevins, & Biedler, 2011), but the potential innovative aspect of this phase of the project was that students were guided (by design in the video game and instructional supports) to expand and confirm their growing understanding of evolution by leveraging the video game as a learning medium. The gains in understanding were recorded using traditional (paper-and-pencil post-lesson tests) and alternative (expert logs) assessment protocols. Based on these initial results (as detailed in Evans, 2010), the *Mission: Evolution* project was translated to a high school biology classroom. Responding to a call from the MacArthur Foundation to challenge educators and learning scientists to propose innovative uses of recreational video games for instruction and learning, the transition was enhanced by allowing students opportunities to engage productively with recreational video games outside of class, dedicating a substantial portion of the time developing their own games to convey scientific ideas to others. In fact, our project was recognized with an award in a competition also sponsored by the MacArthur Foundation (see Evans, 2010; and Evans & Bielder, 2012, for further information about this phase of the project).

The next iterations of *Mission: Evolution* were a MacArthur Foundation, Digital Media & Learning Competition sponsored project. In these phases, the improvements to the project were twofold. First, we invited tenth-grade biology students to apply knowledge of evolutionary biology covered in daytime course work to detect errors and misconceptions of science while playing *Spore* (phase two). These activities took place over two months in Fall 2010. Second, the classroom science teacher and graduate students from science education and computer science mentored students in game design as they built individualized games in *Spore Galactic Adventures*, an expansion pack for *Spore* that allows players to develop self-generated levels and challenges in a structured environment where tutorials guide the student in-game (phase three). In Spring 2011, students completed the final phase of the project prior to presentation at the Digital Media & Learning (DML) Conference in early March of that year. Students adopted insights gained during the *Spore* analysis and planned ways to incorporate these insights into a final *Spore Galactic Adventures*–generated game. The science teacher judged final video game products on how well they conveyed a specific scientific concept, such as speciation (the evolutionary process that results in new species). The teacher based assessment on standards, objectives, and lesson plans from the daily curriculum. In parallel, graduate students evaluated final deliverables on how well the games leveraged sound game design principles—such as whether the games provided challenging yet achievable goals—and assigned behaviors to characters that supported players in succeeding to win the game. The highest-judged games, along with supporting media and materials, were presented at the DML conference in March 2011 at an invited session (see Evans & Biedler, 2012, for details on these phases of the project).

Overall, the different phases of the *Mission: Evolution* project addressed specific learning needs. For the middle school phase (phase one) conducted in Spring 2009, the learning goals focused on mastering curriculum taught in a life science classroom. The objectives took into consideration the standards of learning (SOL) set forth by the Commonwealth of Virginia, and the need to establish a motivational classroom climate for participants. A significant SOL objective taken from existing curricula was to conduct a scientific investigation, which was accomplished through game play of *Spore Origins* on the iPod Touch and *Spore* on a desktop computer projected onto an interactive whiteboard. For this assignment, students were tasked with organizing data into tables, creating models to demonstrate and explain content, interpret data through evaluation, and to contemplate the nature of science (Reiber, 2005). A secondary SOL objective included investigating how organisms interacted with each other, which focused on competition, cooperation, and territorial imperative among species. A tertiary SOL objective was to investigate and understand how organisms changed over time, including changes through mutation, adaptation, extinction, and natural selection. Thus, for this standard, students were challenged to particularly focus on the components of natural selection present in *Spore*. They also investigated environmental influences on change in organisms, and the role of genetic variation during evolution. While addressing the SOL objectives, students were challenged to extend their knowledge and to formulate their own definition of evolution by creating an actualized representation of their knowledge via a creature developed in *Spore*.

As students analyzed the game, they needed to exercise analytical skills useful in science and to use technical language while making claims based on observation. A further challenge was to function as budding scientists in a collaborative setting. Students were given the task of discussing their findings in an open classroom forum, and reconciling their conflicting conclusions to come to an eventual consensus. The instructional program provided scaffolds with the intent that students would extend their conceptual knowledge about biological evolution. Students combined their knowledge and skills to document findings in a readable data format while experiencing the scientific method in an authentic setting. Overall, the program aimed to develop confidence and motivation in students first through individual success and then through computer-supported collaborative learning (Evans & Biedler, 2012).

Research and Theories Used to Analyze Students' Motivation

We selected the MUSIC Model of Academic Motivation (Jones, 2009) to analyze students' motivation, because the model was designed as an operational guide to translate and organize motivational theory and research into practical strategies that could be applied by instructors. Five key principles/components of the model are that students are more motivated learners when they perceive that they are *eMpowered*, the content is *Useful*, they can be *Successful*, they are *Interested*, and they feel *Cared* for by others in the learning environment. These principles were derived from research and theory as pertinent to students' engagement in academic settings (Jones, 2009; see wwwssotivatingStudents.info for more information). The MUSIC model has been used by researchers and instructors at the K–12 levels in formal schooling settings (e.g., Jones & Wilkins, 2013b) and informal settings (e.g., Evans, Jones, & Akalin, 2012; Schnittka, Brandt, Jones, & Evans, 2012), and in higher education with traditional face-to-face courses (e.g., Jones, Ruff, Snyder, Petrich, & Koonce, 2012) and online courses (e.g., Jones, 2010). The model has also been used to examine students' motivation in different types of courses (e.g., Jones & Wilkins, 2013a) that used varied instructional approaches, including courses that were online (e.g., Jones, Watson, Rakes, & Akalin, 2012; Hall, Jones, Amelink, & Hu, 2013), that incorporated problem-based learning (e.g., Jones, Epler, Mokri, Bryant, & Paretti, 2013), and that implemented interventions to increase students' motivation (e.g., McGinley & Jones, in press). Several features of the MUSIC model make it particularly useful to instructors at all levels:

- It organizes major motivational concepts into one framework that can be used to guide instruction.
- It aims to translate motivational jargon into comprehensible instructional strategies for instructors.
- It brings an awareness to instructors of the importance of all five key motivational components in educational settings.
- It enables instructors to assess the effectiveness of their instruction with respect to each MUSIC component to collect data to assess and/or revise instruction.

In the sections that follow, we further explain the components of the MUSIC model and the research and theories associated with them.

EMPOWERMENT

The *empowerment* component of the MUSIC model refers to the amount of autonomy that students perceive they have within their learning environment.

When students feel empowered, they believe that they are able to make choices and decisions. Much of the research related to the empowerment components has been conducted by researchers studying autonomy within the framework of self-determination theory (Deci & Ryan, 2000). In fact, the need for autonomy is one of the three basic psychological needs, along with the need for competence and relatedness, that self-determination researchers have identified as critical to understanding individuals' goal-directed behavior, psychological development, and well-being (Deci & Ryan, 2000). To empower students, teachers need to provide students with choices and allow them to make decisions about some aspect of their learning environment (Jones, 2009).

USEFULNESS

The *usefulness* component of the MUSIC model involves the extent to which students believe that instruction is useful for their short- or long-term goals. This component is important because students' motivation is affected by their perceptions of the usefulness of what they are learning for their future. Research related to usefulness has been conducted by Eccles and her colleagues (Eccles et al., 1983; Wigfield & Eccles, 2000) who have studied the utility value construct as part of their work on the expectancy-value model of motivation, and by future time perspective theorists who have studied instrumentality or "the perception that completion of a task will directly increase the probability of achieving a future goal" (Husman, Derryberry, Crowson, & Lomax, 2004, p. 64). Instrumentality focuses on the usefulness of a present behavior for some future goal. Teachers can incorporate usefulness into their pedagogy by making activities relevant to students' career goals and interests, and relevant to the "real-world" (Jones, 2009).

SUCCESS

The *success* component of the MUSIC model is important because when students feel successful, they are more likely to be motivated to engage in those activities in the present and future. Conversely, students who do not feel successful at particular activities will not be as likely to engage in them. Students feel successful when they perceive that they are or can be competent in activities. Self-perceptions of competence (i.e., one's beliefs about one's abilities) are central to many motivation theories, such as self-concept theory (Marsh, 1990), self-efficacy theory (Bandura, 1986), self-worth theory (Covington, 1992), goal orientation theory (Ames, 1992), and expectancy-value theory (Wigfield & Eccles, 2000). Instructors can foster students' success beliefs in a variety of ways, including making the course expectations clear, challenging students at an appropriate level, and providing students with feedback regularly (Jones, 2009).

INTEREST

The *interest* component of the MUSIC model can be separated into two theoretically distinct components: situational and individual interest (Hidi & Renninger, 2006; Jones & Wilkins, 2013a). *Situational interest* refers to students' positive emotion and attention that is activated by the environment. That is, factors in any learning environment can stimulate students' situational interest by catching their attention and being associated with productive emotions. Therefore, when students are situationally interested, they enjoy what they are doing. Conceptually, situational interest is similar to constructs such as intrinsic motivation (Deci, 1975) and intrinsic interest value (Wigfield & Eccles, 2000), whereby anticipation of an external reward is not the basis for the interest. Teachers can stimulate situational interest by including one or more of the following elements in course activities: novelty, social interaction, games and puzzles, fantasy, humor, or physical movement (Bergin, 1999).

Individual interest emerges from interaction with content perceived as personally important and valuable. When students have an individual interest, they seek out opportunities to reengage in activities related to the topic (Hidi & Renninger, 2006). Individual interest is similar to identification with a domain (Osborne & Jones, 2011) and attainment value (Eccles, 2009), which are defined, in part, by the extent to which individuals believe that a domain is central to their self-definition. Instructors can develop students' individual interest in a topic by providing them with opportunities to become more knowledgeable about the topic and by helping them understand its value (Hidi & Renninger, 2006).

CARING

The *caring* component of the MUSIC model specifies that students have a need to establish and sustain caring interpersonal relationships, either with an instructor or classmates. The importance of interpersonal relationships is derived from research in the areas of belongingness, relatedness, connectedness, affiliation, involvement, attachment, commitment, bonding, and sense of community (e.g., Baumeister & Leary, 1995; Deci & Ryan, 2000). When students have close relationships with their teachers, they tend to show higher levels of motivation and achievement (Bergin & Bergin, 2009). The caring component can be divided into two components: academic caring and personal caring (Jones & Wilkins, 2013a). *Academic caring* concerns students' need to believe that their instructor cares about whether specified learning objectives have been met successfully. In the case of *personal caring*, students need to perceive that their instructor cares about their general well being. To support academic caring, instructors can demonstrate that they care about academic success in the class and to support personal caring, instructors can demonstrate that they care about students' general welfare (Jones, 2009).

Student Motivation in the *Mission: Evolution* Project

In our research related to *Mission: Evolution*, we used the MUSIC Model of Academic Motivation as a lens through which to examine students' motivation and engagement. In our design-based research approach (Brown, 1992; Edelson, 2002; Lamberg & Middleton, 2009; Wang & Hannafin, 2005), we used interviews and participant-observer techniques to examine students' motivation (for details on these methods, please see Evans, Jones, & Akalin, 2012, and Evans, Holbrook, Blevins, & Biedler, 2011). Because this research was situated in real-world, informal learning, and after-school settings, there were many factors that influenced students' motivation besides the recreational video games played. For ease of discussion, we organized the settings into three categories as shown in Figure 19.1: (1) a student's life goals (e.g., achievement in a sport, career aspirations, family-related goals); (2) the learning environment attributes (e.g., interactions with others, task difficulty, reward structures, and content topics); and (3) the recreational video game attributes (e.g., calibrated game levels, mission-specific choices, and responsive feedback). Figure 19.1 shows that some of these factors are nested in others. For example, when a student is motivated to play a game, the attributes of the game are critical to maintaining the student's engagement. However, the characteristics of the learning environment may either support or thwart a student's continued engagement in the game. For instance, a student might choose to stop playing an engaging game if his peers do not think the game is "cool" or if the results of the game play will not be included as part of his class grade. Further, when students participate in an after-school activity voluntary, students' life goals compete with the learning environment for students' attention. An example would be when students—whose life goals include athletic performance—choose to attend their team's soccer practice instead of participating in an after-school academic activity or playing a video game. Thus, to understand students' motivation in a real-world setting, it is necessary to consider all three aspects of the ecology in which their behavior is based.

EMPOWERMENT

Most students believed that they had control over various aspects of the *Mission: Evolution* project. Students reported that they were given supportive guidelines, but that they had control over many aspects of the project, including the topic about evolution to be featured in the video game, the plot chosen to pursue the topic, and the characters that would carry out the academic message chosen. Consistent with the empowerment component of the MUSIC model, students reported that the level of autonomy that they were given in the game motivated them. From the teacher's perspective, it was necessary to incorporate

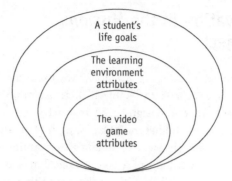

Figure 19.1 Factors that affect student motivation.

choice as students proceeded through the learning process, but in doing so, the teacher felt that she needed to be vigilant that the choices focused on biology curriculum content in a scientifically rigorous fashion. For example, if a student was deciding how to design a creature, the teacher guided the student to make choices that demonstrated natural selection, instead of those based on the options that the game had to offer that may not have pertained to natural selection.

USEFULNESS

Because we designed the *Mission: Evolution* project as informal and inquiry-driven, and for phases two and three we designed it as free-choice, the games required students to consider their life goals and choose what they perceived as most useful to them, in the short- and long-term. In phase one of the project, some students chose not to participate in the classroom intervention because of personal beliefs about evolution. In phases two and three, some students explained that they wanted to participate, but could not do so because it conflicted with sports or homework obligations. Some students had to drop out because participation prevented successful completion of school tasks and homework, thus affecting school grades. These situations exemplify how students' life goals can influence their motivation to participate in a learning environment. In these cases, even if the learning environment and game attributes were designed to engage students, students' could not participate because of conflicting life goals.

Once students were involved in the project, there were multiple aspects to the games that were perceived as being useful. Some students perceived that learning about technology was useful to their future goals. For those students, the game attributes mattered less than simply learning about the technology itself. For other students, the science content in the game was useful for their future careers in science-related fields. The teacher speculated that students might have found the project even more useful if they had realized that participation would increase their academic performance in school. Phases two and three of the project, which targeted information regarding biological evolution, took place well after students had completed lessons on biological evolution in the classroom. In retrospect, the teacher realized that she could have remedied this issue different ways. For instance, she could have offered extra credit on evolution assignments and tests in her class. Another possibility would have been to structure the project so that game topics directly corresponded with specific assessment questions that students needed to master during the day. In doing so, students could have viewed the game play as mental rehearsal for their classroom tests. Another approach would have been to empower students by presenting a democratic system whereby they could propose how they could be rewarded academically for their project. The teacher could oversee this process to ensure fairness to students not participating in the project and a reward appropriate for performance during the project. We speculate that these types of efforts to better coordinate the after-school experience with students' in-school experience would have better fostered the transfer of students' knowledge from the game environment to other school-based contexts.

SUCCESS

Attributes of the game title, *Spore Galactic Adventures* (phase three of the project), allowed the students to receive differentiated instruction so that goals were within reach for all participants. For example, all students chose one topic to incorporate into their game, but varied in the degree of complexity that they included in their games. Students also differed in how much of the game they created, depending on how long they needed to formulate ideas around their topic, and how long it took to understand the game mechanics involved with executing their game plan. Regardless of how much of the game was actually created, students could feel successful that they had decided on a topic and how it should be shown within a game. These findings demonstrate that the game attributes of *Spore Galactic Adventures* were appropriate for this population of students in this setting. Some of the key learning environment attributes that we identified were having a teacher who was knowledgeable about the biology content and technology specialists available to help with ensuring that the game ran smoothly on the school computers. The latter was no insignificant feat given that existing school laptops were replaced by a set purchased through the grant, then adopted into the school district's technology policy and infrastructure. The successful integration of technology into existing classrooms and schools is, thus, a key attribute contributing to a feeling of success (Evans, 2008).

INTEREST

The project teacher believed that the novelty of *Spore Galactic Adventures* was a factor that interested students because they did not typically use video game technology to demonstrate their academic achievement. Students generally reported that they were interested in the project for a variety of reasons. One student who was less situationally interested at the onset became more interested as he became more challenged by the activity. Students' individual interest was related to the usefulness of the project to their future goals. For example, a student who was interested in a career in technology was drawn to the project by the technology aspects of *Spore Galactic Adventures* and a student who was considering science-related careers was motivated by the game's science content. In this way, the game attributes were important for triggering and maintaining students' interest in the project. Specifically, games that incorporate various topics allow students with different individual interests and goals to become more motivated to engage in the project.

CARING

Students in the project reported that their teacher showed her sense of caring through her support. They said that she wanted them to succeed and ensured that the project went smoothly. The teacher attributed her ability to provide adequate academic and personal caring to the small size of the group, which included eight tenth- and eleventh-grade students. She reported that the small size allowed her to develop individualized plans to students according to their needs. Although another possible source of caring is through the relationships students develop with other students in the project, students in the *Mission: Evolution* project did not use these relationships as primary motivators for their game play. Students' comments led us to conclude that the students supported one another and wanted others to succeed, but did not rely on one another for their motivation or success in the project. In this case, it appeared that a caring teacher in a caring environment was sufficient to support students' motivation.

SUMMARY

Our research on the *Mission: Evolution* project led us to several conclusions. First, the game attributes were critical to students' motivation to engage in the project. Attributes that were of particular importance to students' motivation were those that were empowering and that allowed students to be successful. These findings are consistent with others who have found that intrinsic motivation (Deci, 1975) and intrinsic integration (Kafai, 1996) are important factors in game design (Habgood & Ainsworth, 2011) because both empowerment and success can lead to intrinsic motivation (Deci & Ryan, 2000). Attributes of the learning environment were also important, especially the caring support of the teacher that led students to believe that they could be successful. Finally, although the attributes of the game and learning environment were important to students' motivation, students' life goals were important to their motivation to participate in this real-world project where they have competing life goals. Thus, we contend that students will not participate in a project, even if it is well designed, if competing life goals (such as attending an athletic team practice) are more important to them.

Knowledge and Beliefs of Science That Might Transfer to Other Academic Settings

Transfer occurs when students use their past learning to learn something new in another setting (Haskell, 2001). Although researchers often discuss the transfer of "knowledge" (e.g., Barnett & Ceci, 2002), knowledge and beliefs are overlapping constructs (for a discussion, see Murphy & Mason, 2006). Thus, it is possible for students to transfer motivational beliefs (e.g., beliefs about success, interest, and usefulness) from one setting to another. For example, students who are successful at learning science concepts through video games may believe that they could learn these concepts in more formal school settings. The fact that students could transfer their beliefs to formal schooling is important because students who expect to do well in a domain are more likely to choose courses and tasks related to it, put forth more effort in domain-related activities, and persist at these activities (Bandura, 1986). Similarly, students who become more interested in science and find it more enjoyable as a result of their participation in science games could transfer their interest to both formal and informal learning tasks. Participating in science games could also increase students' beliefs about the usefulness of science, which could transfer to them believing that science is useful in other contexts.

Teachers could help students transfer these beliefs to academic and real-world settings by explaining to them how these beliefs could be used in other situations. Alternatively, teachers could provide students with activities that allow them to understand more directly the connections between their beliefs about gaming and other settings. Thus, games could be used to provide a broad vision of what constitutes a subject area. For example, students might believe that "science" only includes the limited topics that are covered in their science courses. Games can be chosen to broaden students' understandings of subject areas in ways that are not possible in a formal school setting because they go beyond the required curriculum.

Our work has been presented in what could be labeled a working example format (Evans & Biedler, 2012). This treatment is structured around the argument of participation and production, and positioned to encourage comment and reflection, focusing attention on how *Spore Origins*, *Spore*, and *Spore Galactic Adventures* served as pedagogical platforms for design-based, inquiry-driven science learning. With a science teacher, and faculty and students from the fields of learning science and educational psychology all working collaboratively, lesson plans and assignments were developed to scaffold learners to construct key concepts about biological evolution through video game play and, later, video game design and development. Our goal has been to focus on ways in which teachers and students adopt video games in a manner that will support motivation, interest, and self-sustained learning, which has built from prior efforts in this area (Evans & Johri, 2008). This chapter presents one example of how an inquiry-driven, technology-infused approach might advance the research in and practice of the learning of science in informal ways with video games within established classroom and after-school settings.

Authors' Note

This research was supported by the MacArthur Foundation (2010–2453), awarded to Jennifer Biedler and Michael A. Evans. We wish to thank the principal, staff, and students at Blacksburg High School, who provided requisite access to school facilities and support throughout this project. We also thank the graduate students from computer science, science education, educational psychology, and instructional design and technology who contributed to project design, implementation, and data collection.

References

Ames, C. (1992). Classrooms: Goals, structures, and student motivation. *Journal of Educational Psychology, 84*, 261–271.

Bandura, A. (1986). *Social foundations of thought and action: A social cognitive theory.* Englewood Cliffs, NJ: Prentice-Hall.

Barnett, S. M., & Cici, S. J. (2002). When and where do we apply what we learn? A taxonomy for far transfer. *Psychological Bulletin, 128*, 612–637.

Baumeister, R., & Leary, M. (1995). The need to belong: Desire for interpersonal attachments as a fundamental human motivation. *Psychological Bulletin, 117*, 497–529.

Bergin, C., & Bergin, D. (2009). Attachment in the classroom. *Educational Psychology Review, 21*, 141–170.

Bergin, D. A. (1999). Influences on classroom interest. *Educational Psychologist, 34*, 87–98.

Blumberg, F. C., & Randall, J. D. (2013). What do children and adolescents say they do during video game play? *Journal of Applied Developmental Psychology, 34*, 82–88.

Bohannon, J. (2008). Flunking Spore. *Science, 322*(5901). Retrieved from http://www.sciencemag.org/cgi/content/full/322/5901/531b

Brown, A. L. (1992). Design experiments: Theoretical and methodological challenges in creating complex interventions in classroom settings. *Journal of the Learning Sciences, 2*(2), 141–178.

Collins, A., & Halverson, R. (2009). *Rethinking education in the age of technology: The digital revolution and schooling in America.* Teachers College Press.

Covington, M. V. (1992). *Making the grade: A self-worth perspective on motivation and school reform.* New York, NY: Cambridge University Press.

Csikszentmihalyi, M. (1990). *Flow: The psychology of optimal experience.* New York, NY: HarperPerennial.

Deci, E. L. (1975). *Intrinsic motivation.* New York, NY: Plenum Press.

Deci, E. L., & Ryan, R. M. (2000). The "what" and "why" of goal pursuits: Human needs and the self-determination of behavior. *Psychological Inquiry, 11,* 227–268.

Eccles, J. (2009). Who am I and what am I going to do with my life? Personal and collective identities as motivators of action. *Educational Psychologist, 44*(2), 78–89.

Eccles, J. S., Adler, T. F., Futterman, R., Goff, S. B., Kaczala, C. M., Meece, J. L., & Midgley, C. (1983). Expectancies, values, and academic behaviors. In J. T. Spence (Ed.), *Achievement and achievement motivation* (pp. 75–146). San Francisco, CA: Freeman.

Edelson, D. (2002). Design research: What we learn when we engage in design. *Journal of the Learning Sciences, 11*(1), 105–121.

Evans, M. A. (2008). Mobility, games, and education. In R. Ferdig (Ed.), *Handbook of research on effective electronic gaming in education,* (Vol. 1, pp. 96–110). Hershey, PA: Information Science Reference.

Evans, M. A. (2009). Promoting mediated collaborative inquiry in primary and secondary science settings: Sociotechnical prescriptions for and challenges to curricular reform. In R. Subramaniam (Ed.), *Handbook of Research on New Media Literacy at the K-12 Level: Issues and Challenges,* (Vol. I, pp.128–143). Hershey, PA: Information Science Reference.

Evans, M. A. (2010). Using commercial off-the-shelf video games to facilitate habits of mind: Spore in the seventh grade life science classroom. In P. Zemliansky & D. Wilcox (Eds.), *Design and implementation of educational games: Theoretical and practical perspectives* (pp. 262–277). Hershey, PA: Information Science Reference.

Evans, M. A., & Biedler, J. (2012). Playing, designing, and developing video games for informal science learning: *Mission: Evolution* as a working example. *International Journal of Learning and Media, 3*(4). doi: 10.1162/IJLM_a_00083

Evans, M. A., Holbrook, H., Blevins, S., & Bielder, J. (2011). *Mission: Evolution—Spore™* as a platform for informal science experiences in high school. Poster presented at the American Educational Research Association Conference, New Orleans, LA, April 8–12.

Evans, M. A., Jones, B. D., & Akalin, S. (2012, April). Leveraging digital game design in an informal science learning environment to motivate high school students in biology. Paper presented at the annual meeting of the American Educational Research Association, Vancouver, Canada.

Gee, J. P., & Hayes, E. R. (2011). *Language and learning in the digital age.* Taylor & Francis.

Green, M. E., & McNeese, M. N. (2011). Using digital games and virtual environments to enhance learning. In M. S. Khine (Ed.), *Learning to play: Exploring the future of education with video games* (pp. 79–105). New York, NY: Peter Lange Publishing, Inc.

Habgood, M. P., & Ainsworth, S. E. (2011). Motivating children to learn effectively: Exploring the value of intrinsic integration in educational games. *Journal of the Learning Sciences, 20*(2), 169–206.

Hall, S., Jones, B. D., Amelink, C., & Hu, D. (2013). Educational innovation in the design of an online nuclear engineering curriculum. *The Journal of Effective Teaching, 13*(2), 58–72.

Haskell, R. E. (2001). *Transfer of learning: Cognition, instruction, and reasoning.* San Diego, CA: Academic Press.

Hidi, S., & Renninger, K. A. (2006). The four-phase model of interest development. *Educational Psychologist, 41*(2), 111–127.

Honey, M. A., & Hilton, M. L. (2011). *Learning Science Through Computer Games and Simulations.* Washington, DC: National Academies Press.

Husman, J., Derryberry, W. P., Crowson, H. M., & Lomax, R. (2004). Instrumentality, task value, and intrinsic motivation: Making sense of their independent interdependence. *Contemporary Educational Psychology, 29,* 63–76.

Jackson, J. (2011). Game changer: How principles of video games can transform teaching. In M. S. Khine (Ed.), *Learning to play: Exploring the future of education with video games* (pp. 107–127). New York, NY: Peter Lange Publishing, Inc.

Jones, B. D. (2009). Motivating students to engage in learning: The MUSIC Model of Academic Motivation. *International Journal of Teaching and Learning in Higher Education, 21,* 272–285.

Jones, B. D. (2010). An examination of motivation model components in face-to-face and online instruction. *Electronic Journal of Research in Educational Psychology, 8,* 915–944.

Jones, B. D., Epler, C. M., Mokri, P., Bryant, L. H., & Paretti, M. C. (in press). The effects of a collaborative problem-based learning experience on students' motivation in engineering capstone courses. *Interdisciplinary Journal of Problem-Based Learning.*

Jones, B. D., Ruff, C., Snyder, J. D., Petrich, B., & Koonce, C. (2012). The effects of mind mapping activities on students' motivation. *International Journal for the Scholarship of Teaching and Learning, 6*(1), 1–21.

Jones, B. D., Watson, J. M., Rakes, L., & Akalin, S. (2012). Factors that impact students' motivation in an online course: Using the MUSIC Model of Academic Motivation. *Journal of Teaching and Learning with Technology, 1*(1), 42–58.

Jones, B. D., & Wilkins, J. L. M. (2013a). Testing the MUSIC Model of Academic Motivation through confirmatory factor analysis. *Educational Psychology: An International Journal of Experimental Educational Psychology, 33*(4), 482–503.

Jones, B. D., & Wilkins, J. L. M. (2013b, May). *Validity evidence for the use of a motivation inventory with middle school students.* Poster presented at the annual meeting of the Society for the Study of Motivation, Washington, D.C.

Kafai, Y. B. (1996). Learning design by making games: Children's development of strategies in the creation of a complex computational artifact. In Y. B. Kafai & M. Resnick (Eds.), *Constructionism in practice: Designing, thinking and learning in a digital world* (pp. 71–96). Mahwah, NJ: Erlbaum.

Khine, M. S. (2011). Let the game begin. In M. S. Khine (Ed.), *Learning to play: Exploring the future of education with video games* (pp. 1–8). New York, NY: Peter Lang Publishing, Inc.

Lamberg, T., & Middleton, J. A. (2009). Design research perspectives on transitioning from individual microgenetic interviews to a whole-class teaching experiment. *Educational Researcher, 38,* 233–245.

Marsh, H. W. (1990). A multidimensional, hierarchical self-concept: Theoretical and empirical justification. *Educational Psychology Review, 2,* 77–172.

McGinley, J., & Jones, B. D. (in press). A brief instructional intervention to increase students' motivation on the first day of class. *Teaching of Psychology.*

McGonigal, J. (2010). Jane McGonigal: Gaming can make a better world [Video file].

Murphy, K. P., & Mason, L. (2006). Changing knowledge and beliefs. In P. A. Alexander & P. H. Winne (Eds.), *Handbook of educational psychology* (pp. 305–324). Mahwah, NJ: Lawrence Erlbaum.

Nielsen, S. E., Smith, J. H., & Tosca, S. P. (2008). *Understanding video games: The essential introduction.* New York, NY: Routledge.

Osborne, J. W., & Jones, B. D. (2011). Identification with academics and motivation to achieve in school: How the structure of the self influences academic outcomes. *Educational Psychology Review, 23*(1), 131–158.

Reiber, L. P. (2005). Multimedia learning in games, simulations, and microworlds. *The Cambridge handbook of multimedia learning,* 549–567.

Rideout, V. J., Foehr, U. G., & Roberts, D. F. (2010). Generation M^2: media in the lives of 8–18 year-olds. Kaiser Family Foundation. Retrieved from http://www.kff.org/entmedia/upload/8010.pdf

Schnittka, C. G., Brandt, C. B., Jones, B. D., & Evans, M. A. (2012). Informal engineering education after school: Employing the studio model for motivation and identification in STEM domains. *Advances in Engineering Education, 3*(2), 1–31.

Squire, K. (2011). *Video games and learning: Teaching and participatory culture in the digital age.* New York, NY: Teachers College Press.

Steinkuehler, C. & Duncan, S. (2009). Scientific habits of mind in virtual worlds. *Journal of Science Education & Technology, 17*(6), 530–543.

Tüzün, H. (2007). Blending video games with learning: Issues and challenges with classroom implementations in the Turkish context. *British Journal of Educational Technology, 38,* 465–477.

Van Staalduinen, J., & deFreitas, S. (2011). A game-based learning framework: Linking game design and learning outcomes. In M. S. Khine (Ed.), *Learning to play: Exploring the future of education with video games* (pp. 29–54). New York, NY: Peter Lang Publishing, Inc.

Wang, F., & Hannafin, M. J. (2005). Design-based research and technology-enhanced learning environments. *Educational Technology Research and Development, 53*(4), 5–23.

Wigfield, A., & Eccles, J. S. (2000). Expectancy-value theory of achievement motivation. *Contemporary Educational Psychology, 25,* 68–81.

20

Video and Computer Games as Grounding Experiences for Learning

JOHN B. BLACK, SAADIA A. KHAN, AND SHIH-CHIEH DOUG HUANG

Introduction

Most of learning in school is thin and shallow: it is not understood very deeply, is quickly forgotten, and does not really become part of the way the learners think about the world. As Dewey (1938) pointed out, learning without experiencing what is being learned is not meaningful. Modern research in embodied and perceptually grounded cognition (Glenberg, 1997; Barsalou, 2008) is based in a similar point: full understanding means that learners build a mental perceptual simulation of what is being learned, and doing that effectively requires as rich a perceptual experience as possible during learning (Black, Segal, Vitale, & Fadjo, 2012). We propose that computer and video games and simulations can provide these grounding experiences and can be effective when used in conjunction with other learning activities.

Advocates for the use of computer and video games in education (e.g., Gee, 2007; Prensky, 2007; Squire, 2011) view them as very effective learning environments. However, recent reviews of the relevant research (National Research Council, 2011; Tobias, Fletcher, Dai, & Wind, 2011; Young et al., 2012) have found that this evidence is at best inconsistent and mixed. Ideally, one would like controlled, experimental studies that show that computer and video games yield more learning than exposure to the same content over the same amount of time in an alternative way. Adams, Mayer, MacNamara, Koenig, and Wainess (2012) recently reported a pair of such studies that showed that students learned more about pathogens in one study and electromechanical devices in another from a matched slideshow presentation than they did from narrative discovery games. Similarly, Egenfeldt-Nielsen (2007) compared learning about European history from playing a history simulation game to learning the same content in a classroom, and found that students learned more in the classroom. Despite these findings, many researchers retain the belief that computer games can be effective for learning (Gee, 2007; Squire, 2011). However, the conditions under which that might happen require further investigation and are not as self-evident as some of the original rhetoric by advocates suggested. We share this belief and propose a different use of computer and video games in learning: namely, that they provide direct experience of what is being learned, which can provide depth when combined with more formal learning experiences.

A Historical Simulation Game as Grounding for Future Learning

Civilization (Meier, 1991) is a popular simulation game with extensive historical content that students have the potential to acquire via game play (Squire, 2004). See Figure 20.1 for a snapshot of game play.

In their study, Hammer, Black, and colleagues (Hammer & Black, 2009; Hammer, Black, Andrews, Zhou, & Kinzer, 2007) recruited as research participants expert *Civilization* players, who were for the most part high school and college students, from online discussion forums for the game, and then gave them a series of tests to see what they had learned from the game. One goal of the study was to determine whether these expert *Civilization* players knew more about

Figure 20.1 Screen shot from *Civilization* History Simulation Game.

the historical content in the game than expert game players who were expert in another popular, content-rich simulation game (*Sim City*; Wright, 1989). The results showed that the expert players did not know any more about the historical content contained in the game than expert players of the other unrelated game (*Sim City*). Another goal of the study was to examine how much the expert *Civilization* players would learn from reading a difficult, college textbook chapter on related historical content. Findings showed that the *Civilization* players learned much more from reading the chapter than the expert players of the *Sim City* comparison game. Table 20.1 shows how much historical knowledge was acquired from reading the history chapter by the two groups of game experts for the propositional, procedural, imagery, and system knowledge contained in the chapter. Propositional knowledge referred to the set of historical facts and their relationships; procedural knowledge referred to the set of strategies for reasoning about these historical facts; system knowledge pertained to the descriptions of the historical dynamics (e.g., how various historical events might change as a function of changes in other historical events); and images were the visual and spatial knowledge (e.g., historical maps). The study participants read the text and then answered a series of free response questions about the content of the chapter. Multiple raters scored these responses (with high inter-rater reliability) for how many propositions, procedural if-then (production) rules, and images they contained. A 0–2 score for system complexity was awarded, whereby 0 indicated that no system was described; 1, that a simple system was described; and 2, that a complex system had been described. As shown in Table 20.1, the *Civilization* experts learned significantly more of all four types of knowledge from reading the history chapter than did the comparison group participants ($p < .05$).

Thus, having the experience of grappling with historical issues in the game may have provided the players with a set of experiences, as Dewey (1938) had stated, that better prepared them for future, more formal learning (Bransford & Schwartz, 2001). These results suggest that the best use of video and computer games in learning might be in providing experience with the subject matter that is to be later acquired via more formal learning settings.

Table 20.1 **Mean Score for Type of History Knowledge Acquired from Book Chapter**

	Civilization Game Experts	Other Game Experts
Propositions	2.33	0.50
Procedures	1.43	0.22
Systems	0.42	0.07
Images	1.52	0.25

Support for this contention also was obtained by Ahn (2007) who examined college undergraduates' learning in the context of an entrepreneurship simulation game (from Harvard Business School), which was incorporated into an entrepreneurship course. Findings showed that students learned more from playing the game multiple times when they also reflected on and articulated their business and game-playing strategies, and related them to background readings in textbooks for the course reminiscent of the college textbook reading in the Hammer and Black study (2009). Notably, students did not learn nearly as much from game play if they did not reflect on how it related to their background reading.

An Archaeological Simulation Game as Grounding for Interpretation

Civilization is sometimes seen as allowing its players an opportunity to experience what it is like to be an historian. Specifically, via game play, players can grapple with the dynamics of history (e.g., change something in history to see how that alters other things). However, this activity differs from that which historians do, which entails collecting and interpreting historical data (e.g., artifacts) to come up with the descriptions of events that are then taught as historical facts (Wineberg, 1991). The *Archaeotype* archaeological simulation game (Black & McClintock, 1996) is designed to allow sixth-grade students to act as archeologists via the simulation of digging up artifacts (from ancient Greek, Assyrian, and Roman history) and measuring them. They then can look up related artifacts that will enable them to interpret what happened at the simulated archaeological site and to argue for their interpretation. Figure 20.2 shows a screenshot of the simulated archaeological site and Figure 20.3 shows the simulated lab where measures are taken of the artifacts that have been found at the site. The students simulate digging and sifting through sectors in the archaeological dig site (Figure 20.2) where they find artifacts, which are then moved to the simulated lab (Figure 20.3). In the lab, they are examined, measured, and compared to background information about artifact characteristics of candidate ancient civilizations potentially relevant to the site.

In the study, students were given a booklet with raw observations in an unfamiliar area accompanied by brief background readings. They then worked in pairs for four hours to prepare a report describing and interpreting the patterns they saw in the observations, and then providing arguments for their interpretations. Experts in the field made a list of 60 points that the students could make in their reports. Students' written reports were then evaluated for the presence of these points. As shown in Table 20.2 the *Archaeotype* students showed significantly better pattern recognition than the control students. The largest difference was in

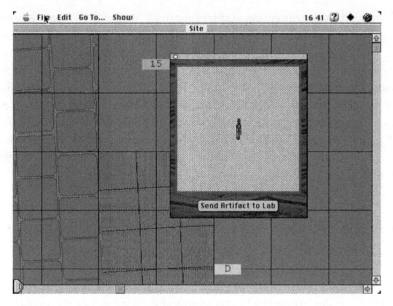

Figure 20.2 Screenshot of the *Archaeotype* Archaeological Simulation Site.

explanation and argumentation where the *Archaeotype* students did much better than the control students.

These findings point to the efficacy of *Archaeotype* as a vehicle for grounding ancient history for the students and for providing them with direct experience with how archaeologists devise interpretations of data, which in turn, facilitated their pattern recognition, interpretation, and explanation and argumentation skills.

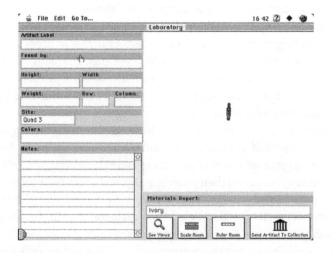

Figure 20.3 Screenshots of the *Archaeotype* Archaeological Simulation Lab.

Table 20.2 **Points by Study Group**

	Pattern Recognition	*Explanation and Argumentation*
Archaeotype	42%	45%
Control	32%	26%

Surrogate Role Playing in *Second Life* as Grounding for Comprehension and Learning

For students to comprehend content presented in a given text, they need to extract ideas (propositions) within the text, link them together (into a propositional network), and imagine the situation and world that are being referred to in the text (Black, 2007; Graesser & MacNamara, 2011; Kintsch, 1998). We (Khan & Black, in press) examined these activities in the context of a study whereby college students read an illustrated text about the history of a Mughal emperor in ancient India. Students then role-played the part of the emperor in an episode of his life in a computer simulation game implemented in *Second Life* (Linden Labs, 2003) as shown in Figure 20.4.

During the study, students in the No Embodiment condition read a text with pictures about a particular event in Indian history. In the Surrogate Embodiment condition, the students were also asked to role play the Mughal emperor in this

Figure 20.4 Screenshot from *Second Life* Surrogate Embodiment Avatars for Indian Mughal History Study.

Table 20.3 *Second Life* **Findings by Condition**

	Surrogate Embodiment	*Imagined Embodiment*	*No Embodiment*
Memory[1]	24	21	19
Transfer[2]	6.7	5.3	4.3

[1] Highest score possible was 30.
[2] Highest score possible was 12.

event by controlling an avatar (their surrogate) in *Second Life*. In the Imagined Embodiment condition, students were told to imagine themselves as the Mughal emperor in the historical event. Student learning was assessed via a 20-item memory test (after a brief delay). Students' scores on the test are shown in Table 20.3. Findings showed that students in the Embodiment conditions remembered significantly more information about the historical event than control group participants (No Embodiment); students who role-played with the avatar (Surrogate Embodiment) remembered the most information. Students also were administered a transfer task that entailed reading a text about another figure from the same era of Indian history and listing the similarities and differences between that figure and the emperor. Students in the Surrogate Embodiment group scored significantly higher than the Imagined Embodiment students, who in turn, scored higher than students in the control group. Afar transfer task, in which students read a literary text instead of a historical one showed the same pattern of results, as did a comprehension test in a follow-up study. Thus, role-playing with a surrogate avatar in a computer simulation game seemed to help students better construct an imaginary world and context for their reading and ultimately, promoted better learning, memory, understanding, and transfer of the content presented in their reading.

In current work, we are exploring (1) the effects of having different historical figures interacting in the same historical events (a multiuser virtual environment); (2) how learning via virtual role-playing with avatars compares to physical role-playing; and (3) how physical and virtual role-playing might be mixed to facilitate learning.

Force Feedback Games for Fuller Grounding

Increasing the perceptual richness of simulations and of video and computer games increases their effectiveness as grounding experiences for learning. Han and Black (2011) provided evidence for this contention by showing that providing force feedback in a simulation of gear ratios increased students' learning. In this

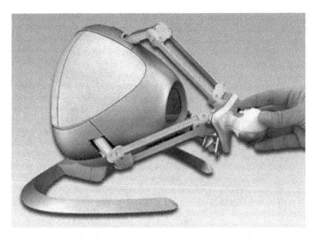

Figure 20.5 3D Force Feedback Joystick Used to *Control the Catapult* Game.

situation the students were learning about work gain and its relationship to gear ratios. Using a graphic interactive simulation yielded better learning than using text and pictures. However, adding force feedback (if the gears in a certain ratio would take more force to turn, the joystick would be harder for the student to turn to control the gear simulation) yielded the greatest learning. (For the study, a simple Microsoft force feedback game joystick was used, whereby feedback was provided by the difficulty involved in moving the joystick in a circular motion.)

Huang, Vea, and Black (2011) expanded this work by using a more sophisticated three-dimensional joystick (see Figure 20.5) that provided a much wider range of force feedback. Specifically, they used it to control the catapult game shown in Figures 20.6a and 20.6b. This game provides students experience with Newton's law relating force with mass and acceleration in physics. Here, the students could vary the mass of the projectiles that they launched with the catapult and also the amount of force they used to pull back the catapult (using the joystick), and then observe how far the projectile travelled.

Students' learning was assessed via a basic physics test including 10 standard multiple-choice physics problems taken from the book *Conceptual Physics* (Hewitt, 2010) and the Force Concepts Inventory (Hestenes, Wells, & Swackhamer, 1992). The advanced physics test included another 10 standard multiple-choice problems from the same sources. No significant differences were found on the initial pre-test of physics knowledge. Table 20.4 shows the post-test results as mean percent correct on these physics problems. For the basic physics test (related to Newton's second law of motion) the Force Feedback students did significantly better than the No Force Feedback students (first row of table), and also they also did significantly better on the transfer advanced physics test (related to gravitation-second row of the table). There was no Force Feedback during the learning of the advanced topic (a gravitation simulation without force feedback capability) so that better

(a)

(b)

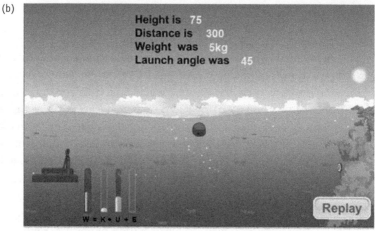

Figures 20.6a and 20.6b Screen shot from the *Control the Catapult* Game (Behind and Side Views).

Table 20.4 **Force Feedback Study Percentage Correct on Basic Physics Test and Advanced Physics Transfer Test**

	Force Feedback	*No Force Feedback*
Basic Physics (Law of Motion)	73%	60%
Advanced Physics (Gravitation)	57%	46%

Note: The differences between Force and No Force Feedback were statistically significant.

performance reflects transfer of the force feedback experience from the basic physics learning.

Overall, these results showed better learning of both the basic physics with the catapult and later transfer of that learning with a different simulation of more advanced physics principles. Huang (2013) replicated these results and showed an even stronger result when a force feedback simulation was used to prime related prior experiences (e.g., experiences with sling shots) before the instruction. These results showed improvement in learning both when the students' had force feedback initial priming of relevant prior experience and also when they had force feedback during instruction of the current content. In fact, the priming effect yielded the strongest improvement. Thus, further examination of this effect in the context of computer and video games is a promising area for future research.

Transfer of Video and Computer Game Learning

The research reported here suggests that a potentially powerful role for video and computer games and simulations in education is providing rich, perceptually grounded experience with the content to be learned. This experience, when combined with the interpretations provided by more formal learning activities, provides deeper, more robust learning that transfers to other situations, activities, and content. The research with the *Civilization* historical simulation game found that becoming expert at playing that game did not seem to increase knowledge of history. However, the experience of grappling with historical dynamics by playing the game prepared students to learn more from reading a difficult college history text chapter. Similarly, efforts to interpret observations in an archaeological site simulation (*Archaeotype*) increased students' ability to interpret and argue using such observations. Others have also found that grappling with observations and phenomena before engaging in more formal learning is particularly effective for learning and transfer (Kapur, 2008; Schwartz & Bransford, 1998; Schwartz, Chase, Oppezzo, & Chin, 2011).

The research on role-playing in *Second Life* showed that having learners use surrogate avatars to role-play historical actors and events in a virtual world simulation increased their learning, and increased their transfer of historical knowledge acquired from reading an illustrated text about the history (similar to the results with *Civilization* and reading a history text). Ostensibly, the grounding experience provided by this virtual role-playing increased students' ability to construct and use the imaginary historical world referred to by the history text (Black, 2007, 2010). Further, this experience enhanced students' memory, understanding, and transfer of knowledge.

The research on force feedback found that increasing the perceptual richness of grounding physics experiences with a simulation game providing force feedback, in addition to the visual and auditory feedback, increased student learning and understanding of basic laws of motion in physics. This knowledge also transferred to improved understanding of more advanced physics.

Collectively, these findings suggest that increasing the richness of the experiences provided by video and computer games may increase the learning, understanding, and transfer of knowledge when used in conjunction with more formal learning activities that provide interpretations of these experiences. Investigating more ways of facilitating these conditions and how best to combine virtual, real world, and academic experiences is an important topic for future research.

References

Adams, R. E., Mayer, R. E., MacNamara, A., Koenig, A. & Wainess, R. (2012). Testing the discovery and narrative hypothesis. *Journal of Educational Psychology, 104*, 235–249.
Ahn, J. (2007). Application of experiential learning cycle in learning from a business simulation game. Unpublished doctoral dissertation. Teachers College, Columbia University, New York, NY.
Barsalou, L. W. (2008). Grounded cognition. *Annual Review of Psychology, 59*, 617–645.
Black, J. B. (2007). Imaginary worlds. In M. A. Gluck, J. R. Anderson, & S. M. Kosslyn (Eds.), *Memory and mind*. Mahwah, NJ: Lawrence Erlbaum Associates.
Black, J. B. (2010). An embodied/grounded cognition perspective on educational technology. In M. S. Khine & I. Saleh (Eds.), *New science of learning: Cognition, computers and collaboration in education*. New York, NY: Springer.
Black, J. B., & McClintock, R. O. (1996). An interpretation construction approach to constructivist design. In B. Wilson (Ed.), *Constructivist learning environments*. Englewood Cliffs, NJ: Educational Technology Publications.
Black, J. B., Segal, A., Vitale, J., & Fadjo, C. (2012). Embodied cognition and learning environment design. In D. Jonassen and S. Lamb (Eds.), *Theoretical foundations of student-centered learning environments*. New York, NY: Routledge.
Bransford, J. D., & Schwartz, D. L. (2001). Rethinking transfer: A simple proposal with multiple implications. *Review of Research in Education, 24*, 61–100.
Dewey, J. (1938). *Experience in education*. New York, NY: Touchstone.
Egenfeldt-Nielsen, S. (2007). Third generation educational use of computer games. *Journal of Educational Multimedia and Hypermedia, 16*, 263–281.
Gee, J. P. (2007). *What videogames have to teach us about learning and literacy*, 2nd ed. New York, NY: Palgrave MacMillan.
Glenberg, A. M. (1997). What memory is for. *Behavioral and Brain Sciences, 20*, 1–55.
Graesser, A. C., & McNamara, D. S. (2011). Computational analyses of multilevel discourse comprehension. *Topics in Cognitive Science, 3*, 371–398.
Hammer, J. & Black, J. B. (2009). Games and (preparation for future) learning. *Educational Technology, 49*, 29–34.
Hammer, J., Black, J., Andrews, G. Zhou, Z., & Kinzer, C. (2007). *Games and learning: A process/PFL approach*. Paper presented at Games Developers Conference, San Jose, CA.
Han, I. & Black, J. (2011). Incorporating haptic feedback in simulations for learning physics. *Computers and Education, 57*, 2281–2290.
Hestenes, D., Wells, M., & Swackhamer, G. (1992). Force Concept Inventory. *The Physics Teacher, 11*, 502–506.
Hewitt, P. G. (2010). *Conceptual Physics, 11th ed*. New York, NY: Pearson.
Huang, S. C. D. (2013). *Grounded learning experience: Helping students learn physics through visuo-haptic priming and instruction*. Unpublished doctoral dissertation. Teachers College, Columbia University, New York, NY.

Huang, S. C. D., Vea, T., & Black, J. B. (2011). Learning abstract physics system with a 3-D force feedback joystick. In *Proceedings of World Conference on Educational Multimedia, Hypermedia and Telecommunications* (pp. 1618–1624). Chesapeake, VA: AACE.

Kapur, M. (2008). Productive failure. *Cognition and Instruction, 26*, 379–424.

Khan, S. A., & Black, J. B. (in press). Surrogate embodied learning in MUVEs: Enhancing memory and motivation through embodiment. *Journal of Immersive Education.*

Kintsch, W. (1998). *Comprehension: A paradigm for cognition.* New York, NY: Cambridge University Press.

Linden Labs (2003). *Second Life.* San Francisco, CA: Linden Labs.

Meier, S. (1991). *Civilization.* Hunt Valley, MD: Microprose.

National Research Council (2011). *Learning science through computer games, and simulations.* Washington, DC: National Academies Press.

Prensky, M. (2007). *Digital game-based learning.* New York: Paragon House.

Schwartz, D. L., & Bransford, J. D. (1998). A time for telling. *Cognition and Instruction, 16*, 475–522.

Schwartz, D. L., Chase, C. C., Oppezzo, M. A., & Chin, D. B. (2011). Practicing versus inventing with contrasting cases: The effects of telling first on learning and transfer. *Journal of Educational Psychology, 103*, 759–775.

Squire, K. (2004). *Replaying history: Learning world history through playing Civilization III.* Unpublished doctoral dissertation. Indiana University, Bloomington, IN.

Squire, K. (2011). *Video games and learning.* New York, NY: Teachers College Press.

Tobias, S., Fletcher, J. D., Dai, D. Y., & Wind, A. P. (2011). Review of research on computer games. In S. Tobias & J. D. Fletcher (Eds.), *Computer games and instruction.* Charlotte, NC: Information Age Publishing.

Wineberg, S. S. (1991). Historical problem solving: A study of the cognitive processes used in the evaluation of documentary and pictorial evidence. *Journal of Educational Psychology, 83*, 73–87.

Wright, W. (1989). *Sim City.* Emeryville, CA: Maxis.

Young, M. F., Slota, S., Cutter, A. B., Jalette, G., Mullin, G., Lai, B.,... Yukhymenko, M. (2012). Our princess is in another castle: A review of trends in serious gaming for education. *Review of Educational Research, 82*, 61–89.

21

Evaluating the Specificity of Effects of Video Game Training

KASEY L. POWERS AND PATRICIA J. BROOKS

Introduction

In recent years, claims have been made that video games make people smarter, for example, by improving their focus of attention, multitasking skills, spatial cognition, and general intelligence (Bavelier, 2012; Hurley, 2012; Jaeggi, Buschkuehl, Jonides, & Shah, 2011; Zichermann, 2011). Video games require players to interact in complex environments, inducing a variety of information-processing demands, which potentially teach "the capacity to quickly learn to perform new tasks—a capability that has been dubbed 'learning to learn'" (Bavelier, Green, Pouget, & Schrater, 2012, p. 392). In any modern video game, players have to navigate complex and potentially unfamiliar environments, determine the most effective ways to avoid enemies or hurdles, and make quick decisions (often under time pressure) while monitoring information in the periphery of the game where informative statistics are typically displayed. Given that skills develop within contexts of engagement, and that video games are a highly engaging, intrinsically motivating activity, task-relevant skills should improve with video game practice (Gee, 2007; Greenfield, 1984, 2009). However, a critical question for application of video games to professional training, education, or rehabilitation is the extent to which skills enhanced through video game play transfer to tasks outside of the game environment.

Recently, researchers have tested the use of commercial games designed for entertainment in the contexts of rehabilitation and cognitive training—that is, choosing video games that reinforce specific skills relevant to the domain of impaired functioning or the training area. For example, as a treatment for amblyopia, a developmental eye disorder that results in impaired vision, researchers have used *Medal of Honor: Pacific Assault* (a first-person shooter game) to support perceptual learning, with adult amblyopic patients showing measurable gains in visual acuity and stereopsis following video game training (see Levi, 2012, for a review). A recent review of applications of video games to improve health-related outcomes reported therapeutic benefits of video game use, especially in contexts of psychological therapy and physical therapy (Primack et al., 2012), but cited concerns about poor study quality.

As early as the 1990s, the Israeli Air Force incorporated *Space Fortress* (an arcade game) into their flight training course after finding that flight skills improved after video game training (Gopher, Weil, & Bareket, 1994). Video game experience has been shown to enhance endoscopic and laparoscopic surgical skills (van Dongen, Verleisdonk, Schijven, & Broeders, 2011) as skill at video games such as *Super Monkey Ball 2* (an arcade game), *Star Wars Racer Revenge* (a sport/racing game), and *Silent Scope* (a first-person shooter game) was found to correlate with enhanced surgical performance (Rosser et al., 2007). Further, in a training study, usage of *Half Life* (a first-person shooter game) was found to improve surgical skills (Schlickum, Hedman, Enochsson, Kjellin, & Felländer-Tsai, 2009). Other studies, however, have failed to demonstrate benefits of video game training (Harper, Kaiser, Ebrahimi, Lambert, Hadley, & Baldwin, 2007; Rosenberg, Landsittel, & Averch, 2005), and others caution that some surgical skills may be more amenable to training than others (Kennedy, Boyle, Traynor, Walsh, & Hill, 2011). What remains unclear across studies is the relationship between the specific features of the video games used for training and the skills acquired.

Prior Meta-analyses of Effects of Video Games on Information Processing

Research demonstrating benefits associated with video game play runs counter to the prevailing negative portrayals of video game–related violence and addiction emphasized in the media (e.g., Graff, 2013; Gross, 2011; Knafo, 2013; Lush, 2011; Sutter, 2012). An early meta-analysis of seven published studies focused on the cognitive effects of violent video game play (first-person shooter games), and documented enhancements in the area of visual-spatial cognition (Ferguson, 2007). Complementing these findings, Dye, Green, and Bavelier (2009) found, via their meta-analysis of seven studies using action/violent video games and visual processing tasks, faster response times in video game players than nonplayers, without any differences in accuracy of responding. They concluded that action/violent video game play reduced the speed-accuracy trade-off in visual processing tasks. Given the proliferation of studies of video game usage in recent years, our lab conducted two meta-analyses of effects of video game play on information-processing skills, with the first focusing on effects of habitual game play, and the second focusing on the effects of targeted video game training (Powers, Brooks, Aldrich, Palladino, & Alfieri, 2013). Most important, Powers and colleagues did not limit their study to the effects of action/violent video games.

Quasi-experimental studies of habitual game players (72 studies, 318 comparisons) comprised three types of comparisons: (1) self-identified video game players compared to nonplayers, (2) self-identified players of action/violent video games compared to self-identified players of other types of video games, and (3) players with high levels of skill compared to players with low skill. The meta-analysis showed a medium effect size of video game play, $d = .61$, 95% CI [.50, .73], with moderating effects of information-processing domain and training game type. Benefits of habitual game use were observed across information-processing domains (coded as auditory processing, executive functions, motor skills, spatial imagery, and visual processing). However, auditory processing and visual processing domains showed medium to large effects, and executive functions, motor skills, and spatial imagery showed small effects. Likewise, significant effects of gaming experience were observed across players of different game types, but varied in magnitude as a function of game type, with players of mimetic games (e.g., Wii) and action/violent games showing larger effects than among players of other game types. However, these effects as observed in quasi-experimental studies did not allow for a determination of causality of video game play on cognitive processing given issues of self-selection. That is, people who enjoy and excel at video game play may have enhanced information-processing skills relevant to successful game play (see Green, this volume).

To evaluate the potential for targeted video game practice to enhance specific information-processing skills, Powers et al. (2013) conducted a meta-analysis of experimental studies utilizing commercial video games (46 studies, 251 comparisons). These studies involved random-assignment of participants to training conditions, and involved one of three types of comparison groups: (1) a no-training control group, (2) a control group trained on a different video game, or (3) a within-subjects design comparing pretest and post-test scores. Overall, the effect of video game training was small to medium, $d = .48$, 95% CI [.35, .60], and varied significantly across information-processing domains. Whereas video game training yielded small to medium effects in auditory processing, motor skills, spatial imagery, and visual processing domains ($ds = .36$ to .76), training yielded negligible effects on executive functions ($d = .17$). A follow-up analysis of effects of video game training on executive function subskills showed significant enhancements only for measures of inhibitory processing, that is, for performance on the Stroop task, the Simon task, and the Flanker task, ($d = .39$), and not for measures of intelligence, task switching, or working memory. In the experimental studies, effect sizes varied across game types, with mimetic and nonaction games showing larger training effects than action/violent and puzzle games. Thus, the effects of game type were inconsistent across the quasi-experimental studies and the experimental training studies. This discrepancy may reflect the usage of diverse games among the habitual video game players—for instance, players who were selected based on their preference for action/violent games might not have restricted their video game usage to such games.

Limitations of Previous Meta-analyses

To explore the issue of transfer of video game training to specific information-processing skills requires additional coding and analysis of the experimental training studies. Powers and colleagues used coarse coding schemes for the type of video game training (action/violent, mimetic, nonaction, puzzle) and for the domains (auditory processing, executive functions, motor skills, spatial imagery, and visual processing) for which putative benefits might be obtained. The coding schemes for game types were based on the quasi-experimental studies in which self-reports indicated preferences for types of games (especially action/violent games) rather than listing the specific games played. Codes for information-processing domains were chosen to ensure large enough groupings to allow comparisons across quasi-experimental studies and true experiments. Powers and colleagues focused on identifying the main effects of moderators, rather than interactions between moderators (video game type and domain)—although in many of the training studies, video games were selected based on features deemed relevant to outcome measures. For instance, De Lisi and Wolford (2002) used *Tetris,* which involves manipulation of 2-D forms to complete patterns, to train mental rotation skills, and Feng, Spence, and Pratt (2007) used *Medal of Honor,* a first-person shooter game requiring participants to aim at a variety of target locations, to enhance participants' functional field of view.

In this chapter, using a more fine-grained coding of game types and outcome measures, we examine the extent to which training involving specific video games enhances various information-processing skills. We anticipated robust effects of training on near-transfer tasks whereby the features of the video game mirror the outcome measures, for example, as described above for *Tetris* and mental rotation skills. It is unknown whether training effects will also be evident for far-transfer tasks; evidence of such effects is crucial to inform debates regarding the specificity of video game training effects. Whereas some researchers have suggested that video game training does not transfer to untrained tasks (Lee et al., 2012), other researchers claim that video game training induces a broad range of effects (Bavelier et al., 2012). Bavelier and colleagues argue that action video games (especially first-person shooter games) require players to make quick and accurate decisions based on limited amounts of noisy data, and thus train participants' ability to extract relevant statistics when performing novel tasks.

Transfer Effects in Experimental Training Studies

To investigate the transfer of video game training to various information-processing skills, we recoded moderators and conducted additional analyses of the 46 training studies compiled by Powers and colleagues (2013). Two moderators were recoded: training game type and information-processing domain. Additional meta-analyses of the recoded dataset were conducted in two steps. First, we examined for each game type whether training benefits were observed in each of four broadly defined information-processing domains. For each game type showing a significant effect of training on a given information-processing domain, we examined effects of training on specific subskills within that domain.

Training Game Type

Games were grouped into seven categories based on attributes of the game play, using a coding scheme adapted from Homer, Hayward, Frye, and Plass (2012). The studies included in the meta-analysis are listed in Table 21.1, organized by game type.

Arcade-style games are ones that originated in an arcade and have been revamped for home play, or ones that were designed in the style of arcade games (e.g., *Centipede for Atari, Crystal Castles, Donkey Kong, Marble Madness, Pac Man, Sink the Ship, Space Fortress, Zaxxon*). Nine of the training studies used arcade-style games.

First-person shooter games (e.g., *Call of Duty, Counter Strike, Halo, Medal of Honor, Unreal Tournament*) are violent, action games where the player chooses and fires weapons at targets. First-person shooter games create an immersive experience in which continuous play leads to improved performance. Twenty of the training studies used first-person shooter games.

Puzzle (non-Tetris) games comprise maze, logic, and board games (e.g., *Portal, Robot Blast, Pharaoh's Needle, Hamlet [a version of Othello], Factory, Enigmo, Copy Cat*) where progressing through the game requires players to solve problems and/or complete patterns. Six training studies used puzzle games.

Sport/racing games are re-creations of sporting or racing events (e.g., *FIFA '10, Mario Kart*). Four training studies used sport/racing games.

Strategy/role-play games (e.g., *Rise of Nations, Stellar 7, World of Warcraft*) require players to create long-term strategies to win territory within the task environment. These often violent games take place in virtual worlds where players may sometimes interact with one another in real time across virtual space, and involve strategy and planning over relatively long time frames. Four training studies used strategy/role-play games.

Table 21.1 **Samples Included in the Meta-analysis by Game Type**

Author(s)	Year	Gaming n	Control n	Total n	Cohen's d	Domain	Game
Arcade-Style							
Boot et al.	2010	19	19		.179	executive functions perceptual processing	Space Fortress
Clark et al.	1987	7	7		1.869	perceptual processing	Donkey Kong and/or Pac-Man
Dorval & Pepin	1986	38	32		.615	spatial imagery	Zaxxon
Drew & Waters	1986			11	.778	executive functions motor skills	Crystal Castles
Gopher et al.	1994	33	25		.391	motor skills	Space Fortress
Lee et al.	2012	25	25		.276	executive functions perceptual processing	Space Fortress
McSwegin et al.	1988	15	15		.768	motor skills perceptual processing	Sink the Ship, Nightmare Gallery
Orosy-Filders & Allan	1989	10	10		1.181	perceptual processing	Centipede for Atari
Subrahmanyam & Greenfield	1996	28	28		.604	spatial imagery	Marble Madness
First-Person Shooter							
Boot	2007	20	19		-.248	executive functions perceptual processing spatial imagery	Medal of Honor

Table 21.1 Continued

Author(s)	Year	Gaming n	Control n	Total n	Cohen's d	Domain	Game
Cohen et al. Exp 1	2008	11	12		.849	perceptual processing	Unreal Tournament
Cohen et al. Exp 2	2008	11	12		.039	perceptual processing	Unreal Tournament
Feng et al. Exp2	2007	10	10		1.345	perceptual processing	Medal of Honor: Pacific Assault
Gagnon	1985	31	27		.156	motor skills spatial imagery	Battle Zone and Targ
Gagnon	1986	30	30		.162	spatial imagery	Battlezone
Green Exp 5	2008	11	12		.431	perceptual processing	Unreal Tournament and Call of Duty
Green & Bavelier Exp 3	2006a	16	16		.498	perceptual processing	Unreal Tournament 2004
Green & Bavelier Exp 2	2006b	9	8		1.097	perceptual processing	Medal of Honor: Allied Assault
Green & Bavelier Exp 2	2007	16	16		.851	perceptual processing	Unreal Tournament 2004
Green et al. Exp 4	2012	19	17		-.176	executive functions	Unreal Tournament Call of Duty
Kearney	2005			14	.809	executive functions	Counter Strike
Li et al. Exp 2	2009	6	7		1.322	perceptual processing	Unreal Tournament 2004 Call of Duty 2

Study	Year	n₁	n₂	d	Cognitive skill	Game
Li et al. Exp 4	2009	13	9	1.093	perceptual processing	Unreal Tournament 2004 / Call of Duty 2
Nelson & Strachen Exp 1	2009	10	10	.121	perceptual processing	Unreal Tournament
Nelson & Strachen Exp 2	2009	10	10	.121	perceptual processing	Unreal Tournament
Sanchez	2012	30	30	.236	spatial imagery	Halo
Spence et al.	2009		20	2.780	perceptual processing	Medal of Honor
Valadez & Ferguson	2012	17	17	.274	spatial imagery	Red Dead Redemptions
Wu et al.	2012	16	9	1.631	perceptual processing	Medal of Honor
Puzzle (Non-Tetris)						
Masson et al.	2011	25	26	.867	motor skills	Enigmo
McClurg & Chaille	1987	19	19	.380	spatial imagery	Factory
Miller & Kapel	1985		88	.306	executive functions / spatial imagery	Robot Blast, Pharaoh's Needle, Hamlet, 3D Maze, Factory
Nelson & Strachen Exp 1	2009	10	10	-.181	perceptual processing	Portal
Nelson & Strachen Exp 2	2009	10	10	.445	perceptual processing	Portal
Smith et al.	2007	38	36	.465	spatial imagery	Copy-Cat
Sport/Racing						
Cherney	2008	10	10	.317	spatial imagery	Antz Extreme Racing (3D)
Fery & Ponserre	2001	40	10	.714	motor skills	Golf

(continued)

Table 21.1 **Continued**

Author(s)	Year	Gaming n	Control n	Total n	Cohen's d	Domain	Game
O'Leary et al.	2011			36	.029	executive functions	Mario Kart
Valadez & Ferguson	2012			16	.127	spatial imagery	FIFA'10
Strategy/Role-play							
Basak et al.	2008	19	20		.214	executive functions perceptual processing spatial imagery	Rise of Nations
Boot	2007	23	19		-.075	executive functions perceptual processing spatial imagery	Rise of Nations
McClurg & Chaille	1987	19	19		.238	spatial imagery	Stellar 7
Whitlock et al.	2012	19	20		.073	executive functions spatial imagery perceptual processing	World of Warcraft
Tetris							
Boot	2007	20	19		-.133	executive functions perceptual processing spatial imagery	Tetris
Cherney	2008	11	10		.206	spatial imagery	Tetrus
De Lisi & Cammarano	1996	29	27		.899	spatial imagery	Blockout
De Lisi & Wolford	2002	23	24		1.113	spatial imagery	Tetris
Goldstein et al.	1997	10	12		.641	executive functions	Super Tetris
Okagaki & Frensch Exp 1	1994	15	13		.426	perceptual processing spatial imagery	Tetris

Okagaki & Frensch Exp 2	1994	15	13	.746	spatial imagery	Tetris
Sims & Mayer Ex 2	2002	8	8	-.180	spatial imagery	Tetris
Wii						
Maillot et al.	2012	15	15	1.111	executive functions motor skills perceptual processing spatial imagery	Wii Sports, Wii Fit, Mario & Sonic on Olympic Games
O'Leary et al.	2011	36	36	-.159	executive functions	Wii Fit
Staiano et al.	2012	36	18	.409	executive functions	Wii Sports

Tetris and its variations (e.g., *Blockout, Tetrus, Super NES Super Tetris*) are tile-matching games involving object rotation. Eight training studies used *Tetris*-style games.

Wii games (e.g., *Wii Sports, Wii Fit*) require participants to mimic on-screen actions using an avatar. Three training studies used Wii games.

Information-Processing Domain

We coded four broad domains of information processing, with subskills where applicable. Comparisons were categorized as one of the following:

- Executive functions comprised executive function batteries, dual/multi-tasking, inhibition tasks, intelligence tests, task switching, and working/short-term memory measures.
- Motor skills comprised measures of hand-eye coordination and gross and fine motor skills.
- Perceptual processing comprised measures of attentional blink, auditory processing (tone location), change detection, enumeration, functional field of view, multiple object tracking, and object detection/matching.
- Spatial imagery comprised spatial batteries, card folding, mental rotation, and spatial visualization tasks.

Reliability of Moderators

Two coders were responsible for recoding the moderators, with 65 comparisons (24.5%) independently coded by both coders. Any disagreements between the two coders were resolved through discussion. Intercoder reliability on all moderators was consistently high (κ = .83 to .89).

Computation and Analysis of Effect Sizes

Because of the range of methodologies used across studies, we used a random-effects model, and conducted statistical analyses using the Comprehensive Meta-analysis, Version 2 (CMA) program (Borenstein, Hedges, Higgins, & Rothstein, 2005). A random-effects model is deemed appropriate as participant samples and experimental factors across studies cannot be assumed to be functionally equivalent. Thus, it cannot be assumed that all effect sizes will share a common effect. Cohen's *d* values are reported here as calculated by the CMA program as a measure of effect size. Cohen's d's between .20 and .50 indicate small effects, d's between .50 and .80 indicate moderate effects, and d's greater than .80 indicate large effects (Cohen, 1988).

Overall Effects

The overall effects matched those previously reported by Powers and colleagues (2013): a meta-analysis at the level of studies (N = 46) generated a small to medium mean effect size, d = .48, 95% CI [.35, .60], with marginal heterogeneity observed across studies, Q (45) = 58.26, p = .089, I^2 = 23.78. A meta-analysis at the level of comparisons (N = 265) generated a small mean effect size, d = .30, 95% CI [.23, .37], with significant heterogeneity, Q (264) = 684.80, p = .001, I^2 = 61.45.

Training game type, analyzed at the level of comparisons, moderated effect sizes, Q (6) = 35.33, p = .001 (see Table 21.2). All game types showed small effects except for Wii games, which showed large effects, and strategy/role-play games, which showed negligible, nonsignificant effects.

Information-processing domain, analyzed at the level of comparisons, moderated effect sizes, Q (3) = 29.93, p = .001 (see Table 21.3). A large effect of training was observed in the domain of motor skills, but this result was based on only 16 comparisons from seven studies. Small effects of training were observed in domains of perceptual processing and spatial imagery; in contrast, negligible effects were found for executive functions.

Table 21.2 **Summary of Effect Sizes Moderated by Training Game Type at the Level of Comparisons**

Training game type	Cohen's d	95% CI	Z	p-value (Z)	k	N	Q (df)	p-value (Q)
Arcade-Style	.31	[.20, .42]	5.33	.001	59	2514		
First-Person Shooter	.23	[.07, .39]	2.78	.005	61	2018		
Puzzle (Non-Tetris)	.31	[–.001, .63]	1.95	.051	23	923		
Sport/Racing	.36	[.13, .60]	3.02	.003	9	366		
Strategy/Role-Play	.06	[–.05, .18]	1.07	.284	35	1334		
Tetris	.28	[.13, .44]	3.50	.001	51	1507		
Wii	.95	[.66, 1.23]	6.58	.001	20	684		
Between-classes effect							35.33 (6)	.001

Table 21.3 **Summary of Effect Sizes Moderated by Information-Processing Domain at the Level of Comparisons**

Domain	Cohen's d	95% CI	Z	p-value (Z)	k	N	Q (df)	p-value (Q)
Executive Functions	.15	[.04, .25]	2.68	.007	96	3848		
Motor Skills	.76	[.54, .98]	6.65	.001	15	627		
Perceptual Processing	.32	[.15, .49]	3.71	.001	71	2216		
Spatial Imagery	.42	[.32, .52]	8.46	.001	79	2655		
Between-classes effect							28.93 (3)	.001

EFFECTS OF GAME TYPE ON INFORMATION-PROCESSING DOMAINS

For each information-processing domain, we conducted a separate meta-analysis to determine whether there was a moderating effect of training game type. As a first step in evaluating how broadly video game training transfers to various outcome measures, these meta-analyses allowed us to determine whether different video games produced differential training effects across domains.

First, we examined effects of video game training on executive functions and found training effects to be moderated by game type, $Q (6) = 23.75$, $p = .001$ (see Table 21.4). Only two game types showed positive effects of video game training on executive functions: Wii games showed a large training effect and arcade-style

Table 21.4 **Summary of Effect Sizes for Executive Functions Moderated by Game Type at the Level of Comparisons**

Game Type	Cohen's d	95% CI	Z	p-value (Z)	k	N	Q (df)	p-value (Q)
Arcade-Style	.22	[.08, .37]	3.03	.002	40	1738		
First-Person Shooter	−.17	[−.47, .14]	−1.08	.281	10	384		
Puzzle (Non-Tetris)	−.33	[−.63, −.03]	−2.15	.013	7	341		
Sport/Racing	.03	[−.43, .49]	.12	.902	0	72		
Strategy/Role-Play	.09	[−.09, .27]	.97	.330	15	620		
Tetris	−.001	[−.37, .36]	−.01	.994	8	309		
Wii	.78	[.35, 1.21]	3.58	.001	10	384		
Between-classes effect							23.75 (6)	.001

games showed a small training effect. First-person shooter, sport/racing, strategy/role-play, and *Tetris* all showed negligible, nonsignificant effects. Puzzle (non-*Tetris*) games showed a small negative effect of video game training on executive functions.

For the two game types (arcade-style and Wiigames) that yielded significant training effects, we conducted additional meta-analyses to examine training effects for specific executive function subskills (see Table 21.5). Although executive function subskill failed to moderate the effects of arcade-style games, Q (4) = 1.08, p = .897, the effect of training was reliable only for inhibition tasks, due to small effect sizes and few comparisons. Executive function subskills moderated effects of Wii training, Q (4) = 17.93, p = .001, with significant, large training effects observed for inhibition tasks, intelligence tests, and task switching.

Table 21.5 **Summary of Effect Sizes for Executive Functions Moderated by Subskill at the Level of Comparisons for Game Types Showing Significant Training Effects**

Game Type	Executive Function Sub-skill	Cohen's d	95% CI	Z	p-value (Z)	k	N	Q (df)	p-value (Q)
Arcade	Dual/ Multitasking	.14	[–.20, .47]	.81	.417	11	532		
	Inhibition	.26	[.05, .47]	2.40	.017	7	356		
	Intelligence	.25	[–.12, .63]	1.32	.187	8	342		
	Task Switching	.44	[–.02, .89]	1.88	.060	1	76		
	Working/ Short-Term Memory	.25	[–.06, .55]	1.57	.117	9	432		
	Between-classes effect							1.08 (4)	.897
Wii	Exec Function Battery	.40	[–.09, .90]	1.60	.109	1	72		
	Inhibition	.83	[.16, 1.49]	2.44	.015	4	192		
	Intelligence	2.06	[1.17, 1.94]	4.56	.001	0	30		
	Task Switching	1.53	[.72, 2.34]	3.68	.001	0	30		
	Working/ Short-Term Memory	.15	[–.43, .73]	.50	.619	1	60		
	Between-classes effect							17.93 (4)	.001

These promising results came from only two studies (Maillot, Perrot & Hartly, 2012; O'Leary, Pontifex, Scudder, Brown, & Hillman, 2011), and there was only one comparison each for intelligence test and task switching subskills. Thus, replication studies are imperative to confirm these far transfer effects of Wii training on executive functions.

The second information-processing domain was motor skills. Training effects on motor skills were moderated by game type, $Q(4) = 19.37$, $p = .001$ (see Table 21.6). (*Tetris* and strategy/role-play games have not yet been used for motor skills training, and therefore could not be included in the meta-analysis.) Whereas arcade-style, puzzle (non-*Tetris*), sport/racing, and Wii games all showed medium to large training effects, first-person shooter games showed negligible, nonsignificant effects. This suggests that a wide range of game types may be used to enhance hand-eye coordination and other fine and gross motor skills, although first-person shooter games may not be well suited for this purpose. Given the small number of training studies targeting motor skills ($N = 7$), we did not attempt a quantitative analysis of the results at the level of motor subskills. However, examination of individual studies shows considerable breadth of transfer. For example, Drew and Waters (1986) demonstrated improved fine motor skills using a rotary pursuit task and the Purdue pegboard task following training with *Crystal Castles* (an Atari arcade-style game), Fery and Ponserre (2001) demonstrated improved gross motor putting skills after playing *Golf* (a sports game), and Maillot and colleagues (2012) demonstrated improved hand-eye coordination using a plate-tapping task following Wii training. Notably, two video game training studies involving surgical skills (Boyle, Kennedy, Traynor, & Hill, 2011; Schlickum et al., 2009) could not be included in our meta-analysis because they did not provide parametric statistics. Boyle and colleagues observed a nonsignificant trend toward improved

Table 21.6 **Summary of Effect Sizes for Motor Skills Moderated by Game Type at the Level of Comparisons**

Game Type	Cohen's d	95% CI	Z	p-value (Z)	k	N	Q (df)	p-value (Q)
Arcade-Style	.65	[.29, 1.01]	3.50	.001	3	132		
First-Person Shooter	.07	[-.31, .45]	.36	.721	1	114		
Puzzle (Non-Tetris)	.87	[.25, 1.48]	2.75	.006	0	51		
Sport/Racing	.69	[.28, 1.10]	3.32	.001	2	150		
Wii	1.17	[.85, 1.48]	7.21	.001	5	180		
Between-classes effect							19.37 (4)	.001

surgical performance following Wii training, whereas Schlickum and colleagues found significant improvements following training with *Half Life* (a first-person shooter game). Thus, the range of transfer of training from video games to motor skills tasks is likely to be underestimated in our meta-analysis.

The third information-processing domain examined was perceptual processing, where in training effects were again moderated by game type, Q (5) = 44.30, p = .001; see Table 21.7. (Because sport/racing games have not yet been used to train perceptual processing skills, they were not included in the meta-analysis.) Only three types of the game types led to benefits for perceptual processing: arcade-style, first-person shooter, and Wii games, with the results for Wii games based on two comparisons from a single study (Maillot et al., 2012). The lack of transfer of training with puzzle (non-*Tetris*), strategy-role play, and *Tetris* games indicates limitations in the types of games that can increase efficiency of perceptual processing, with only the faster-paced game types generating benefits. Bavelier and colleagues (Bavelier, Green, Pouget, & Schrater, 2012) have suggested that action/violent games increase participants' ability to extract patterns and regularities in the environment—what they describe as probabilistic inference. The results of our meta-analysis indicate that these perceptual processing benefits extend to arcade-style and Wii games, in addition to the first-person shooter games used in Bavelier and colleagues' studies.

To gain more precise information regarding which perceptual skills were enhanced through video game training, we conducted a follow-up meta-analysis for each game type yielding a significant overall effect, using perceptual processing subskill as a moderator. Seven perceptual subskills were identified, all of which were tested in the visual modality, with the exception of auditory (tone) localization (see Table 21.8). Fourteen of the 23 studies of perceptual processing

Table 21.7 **Summary of Effect Sizes for Perceptual Processing Moderated by Game Type at the Level of Comparisons**

Game Type	Cohen's d	95% CI	Z	p-value (Z)	k	N	Q (df)	p-value (Q)
Arcade-Style	.42	[.23, .61]	4.27	.001	12	518		
First-Person Shooter	.45	[.17, .72]	3.19	.001	35	951		
Puzzle (Non-Tetris)	.12	[−1.50, 1.73]	.14	.887	3	80		
Strategy/Role-Play	−.14	[−.37, .08]	−1.24	.214	8	359		
Tetris	−.08	[−.40, .24]	−.50	.617	6	248		
Wii	1.72	[1.13, 2.32]	5.69	.001	1	60		
Between-classes effect							44.30 (5)	.001

Table 21.8 **Summary of Effect Sizes for Perceptual Processing Moderated by Subskill at the Level of Comparisons for Game Types Showing Significant Training Effects**

	Perceptual Processing Subskill	Cohen's d	95% CI	Z	p-value (Z)	k	N	Q (df)	p-value (Q)
Arcade-Style	Attentional Blink	.32	[.02, .62]	2.10	.036	3	176		
	Change Detection	−.02	[−.41, .37]	−.09	.925	1	100		
	Object Detection/ Matching	.68	[.41, .94]	4.98	.001	6	242		
	Between-classes effect							8.79 (2)	.012
First-Person Shooter	Attentional Blink	.66	[.01, 1.31]	1.98	.047	5	167		
	Auditory (Tone) Localization	.45	[−.47, 1.36]	.96	.339	1	50		
	Enumeration	.59	[−.24, 1.42]	1.39	.166	2	72		
	Functional Field of View	.70	[.27, 1.13]	3.20	.001	10	295		
	Multiple Object Tracking	−.19	[−.69, .32]	−.73	.467	6	202		
	Object Detection/ Matching	.43	[−.45, 1.31]	.96	.335	7	165		
	Between-classes effect							7.90 (5)	.162
Wii	Object Detection/ Matching	1.72	[1.13, 2.32]	5.69	.001	1	60		

used first-person shooter games (with 8 out of 14 conducted by Bavelier and her colleagues). These training studies examined six perceptual processing subskills: attentional blink, auditory (tone) location, enumeration, functional field of view, multiple object tracking, object detection/matching. Although perceptual processing subskill failed to be a statistically significant moderator of the

Table 21.9 **Summary of Effect Sizes for Spatial Imagery Moderated by Game Type at the Level of Comparisons**

Game Type	Cohen's d	95% CI	Z	p-value (Z)	k	N	Q (df)	p-value (Q)
Arcade-Style	.61	[.24, .98]	3.27	.001	1	126		
First-Person Shooter	.17	[.01, .34]	2.05	.040	11	569		
Puzzle (Non-Tetris)	.84	[.65, 1.04]	8.43	.001	10	451		
Sport/Racing	.23	[–.10, .56]	1.36	.174	5	144		
Strategy/Role-Play	.23	[.02, .44]	2.12	.034	10	355		
Tetris	.46	[.28, .64]	4.95	.001	35	950		
Wii	.53	[–.01, 1.06]	1.94	.052	1	60		
Between-classes effect							31.95 (6)	.001

effects of first-person shooter games, Q (5) = 7.90, p = .162, positive trends were not significant for auditory (tone) localization, enumeration, and object detection/matching, given either too few comparisons or variability in research findings. A negative trend was observed for multiple object tracking (7 comparisons from two studies: Boot, 2007; Cohen, Green, & Bavelier, 2008, Exp 2). Robust medium effects were observed for attentional blink and functional field of view subskills. That is, training with first-person shooter games significantly shortened the attentional blink (i.e., the recovery time between presentations of a repeated stimulus) and expanded the size of the functional visual field.

Arcade-style games (N = 5 studies) were used to train three perceptual processing subskills: attentional blink, change detection, and object detection/matching. Perceptual processing subskill proved to be a significant moderator of effects, Q (2) = 8.79, p = .012, with significant enhancements in visual processing evident for attentional blink and object detection/matching subskills, and a negligible, nonsignificant effect for change detection. Wii games were used to train only one perceptual processing subskill (object detection/matching) in only one study (Maillot et al., 2012), which showed a large effect. Clearly additional studies are needed to confirm this result, and to extend studies of Wii training to other perceptual processing sub-skills.

The final information-processing domain examined was spatial imagery, with game type again moderating training effects, Q (6) = 31.95, p = .001 (see Table 21.9). All game types, with the exception of sport/racing games, yielded significant training effects. These effects, however, varied in size with puzzle (non-*Tetris*) games showing a large effect size, arcade-style games and Wii games showing medium effect sizes, strategy/role-play and *Tetris* showing small effect sizes, and first-person shooter games showing a negligible effect. Thus, counter to expectations, *Tetris* games failed to yield larger training effects for spatial imagery than other game types, notably other puzzle games and arcade-style games (see confidence intervals in Table 21.9). The superiority of puzzle (non-*Tetris*) training over other types of video games should be interpreted cautiously given the small number of studies involved (N = 3; McClurg & Chaille, 1987; Miller & Kapel, 1985; Smith, Morey, & Tjoe, 2007). Additional studies are needed to identify which features of puzzle (non-*Tetris*) games are most beneficial for enhancing spatial imagery.

For each game type that yielded a significant training effect on spatial imagery, we conducted a follow-up meta-analysis, using spatial imagery subskill as a moderator (see Table 21.10). Four outcome measures were identified: spatial batteries, card/paper folding tasks, spatial visualization tasks, and mental rotation. In none of these follow-up analyses was spatial imagery subskill a significant moderator of effect sizes. Most game types were tested using only a limited number of outcome measures, with too few studies and comparisons.

Transfer of Game Training Across Information-Processing Domains

As a second step toward evaluating how broadly video game training transferred across information-processing domains, for each game type we examined the range of training effects. Arcade-style games (N = 9 studies) yielded significant training effects across all four domains, with medium effects observed for motor skills and spatial imagery, and small effects observed for executive functions and perceptual processing. Note, however, that many of these studies were conducted in the 1980s and 1990s, in the early years of home video game usage (see Table 21.1). The two recent studies (Boot et al., 2010; Lee et al., 2012) appeared to have yielded smaller effects than the earlier studies (i.e., smaller differences between training and control groups); this pattern suggests possible generational differences in the impact of video games on cognitive skills—a finding warranting confirmation in future studies. The ubiquity of video games and mobile apps in today's society, accessed through smartphones, computers, and other devices, may be minimizing differences between training and control groups, with participants in present-day studies increasingly likely to have had daily exposure to games through a variety of technology interfaces. Thus, arcade-style games, with their long history of usage (often dated from the release of *Pong* in 1972 and *Space Invaders* in 1978), may be ideally suited for the comparison of video game training effects across generations of players.

Training with Wii games also showed positive effects across information-processing domains, with large effects for executive functions, motor skills, and perceptual processing, and a medium (marginally significant) effect for spatial

Table 21.10 **Effect Sizes for Spatial Imagery Moderated by Subskill at the Level of Comparisons for Game Types Showing Significant Training Effects**

	Spatial Imagery Subskill	Cohen's d	95% CI	Z	p-value (Z)	k	N	Q (df)	p-value (Q)
Arcade-Style	Spatial Battery	.62	[.11, 1.12]	2.41	.016	0	70		
	Spatial Visualization	.60	[.07, 1.14]	2.21	.027	0	56		
	Between-classes effect							.001 (1)	.977
First-Person Shooter	Spatial Battery	.23	[.02, .44]	2.18	.029	7	371		
	Card/Paper Folding	.23	[-.47, .93]	.66	.511	1	120		
	Mental Rotation	-.17	[-.61, .28]	-.73	.466	1	78		
	Between-classes effect							2.54 (2)	.282
Puzzle (Non-Tetris)	Spatial Battery	.98	[.75, 1.20]	8.48	.001	7	339		
	Mental Rotation	.37	[-.34, 1.07]	1.02	.310	1	38		
	Spatial Visualization	.47	[-.01, .94]	1.91	.056	0	74		
	Between-classes effect							5.50 (2)	.064
Strategy/Role-Play	Card/Paper Folding	.40	[-.24, 1.03]	1.23	.218	0	39		
	Mental Rotation	.20	[-.04, .44]	1.62	.106	8	277		
	Spatial Visualization	.27	[-.36, .90]	.84	.404	0	39		
	Between-classes effect							.34 (2)	.843
Tetris	Card/Paper Folding	.04	[-1.05, 1.13]	.07	.942	0	16		
	Mental Rotation	.50	[.30, .71]	4.79	.001	29	829		
	Spatial Visualization	.24	[-.19, .66]	1.09	.274	4	105		
	Between-classes effect							1.79 (2)	.409

imagery. Given that Wii games were released only recently (in 2006), results for Wii training studies are only now appearing in the literature. Consequently, three studies were available to be included in our meta-analysis, with only one study (Maillot et al., 2012) exploring training effects across multiple information-processing domains. Maillot and colleagues introduced Wii games in the context of cognitive and physical skills training for elderly adults (mean age 73 years), inspired by evidence of beneficial effects of physical activity on cognitive functioning (e.g., Colcombe & Kramer, 2003; Colcombe et al., 2004; Erickson & Kramer, 2009; Erickson et al., 2011). Following 12 weeks of Wii game training, elderly adults showed significant improvements, relative to a no-contact control group, on physical fitness tests of flexibility, strength, and balance, in addition to showing training effects across all four of the information-processing domains examined here. Whether these benefits reflect the physical activity required to play Wii games or, alternatively, the demands of navigating through virtual environments, requires further investigation. Anderson-Hanley et al. (2012) found that the combination of riding a stationary bike with a virtual reality display led to greater improvements in executive functions for elderly adults than riding a stationary bike alone. This result suggests that both exercise and mimetic experience might underlie the beneficial effects of Wii use.

In contrast to the broad transfer effects observed for arcade-style and Wii games, other game types yielded more restricted training effects. Puzzle (non-*Tetris*) games yielded large effects for motor skills and spatial imagery, although the effect for motor skills was based on only one comparison from a task that required participants to draw the trajectories of objects moving through space (Masson, Bub, & LaLonde, 2011). No significant effect of puzzle (non-*Tetris*) training was evident for perceptual processing, and a small, negative effect was observed for executive functions. Likewise, benefits of *Tetris* training were limited to the spatial imagery domain (small effect), with no effects on executive functioning or perceptual processing. (*Tetris* has not been used for training motor skills.) The view that puzzle (non-*Tetris*) and *Tetris* training enhances performance only on near transfer tasks is further supported by the work of Bavelier and colleagues (e.g., Cohen, Green, & Bavelier, 2008; Green & Bavelier, 2006a, 2006b, 2007), using *Tetris* training as the control condition for studies of the effects of first-person shooter games on perceptual processing.

Training using first-person shooter games produced significant effects on perceptual processing and spatial imagery, but not on executive functions and motor skills. However, while the training effect size was small for perceptual processing, it was negligible for spatial imagery. This finding suggests that first-person shooter games yield a pattern of near transfer effects, which runs counter to the claim of Bavelier and colleagues (2012, p. 394) that "action video game play bears little resemblance in terms of stimuli and goals to perceptual, attentional, or cognitive tasks at which VGPs [video game players] are found to excel in the laboratory." Indeed, when we conducted follow-up analyses of players of action/violent video games in the meta-analysis of quasi-experimental studies (Powers et al., 2013), we found a large mean effect size of video game experience on perceptual processing ($d = .73$), a medium mean effect on executive functions ($d = .51$), and a small mean effect on spatial imagery ($d = .29$). (There were no quasi-experimental studies involving action game players and motor skills tasks.) This discrepancy, between the findings of the quasi-experimental studies comparing habitual video game players and nonplayers and the training experiments, might partially reflect self-selection, wherein players with enhanced information-processing skills might be more likely to excel at and enjoy action/violent games. Also, with the strategic recruitment of video game players to perform computer-based tasks in quasi-experimental studies, Hawthorne effects might contribute to the larger effects observed in the nonexperimental studies (cf. Boot, Blakely, & Simons, 2011). That is, participants may be aware of research claims about the effects of gaming (e.g., from media coverage), leading video game players to expect to perform well in studies that target their skills in recruitment.

The remaining two game types, sport/racing games ($N = 4$ studies) and strategy/role-play games ($N = 4$ studies) have been used in relatively few training studies, and have yielded limited effects. Sport/racing games yielded a medium training effect for motor skills based on three comparisons from one study (Fery & Ponserre, 2001), and no significant effects for executive functions or spatial imagery. (Sport/racing games have not been used to train perceptual processing.) Strategy/role-play games yielded a small effect for spatial imagery, and no significant effects for executive functions or perceptual processing. (Strategy/role-play games have not been used to test motor skills.) Of the four studies to use strategy/role-play games for cognitive training, three (Basak, Boot, Voss, & Kramer, 2008; Boot, 2007; Whitlock, McLaughlin & Allaire, 2012) tested effects across information-processing domains, which provides a stronger basis for concluding that training benefits are restricted to spatial imagery tasks and do not extend to executive functions and perceptual processing.

Applying Findings to Education and Cognitive Training

Given the technological saturation of today's youth culture, it is becoming nearly impossible for studies to include youth control groups with limited or no prior gaming experience. In Powers et al. (2013), the effects of game training were larger in elderly adults than in young adults, which might reflect less prior game experience among the elderly, resulting in a lower baseline. To date, very few training studies have been conducted with youth ($N = 7$ in our sample, defined as studies involving children of ages 7 to 17), and the widespread popularity of Wii, Xbox, PlayStation and other game platforms makes it increasingly difficult to evaluate effects of commercial games in children. Thus, the implications of video game training studies for the field of education remain unclear: first, because too few studies have tested youth, which limits our knowledge of how skills acquired through video game play affect information processing in childhood; second, because crucial educational outcomes, such as critical thinking, oral and written communication skills, appear to be distant from the types of skills sharpened through video game training (Greenfield, 2009).

Only two studies in our meta-analyses used video games to train executive functions in youth (Miller & Kapel, 1985; Staiano, Abraham, & Calvert, 2012). Miller and Kapel (1985) used a variety of puzzle games in training seventh and eighth graders, and found negligible effects on abstract reasoning (intelligence) tests. Staiano and colleagues (2012) introduced 10 weeks of Wii training to 15- to 19-year-old obese teenagers, and contrasted effects of competitive play, cooperative play, and a no-play control group. This study documented enhancement in performance on an executive function battery (Delis-Kaplan Executive Function System) only in the competitive group—a pattern attributed to the increased demands of competitive exercise on the prefrontal cortex (Best, 2010; Decety et al., 2004). Thus, the only study to demonstrate broad transfer of video game training in youth suggests that the benefits of Wii training are tied to the cognitive effects of competition, as opposed to other game features such as virtual reality.

With regard to cognitive training for elderly adults, more research needs to examine whether benefits extend beyond studies of exergaming, as described above. Our meta-analysis included only four studies (Basak et al., 2008; Drew & Waters, 1986; Goldstein et al., 1997; Whitlock, McLaughlin & Allaire, 2012) that tested for effects of video game training on executive functioning among the elderly, using games other than Wii. Basak and colleagues (2008) and Whitlock and colleagues used strategy/role-play games and examined effects on various executive function subskills. Unfortunately, the results across these two studies are contradictory, with positive effects for inhibition in Whitlock et al. (2012), but not Basak et al. (2008), and positive effects for nonverbal intelligence (progressive matrices) in Basak et al. (2008) but not Whitlock et al. (2012). Results for other executive function subskills (battery, working memory, task switching) in these two studies were also equivocal. Goldstein and colleagues examined transfer of *Super Tetris* to the Sternberg task, a measure of working memory, and the Stroop task, a measure of inhibition. Goldstein found improved performance on the Sternberg task, but not the Stroop task, post training. Drew and Waters (1986) trained elderly adults on *Crystal Castles* (an arcade game) and reported an improvement in general intelligence. However, this study lacked an adequate control group, and therefore used a within-subjects pretest/post-test comparison. Taken together, these mixed effects indicate the need for future studies to evaluate the utility of video games for cognitive training in elderly adults. In particular, studies are needed that use games that elderly adults can play with success, regardless of their physical mobility.

Future Directions

Mobile devices have drastically increased in popularity in recent years, with estimates that 85% of 15- to 18-year-olds own cell phones as of 2009 (Rideout, Foehr, & Roberts, 2010). These devices provide nearly continuous access to games; hence, studies are needed to determine whether training effects of video games, especially in the domain of perceptual processing, vary as a function of screen size. Unfortunately, no study has yet examined this question. However, training studies that use mobile devices are now appearing. For example, Oei and Patterson (2013; not included in our meta-analysis) used five games played on an iPhone or iPod Touch, with outcome measures in domains of perceptual processing and executive functions. In the domain of perceptual processing, the first-person shooter game *Modern Combat: Sandstorm* yielded benefits for measures of attentional blink and multiple-object tracking, but not object detection [visual search]. A contrasting pattern was observed for puzzle games (*Hidden Expedition Everest, Memory Matrix, Bejeweled 2*) with benefits observed for object detection, but not attentional blink or multiple-object tracking measures.

In the domain of executive functions, the first-person shooter game yielded benefits for inhibition, but not working memory, whereas the opposite pattern was observed for puzzle games. Only the simulation game, *The Sims 3*, showed no apparent training benefits. These complementary patterns were interpreted as support for task-specific transfer effects for each game type. Note, however, that the observed results for executive functions did not match our findings, where non-*Tetris* puzzle games and first-person shooter games failed to yield any benefits (see Table 21.4).

The inconsistencies of findings across video game training studies warrant the use of meta-analysis to evaluate the impact of moderators, such as game type, as the literature continues to grow. However, in moving forward, greater attention needs to be paid to methodological issues such as control conditions (cf. Boot, Simons, Stohart, & Stutts, 2013), and participants' prior gaming histories as moderators of effects. Generational changes in information processing due to the technological revolution are likely to affect training as well, in ways that may be difficult to quantify.

Authors' Notes

This research was partially funded by CUNY Doctoral Student Research Grant to K. Powers. We thank Naomi Aldrich, Louis Alfieri, and Melissa Palladino for their work in creating the dataset for this study.

Notes

1. There were 265 comparisons in our dataset rather than the 251 comparisons in the dataset of Powers et al. (2013): 14 comparisons from one study (Boot, 2007) were expanded to allow for comparison of two different commercial video games.
2. References marked with an asterisk are included in the meta-analysis.

References[2]

Anderson, S. (2012, April 8). Just one more game...Angry Birds, Farmville, and other hyper-addictive "stupid games." *New York Times Sunday Magazine* (p. MM28). Retrieved from http://www.nytimes.com/2012/04/08/magazine/angry-birds-farmville-and-other-hyperaddictive-stupid-games.html

Anderson-Hanley, C., Arciero, P. J., Brickman, A. M., Nimon, J. P., Okuma, N., Westen, S. C.,...Zimmerman, E. A., (2012). Exergaming and older adult cognition: A cluster randomized clinical trial. *American Journal of Preventative Medicine, 42*, 109–120.

*Basak, C., Boot, W., Voss, M., & Kramer, A. (2008). Can training in a real-time strategy video game attenuate cognitive decline in older adults? *Psychology and Aging, 23*, 765–777.

Bavelier, D. (2012, November). Daphne Bavelier: Your brain on video games [Video file]. Retrieved from http://www.ted.com/talks/daphne_bavelier_your_brain_on_video_games.html

Bavelier, D., Green, C. S., Pouget, A., & Schrater, P. (2012). Brain plasticity through the life span: Learning to learn and action video games. *The Annual Review of Neuroscience, 35*, 391–416.

Best, J. R. (2010). Effects of physical activity on children's executive function: Contributions of experimental research on aerobic exercise. *Developmental Review, 30*, 331–351.

*Boot, W. R. (2007). *The effects of video-game playing on perceptual and cognitive abilities.* University of Illinois at Urbana-Champaign). *ProQuest Dissertations and Theses*, Retrieved from http://ezproxy.gc.cuny.edu/login?url=http://search.proquest.com/docview/304857335?accountid=7287. (304857335).

*Boot, W. R., Basak, C., Erickson, K. I., Neider, M., Simons, D. J., Fabiani, M., & Kramer, A. F. (2010). Transfer of skill engendered by complex task training under conditions of variable priority. *Acta Psychologica, 135*, 349–357.

Boot, W. R., Blakely, D. P., & Simons, D. J. (2011). Do action video games improve perception and cognition? *Frontiers in Psychology, 2*, 1–6.

Boot, W. R., Simons, D. J., Stothart, C. & Stutts, C. (2013). The pervasive problem with placebos in psychology: Why active control groups are not sufficient in rule out placebo effects. *Perspectives on Psychological Science, 9*, 445–454.

Boyle, E., Kennedy, A., Traynor, O., & Hill, A. D. K. (2011). Training surgical skills using nonsurgical tasks—can Nintendo Wii improve surgical performance? *Journal of Surgical Education, 68*(2), 148–154.

Borenstein, M., Hedges, L., Higgins, J., & Rothstein, H. (2005). *Comprehensive Meta-Analysis Version 2.* Englewood, NJ: Biostat.

*Cherney, I. (2008). Mom, let me play more computer games: They improve my mental rotation skills. *Sex Roles, 59*, 776–786.

*Clark, J., Lanphear, A., & Riddick, C. (1987). The effects of videogame playing on the response selection processing of elderly adults. *Journal of Gerontology, 42*(1), 82–85.

Cohen, J. (1988). *Statistical power analysis for the behavioral sciences* (2nd ed.). Hillsdale, NJ: Lawrence Erlbaum Assoc.

*Cohen, J. E., Green, C. S., & Bavelier, D. (2008). Training visual attention with video games: Not all games are created equal. In H. F. O'Neil & R. S. Perez (Eds.), *Computer games and team and individual learning* (pp. 205–227). Oxford, UK: Elsevier Ltd.

Colcombe, S. J., Kramer, A. F., McAuley, E., Erickson, K. I., & Scalf, P. (2004). Neurocognitive aging and cardiovascular fitness. *Journal of Molecular Neuroscience, 24,* 9–14.

Colcombe, S. J., & Kramer, A. F. (2003). Fitness effects on the cognitive function of older adults: A meta-analytic study. *Psychological Science, 14,* 125–130.

Decety, J., Jackson, P. L., Sommerville, J. A., Chaminade, T., & Meltzoff, A. N. (2004). The neural bases of cooperation and competition: An fMRI investigation. *Journal of NeuroImage, 23,* 744–751.

*DeLisi, R., & Cammarano, D. (1996). Computer experience and gender differences in undergraduate mental rotation performance. *Computers in Human Behavior, 12,* 351–361.

*DeLisi, R., & Wolford, J. (2002). Improving children's mental rotation accuracy with computer game playing. *Journal of Genetic Psychology, 163,* 272–282.

*Dorval, M., & Pepin, M. (1986). Effect of playing a video game on a measure of spatial visualization. *Perceptual and Motor Skills, 62*(1), 159–162.

*Drew, B., & Waters, J. (1986). Video games: utilization of a novel strategy to improve perceptual-motor skills in the non-institutionalized elderly. *Cognitive Rehabilitation, 4*(2), 26–31.

Dye, M. W., Green, G. C., & Bavelier, D. (2009). Increasing speed of processing with action video games. *Current Directions in Psychological Science, 18,* 321–326.

Erickson, K. I., & Kramer, A. F. (2009). Aerobic exercise effects on cognitive and neural plasticity in older adults. *British Journal of Sports Medicine, 43,* 22–24.

Erickson, K. I., Voss, M. W., Prakash, R. S., Basak, C., Szabo, A., Chaddock, L.,..., Kramer, A. F., (2011). Exercise training increases size of hippocampus and improves memory. *Proceedings of the National Academy of Sciences, 108,*3017–3022.

*Feng, J., Spence, I., & Pratt, J. (2007). Playing an action video game reduces gender differences in spatial cognition. *Psychological Science, 18,* 850–854.

Ferguson, C. J. (2007). The good, the bad and the ugly: A meta-analytic review of positive and negative erects of violent video games. *Psychiatric Quarterly, 78,* 309–316.

*Fery, Y. A., & Ponserre, S. (2001) Enhancing the control of force in putting by video game training. *Ergonomics, 44,* 1025–1037.

*Gagnon, D. (1985). Videogames and spatial skills: An exploratory study. *Educational Communication and Technology Journal, 33,* 263–275.

*Gagnon, D. (1986). Interactive versus observational media: The influence of user control and cognitive styles on spatial learning. *ProQuest Dissertations and Theses.*

Gee, J. (2007). *What video games have to teach us about learning and literacy.* New York, NY: Palgrave Macmillan.

*Goldstein, J., Cajko, L., Oosterbroek, M., Michielsen, M., Van Houten, O., & Salverda, F. (1997). Video games and the elderly. *Social Behavior and Personality, 25,* 345–352.

*Gopher, D., Weil, M., & Bareket, T. (1994). Transfer of skill from a computer game trainer to flight. *Human Factors, 36,* 387–405.

Graff, A. (2013, February 22). Do violent video games lead kids to be violent in the real world? *SFGate.* Retrieved from http://blog.sfgate.com/sfmoms/2013/02/22/do-violent-video games-lead-kids-to-be-violent-in-the-real-world/

*Green, C. S. (2008). The effects of action video game experience on perceptual decision making. *Dissertation Abstracts International, 69*(5-B), pp. 3287.

*Green, C. S., & Bavelier, D. (2006a). Effect of action video games on the spatial distribution of visuospatial attention. *Journal of Experimental Psychology, 32,* 1465–1478.

*Green, C. S., & Bavelier, D. (2006b). Enumeration versus multiple object tracking: The case of action video game players. *Cognition, 101,* 217–245.

*Green, C. S., & Bavelier, D. (2007). Action-video game experience alters the spatial resolution of vision. *Psychological Science, 18*(1), 88–94.

*Green, C. S., Sugarman, M. A., Medford, K., Klobusicky, E., Bavelier, D. (2012). The effect of action video game experience on task-switching. *Computers in Human Behavior, 28,* 984–994.

Greenfield, P. M. (1984). *Mind and media: The effects of television, videogames, and computers.* Cambridge, MA: Harvard University Press.

Greenfield, P. M. (2009). Technology and informal education: What is taught, what is learned. *Science, 323*(69), 69–71.

Gross D. (2011, June 29). The 10 biggest violent video game controversies. Retrieved from http://articles.cnn.com/2011-06-29/tech/violent.video.games_1_sale-of-violent-video-mortal-kombat-entertainment-software-rating-board?_s=PM:TECH

Harper, J. D., Kaiser, S., Ebrahimi, K., Lambert, G. R., Hadley, H. R., & Baldwin, D. D. (2007). Prior videogame exposure does not enhance robotic surgical performance. *Journal of Endourology, 21*, 1207–1210.

Homer, B. B., Hayward, E. O., Frye, J., & Plass, J. L. (2012). Gender and player characteristics in video game play of preadolescents. *Computers in Human Behavior, 28*, 1782–1789. doi: 10.1014/j.chb.2012.04.018

Hurley, D. (2012, April 18). Can you make yourself smarter? *New York Times Magazine.* Retrieved from http://www.nytimes.com/2012/04/22/magazine/can-you-make-yourself-smarter.html?pagewanted=all

Jaeggi, S. M., Buschkuehl, M., Jonides, J., & Shah, P. (2011). Short- and long-term benefits of cognitive training. *PNAS Proceedings of the National Academy of Sciences of the United States of America, 108*, 10081–10086.

*Kearney, P. R. (2005, June). Cognitive calisthenics: Do FPS computer games enhance the player's cognitive abilities? *Proceedings of the Digital Games Research Association 2005 Conference: Changing Views—Worlds in Play. Vancouver, British Columbia, Canada.* Retrieved from http://www.digra.org/dl/db/06276.14516.pdf

Kennedy, A. M., Boyle, E. M., Traynor, O., Walsh, T., & Hill, A. D. (2011). Video gaming enhances psychomotor skills but not visuospatial and perceptual abilities in surgical trainees. *Journal of Surgical Education, 68*, 414–420.

Knafo, S. (2013, January 17). Joe Biden talks violent video games with industry reps in wake of Newtown shooting. *Huff Post Tech.* Retrieved from http://www.huffingtonpost.com/2013/01/11/joe-biden-violent-video games_n_2458161.html

*Lee, H., Boot, W. R., Basak, C., Voss, M. V. Prakash, R. S., Neider, M.,...Kramer, A. F. (2012). Performance gains from directed training do not transfer to untrained tasks. *Acta Psychologica, 139*, 146–158.

Levi, D. M. (2012). Prentice Award Lecture 2011: Removing the brakes on plasticity in the amblyopic brain. *Optometry and Vision Science, 89*, 827–838.

*Li, R., Polat, U., Makous, W., & Bavelier, D. (2009). Enhancing the contrast sensitivity function through action video game training. *Nature Neuroscience, 12*, 549–551.

Lush, T. (2011, August 29). At war with *World of Warcraft*: An addict tells his story. *The Guardian.* Retrieved from http://www.guardian.co.uk/technology/2011/aug/29/world-of-warcraft-video game-addict

*Maillot, P., Perrot, A., & Hartly, A. (2012). Effects of interactive physical-activity video game training on physical and cognitive function in older adults. *Psychology and Aging, 27*, 589–600.

*Masson, M., Bub, D., & Lalonde, C. (2011). Video game training and naïve reasoning about object motion. *Applied Cognitive Psychology, 25*, 166–173.

*McClurg, P., & Chaille, C. (1987). Computer games: Environments for developing spatial cognition? *Journal of Educational Computing Research, 3*(1), 95–111. doi: 10.2190/9N5U-P3E9-R1X8ORQM

*McSwegin, P., Pemberton, C., & O'Banion, N. (1988). The effects of controlled videogame playing on the eye-hand coordination and reaction time of children. In J. E. Clark & J. H. Humphery (Eds.), *Advances in motor development research* (Vol. 2, pp. 97–102). New York, NY: AMS Press.

*Miller, G., & Kapel, D. (1985). Can non-verbal, puzzle type microcomputer software affect spatial discrimination and sequential thinking skills of 7th and 8th graders. *Education, 106*(2), 161–167.

*Nelson, R., & Strachen, I. (2009). Action and puzzle video games prime different speed/accuracy tradeoffs. *Perception 38*, 1678–1687.

Oei, A. C., & Patterson, M. D., (2013). Enhancing cognition with video games: A multiple game training study. *PLoS ONE, 8*, e58456.

*Okagaki, L., & Frensch, P. A. (1994). Effects of video game playing on measures of spatial performance: Gender effects in late adolescence. *Journal of Applied Developmental Psychology, 15*, 33–58.

*O'Leary, K. C., Pontifex, M. B., Scudder, M. R., Brown, M. L., & Hillman, C. H. (2011). The effects of single bouts of aerobic exercise, exergaming, and video game play on cognitive control. *Clinical Neurophysiology, 122*, 1518–1525.

*Orosy-Fildes, C., & Allan, R. W. (1989). Psychology of computer use: XII. Video-game play: Human reaction time to visual stimuli. *Perceptual and Motor Skills, 69*, 243–247.

Powers, K. L., Brooks, P. J., Aldrich, N. J., Palladino, M. A., Alfieri, L. (2013). Effects of video-game play on information processing: a meta-analytic investigation. *Psychonomic Bulletin and Review, 20*(6), 1055–1079.

Primack, B. A., Carroll, M. V., McNamara, M., Klem, M. L., King, B., Rich, M., ... Nayak, S. (2012). Role of video games in improving health-related outcomes. *American Journal of Preventive Medicine, 42*, 630–638.

Rideout, V. J., Foehr, U. G., & Roberts, D. F. (2010). *Generation M2 media in the lives of 8- to 18-year-olds.* Menlo Park, CA: The Henry J. Kaiser Family Foundation. Retrieved from www.kff.org

Rosenberg, B. H., Landsittel, D., & Averch, T. D. (2005). Can video games be used to predict or improve laparoscopic skills? *Journal of Endourology, 19*, 372–376.

Rosser, J. C., Lynch, P. J., Cuddihy, L., Gentile, D. A., Klonsky, J., & Merrell, R. (2007). The impact of video games on training surgeons in the 21st century. *Archives of Surgery, 142*(2), 181–186.

*Sanchez, C. A. (2012). Enhancing visuospatial performance through video game training to increase learning in visuospatial science domains. *Psychonomic Bulletin and Review,19*, 58–65.

Schlickum, M. K., Hedman, L., Enochsson, L., Kjellin, A., & Felländer-Tsai, L. (2009). Systematic video game training in surgical novices improves performance in virtual reality endoscopic surgical simulators: A prospective randomized study. *World Journal of Surgery, 33*, 2360–2367.

*Sims, V. K., & Mayer, R. E. (2002). Domain specificity of spatial expertise: The case of video game players. *Applied Cognitive Psychology, 16*, 97–115.

*Smith, G., Morey, J., & Tjoe, E. (2007). Feature masking in computer game promotes visual imagery. *Journal of Educational Computing Research, 36*, 351–372.

*Spence, I., Yu, J. J., Feng, J., & Marshman, J. (2009). Women match men when learning a spatial skill. *Journal of Experimental Psychology, 35*, 1097–1103.

*Staiano, A. E., Abraham, A. A., & Calvert, S. L. (2012). Competitive versus cooperative exergame play for African American adolescents' executive function skills: Short-term effects in a long-term training intervention. *Developmental Psychology, 48*, 337–342.

*Subrahmanyam, K., & Greenfield, P.(1996). Effect of video game practice on spatial skills in girls and boys. *Journal of Applied Developmental Psychology, 15*, 13–32.

Sutter, J. D. (2012, August 6). 5 warning signs of gaming addiction. Retrieved from http://www.cnn.com/2012/08/05/tech/gaming-gadgets/gaming-addiction-warning-signs

*Valadez, J. J., & Ferguson, C. J. (2012). Just a game after all: Violent video game exposure and time spent playing effects on hostile feelings, depression, and visuospatial cognition. *Computers in Human Behavior, 28*, 608–616.

van Dongen, K. W., Verleisdonk, E. M. M., Schijven, M. P., & Broeders, I. A. M. J. (2011). Will the PlayStation generation become better endoscopic surgeons? *Surgical Endoscopy, 25*, 2275–2280.

*Whitlock, L. A., McLaughlin, A. C., & Allaire, J. C. (2012). Individual difference in response to cognitive training: Using a multi-modal, attentionally demanding game-based intervention for older adults. *Computers in Human Behavior, 28*, 1091–96.

*Wu, S., Cheng, C. K., Feng, J., D'Angelo, L., Alain, C., & Spence, I. (2012). Playing a first-person shooter video game induces neuroplastic change. *Journal of Cognitive Neuroscience, 24*, 1286–1293.

Zichermann, (2011, November). Gabe Zichermann: How games make kids smarter [Video file]. Retrieved from http://www.ted.com/talks/lang/en/gabe_zichermann_how_games_make_kids_smarter.htm

Part Five

CONCLUSION

22

Games in a Digital Age: Supporting a New Ecology of Learning[1,2]

MICHAEL H. LEVINE, LORI TAKEUCHI, AND SARAH E. VAALA

Something Old, Something New: Anchoring a Modern Family Ecology

Since its inception in the 1970s, Urie Bronfenbrenner's ecological systems theory (EST) has provided a generation of scholars and practitioners with a powerful tool for understanding human development. According to Bronfenbrenner's theory, children grow and learn within a set of nested and interrelated contexts (Bronfenbrenner, 1977, 1979). These contexts span from children's immediate surroundings, such as their homes, community centers, and schools; to settings that indirectly influence their lives, such as their parents' workplaces; to broader societal contexts, including the culture children are immersed in and the historical time period in which they live. All of these contexts shape children's development, relationships, and interactions with the environment around them. In turn, children reciprocally influence these contexts. Conceived during a period of increasing economic disparity, EST provided the basis for a strong argument for the design and establishment of key family support programs that remain pillars of the U.S. social welfare system today, including Head Start and many other family support programs.

In the decades that have passed since Bronfenbrenner first introduced EST, we have moved out of the Industrial Age and into the Information Age. Most citizens of the United States have had their work and personal lives transformed by two developments in the information and communications technology (ICT) sector. First, advancements in microprocessor technology have rendered computing technologies faster, more powerful, more affordable, and more mobile at an exponential rate.[3] Second, the advent of the Internet (c. 1969) has opened up multiple channels for communication and information sharing that are remarkably cost-effective and flexible compared to older systems (i.e., telephone and print). Together, these events have led to a burgeoning consumer electronic marketplace and revolutionary changes in how business gets done across all sectors of the U.S. workforce, and set the historical context—what Bronfenbrenner called the *chronosystem*—for children growing up today (Takeuchi & Levine, in press). In this changing ecology of human development, digital games are emerging as a promising new way to promote children's learning.

Gone Digital: How Children Now Play...and Learn

Mass media consumption is a norm in today's highly networked digital age, driven by transformative changes in commerce, the workplace, and in family life itself. In 2012, U.S. sales of consumer electronics were expected to exceed $206 billion, up from $94.2 billion spent a decade before, in 2002 (Consumer Electronics Association, 2012). Families with young children are major contributors to this trend: in 2009, consumer research firm NPD Group (2009a) reported that households with children aged 4 to 14 owned an average of 11 electronic devices. As the prices of devices continue to drop, parents are increasingly inclined to purchase TV sets, cell phones, and laptops for their children's individual use, too. In 2011, 42% of children under the age of 8 had a TV in their bedroom and 24% had their own handheld gaming device (Rideout, 2011). Content geared toward children helps drive sales of these platforms, and its production has grown to become billion-dollar industries as well. Annual video game revenues in the US ($25 billion; Entertainment Software Association, 2012) currently surpass those of the film and music industries, and families with children under the age of 12 account for 45% of these sales (NPD, 2009b).

In effect, digital media are invading what Bronfenbrenner referred to as children's "microsystems"—their homes, classrooms, and other settings they frequent—and altering communication, learning, and entertainment routines. In general, children's digital consumption is on the rise: 60% of children aged 5–8 have played a handheld game, 81% have played a console game, and 90% have used a computer. Book reading, regrettably, is on the decline: in 2011, children between the ages of 6 months and 6 years spent 29 minutes per day reading or being read to, compared to 40 minutes per day in 2005 (Rideout, 2011). Children as young as 4 have increasingly sophisticated digital lives, and 10-year-olds partake in more than seven hours of media consumption a day—almost an hour and a quarter of which is used to play digital games.

Digital Games: One Opportunity to Harness Digital Technology for Learning

The high consumption rates of digital media—especially age-inappropriate video games and untethered social networks—have inspired understandable concern among parents and in research and policy circles about how smartphones, tablets, and gaming devices may be both compromising childhood and complicating parenting. Multiple observers cite former FCC chairman Newton Minow's famous summary of available television choices—the "vast wasteland" of the 1960s—as an apt metaphor for current-day offerings. Many professionals and children's advocates are concerned that the panoply of media choices, many of which have limited educational value (Shuler, 2007) has become a new "vast wasteland." Others are worried that online social networking forums and virtual worlds, and the fact that children are "always connected" (Wallis, 2010), pose privacy, health, and safety concerns, especially for younger children (Grimes and Fields, 2012).

Five decades after Minow's speech, the marketplace of digital media choices, of course, is remarkably different. In this chapter, we suggest that an exciting crossroads may be at hand. Unlike in the early days of television, when the EST was first developed, and where pioneers such as *Sesame Street* and *Mr. Rogers' Neighborhood* were few and far between, digital media and in particular, games, have attracted investors, creators, and policymakers to explore their largely untapped potential (Richards, Stebbins, & Moellering, 2013).

Today's gamers have evolved to include just about everyone. The Entertainment Software Association reports that 70 % of households play on gaming consoles, while 38 % of households play on their smartphone and 26 % play digital games on other wireless devices (e.g., iPads, ESA, 2012). Notably, 59 % of parents play digital games with their children. Of those parents, 90 % think that games are "fun for the entire family," while 66 % think games "provide mental stimulation" (ESA, 2012).

The digital games industry is perhaps still best known as a $55 billion worldwide video game entertainment behemoth that conjures images of mayhem and adolescent bonding (e.g., American Academy of Pediatrics, 2009; Ferguson, 2008; Kutner, Olson, Warner,& Hertzog, 2008). But as the articles in this volume illustrate, digital games have emerged as much more than that. Driven by their highly visual and engaging nature, games are now found everywhere: in medical and military simulations, physical education courses, publishing, advertising, and corporate training. This volume expertly draws on new research that shows how and why digital games may help advance an exciting new frontier of research on the changing ecology of human development (see Takeuchi, 2011; Takeuchi & Levine, in press).

In the past few years, a great deal of attention has been paid to the potential of digital games for good—President Barack Obama recently appointed an expert adviser to fashion the first national policy initiative on digital games' role in education, health, civic engagement, and numerous other areas (Toppo, 2012). The Department of Defense, National Science Foundation, DARPA, and National Institutes of Health have all expanded research and development funding to tease out the range of effects that games, when well deployed, can play.

To fully engage and inspire children on subjects like math and science, educators and parents are now taking advantage of children's natural affinity for digital games. Games have attracted foundations' and policymakers' interest and may emerge as a new place to find common ground. For example, the charter school Quest to Learn in New York City, which is supported by the MacArthur Foundation and others, is the nation's first public school grounded in principles of game design. Chicago Quest, following the Quest to Learn model, opened in 2011. The premise behind these schools is simple: allow young people, through gaming and game design, to construct their own learning environments. They will, in turn, develop the essential skills necessary to cooperate and problem-solve in the twenty-first-century economy.

There are several other significant examples of the new national interest in gaming as an emerging educational tool. In 2010, the Obama Administration launched a national effort to develop educational digital games—The National STEM [science, technology, engineering and math] Video Game Challenge—in cooperation with a wide range of philanthropic, nonprofit children's organizations and industry partners. The effort seeks to overcome what the Gates Foundation has labeled a national "student engagement crisis" (Civic Enterprises, 2006) by encouraging youth to create their own game-based solutions to teach essential knowledge and skills. In 2011, Congress also launched a bipartisan E-Tech Caucus and supported a new Digital Promise initiative to promote public-private partnerships that advance innovation (including game-based solutions) in education (Levine, 2011).

Toward a New Research and Policy Framework

This volume delves deeply into some of the issues that scholars, as well as program and policy experts, need to consider as they form a critical analysis of the emerging game-infused educational marketplace. We turn to some of the key themes that scholars and practitioners should consider in framing digital gameplay within an ecological theory of human development. To harness the power of digital games for learning, it is important to dig more deeply into what Bronfenbrenner called the "microsystem" by prioritizing different features of engagement, to consider variability among learners and games, and to fully contextualize gameplay within settings and relationships.

Engagement is a theme that weaves across much of the research both in this volume and in a recent issue of *New Directions for Child and Adolescent Development* (Vol. 139) on digital games. Games have great potential to engage children in learning. Fisch (2013) argues that digital media—including digital games—are particularly suited for engaging children because they offer children multiple points of entry into educational content. With many digital media options, children are able to choose media that most appeal to their interests to explore educational content between and across platforms (i.e., allowing "transmedia" engagement).

However, not all games are equally engaging, and engagement plays an important role between game exposure and educational impact. In light of this situation, several authors underscore the need to design high-quality educational games that appeal to youth as much as entertainment games do (i.e., Blumberg, Altschuler, Almonte, & Mileaf, 2013; Deater-Deckard, Change, & Evans, 2013; Sherry, 2013). Since today's youth are often referred to as "digital natives"—people whose lives have been immersed in technologies since birth—they are incredibly tech-savvy even at young ages (Prensky, 2001). They can tell instantly when a game has high-quality graphics, strong narratives, and the other hallmarks of popular commercially available entertainment games, even if they cannot discern the educational value or the disruptive stress that overconsumption of digital media can have on interpersonal relationships (Turkle, 2012). Blumberg and colleagues stress that "[educational] game development efforts often fail to adequately consider the cognitive sophistication or relative immaturity of its child and adolescent audience, and the appeal of the games compared to more recreational ones" (pg. 43). Attention to game appeal is crucial: we can make the most educational games possible—games that teach everything from algebra to art to astronomy— but if they do not attract and engage youth, our efforts will go to waste.

Moreover, not all children are engaged by the same types of games. Digital games are not monolithic and neither are young people or their circumstances, abilities, and needs—thus we should not expect that all games will affect all children in the same way. When examining the dynamic forces that video game play can have on microsystem relationships, it is crucial to consider issues that span engagement levels across developmental stage, gender, and socioeconomic factors. Research suggests that children of different ages are attracted to different games (Olson, 2010). For example, compared with preteens and teens, children under 10 seem to be less interested in games with complex plot features (Greenberg et al., 2008). Moreover, the learning impact associated with particular game features varies by age as well (Blumberg, 1998). Another key variable to consider is gender (Dickey, 2006). Kafai's (1994) landmark study on gender differences in gaming revealed that girls tend to prefer realistic settings and non-gender-specific characters, while boys do not show such preferences. Research suggests that game preferences vary along socioeconomic lines as well. For example, compared with their middle-class peers, children from low socioeconomic backgrounds tend to prefer action-oriented games (Andrews, 2008). Research methodology should match the multidimensionality of our youth and the digital games with which they engage. It is our opinion that overly simplistic research questions and designs are in part to blame for the lack of clear or consistent findings in this area (see also Young et al., 2012). Examining the context of gameplay from the varied and diverse needs of different learners and different institutional settings that comprise the microsystem is crucial to advancing the field and informing game development.

In this light, researchers should take an ecological approach that contextualizes gameplay within settings and relationships. Research should investigate the potential mechanisms and contexts operating between children's digital gaming and the key settings that drive healthy development and learning. Investigating the forces at work between inputs (i.e., exposure to digital games), settings (home, community, formal school), and outputs (e.g., learning, healthy behavior) will shed light on which features are successful or unsuccessful for accomplishing certain goals in certain contexts. Explicating potential mechanisms introduces to the field testable predictions of what is happening in the "black box" that exists between digital gameplay and child outcomes. Testing those predictions will then result in tangible, research-driven insights for best practices in designing digital games that will be most advantageous.

Within the ecological framework, more research is needed on children's co-play of digital games with parents as well (Takeuchi & Stevens, 2011). There has been a long history of focus on the benefits of parent-child "co-viewing" of television for boosting learning and mitigating potential harmful effects; we believe that co-engagement with digital games may have similar salutary impact for families (see Chiong, 2009; Takeuchi & Stevens, 2011). When digital games are designed such that each party is engaged in play, parents can scaffold the educational content for their children and extend the learning outside the context of play. In addition, many parents report that they learn technological skills from their children (Takeuchi, 2011). Using intergenerational digital gameplay as a method for promoting learning and parent-child bonding seems quite promising given the proportion of adults who report regular gameplay themselves (Entertainment Software Association, 2012).

To promote co-play that fosters learning, it is necessary for parents to understand that games can be effective learning tools. We know that despite the great appeal that video games have for many youth, parents often hold mixed perceptions of the role and repercussions of these media in their children's development. Many are concerned with the possible antisocial influence of violent games, as well as the time gameplay may displace from other activities (e.g., Gentile & Walsh, 2002; Kutner et al., 2008; Woodard & Gridina, 2000). Increasingly, however, parents feel that digital games can have a positive effect on children's learning (Entertainment Software Association, 2012). However, a 2007 parent survey conducted by the Joan Ganz Cooney Center, Common Sense Media, and Insight Research Group suggested that while parents of 6- to 14-year-olds believed that digital media broadly had great potential for children's learning, relatively few felt digital games boosted their curiosity and interest in learning, math and science skills, or reading and writing skills (Levine, Steyer, & Henry, 2008). Clearly, more should be done to develop high-quality educational games and make them known to parents.

Last, it is important to recognize the powerful learning and social exchange that that can result across the ecological levels when children design and program their own games. Kevin Clark and his colleagues at George Mason University have built a research program in which underserved youth are taught to design and create their own digital games at after-school programs and with the help of mentors (see Clark, Brandt, Hopkins, & Wilhelm, 2010; Clark & Sheridan, 2010). These scholars and others have found that learning to design and program digital games helps youth to learn game programming skills and math, problem-solving, critical thinking, systems-thinking, and metacognitive skills (Clark et al., 2010; Torres, 2009). The process is empowering and can build self-esteem as well. More research is needed to explicate the full nature and extent of learning that may accompany game design and programming training, and methods for efficiently incorporating such curricula into formal education.

The work reflected in the current volume moves the needle on our current understanding of the healthy development of youth in an increasingly digital world, and in particular the positive roles that well-designed digital games can play in their lives. But we hope this is only the beginning. Below we suggest some next steps that our nation can take to clarify how a new learning ecology around gameplay can emerge and to incent best practices in digital game design to facilitate learning from the game to more academic tasks.

Next Steps: The Potential of Digital Games for Healthy Development and Learning

At a White House event in 2011, U.S. Secretary of Education Arne Duncan announced the establishment of the Digital Promise, a nonprofit initiative created to promote digital technologies with the potential to transform teaching and learning. Experts on digital media and learning cheered this latest signal that robust experimentation with technology based on rigorous research and development would take a more prominent place in the national education reform debate. Here are some of the key challenges that more research and development work on well-designed game-based learning platforms might help address in the decade ahead.

The Nation's Literacy Crisis
Foundational literacy skills are completely stagnant among low-income and minority students; despite billions of dollars spent on early intervention in

literacy, we have made scant progress in 25 years. Tragically, only one in six African-American or Hispanic fourth-graders is proficient in reading, according to the 2011 National Assessment of Educational Progress; time has run out on our twentieth-century approach to this wholly preventable national disgrace. New evidence from the U.S. Department of Education's Ready to Learn programs have shown significant gains in vocabulary-development and reading-comprehension skills that can be facilitated by embedded media, like games, that personalize and deepen literacy learning (e.g., Penuel et al., 2009). We need to know much more about how engaging games can be delivered in multiple digital formats anytime, anywhere to promote learning "right from the start."

The Engagement Crisis

Too many children are "bored to tears" with conventional learning options, and low-income youth are dropping out of school in droves. According to Child Trends (2012), nearly one in five minority youths is dropping out of school, and in some lower socioeconomic communities, this number approaches 50% (as of 2007; Swanson, 2010). Can we square these data constructively with better designed, game-infused curricula such as those being offered by pioneers such as Quest to Learn?

The STEM and College Graduation Crises

According to recent international comparison data, U.S. students are falling further behind other industrialized countries in everything from math (25th place) and science scores (17th) to the proportion of young people with college degrees (14th; see Hechinger, 2010; U.S. Department of Education, 2012). The challenges our young people now face in an interconnected, digitally driven global landscape require a new set of competitive and cooperative skills. Design competitions and more active uses of project- or inquiry-based learning are gaining currency in high performing schools. Can games be more integrated in these increasingly popular "active learning" approaches to education, seeing as how they are interactive and participatory?

Cooperative Learning

Games are increasingly social. Whether they involve teams jointly accomplishing missions, asynchronous collaboration over social networks, or sourcing advice from interest-driven communities to help solve tricky challenges, games may naturally drive peer-to-peer and peer-to-mentor social interactions. We need to test whether such social interaction can be a boon for learning or simply a "time dump" for bored and disengaged youth.

Development of Twenty-First-Century Skills

Good games are complex. Whether it is a 5-year-old parsing a Pokémon card or a 15-year-old building in SimCity, games can foster critical skills such as problem-solving, critical thinking, creativity, collaboration, and systems thinking (Gee, 2007). Given that many of the jobs that will emerge in the twenty-first century have not yet been invented, these skills are particularly important. Will the current push to deeper "common core" standards be aligned with the unique affordances of digital games to personalize and assess skills, knowledge, and perspectives?

Although many good models are beginning to be scaled up, a significant gap exists between the promise of game-based learning and the current reality. This gap is especially evident in transforming games from effective research trials into financially sustainable products that can reach and affect students through either formal or informal channels. To help close this gap, the Joan Ganz Cooney Center has recently undertaken a major project with the support of the Bill & Melinda Gates Foundation. The Games and Learning Publishing Council has conducted a business-market analysis (Richards et al., 2013), video documentation studies of effective models (Millstone, 2012b), and a national survey of teachers to understand market dynamics, practitioner perspectives, and areas of innovation that are ready for scaling up (Millstone, 2012a). The council is releasing, on an ongoing basis, other market and policy analyses, along with research-based resources such as a new game and learning website for researchers, entrepreneurs, practitioners, and funders.

To increase the capacity of researchers and industry to address the issues raised here, we join others in calling for more robust investments in research. Most R&D is provided by the government—the Department of Defense, the Department of Education, the National Science Foundation (NSF), and the National Institutes of Health (NIH) all support game-based experimental research. However, it is unevenly distributed and highly fragmented, and it lacks shared research priorities or mechanisms to foster interagency coordination and collaboration. The Federal Games Working Group led by the White House Office on Science and Technology Policy has made progress in establishing a mechanism for interagency collaboration, planning and data sharing that should help guide future programs for research and development. As research advances, we need to know more precisely what is being done in the field: government should regularly publish inventories that track what research is being funded and by which agencies.

Conclusion

Despite a remarkable rise in ICTs and other digital technologies and vast corresponding changes to our daily lives and culture, Bronfenbrenner's ecology of human development seems as fresh and relevant today as it was nearly four decades ago. The proliferation of digital games and other media need not be considered a crisis within the modern family ecology, but rather a potential vehicle for learning and engagement that cuts and transfers across the spheres of children's lives and development. While more research on the enduring impact of digital media on tangible measures of learning and development is certainly needed, we are optimistic that technologies can offer both creative and tangible solutions, when well deployed by knowledgeable teachers and other caring adults. If every stakeholder encircling the developing child—parents, teachers, faith leaders, technology manufacturers, media producers, researchers, journalists, policymakers—indeed if every pivotal sector can commit to understanding its role in influencing the new ecology of human development, children will have a better chance of realizing the as yet unfulfilled promise of digital media.

As this volume makes clear, much work remains to harness the distinctive qualities of games to promote personalized learning and promote learning from games to contexts outside it. As the technology industry disrupts old practice models, policymakers and industry leaders may well look to the power of digital games to help build a modern learning ecology.

Notes

1. Sections of this chapter are directly adapted from the following: Takeuchi, L., & Levine, M. H. (in press). Learning in a digital age: Towards a new ecology of human development. In A. Jordan & D. Romer (Eds.), *Media and the well-being of children and adolescents.* New York: Oxford University Press.
   Levine, M. H., & Vaala, S. E. (2013). Games for learning: Vast wasteland or a digital promise? In F. C. Blumberg & S. M. Fisch (Eds.), Digital Games: A Context for Cognitive Development and Learning. *New Directions for Child and Adolescent Development, 139,* 71–82.
2. The authors greatly appreciate the editorial advice and review of relevant literature conducted by Christina Hinton and Anna Ly in preparing this chapter.
3. According to Moore's Law, which is the observation that over the history of computing hardware, the number of transistors on integrated circuits doubles about every two years (Moore, 1965).

References

American Academy of Pediatrics. (2009). Policy statement—media violence. *Pediatrics, 124,* 1495–1503.

Andrews, G. (2008). Gameplay, gender, and socioeconomic status in two American high schools. *E-Learning and Digital Media, 5,* 199–213.

Bronfenbrenner, U. (1977). Toward an experimental ecology of human development. *American Psychologist, 32,* 513–531.

Bronfenbrenner, U. (1979). *The ecology of human development: Experiments by nature and design.* Cambridge, MA: Harvard University Press.

Blumberg, F. C. (1998). Developmental differences at play: Children's selective attention and performance in video games, *Journal of Applied Developmental Psychology, 19*, 615–624.

Blumberg, F. C., Altschuler, E. A., Almonte, D. E., & Mileaf, M. M. (2013). The impact of recreational video game play on children and adolescents' cognition. In F. C. Blumberg & S. M. Fisch (Eds.), Digital Games: A Context for Cognitive Development and Learning. *New Directions for Child and Adolescent Development, 139*, 41–50.

Child Trends. (2012). High school dropout rates: Indicators on children and youth. Retrieved fromhttp://www.childtrendsdatabank.org/sites/default/files/01_Dropout_Rates.pdf

Chiong, C. (2009). *Can video games promote intergenerational play and literacy learning? Report from a research and design workshop.* New York, NY: Joan Ganz Cooney Center at Sesame Workshop. Retrieved from http://joanganzcooneycenter.org/upload_kits/intergen_final_021210.pdf

Civic Enterprises in association with Peter D. Hart Research Associates. (2006, March). The silent epidemic: Perspectives of high school dropouts. Seattle, Washington: The Bill & Melinda Gates Foundation. Retrieved from http://www.civicenterprises.net/pdfs/thesilentepidemic3-06.pdf

Clark, K., Brandt, J., Hopkins, R., & Wilhelm, J. (2010). Making games after school: Participatory game design in non-formal learning environments. *Educational Technology, 49*(6), 40–44.

Clark, K., & Sheridan, K. (2010). Game design through mentoring and collaboration. *Journal of Educational Multimedia and Hypermedia, 19*(2), 5–22.

Consumer Electronics Association. (2012). CE industry to reach record-high revenues in 2012, according to CEA. Retrieved from http://www.ce.org/News/News-Releases/Press-Releases/2012-Press-Releases/CE-Industry-to-Reach-Record-High-Revenues-in-2012,.aspx

Deater-Deckard, K., Change, M., & Evans, M. E. (2013). Engagement states and learning from educational games. In F. C. Blumberg & S. M. Fisch (Eds.), Digital Games: A Context for Cognitive Development and Learning. *New Directions for Child and Adolescent Development, 139*, 21–30.

Dickey, M. D. (2006). Girl gamers: the controversy of girl games and the relevance of female-oriented game design for instructional design. *British Journal of Educational Technology, 37*, 785–793.

Entertainment Software Association (2012). 2012 Essential facts about the computer and video game industry. Retrieved from http://www.theesa.com/facts/pdfs/ESA_EF_2012.pdf

Ferguson, C. J. (2008). The school shooting/violent video game link: Causal relationship or moral panic? *Journal of Investigative Psychology and Offender Profiling, 5*, 25–37.

Fisch, S. M. (2013). Cross-platform learning: On the nature of children's learning from multiple media platforms. In F. C. Blumberg & S. M. Fisch (Eds.), Digital Games: A Context for Cognitive Development and Learning. *New Directions for Child and Adolescent Development, 139*, 59–70.

Gee, J. P. (2007). *What video games have to teach us about learning and literacy*, 2nd ed. New York, NY: Macmillan.

Gentile, D. A., & Walsh, D. A. (2002). A normative study of family media habits. *Applied Developmental Psychology, 23*, 157–178.

Greenberg, B. S., Sherry, J., Lachlan, K., Lucas, K., & Holmstrom, A. (2010). Orientations to video games among gender and age groups. *Simulation & Gaming, 41*(2), 238–259.

Grimes, S. M., & Fields, D. A. (2012). *Kids online: A new research agenda for understanding social networking forums.* New York, NY: The Joan Ganz Cooney Center at Sesame Workshop.

Hechinger, J. (2010). U.S. teens lag as China soars on international test. Retrieved from http://www.bloomberg.com/news/2010-12-07/teens-in-u-s-rank-25th-on-math-test-trail-in-science-reading.html

Kafai, Y. B. (1994). *Minds in play: computer game design as a context for children's learning.* Hillsdale, NJ: Lawrence Erlbaum Associates.

Kutner, L. A., Olson, C. K., Warner, D. E., & Hertzog, S. M. (2008). Parents' and sons' perspectives on video gameplay: A qualitative study. *Journal of Adolescent Research, 23*(1), 76–96.

Levine, M. H. (2011, March 11). Congress launches caucus for competitiveness in entertainment technology. [Blog post.] Retrieved fromhttp://www.joanganzcooneycenter.org/Cooney-Center-Blog-127.html

Levine, M. H., Steyer, J., & Henry, A. (2008, May). *Growing up digital: Adults rate the educational potential of new media and 21st century skills.* New York, NY: Joan Ganz Cooney Center at Sesame Workshop in collaboration with Common Sense Media and Insight Research. Retrieved from http://www.joanganzcooneycenter.org/wp-content/uploads/2012/11/growingupdigitalppt.pdf/

Levine, M. H., & Vaala, S. E. (2013). Games for learning: Vast wasteland or a digital promise? In F. C. Blumberg & S. M. Fisch (Eds.), Digital Games: A Context for Cognitive Development and Learning. *New Directions for Child and Adolescent Development, 139,* 71–82.

Millstone, J. (2012a). *Teacher attitudes about digital games in the classroom.* New York, NY: Joan Ganz Cooney Center at Sesame Workshop and BrainPop. Retrieved from http://www.joanganzcooneycenter.org/images/presentation/jgcc_teacher_survey.pdf

Millstone, J. (2012b). *Teacher attitudes about digital games in the class room: Video case studies.* New York, NY: Joan Ganz Cooney Center at Sesame Workshop and BrainPop. Retrieved fromhttp://joanganzcooneycenter.org/Reports-34.html

NPD Group. (2009a). Households with kids up to 12 years of age account for 45 percent of video game industry revenue. Retrieved from http://www.npd.com/press/releases/press_090910.html

NPD Group. (2009b). Kids' use of consumer electronics devices such as cell phones, personal computers and video game platforms continue to rise (Vol. 2009). Port Washington, NY: NPD.

Olson, C. K. (2010). Children's motivations for video gameplay in the context of normal development. *Review of General Psychology, 14,* 180–187.

Penuel, W. R., Pasnik, S., Bates, L., Townsend, E., Gallagher, L. P., Llorente, C., & Hupert, N. (2009). *Preschool teachers can use a media-rich curriculum to prepare low-income children for school success: Results of a randomized controlled trial.* New York, NY, and Menlo Park, CA: Education Development Center, Inc., and SRI International.

Prensky, M. (2001). Digital natives, digital immigrants. *On the Horizon, 9,* 1–6.

Richards, J., Stebbins, L., & Moellering, K. (2013). *Games for a digital age: K–12 market map and investment analysis.* New York, NY: Joan Ganz Cooney Center at Sesame Workshop. Available from: http://www.joanganzcooneycenter.org/wp-content/uploads/2013/01/glpc_gamesforadigitalage1.pdf

Rideout, V. J. (2011). *Zero to eight: Children's media use in America.* San Francisco, CA: Common Sense Media.

Sherry, J. L. (2013). The challenge of audience reception: A developmental model for educational game engagement. Digital Games: A Context for Cognitive Development and Learning. *New Directions for Child and Adolescent Development, 139,* 11–20.

Shuler, C. (2007). *D is for digital. An analysis of the children's interactive media environment with a focus on mass marketed products that promote learning.* New York, NY: Joan Ganz Cooney Center at Sesame Workshop. Retrieved from http://joanganzcooneycenter.org/upload_kits/disfordigital_reports.pdf

Swanson, C. B. (2010, June 2). U.S. graduation rate continues decline. Retrieved from http://www.edweek.org/ew/articles/2010/06/10/34swanson.h29.html

Takeuchi, L. (2011). *Families matter: Designing media for a digitalage.* New York, NY: Joan Ganz Cooney Center at Sesame Workshop. Retrieved fromhttp://joanganzcooneycenter.org/Reports-29.html

Takeuchi, L., & Levine, M. H. (in press). Learning in a digital age: Towards a new ecology of human development. In A. Jordan & D. Romer (Eds.), *Media and the well-being of children and adolescents.* New York, NY: Oxford University Press.

Takeuchi, L., & Stevens, R. (2011). *The new coviewing: Designing for learning through joint media engagement.* New York, NY: Joan Ganz Cooney Center at Sesame Workshop.

Toppo, G. (2012, January 31). White House offices studies benefits of digital games. Retrieved fromhttp://www.usatoday.com/news/washington/story/2012-01-26/edcuational-video-games-white-house/52908052/1

Torres, R. J. (2009). *Learning on a 21st century platform: Gamestar Mechanic as a means to game design and systems-thinking skills within a nodal ecology*. ProQuest.

Turkle, S. (2012). *Alone together: Why we expect more from technology and less from each other.* New York, NY: BasicBooks.

U.S. Department of Education. (2012, September 21). Ed review. Retrieved from http://www2.ed.gov/news/newsletters/edreview/2012/0921.html

Wallis, C. (2010). The impacts of media multitasking on children's learning &development: Report from a research seminar. The Joan Ganz Cooney Center and Stanford University.

Woodard, E. H., & Gridina, N. (2000). *Media in the home: The fifth annual survey of parents and children*. Philadelphia, PA: The Annenberg Public Policy Center.

Young, M. F., Slota, S., Cutter, A. B., Jalette, G., Mullin, G., Lai, B.,...Yukhymenko, M. (2012). Our princess is in another castle: A review of trends in serious gaming for education. *Review of Educational Research, 82*(1), 61–89.

Index